PROFITABLE OFFICES

PITT LATIN AMERICAN SERIES
CATHERINE M. CONAGHAN, EDITOR

PROFITABLE OFFICES

CORRUPTION, ANTICORRUPTION, AND THE FORMATION OF VENEZUELA'S NEOPATRIMONIAL STATE, 1908-1948

DOUG YARRINGTON

UNIVERSITY OF PITTSBURGH PRESS

Published by the University of Pittsburgh Press, Pittsburgh, Pa., 15260
Copyright © 2025, University of Pittsburgh Press
All rights reserved
Manufactured in the United States of America
Printed on acid-free paper
10 9 8 7 6 5 4 3 2 1

Cataloging-in-Publication Data is available from the Library of Congress

ISBN 13: 978-0-8229-4850-6
ISBN 10: 0-8229-4850-8

Cover art (*clockwise from top left*): Generación del 28, 1928; Juan Vicente Gómez during his last years, 1930s; Rómulo Betancourt, 1936; Juan Vicente Gómez and Eleazar López Contreras in Maracay, 1934.
Cover design: Melissa Dias-Mandoly

CONTENTS

Note on Currency
vii

Acknowledgments
ix

INTRODUCTION:
Approaching Corruption and Anticorruption
in Venezuela, 1908–48
3

CHAPTER 1:
The Formation of a Neopatrimonial State, to 1935
21

CHAPTER 2:
The Gomecista Cattle Monopoly: A Patrimonial Enterprise
49

CHAPTER 3:
Bureaucratic Reform as Anticorruption: The Liquor Tax and
Neopatrimonialism
73

CHAPTER 4:
Opponents and Prisoners: Middle-Class Honor and Anticorruption
99

CHAPTER 5:
Oil Money: Petroleum Concessions, Chapter VII Payments, and Ambiguous Corruption
126

CHAPTER 6:
Transition, 1935–45
157

CHAPTER 7:
The Corruption Trials, Public Opinion, and the Middle Class
183

CONCLUSION:
Twentieth-Century Venezuela and the Historical Study of (Anti)Corruption
215

Notes
229

Bibliography
273

Index
293

NOTE ON CURRENCY

The Venezuelan currency throughout the period 1908–48 was the bolívar (plural, bolívares). For stylistic reasons, the currency is occasionally referred to with the abbreviation "Bs.," especially in passages that contain numerous, concentrated references to sums of money and repetition of "bolívares" would clutter the text.

ACKNOWLEDGMENTS

This book has been a long time in the making. I began the research for it in 1999 with the assistance of a summer grant from the National Endowment for the Humanities, for which I am grateful. But my curiosity in the topic of this study began even earlier, while I conducted dissertation research on a local Venezuelan coffee economy at the Registro Principal del Estado Lara in Barquisimeto in 1988–90. Those two years coincided with the beginning of the unraveling of the democratic system that dated back to 1958. As I sat reading through land sales, loans to coffee growers, court cases, and wills from the nineteenth and early twentieth centuries, I shared a table with Venezuelans from every walk of life who came to the archive with much more immediate, concrete concerns. The conversation at the table sometimes turned to politics, and when a politician's name was mentioned, someone would often interject to categorize the official as either corrupt or honest.

ACKNOWLEDGMENTS

Such offhand accusations of corruption held obvious significance by early 1989, as the government imposed economic austerity measures, which provoked protests repressed by the killing of perhaps 1,200 Venezuelans. People pointedly asked why such hardship was necessary in a nation blessed with vast, publicly controlled petroleum reserves. Meanwhile, the story emerging from the historical documents in front of me featured political insiders using their positions and influence to seize land that small cultivators had made into a thriving coffee economy. A decade after my stay in Barquisimeto, as I formulated a new research project, the interrelated themes of corruption, anticorruption, state formation, and their social impact seemed both feasible as a historical topic and relevant to Venezuela's ongoing political transformation. My earliest debt, then, is to the people who passed through the archive in Barquisimeto all those years ago. They helped me to appreciate that citizens' attitudes toward corruption are as worthy of attention as whatever nefarious doings their government officials might be up to.

During my research for this project, I visited archives in Venezuela, the United Kingdom, the United States, and Spain. I'm thankful to the staff at each of the archives listed in the bibliography, as well as to everyone at the Benson Latin American Collection at the University of Texas at Austin, which I have visited repeatedly over the years. I owe a special debt to David Irvin, at Arizona State University's library, for facilitating my research visit during the waning days of the COVID pandemic.

As research in Venezuela became increasingly problematic over the past fifteen years, I came to depend on published collections of historical documents and on interlibrary loan. I gratefully acknowledge that my project would have been impossible without the work of Ramón J. Velásquez, Yolanda Segnini, Naudy Suárez Figueroa, Elías Pino Iturrieta, and others who have dedicated themselves to gathering and editing collections of documents related to Venezuela during the first half of the twentieth century. I have also relied on the interlibrary loan staff at Colorado State University, who have attended to my endless requests over the years and were especially resourceful in obtaining some rare volumes late in my research. To Maggie Cummings, Cristi MacWaters, and everyone who works in their office, my heartfelt thanks.

Numerous colleagues have offered comments, encouragement,

and advice in response to the conference papers, journal articles, and chapter drafts that I wrote along the way to completing the book. Judy Ewell, a wonderful mentor during my undergraduate years at the College of William and Mary, read many of these early pieces and generously offered her encouragement and unparalleled insight. I regret that I did not complete the manuscript before her untimely death. It is no exaggeration to say that everything I write on Venezuela has been touched by Judy's influence, even when I've formulated arguments with which she disagreed. My conversations with Peter Linder, though not as frequent as either of us would wish, have also deepened my understanding of Venezuela's past, especially the Gómez era. Reuben Zahler applied his razor-sharp intellect to drafts of more than one of the essays that preceded the present volume and provided honest and constructive feedback. Christoph Rosenmüller used his expertise on the history of corruption and anticorruption in Latin America to comment on an early draft of the introduction, and Bob Ferry and Erick Langer commented on conference papers. Finally, I am indebted to Kim Morse for her close reading of the entire manuscript, her detailed comments, and her forthright reaction to my ideas. Our exchanges after she read each chapter were some of the most rewarding intellectual dialogues of my career thus far. Each of these colleagues helped me to write a better book but none of them, of course, is responsible for any errors that remain.

I owe a particular debt to Klaus Buchenau and Dragos Radu at the University of Regensburg, Germany, for organizing and hosting the conference "Corruption in Eastern and Southeastern Europe and Latin America: Comparative Perspectives," in the summer of 2017. This gathering of interdisciplinary scholars broadened my thinking at a crucial time. I am particularly grateful to Klaus for his comments on my conference paper and for sharing comparisons with his own work on Eastern Europe. Special thanks are also due to Elizabeth Jones, who went out of her way to alert me to the conference. Paulo Drinot graciously facilitated two opportunities for me to present papers related to this project at the University of London, first in 2011 by including me in the conference on the Great Depression in the Americas and again in 2015 by inviting me to speak to his seminar on Latin American history.

Since the fall of 2000, I've had the good fortune to work in the History Department at Colorado State University. My colleagues read and discussed early drafts of several articles and chapters at our faculty research seminars, providing stimulating insights from their own fields of specialization. I'm deeply appreciative of the colleagues who nurtured my scholarly work—and of those who offered solidarity during my two terms as department chair—here at CSU. My thanks also go to Madzie Boyles and Sophia Linn at the CSU Geospatial Centroid for creating the book's map. Go Rams!

Josh Shanholtzer, the acquisitions editor for the Latin American studies series at the University of Pittsburgh Press, deserves credit for his acceptance of a somewhat idiosyncratic project. I also appreciate the many hours that the editorial team of Amy Sherman, Kelly Lynn Thomas, and Matthew Somoroff dedicated to polishing the manuscript and responding to my queries.

This book includes material that has been previously published in several articles. The research that originally appeared in my article "Cattle, Corruption, and Venezuelan State Formation During the Regime of Juan Vicente Gómez, 1908–35," *Latin American Research Review*, 38 no. 2 (2003): 9–33, is reprinted here with permission from the University of Texas Press. Most of chapter 3 was originally published as "Tax Farming, Liquor, and the Quest for Fiscal Modernity in Venezuela, 1908–1935," *Hispanic American Historical Review* 94, no. 2 (2014): 237–269, and is reprinted with permission from Duke University Press. Parts of chapters 5 and 7 were originally published in "Venezuelan Presidents' Discretionary Payments to Allies and Followers: Neopatrimonialism and Gray Corruption, 1919–1948," *Südost-Forschungen*, no. 77 (2018): 95–120, and appear here with permission from the Leibniz Institute for East and Southeast European Research. Much of chapter 7 was included in my article "Public Opinion and Modernity in Venezuela's Anti-Corruption Trials, 1945–1948," *Journal of Latin American Studies* 51, no. 1 (2019): 59–83, and is reprinted with permission from Cambridge University Press.

My family has provided much love and support as I've gone about my research and writing, and they've patiently listened to my evolving explanations of what the project was about, all while somehow maintaining their faith that I'd complete it. Lynda, my mother, and Jeff, my younger brother, never failed to express an interest, while my older brother, Peter, and his wife Pam repeatedly shared their home with me during my stints at the Library of Congress and the US National Archives. My son Ben, barely more than a toddler when

ACKNOWLEDGMENTS

I began this endeavor and now a fine young man (as well as a better writer than I'll ever be), gave me priceless encouragement. Maria, my partner in life for almost forty years, has experienced many periods when I was not physically or mentally present while I focused on "the book." More happily, she and I share many fond memories of some of the travels associated with this research. Our peregrinations together, whatever the occasion or destination, will always be a source of joy.

PROFITABLE OFFICES

INTRODUCTION

APPROACHING CORRUPTION AND ANTICORRUPTION IN VENEZUELA, 1908-48

As he wrote his memoirs recounting his years of service in the regime of Juan Vicente Gómez (1908–35), Gumersindo Torres found himself returning again and again to the issue of corruption. Trained as a medical doctor, Torres was pulled into politics as a young man, and Gómez eventually appointed him to a series of official positions, including two stints as minister of development (1917–22, 1929–31). Torres took pride in his public service and believed that Gómez's long rule, despite its manifest faults, had benefited Venezuela. The dictator could be credited with ending a century of civil wars, establishing the authority of the central government, constructing a national system of highways, and creating Venezuela's first professional treasury bureaucracy and military. Working on his memoirs periodically during the dictatorship and after Gómez's death in 1935, Torres continued to defend the ruler who, in the eyes of his supporters, had done more than any other to make Venezuela a modern nation-state.

Nevertheless, as a rigorous administrator imbued with the ideals of public service, Torres could not avoid deploring the abuses of power that he witnessed regularly for more than a quarter century. We can imagine his narrow face set firmly and his piercing eyes filled with frustration as he wrote pages denouncing cabinet ministers who enriched themselves from the public treasury, state governors (then referred to as state presidents) who ran illegal monopolies, and public officials who reaped personal fortunes from the early development of the nation's petroleum industry.[1] Torres felt compelled to assert his own financial probity, a claim supported by others, and to recount the occasions when he thwarted officials' attempts to misuse public power for personal profit. The dilemma of how to reconcile these rampant abuses of government office with his belief in the positive impact of the Gómez regime hangs over much of Torres's memoir, unresolved until he could avoid it no longer.

Torres's most direct engagement with the issue of systemic corruption came during his discussion of the two years he served as chief administrator of the Venezuelan Industrial Cattle Company, a business partnership that joined Gómez with many of his state presidents and other collaborators in what the regime publicized as an effort to modernize the cattle industry. Once installed as manager, however, Torres was distressed to learn that the partners in the company, which received large subsidies of public money, treated the enterprise primarily as a source of easy cash. Popular riots against the company following Gómez's death left Torres concerned that his involvement in the enterprise might be perceived as a stain on his otherwise clean reputation.[2] And so he returned to work on his manuscript, reflecting on corruption not as the individual failings of unscrupulous officials but rather as a central problem in explaining the nature of Gómez's power—a topic Torres felt freer to explore, no doubt, now that Gómez had died. "In Venezuela," he wrote,

> public functionaries, from the President of the Republic to the office doorman or simple police agent, are accustomed to using their political position to make money with business dealings of every kind. Naturally there are honorable exceptions, and many are the public employees who have not played that game [*que no han comulgado con esa hostia*] and have left their offices as poor as when they entered. General Gómez was not an exception, but rather followed the general

rule, as did the absolute majority of men who served him; he left their hands free so that they might enrich themselves. Perhaps this was one of the most effective methods by which he imposed himself on them with all that force of authority which he maintained in Venezuela until his death. General Gómez, a man of business, used his power and great authority to do business and thus died a millionaire, and such abuses were in accordance with his exercise of power.[3]

Torres's comments convey an insight that serves as a point of departure for this study of the relationship between corruption and state formation: the use of public office for private profit was intimately intertwined with the style of rule developed by Gómez and his allies, and it advanced their efforts to create the most powerful national state Venezuela had ever known. At the same time, Torres's memoir reminds readers of Venezuelans' efforts to curb corruption (or "abuses," as Torres wrote in the quotation above). These anticorruption efforts also shaped the new state in decisive ways. Some officials within the regime sought to limit the malfeasance committed by other officials, and more numerous Venezuelans outside the regime protested its corruption with much greater vigor. Following Gómez's death, for example, the citizenry attacked the properties owned by the dictator and his allies in an outpouring of pent-up popular rage. These protests forced Gómez's successor, president and general Eleazar López Contreras (1935–41), to curtail the most hated forms of corruption, even though more discreet methods of malfeasance continued in the years that followed.

The most dramatic anticorruption drive began in 1945, when a coalition of young military officers and civilian reformers overthrew president and general Isaías Medina Angarita (1941–45), López Contreras's hand-picked successor. The reformers put López Contreras, Medina Angarita, and 165 former officials from their administrations and from the Gómez era on trial for corruption as part of their larger project to create a modern democratic state. These anticorruption trials, which received widespread support at first, soon became so controversial that they contributed to the downfall of the reformist government in 1948.[4] In sum, corruption and anticorruption—the themes that Torres grappled with in his writing and his life—were both central to Venezuelan politics throughout the period from 1908 to 1948, the years when the national state was consolidated. This book's overarching thesis is that these two competing tendencies shaped the process of state formation.

The History of Corruption and Anticorruption: Problems and Concepts

Latin American protests against corruption have become so commonplace in recent decades that it is surprising historians have not devoted more attention to the topic.[5] From the 1990s onward, allegations of corruption have forced presidents out of office in several Latin American nations. The bribery scandal involving the transnational Brazilian firm Odebrecht rocked the entire region in the 2010s, and public opinion surveys often rank corruption as a top concern among Latin American citizens. Transparency International, the nongovernmental organization that publishes a widely read annual index of perceptions of corruption, currently gives Venezuela the most unfavorable ranking of any nation in the Americas, and Venezuelans have protested against corruption for years.[6] If one purpose of history is to expand our understanding of present-day problems—problems as diverse as environmental degradation, racism, and economic inequality—then why have Latin Americanists paid relatively little attention to the history of corruption?

Some historians are deterred by a perceived lack of sources, especially for studies of the period after most Latin American nations won independence in the early nineteenth century. Although the crowns of Spain and Portugal investigated the malfeasance of colonial officials, thus providing a substantial documentary base for studies of corruption during the three centuries of European rule, postcolonial governments proved less likely to investigate and document corruption by their officials.[7] One goal of this book is to demonstrate that research into the history of post-independence corruption and anticorruption may be more feasible than historians have generally believed. In researching this project, I have found ample materials related to corruption and anticorruption in government officials' correspondence, reports from the Treasury Ministry, dispatches from diplomats in Venezuela representing the United States, Britain, Spain and the Vatican, political pamphlets and broadsheets, congressional debates, newspapers, the records of the anticorruption trials of the mid-1940s, and memoirs and private correspondence written by Gómez's allies and enemies.

INTRODUCTION

Another methodological issue hindering historians' investigation of this topic is the thorny question of how to define *corruption*. Scholars who study the phenomenon from a diversity of disciplinary perspectives—including anthropology, political science, and economics, as well as history—are far from a consensus.[8] Some insist that public officials' use of their power for private enrichment is corrupt only if it violates a law, but this approach is clearly unsatisfactory for cases in which unscrupulous cliques created laws with self-serving loopholes.[9] Other scholars debate whether the concept of corruption should focus exclusively on the actions of government officials or be defined to include others, such as business leaders, whose actions may also violate public trust and undermine public well-being.[10] Moreover, just as social scientists often search for a culturally neutral definition to apply across diverse societies, historians face the challenge of formulating a definition that avoids the projection of current ideas or attitudes regarding corruption onto the past.[11] In particular, a historical study that examines *anticorruption* as well as corruption needs to employ a definition that incorporates the attitudes of historical actors themselves so as to illuminate a past society's discourses and actions against "corruption."[12]

In this book, I follow scholars who emphasize that the "concept of corruption is heavily contested and socially constructed"[13] by historical actors. This constructivist approach draws our attention to how past societies' understanding of the boundary between corruption and acceptable behavior has changed (or not) over time. By highlighting how political debates and protests have shaped a society's definition of corruption, such an approach acknowledges that consensus on the definition of *corruption* was often elusive in the past, just as it is today. Political scientist Michael Johnston, a proponent of the constructivist approach, emphasizes that "it is an irony of corruption that where it is most important it can also be most difficult to define."[14] This observation certainly aligns with the situation in Venezuela between 1908 and 1948, an era of rapid change when many Venezuelans saw corruption as an important issue but agreement on defining and punishing it often proved elusive. With these considerations in mind, I define corruption as *the use of public office and other public resources for private benefit in ways that were condemned by significant segments of public opinion in the society under study*. Throughout this book, I use *corruption* and its synonyms, such as *malfeasance* and *profiteering*, only as reflections of public perception during the historical period being discussed, and never as a legal or moral judgment.

This definition, by emphasizing the "social meaning"[15] of corruption, recognizes that societies' perceptions of corruption have varied across historical time and geographical space. As one research team of historians who embrace the constructivist approach has argued, "corruption actually acquires its meaning in relation to its social setting and historical context."[16] It follows that the nuances of each nation's understanding of corruption will reflect its particular experience at any given moment in time. For example, by the early twentieth century, Venezuelans had a long and bitter history of living under monopolies that, through legal or illegal means, reserved some areas of the national economy as the exclusive preserve of powerful individuals or the groups they favored, to the detriment of much of the population. During the eighteenth century, many Venezuelans condemned and resisted the monopoly over the lucrative cacao economy granted by the Spanish crown to a company of Basque merchants.[17] And, as I outline in the next chapter, the final three decades of the nineteenth century witnessed a steady stream of monopoly concessions granted by national officials who were widely perceived to profit personally from the cartels they created. The hardship imposed on the consumers, workers, and entrepreneurs whose livelihoods were ruined or undermined by monopolies reached its peak during the Gómez dictatorship. Thus, throughout the four decades examined in this book, as Venezuelans considered whether certain activities constituted corruption, they were most unified when denouncing monopolies established by their rulers.

This book's constructivist approach is in keeping with historians' tendency to study corruption (and other phenomena) from an emic perspective, that is, from the viewpoint of historical actors.[18] Nevertheless, emic approaches to corruption, like all analytical tools, have their limitations and potential problems. Like other scholars, I recognize that historical actors' notion of crucial elements of corruption, such as the boundary between "public" and "private," was often blurry and flexible, and that written sources for deciphering "public opinion" are usually weighted (certainly in early twentieth-century Venezuela) toward the minority of the population in the middle and upper classes.[19] But the advantages of this emic perspective outweigh the disadvantages, especially when compared to alternative approaches.

Adopting a supposedly "universal" concept of corruption to understand Venezuelans who fought against it a century ago would ignore political and cultural context. As historian Jens Ivo Engels has argued, it is precisely by exploring such context and nuance that historical studies can contribute to interdisciplinary understanding of struggles over corruption, in both the past and the present.[20]

Moreover, a close examination of Venezuelans' debates over corruption during the first half of the twentieth century allows us to make useful distinctions between two types of profiteering that elicited different responses. I use the term *predatory corruption* to refer to public officials' use of their positions to extract resources *directly* from the population for their private benefit. As recounted in subsequent chapters, Gómez and his subordinates used their power to create monopolies over cattle, beef, liquor, and other commodities, as well as to seize properties and extract coerced payments from those they ruled. Criticisms of Gómez's monopolies echoed long-standing Venezuelan complaints that their rulers created such cartels as a method of solidifying their political networks and enriching themselves at the expense of consumers (who had to pay monopoly prices) and entrepreneurs (who were often obliged to sell their operations cheaply to predatory officials). Venezuelans roundly condemned Gómez and his officials for enriching themselves by extracting wealth directly from those they ruled. These predatory abuses therefore may also be referred to as *generally condemned corruption*—that is, practices reviled throughout society and widely deemed to be worthy of punishment.[21]

By contrast, what I refer to as *ambiguous corruption* or *financial corruption* occurred when officials manipulated public assets such as treasury funds or petroleum contracts for their private benefit, a practice that evoked more mixed or ambivalent responses from Venezuelans during the first half of the twentieth century. This mode of profiteering was more likely to provoke disagreements over the precise boundaries between the public and private spheres, making attempts at punishment controversial. The financial malfeasance denounced by anti-Gomecistas (opponents of Gómez) often constituted ambiguous corruption, because during the period under study Venezuelans vehemently disagreed over whether it deserved condemnation and punishment.[22] This distinction between generally condemned predatory corruption and ambiguous financial corruption becomes especially illuminating when analyzing the post-Gómez transition and the controversy surrounding the anticorruption trials of the 1940s. The rulers who succeeded Gómez in 1935–45 defended cash payments to their allies and to a wide array of citizens who requested aid—payments made at the president's discretion—as necessary to maintain political stability, a public good. Prosecutors, in contrast, argued that the officials had used public funds improperly to build networks of personal political support, or to enrich themselves. While debates raged over the probity of these financial transactions, prosecutions for predatory forms of corruption provoked no real controversy. This distinction between widely condemned predatory corruption and ambiguous financial corruption, then, proves useful for exploring Venezuelans' perceptions of malfeasance and may provide insights for historical studies beyond Venezuela.

Corruption, Anticorruption, and Neopatrimonial State Formation

The contradictory tendencies in Gómez's regime that nagged at Gumersindo Torres—the harmful abuses of power versus the welcome creation of political stability and economic growth—are reflected in historians' contrasting assessments of the dictator. Gómez's defenders have usually acknowledged his abuses, such as his profiteering and his cruel treatment of political opponents, but have emphasized his success in pacifying the country, building infrastructure, overseeing the early development of the oil economy, and laying the foundation of a modern state.[23] In the opposing camp, critical scholars argue that his twenty-seven-year rule represented the opposite of national ideals: Gómez's repression delayed the development of democratic institutions; his generally cozy relationship with foreign oil companies and their governments locked the nation into neocolonial dependency; his imprisonment, torture, and murder of political foes belied claims that he brought "peace" to the nation; and his blatant corruption set a low bar for standards of public probity.[24] Each side in the debate has ample evidence to support its point of view, but neither perspective offers a wholistic synthesis of state formation under Gómez or an altogether satisfying way of explaining the place of the Gómez era in the nation's history.

This book argues that in Venezuela between 1908 and 1948 corruption and anticorruption contributed to a neopatrimonial process of state formation, one that included both patrimonial practices and attempts to implement modern bureaucratic forms of rule.[25] Neither of these two modes of governance was new to Venezuela in the early twentieth century, but tensions between them became more pronounced than at any previous time in the nation's history, and they require discussion here. Patrimonialism—the continual intermixing of public and private interests—provides context for understanding corruption and anticorruption during the first half of the twentieth century in Venezuela. In a patrimonial regime, the ruler generally fills important political and administrative positions with his kin and business associates, who accept subordination to the ruler in exchange for the economic and political benefits he allows them as his clients. In their administration of the state, the ruler and these clients pursue their joint interests, which override any institutional or legal considerations. Goods formally identified as public, such as government funds and the powers attached to public office, are in practice used to advance the personal interests of the ruler and his clique, including their private accumulation of wealth and their continuation in power. These private interests provide the central logic of a patrimonial regime, maintaining cohesive bonds of loyalty within the regime and leading to coercive, often predatory relations between rulers and citizens. Thus, corruption (the use of public power for private benefit in ways that are condemned by significant segments of society) is an inherent aspect of patrimonialism.[26] When Venezuelans opposed to the Gómez regime denounced its "personalism" (*personalismo*), they had in mind the same characteristics that scholars associate with patrimonialism.

Under Gómez, profiteering became more pervasive and systematic than under past regimes, so people resented it as never before.[27] Gómez's opponents denounced his economically motivated "abuses," "robbery," "monopolies," and "embezzlement" (*peculado*)[28]—all of which they only occasionally labeled as "corruption"—as much as they denounced any other aspect of his regime. Indeed, even some of Gómez's closest collaborators conceded that the dictator and many of his allies used their power improperly to enrich themselves; Torres was hardly alone among Gomecistas (allies and supporters of Gómez) in his criticism of patrimonial excesses. Román Cárdenas, who served as treasury minister from 1913 to 1922, denounced the practice of tax farming, which continued intermittently into the early 1930s, as inherently corrupt because it allowed favored individuals to profit from the collection of state revenues.[29] Carlos Siso, another civilian functionary of the regime, deplored the "monopoly" over cattle markets exercised by Gómez and his allies.[30] López Contreras, one of Gómez's leading generals and his successor as president, lamented the use of Venezuelan army units as agricultural laborers on Gomecistas' estates and denounced officials who used their positions to embezzle public funds and secure lucrative petroleum concessions.[31] Still, these critics understood that such patrimonial abuses created much of the regime's internal cohesion, as Gómez and his allies cooperated to use their political clout to accumulate private wealth. Without the bonds of loyalty created by personalistic exchanges, they realized, the regime's accomplishments of political centralization and economic stabilization would have been impossible.

But just as patrimonialism provided one source of the regime's strength, the selective development of bureaucratic expertise and efficiency in strategic areas of the state apparatus provided another, distinct form of power in the neopatrimonial regime. The treasury bureaucracy and the military—two pillars of any modern state—were professionalized to a greater extent under Gómez than previously. The military reform of 1910–13 created the nation's first professional army with standardized training and equipment; it was implemented, in part, by graduates of the newly created military academy, though Gómez reserved the highest ranks for men personally loyal to him.[32] Significantly, the military's quasi-professionalization became intertwined with an initiative to create a modern treasury bureaucracy to provide the necessary revenues—an innovation proposed by Treasury Minister Cárdenas as necessary to curtail corruption, boost the economy, and fund the government's state-building projects.[33] Cárdenas's drive to root out corruption in tax collection by adhering to what he called "the modern science of finances"[34] led to the creation of a professional fiscal bureaucracy and dramatically improved government finances before the oil economy took off in the mid-1920s. Thus, anticorruption sentiment within the regime animated the increasing bureaucratic power of the state at the same time that intensified patrimonial abuses by other officials—viewed as corrupt by many Venezuelans—cemented alliances among Gómez and many of his key collaborators. Both corruption and anticorruption were fundamental to Venezuela's neopatrimonial process of state formation.

Such dynamics did not fade away entirely during the post-Gómez transition of 1935–45. Instead, neopatrimonialism was refined by Gómez's two successors, both military men from the Andean state of Táchira, like Gómez. Presidents López Contreras and Medina Angarita initiated a gradual transition toward limited democracy, expanded the federal bureaucracy, increased state oversight of the oil industry, and established a national comptroller's office to audit government finances, though the office was widely regarded as weak.[35] While López Contreras and Medina Angarita ended the systemic predatory corruption that had marked the dictatorship, their opponents criticized their continuation of payments to allies and supporters through the discretionary fund known as Chapter VII of the budget of the Ministry of Interior Relations. The ongoing process of neopatrimonial state formation, with its combination of bureaucratic and patrimonial power, was now paralleled by a public debate aimed at distinguishing corruption from acceptable government practices. A variety of opposition groups led by middle-class reformers criticized López Contreras and Medina Angarita for continuing the "personalist" practices of Gómez—especially the Chapter VII payments—and called for a "modern" state free of corruption. In response, government officials defended the expenditures from Chapter VII as a necessary mechanism of effective governance in what they viewed as a paternalistic political culture ingrained in Venezuelan society.

The failure of the anticorruption trials to resolve this dispute, following reformers' seizure of power in 1945, facilitated the continuation of a neopatrimonial state as Venezuela's economy became ever more dependent on oil. Indeed, scholars who have examined Venezuela during and after the mid-twentieth century offer interpretations of the nation's petrostate that are compatible with the concept of neopatrimonialism or embrace it explicitly. The anthropologist Fernando Coronil provides a theoretically sophisticated analysis of the peculiar interweaving of modernity and rent-seeking (the tendency to seek wealth from the state's resources rather than through productive enterprises) within Venezuelan political culture during most of the twentieth century.[36] More recently, historian Margarita López Maya, in her studies of the Hugo Chávez era (1999–2013), as well as the post-Chávez era, has argued that the concept of neopatrimonialism offers insight into the Venezuelan state of the early twenty-first century, a view echoed by political scientists.[37]

Other Historiographical Contexts and Contributions

This study builds on insights into the history of anticorruption, a topic which has inspired recent research among historians of Europe even while it remains an undeveloped theme in the historiography of post-independence Latin America.[38] Scholarly work on the history of anticorruption in Europe has succeeded in making the point that the histories of corruption and anticorruption need to be studied together. Indeed, if one adopts an emic definition of corruption, it follows logically that there is no corruption without anticorruption sentiment, a perspective also emphasized by anthropologists.[39] But as the editors of a volume of cutting-edge essays on the history of anticorruption observe, these studies tend to treat anticorruption campaigns as political instruments utilized to damage opponents.[40] *Profitable Offices* departs from that anticorruption paradigm in at least two ways. First, in my examination of the campaign by Cárdenas, Gómez's treasury minister, to replace tax farming with tax collection by salaried, professionally trained bureaucrats, I emphasize Cárdenas's vision of fiscal modernity rather than any political motivation, such as rivalry between factions within the regime. Cárdenas saw tax farming as a form of corruption which deprived the treasury of revenue and constrained economic growth. Ironically, the success of Cárdenas's bureaucratic reforms led to a growth of treasury revenues which Gómez often spent in a patrimonial fashion. Thus, a reform that Cárdenas framed as "modern" ultimately served patrimonial ends, a scenario that illuminates the dynamics of neopatrimonial state formation rather than appearing as a political win or loss for Cárdenas and his fiscal bureaucracy.

This study also departs from a purely political paradigm of anticorruption in its treatment of Gómez's opponents. I take seriously the emotional tropes of humiliation and wounded honor used by men and women to describe their suffering under the predatory corruption of Gómez and his allies. While their denunciations of corruption had obvious political goals, the sentiments they expressed offer insight into the lived experiences of many Venezuelans in the face of official predation. Anticorruption struggles thus deserve a place in scholars' consideration of the affective dimension of state formation, if we take *affect* to refer to shared sentiments that lead to action.[41]

Similarly, as I explore the anticorruption rhetoric and actions of

Rómulo Betancourt and other young anti-Gomecista reformers from 1928 through the 1930s and '40s, I acknowledge their political motives but also take as sincere their desire to establish a modern democratic state distinct from the personalist one they associated with the corruption of Gómez, López Contreras, and Medina Angarita. Democratic reformers' condemnations of corruption as incompatible with modernity, along with Treasury Minister Cárdenas's similar justification of reforms under Gómez, open an interpretative perspective on anticorruption struggles that goes beyond narrow political interpretations. Despite their political differences, Gomecista technocrats and younger populist reformers both viewed corruption as the antithesis of modern state practices—and they did so well before the emergence of modernization theory in the United States and Europe in the 1950s.[42]

Finally, this study contributes to the historical literature on Latin America during the national period by offering a book-length, interdisciplinary analysis of how both corruption and anticorruption contributed to the process of state formation. In recent decades, historians of Latin America have viewed the state's internal dynamics and its relationship to society from the diverse perspectives of political economy, discourse analysis, cultural studies, and gender studies.[43] My analysis borrows from each of these approaches as it explores the material and symbolic forces at work in the construction of state power and resistance to it. Just as some of the best work on state formation illuminates how systems of power are negotiated from above and below, the present study seeks to demonstrate that placing corruption and anticorruption at the center of the negotiation of rule can deepen our understanding of this process.[44]

The Book's Organization

The chapters that follow are organized both thematically and chronologically. Chapter 1 provides an overview of Venezuelan politics before Gómez and then examines, in broad strokes, the course of neopatrimonial state formation during his twenty-seven-year rule, providing the context for what follows. As outlined below, chapters 2 through 5 then explore specific aspects of the Gómez regime, adhering to a thematic scheme. Chapters 6 and 7 discuss the post-Gómez era, 1935–48, proceeding in a chronological fashion.

Chapter 2 analyzes the Gomecistas' cattle monopoly, the most important economic enterprise that bound together the dictator and his collaborators from the earliest years of their regime. It argues that Gomecistas' partnerships in the cattle business served an integrative function by promoting the internal unity of the regime as its principal members cooperated to centralize political power and use it for private profit. The cattle monopoly also shaped the relationship between the state and society as non-Gomecista ranchers were forced out of business and as consumers buying beef had little choice but to submit to the cartel.

Chapter 3 examines the drive by Treasury Minister Cárdenas to replace the regime's corrupt system of tax farming, in which the treasury contracted with leading Gomecistas to collect the liquor tax, with a new bureaucracy staffed by salaried state revenue collectors. Gómez's decision to allow Cárdenas to curb tax farming, despite the harm to his collaborators, reflected the dictator's need to increase domestic revenues as World War I disrupted international trade. Although not all Cárdenas's hard-won victories against corruption survived his retirement, his pursuit of fiscal reform demonstrates that the discursive contrast between corruption and modernity shaped segments of the Gomecista state from within as well as providing an eventual rallying cry for anti-Gomecistas. Chapters 2 and 3, taken together, argue that cattle and liquor played central roles in Venezuelan state formation and that, at least during the first half of the Gómez era, their significance outweighed that of oil, the commodity scholars most often associate with political centralization in Venezuela.

In Chapter 4, I explore the experiences and discourses of middle-class anti-Gomecistas who suffered the regime's predatory corruption. These opponents framed submission to Gomecista predation as a cause of humiliation within the highly gendered norms of bourgeois honor. Studies of opposition to Gómez usually emphasize either the political opportunism of rival *caudillos* (political strongmen) or the democratic aspirations of younger urban protesters,[45] but this chapter's analysis highlights the resonance of an opposition discourse that framed anticorruption as a defense of male and female honor within the patriarchal assumptions of the era. The innovation of the later, younger anti-Gomecistas who burst onto the scene in 1928 was to link such anticorruption sentiment to democratic ideals as the basis for mass political mobilization. Rómulo Betancourt, the leader of the young activists, concluded that middle-class deprivation under Gomecista monopolies would drive this social sector to join with peasants and workers in a new, multi-class political movement.

Chapter 5 discusses how the oil boom that began in the 1920s funded two modes of financial profiteering. First, as many scholars have discussed, Gómez used the state's control over subsoil deposits to grant concessions for oil production to his family and political allies; many concessions went to a company Gómez himself controlled. Foreign companies purchased these concessions for large sums, enriching individual Venezuelans rather than the nation.[46] A second, much less studied mode of profiteering occurred when rising oil revenues funded a substantial expansion of payments from Chapter VII of the budget of the Ministry of Interior Relations, the presidential slush fund. While scholars such as Coronil have pointed to the connection between Venezuela's petroleum riches and its rent-seeking political culture, none has offered a detailed examination of Chapter VII, which benefited thousands more Venezuelans—including many in the middle class—than ever received the famous petroleum concessions. Significantly, both the oil concessions and Chapter VII payments allowed Venezuelans who enjoyed the regime's favor to benefit from the state's largesse without extracting resources directly from the citizenry. As a result, Venezuelans' responses were more divided and ambivalent than their reactions to predatory corruption. Many denounced the concessions and Chapter VII payments as corrupt, but many others either defended these practices or regarded them with ambivalence, in contrast to the widespread condemnations of predatory corruption.

Chapter 6 argues that anticorruption sentiment and politics played an essential role in shaping the post-Gómez transition of 1935–45. Following the dictator's death, the protests that targeted the properties of officials perceived as corrupt led to the nationalization of Gómez's fortune, and President López Contreras's curtailment of predatory corruption was crucial to the stabilization of his administration. Nevertheless, debates in the press and the congress over López Contreras's and Medina Angarita's continuation of Chapter VII revealed deep disagreements over the probity of these discretionary payments, indicating that they exemplified ambiguous financial corruption during the post-Gómez transition. Critics of Chapter VII gained the most political traction when, late in Medina Angarita's administration, they integrated their denunciations into a larger narrative of presidential personalism (which, again, I regard as synonymous with the patrimonial dimension of neopatrimonialism).

Chapter 7 examines the anticorruption trials organized by the Democratic Action Party (Acción Democrática, AD) following the 1945 coup that overthrew Medina Angarita. AD justified these ad hoc proceedings against 167 individuals associated with the governments of Gómez, López Contreras, and Medina Angarita by arguing that punishing past corruption was necessary to root out personalism and create a modern state. I argue that the trials initially enjoyed widespread support, especially among the middle classes, and that public support for the punishment of predatory corruption remained strong throughout the reformist *trienio* (three-year period of AD rule, 1945–48). Nevertheless, the trials lost much public support due to ongoing disagreements over the appropriateness of payments from Chapter VII. Enthusiasm for the trials dwindled as the tribunal created by AD punished large numbers of defendants for making or accepting payments from Chapter VII. Rather than laying a foundation for the modern state promised by AD, the anticorruption campaign of 1945–48 highlighted divisions over reformers' claim that discretionary payments from Chapter VII were often corrupt. More broadly, I suggest that disputes over the trials revealed the middle class's mounting ambivalence toward AD's professed ideal of an impersonal bureaucratic state.

Such ambivalence was hardly unique to Venezuela. Other historians have found that Latin America's middle classes often espoused the modernist ideals of a merit-based society while simultaneously employing antithetical means, such as personal relationships, to obtain favored access to public resources and to protect their status and careers.[47] This book supports scholars' emphasis on middle-class vacillation as its members navigated such contradictions during the mid-twentieth century.[48] The controversy over Venezuela's anticorruption trials indicates that while AD's notion of a modern state exerted appeal in the abstract, the prospect of severing ties to state patronage—of creating an impersonal state that allowed officials little space for the consideration of individual status or circumstances in the distribution of public resources—represented too great an innovation for many in the middle class that AD sought to represent.

Scholars who frame their discussion of corruption and anticorruption by examining historical actors' halting pursuit of modernity remind us that while modernist aspirations promise to dispel ambiguity and uncertainty, they rarely do.[49] To be sure, the Venezuelan nation-state that existed in 1948, the year that marks the close of this book's narrative, conformed more closely to the principles of modern state organization than the state Gómez seized control of in 1908. Ultimately, however, the history of corruption and anticorruption underscores the development of enduring neopatrimonial dynamics rather than a stage in the more or less linear development of modern forms of governance, as envisioned by some of the reformers who appear in this study. The continuation of neopatrimonial dynamics in the Venezuelan state of the early twenty-first century suggests that the period examined here witnessed the creation of patterns that would continue to ripple through the nation's history for decades to come.

CHAPTER 1
THE FORMATION OF A NEOPATRIMONIAL STATE, TO 1935

Venezuelans living under Gómez's dictatorship often remarked, albeit in hushed voices, that he governed the country as though it were one of his landed estates. "We are all just tenants on Gómez's big farm," one man confided to a US diplomat in 1925.[1] His comment neatly captured both the patrimonial dimension of the dictatorship, in which Gómez treated the state and the nation as personal possessions, and the pervasive sense that Gómez and his allies had organized much of the economy to funnel wealth to themselves, as though Venezuelans were obliged to allow their rulers to profit from their labor and the nation's resources.

Such analogies between Gómez's style of government and his management of his landed estates echoed sociologist Max Weber's belief that patrimonial forms of rule grew out of the authority that powerful patriarchs—such as large landowners—exercised over kinfolk and dependents within their households.[2] Recent scholars who have adopted and refined Weber's concept of patrimonialism have underscored the significance of the patriarchal household as the social and ideological foundation for patrimonial rulers' discretionary authority over public resources and their reliance on personal relationships to advance their interests.[3] As I argue in this chapter, Venezuela had a history of patrimonial rule since gaining independence in the nineteenth century, which Gómez continued but also fundamentally altered. Gómez's signal innovation was to advance the bureaucratization of selected pockets of the state so that they functioned more in accordance with written rules, clear hierarchies, merit-based appointments, and relative efficiency, but he did so only to the extent that such changes augmented, rather than undercut, his personal power and autonomy. To be sure, Gómez did not control everything—not the pandemic that killed his favorite son in 1918, or the spread of democratic ideals that inspired student protests in 1928, or the timing and fluctuations of the oil boom—but he did maintain considerable discretion in the exercise of power. Precisely because neopatrimonialism is a "style of rule,"[4] this chapter begins with a description of Gómez's daily routine during his dictatorship. It then backs up in time and provides an overview of the development of neopatrimonialism in Venezuela, concentrating on the process of state formation under Gómez and setting the stage for the chapters that follow.

Neopatrimonialism in Motion: Gómez's Daily Routine

Although Caracas was the national capital, Gómez chose to reside primarily in Maracay, a town 60 miles to the west, near many of his ranches, farms, and other businesses, from about 1914 onward. In his house bordering the town's plaza, he rose before dawn, dressed, and drank coffee prepared by a long-time bodyguard.[5] By 6 a.m., Gómez was at work with his private secretary, reviewing and responding to reports from officials and loyalists around the country, especially from state presidents—all of whom were selected by Gómez, even during the years that the constitution called for them to be elected by state legislatures. These messages alternated between reporting on political developments and providing Gómez with information regarding his businesses. Telegrams and letters describing efforts to build roads, collect taxes, apprehend criminals, and other matters of public concern merged easily with communications regarding the sale of cattle owned by Gómez or his allies, the creation of new companies by regime insiders, or (especially after World War I) the distribution of petroleum concessions. The dictator and his allies trumpeted the advancement of such business enterprises as evidence of national progress, along with their administration of public affairs.

Around 8 a.m., Gómez had breakfast with some of his children. Gómez never married, but over the course of his life he informally acknowledged and provided economic support to seventy-four children he fathered with thirty-three different women. He legally recognized only the children he had with Dionisia Bello, a longtime companion from his native state of Táchira, and Dolores Amelia Núñez, his companion since 1907, who lived in Maracay with their children in a house near Gómez's residence.[6] Gómez considered two of his recognized sons as potential successors to rule Venezuela. Alí, his favorite and the one most highly regarded by others, died in the influenza pandemic of 1918.[7] José Vicente, who served as inspector general of the army for a decade despite having no military experience or formal training, and who was named vice president in the early 1920s, was likewise considered the dictator's political heir for a time. Like his father, José Vicente amassed a fortune, but he never inspired the same respect in governing circles, and his widespread unpopularity became a political liability. During the political protests that erupted in 1928, Gómez ordered José Vicente into exile, where he died in 1930.[8] Thereafter, Gómez accepted that his successor would not come from his immediate family, though many of his relatives—cousins, sons-in-law, and brothers-in-law—continued to hold high positions in his regime and accumulated substantial wealth through their connections to the dictator.

Following breakfast, Gómez usually met with one of his cabinet ministers. He had grown frustrated with the quarrels among ministers early in his rule and, once he moved to Maracay, he preferred to meet with them individually as they visited him in turn. They typically came from backgrounds very different from Gómez. He was born into a rural family dedicated to agriculture and ranching, with little formal education, and did not see Caracas until he was over forty years of age. His cabinet ministers, by contrast, tended to be well educated, urbane, and often from elite families. Gómez tolerated some ministers' proclivity for diverting public funds to private use so long as their malfeasance did not threaten the solvency of the national treasury. For their part, ministers followed Gómez's instructions throughout his twenty-seven-year rule, regardless of whether he occupied the office of president, as in 1909–14, 1922–29, and 1931–35, or one of his hand-picked presidents occupied the office, as in 1914–22 and 1929–31, while Gómez continued as commander-in-chief of the army.

He usually visited his cattle ranches and farms near Maracay twice a day, once in the morning and again in the late afternoon. A large entourage accompanied him on these excursions. Government officials, foreign diplomats, office-seekers, businessmen, and military officers all sought to speak with Gómez or to demonstrate their loyalty by accompanying him. Officials leaving Caracas for new positions in the provinces were expected to go to Maracay for an audience with Gómez and often joined the entourage. Nemecio Parada, a telegraph operator traveling to a new assignment, met Gómez at his estate called Las Delicias one afternoon in 1925 and described the scene. During his conversation with Gómez, "none of the persons in attendance—not one cabinet minister, general, doctor [i.e., university graduate], man of finance or commerce from Caracas, nor anyone from the so-called high society of the capital—spoke or moved. They all listened in silence with an attitude that conveyed submission and admiration."[9] Despite his reputed reticence, Gómez seemed at ease discussing official and personal business on his farms and ranches, often speaking emphatically and smiling broadly while those around him remained anxious to avoid any offense.

For part of the afternoon, Gómez would meet privately with the manager of his properties. This administrator and a team of roughly twenty employees worked at a house in Maracay overseeing Gómez's rural estates, factories, urban real estate (he owned hundreds of houses across the country), petroleum concessions, shares of stock in various companies, and his accounts with various merchant houses and banks.[10] Historians and contemporary writers disagree over the total value of Gómez's holdings, in part because some assets were in the names of front men, but the most careful estimate places his fortune at around 150 million bolívares (between US$29 million and US$37 million, depending on exchange rates) during the last five years of his life.[11] He was clearly the wealthiest man in Venezuela during most of his dictatorship; some believed he had become the richest man in South America by the time of his death.[12] Although only 10 percent of his holdings were tied directly to petroleum, his fortune grew most rapidly during the heyday of Venezuela's oil boom (1923–29), as government revenues climbed steadily before the Depression.[13]

At any point in the day, Gómez might demonstrate his generosity as a patron. A loyalist visiting Maracay might leave with a stipend of several hundred bolívares a month, ordered by Gómez to be paid from a government account.[14] Gómez routinely played the openhanded benefactor when he traveled south from Maracay to the thermal baths at San Juan de los Morros. As he passed through the town of Villa de Cura, located along the road used to bring cattle from the plains northward to Caracas, he would stop to greet the townspeople and hand money to a local woman, Juana Méndez, for her to distribute among them.[15] Gómez often received personal requests for money from his cabinet ministers and other civilian allies, which he approved or declined during his early morning meeting with his private secretary.[16] Those who gathered at Maracay had their final opportunities to approach the General at dinner, where he favored traditional Andean foods, and later in the evening at a cinema, before he retired to his plain, sparsely furnished bedroom around ten o'clock.

The regime's propagandists made no effort to hide the personalist nature of Gómez's rule; they often celebrated it, just as they celebrated his businesses as evidence of national progress. Laureano Vallenilla Lanz, the editor of the regime's newspaper, *El Nuevo Diario*, wrote that Gómez "is loved, he is venerated among his followers as the patriarch of the Venezuelan family."[17] In this role, it was understood, the General had the freedom to grant or deny his favor to whomever he wished. The personal discretion of the patriarch was also mirrored in Gómez's use of state power and public resources to advance his personal economic interests, even though many Venezuelans, including some of his collaborators, viewed such activity as improper.

But the personalist dimension of Gómez's regime, as pervasive and consequential as it was, formed only one aspect of his system of rule. He also oversaw significant advances in the institutionalization of a professional military and a fiscal bureaucracy to administer national finances. By the mid-1910s, roughly a decade before the onset of Venezuela's oil boom, the accounts of public revenues and expenditures that Gómez received from his treasury minister in Maracay were the most orderly—and showed the most positive balances—of any such accounts in the nation's history. The army units stationed in Maracay and Caracas were the most professional, best trained, and best equipped Venezuela had known. *El Nuevo Diario* recognized these institutional advances of the regime when, in 1916, it praised Gómez's military reform for proceeding "in accord with the demands of modernity" (*de acuerdo con las exigencias de la modernidad*) and again in 1918 as it lauded the "fiscal modernization" (*modernización fiscal*) of the treasury administration.[18] It was Gómez's ability to combine the selective modernization of the state with his personalist exercise of power that set him apart from previous Venezuelan rulers and left a lasting imprint on the national state. We now turn to an overview of the neopatrimonial process of state formation—in which personal, patrimonial power was intertwined with modern bureaucratic authority—to provide context for the chapters that follow.

Venezuelan Caudillismo

Gómez's blending of personal and public interests was rooted in the logic of caudillo politics that had prevailed ever since Venezuela's war for independence (1810–21). In the new nation, formal state institutions proved weaker than the personal networks of authority that grew out of the daily struggle for security in the countryside. *Caudillos* (regional strongmen) built networks of followers who depended on them for access to land, work, political office, or other benefits. Mobilizing these subordinates to fight in the civil wars that raged during much of the nineteenth century provided caudillos with political clout, whether they held political office or not. Historian John Lynch aptly characterized *caudillismo* (the practice of caudillo politics) as a patron-client system based on "an informal and personal exchange of resources, economic or political, between parties of unequal status."[19] The typical caudillo was a landowner with dependent workers and connections to the incipient middle class of the small towns and cities. If he aspired to national dominance, he would need to incorporate other regional strongmen into his patronage network as well. Caudillos who captured state power, whether at the local, regional, or national level, were expected to channel public resources to their allies and clients. This openly transactional logic meant that formal ideologies played relatively little part in Venezuelan politics. Some caudillos identified as Liberal or Conservative (the latter label was absorbed into the Nationalist movement in the late nineteenth century), but the ideological or cultural differences attached to these labels remained weak and fluid.

Of course, many Venezuelans longed for a different kind of politics, one built on the ideas and institutions associated with political liberalism, the dominant philosophy of the North Atlantic world to which Venezuela was increasingly connected through its exports of coffee, cattle hides, and cacao.[20] Venezuelan liberals (regardless of whether they identified with the Conservative or Liberal movements) favored adherence to constitutional and legal norms rather than the personalism of caudillismo, and they scored periodic successes, especially in the first decades following independence. As the historian Reuben Zahler has demonstrated, liberals took advantage of the stability imposed by the caudillo general José Antonio Páez (1830–48), a Conservative, to promote the ascendancy of written law over other sources of authority, such as custom or religion, at least in the courts. Belief in some liberal principles, such as legal equality among male citizens, also became increasingly widespread.[21] But these changes relied upon the relative peace and order guaranteed by Páez, described by Lynch as "the perfect caudillo" who excelled at the personalist exchanges of the patron-client system and who received "much criticism for building a private fortune by 'scandalous speculation' in the land vouchers of his officers and men" which they received as compensation for military service.[22] Despite the patchy spread of liberal values, it was caudillismo, with its patrimonial mixing of private and public interests and its readiness to resort to violence, that drove national politics. Even the rule of Antonio Guzmán Blanco (1870–1888), a Liberal who managed some centralizing reforms—such as a national telegraph system, growth in the federal bureaucracy, and some centralization of government finances—was marked by constant regional conflicts as lesser caudillos jostled for local supremacy.[23] Between 1830 and 1902, cycles of caudillo violence allowed Venezuela only eight years of peace.[24]

Guzmán Blanco introduced new forms of patronage into the repertoire of caudillo politics, including some that were widely denounced as abuses of public authority for private gain. While continuing Páez's practice of acquiring large landholdings, Guzmán Blanco seized greater wealth by taking generous "commissions" on foreign loans that he negotiated on behalf of the nation. Most significantly for the future of corruption and state formation, he granted monopoly concessions to foreign and domestic investors to develop natural resources or to build public services, and in exchange he demanded stock in the investors' companies, a custom that would loom large in the regimes of Gómez's predecessor, Cipriano Castro (1899–1908), and Gómez himself.[25] These monopoly contracts became attractive to investors from the 1870s onward, as growing coffee exports expanded Venezuela's economy and as capital accumulation and technological innovations in the industrial nations of the North Atlantic led to the "great acceleration" of global capitalism.[26] Aside from enriching Guzmán Blanco, the distribution of monopoly contracts garnered him support among the political and economic elites who received them, a practice followed by subsequent presidents.

But Guzmán Blanco and his Liberal successors also received much criticism for such profiteering and patronage. Even through government critics rarely used the word *corruption* to denounce the malfeasance of Guzmán Blanco and other rulers, they condemned the use of public office to enrich presidents and their cronies. The legislature of Bolívar state—where Guzmán Blanco granted important mining concessions—decried "the monopolies created to open space for ruinous speculation," charging that the dictator's actions revealed "an unworthy sentiment of seeking personal profit, which is more than reprehensible in a Magistrate."[27] An anti-Liberal political society organized in 1889, the Democratic Union, denounced "any contracts, monopolies, or concessions that, under the pretext of developing public wealth, destroy liberty of commerce or industry." Such dealings, according to Union leaders, violated "economic science [and] moral and material progress"; their movement promised, in contrast, "to ensure the morality of administration."[28] Disaffected Liberals voiced similar complaints. Jesús Muñoz Tébar, a minister of public works and minister of development under Guzmán Blanco who broke with the former ruler and published *El personalismo i el legalismo* (Personalism and Legalism) in 1890, lamented leaders who failed to respect "liberty of industry because this [principle] would ruin various friends, good servants and faithful partisans, who live from monopolies."[29]

José Manuel Hernández, the leader of the Nationalist Party that challenged Liberal dominance in the late nineteenth century, gained a mass following as he integrated this anti-monopoly sentiment into his critique of Guzmán Blanco's Liberal successors. In debates over a new constitution during 1892–93, Hernández charged that the concessions and monopolies Liberal rulers distributed to their clients smothered opportunities for smaller, local entrepreneurs, a stance that may account for his appeal among the provincial middle class.[30] As the presidential candidate of the newly formed Nationalist Party in 1897, Hernández continued to denounce monopolies that only served the private interests of public officials and allied investors.[31] Barnstorming the country in the first grassroots campaign of a major candidate, Hernández won enthusiastic support, only to see the Liberals manipulate the electoral machinery to produce a victory for Ignacio Andrade, who enjoyed the backing of the dominant Liberal caudillo and outgoing president, General Joaquín Crespo (1892–98). The Nationalists then rose in revolt and Crespo died on the battlefield while subduing the rebels. Gómez's political patron and mentor, Cipriano Castro, exploited the political opening.

Castro came from a different background than most nineteenth-century caudillos. He did not command a clientele of dependent workers, nor could he boast a prominent family lineage. Rather, he relied on audacity and an ability to articulate the grievances and aspirations of the middling social sectors of his western state of Táchira. Young *tachirenses* (people of Táchira) identified with his assertions that their state, a leader in Venezuelan coffee production, was unjustly marginalized in national politics.[32] Castro championed these feelings, winning a variety of political offices, and he remained popular even after his opposition to Crespo's successful rebellion of 1892 forced him to flee to Colombia. As President Andrade's authority slipped away following Crespo's death in 1898, Castro sensed his opportunity. He crossed back into Táchira in May 1899 and declared himself the leader of the Liberal Restorative Revolution against Andrade's government.

Gómez was Castro's second in command in 1899, reflecting the personal bond that had developed between the two men over the previous decade. Born in 1857 to hardworking farmers, Gómez was the eldest of nine children and thus became the head of his family after his father's death in 1883. By the time he met Castro a few years later, he had built a prosperous business raising livestock and supplying local slaughterhouses. The friendship between the two led Castro and his wife, Ziola, to become the godparents of Gómez's son José Vicente.[33] In 1892, Gómez served as quartermaster in Castro's forces that resisted Crespo's bid for power; in defeat, the two tachirenses settled on nearby farms across the Colombian border.[34] Gómez spent his years in exile expanding his cattle business and caring for his growing family. By the time he followed Castro to Venezuela in the Liberal Restorative Revolution in 1899, the priorities that guided the remainder of Gómez's life—dedication to his business interests and to his clan, and the use of political force to protect them both—were already taking shape.[35]

Castro, Gómez, and the Politics of Monopolies

Castro's men marched into Caracas later that year, owing their victory to their leader's boldness, disunity among top Liberal caudillos, and a measure of good fortune.[36] Castro began the transition toward a more centralized—and more predatory—national state, which Gómez would accelerate after 1908. Soon after taking power, Castro made several moves to break the hold of the regional strongmen and concentrate authority in his own hands. His forces swept through rural areas to confiscate weapons from caudillos and their clients; he appointed his loyalists to govern the states of strongmen long accustomed to regional control; and he eliminated the constitutional provision that required a state president's permission for federal troops to enter his territory. To build up the national military, Castro spent heavily on imported arms and announced plans for a military academy to professionalize officers. The caudillos' only chance for political survival was to rebel before Castro consolidated power.[37]

Castro's victory over the ensuing revolt of 1901–3 guaranteed his continuation as president, but it also marked the beginning of Gómez's eclipse of his mentor. The rebellion, dubbed the *Revolución Libertadora* (Liberating Revolution), was led by Manuel Antonio Matos, a wealthy financier and political figure, but the forces under his nominal command were mobilized and led by entrenched caudillos. Castro dispatched Gómez to confront the rebels, and to the surprise of many his untested subordinate defeated one famous chieftain after another. Many of the men who fought under Gómez in these campaigns would go on to become his business partners and to serve him as state presidents and military commanders following his seizure of power in 1908. Predominantly tachirenses, they gained confidence in Gómez as they observed his steady, brave, and seemingly intuitive leadership. Castro occasionally led government forces against the rebellion, and he survived an international threat to Venezuelan sovereignty when, near the end of the Libertadora, warships from

Britain, Germany, and Italy blockaded major ports to force payment of financial claims.[38] But by the time Gómez won the final battle against the rebels in July 1903, it was clear that his military leadership rivaled, or perhaps surpassed, that of Castro.

Gómez greatly expanded his cattle enterprise during Castro's presidency, always attentive to the interplay between business and politics. He bought land and livestock in Táchira and, increasingly, in the north-central region between Caracas and Valencia.[39] He offered employment on his estates to tachirenses who had either arrived with Castro's army in 1899 or had come to the capital later in hopes of finding positions now that men from their region controlled the government. As Castro pursued alliances with elites of the north-central region, tachirenses found Gómez to be the more reliable patron.[40]

Despite growing tensions between the two, Castro and Gómez continued to be partners in the livestock operations they had begun early in Castro's presidency. Both men reportedly exercised de facto monopolies over the supply of cattle to markets and ports in the north-central region from 1903 onward.[41] In 1905, as Castro became suspicious that Gómez was conspiring to replace him as president, he sought to ruin Gómez financially by ending this partnership and demanding immediate payment of some 200,000 bolívares to settle accounts. Gómez was saved by a generous loan from Antonio Pimentel, a wealthy landowner, cattle rancher, and military caudillo based near Valencia who became his longtime ally and business partner.[42] The episode must have impressed upon Gómez that the only businesses that were truly secure were those of the president.

Castro failed to ruin Gómez, but he proved himself an adroit wielder of patrimonial power in other ways, especially as he expanded the distribution of public contracts for monopolies and other concessions. Castro decreed new monopolies (e.g., on salt, glass, flour, guano, and regional shipping) while also creating federal taxes (e.g., on tobacco and liquor) that he administered so as to create de facto private monopolies.[43] Like Guzmán Blanco, Castro was widely criticized by Venezuelans who saw monopolies as a means of illicit enrichment for the president and his inner circle.[44] But there was a crucial difference. Because Castro oversaw the monopolization of so many items of daily consumption, his concessions cut more deeply into citizens' lives. To take one example, the monopoly he created on cigarettes centralized production in Caracas, forcing factories in the interior to shut down and lay off thousands of workers. Meanwhile, Castro received one-fourth of the shares in the new monopoly company.[45] The Spanish legation in Caracas reported the public perception that such monopolies "have been established by the president and the clique of favorites who surround him for their personal benefit."[46]

Castro's enrichment through monopolies that imposed hardship on workers and aspiring entrepreneurs provoked armed opposition. Antonio Paredes, a leading anti-Castro rebel who was eventually executed on the president's orders, called in a book published posthumously in 1907 for the abolition of "monopolies of all kind with which Castro and his men are ruining the country."[47] His brother, Héctor Luis Paredes, accused Castro of "having monopolized all the basic commodities [*artículos de primera necesidad*] in Venezuela" and of ordering Antonio's execution "to secure the reign of monopoly, robbery, and assassination."[48] According to historian William Sullivan, many Venezuelans felt "bitter resentment" toward Castro not only for his monopolies but also for his acquisition of large ranches and other properties out of proportion to his presidential salary.[49]

Resentment over Castro's monopolies contributed to his overthrow, but there were other factors as well.[50] The United States, France, and the Netherlands broke off relations with Castro's government due to unresolved financial claims, and in late 1908 the navy of the latter nation threatened Venezuelan shipping, raising fears of isolation from foreign markets. Caudillos, still smarting from defeat in the Libertadora, believed their return to power would be easier with Castro removed, while civilian leaders had grown disenchanted with Castro because of his rash character and indiscreet sexual relationships.[51] Gómez's sobriety and reserved demeanor appealed to those who believed that steadier leadership was needed. Moreover, his attention to the needs of the tachirenses paid dividends, especially in the army, as many officers hailed from that state. When, in November 1908, Castro departed Venezuela for medical treatment in Europe and left Gómez as provisional president, the anti-Castro reaction quickly erupted. Crowds cheered Gómez while denouncing Castro, caudillos rallied around Gómez, and foreign powers reacted positively to his offer to settle claims. President Theodore Roosevelt sent US warships to Venezuela to support Castro's ouster. On December 19, when Gómez moved decisively to seize power, there was little resistance. Many supporters of the coup saw Gómez merely as a convenient means to rid themselves of Castro; they did not believe him capable of holding onto power for long. One ambitious caudillo commented that Gómez was "a six-month problem."[52]

Gómez, however, demonstrated unexpected political skill, in part through his manipulation of the politics surrounding monopolies. Less than three weeks after he seized power, the Spanish legation in Caracas reported that "the reaction against President Castro is an accomplished fact. The proof is that all the acts of the new Government are aimed at bringing down the monopolies and obstacles that hinder industry, commerce, and freedom of transit."[53] More than a month later, Gómez maintained a popular anti-monopoly policy. "One of the principal tendencies of the new Government, acceding to the repeated clamor of the public," wrote the minister, "has been the termination of existing monopolies."[54]

But by early 1910, Gómez's government had reversed itself and reestablished some monopolistic concessions. Having already lasted longer than the predicted six months in power, Gómez judged that the political benefits of distributing monopolies among political and economic elites now outweighed the cost to his popularity. The newspaper *El Grito del Pueblo* criticized the reimposition of monopolies in an editorial published on January 7, accusing the government of undermining the "freedom of industry" and stating that "monopolies and arbitrary taxes cost the country one-half of its means of existence."[55] The governor of Caracas summoned the staff of the paper to his office, informed them that such criticisms were not allowed, and imprisoned the editor. The following year, the British minister reported that a new monopoly granted to a company fronted by two of Gómez's generals, Román Delgado Chalbaud and Manuel Corao, with exclusive rights to river transport, salt mining, and colonization and trade in Venezuela's Amazonian region, "is very unpopular among the general population of Venezuela" and almost certainly violated the constitutional guarantee of "liberty of industry."[56] A few months later, the British added, "As regards concessions, it is notorious that the President and his Ministers exact large sums from all concessionaires, dividing the spoils among themselves."[57] As under Castro, some companies paid off Gomecista officials with shares in the new enterprises. The legation's report summarizing developments in 1912 emphasized the public's rejection of such profiteering, observing that "from every quarter one hears of the large profits

[Gómez] is making from monopolies, 'commissions' on contracts, and concessions."[58]

By March 1913, as suspicion spread that Gómez would flout the constitution and impose a dictatorship, he had firmly embraced monopoly concessions as a technique of political consolidation. The Spanish legation sent a somber report—"without euphemisms"—arguing that "domestic policy within Venezuela is reduced to a matter of caudillo rule [*caudillaje*]. . . . The President, with ominous authority, distributes public offices among his friends and close allies [*allegados*], and under the cover of these [offices], he and they facilitate for themselves every business or monopoly, either openly or concealed, with complete venality and favoritism. This is the principal basis for the self-interest and fervor with which each of the caudillo's [i.e., Gómez's] partisans supports him."[59] The British legation reiterated the pervasive resentment over monopolies in early 1913, emphasizing the damage they inflicted on the population and on Gómez's waning popularity. "The system of virtual or actual monopolies in the production and sale of every necessary of life presses very severely on the working classes," wrote the British minister, adding that Gómez's "avarice and cupidity and that of his relations and confidants have certainly made him very unpopular in the provinces."[60] Gómez's decision to cancel elections and impose a dictatorship under the guise of a new constitution in 1914 enabled him to clamp down on the discontent caused in part by his turn toward monopolies. Just as important, the decision of his allies—including his military commanders, as described below—to support his continuation in power suggested an interest in protecting the economic interests that Gómez had distributed among them.

The Army and Neopatrimonial State Formation under Gómez

Gómez remained in power for twenty-seven years in part by fulfilling the expectation that a leader would distribute benefits to his allies in the personalist, patrimonial tradition of caudillo politics. But he also introduced reforms in segments of the state apparatus that departed from established practices. His advancement of military professionalization and bureaucratic administration of the treasury involved the promotion of impersonal criteria such as technical expertise, individual merit, and compliance with written regulations. But such innovations remained selective and limited. Gómez never allowed the reforms to advance to the point that they threatened his personal authority or interests. He pursued a more modern state apparatus only to the extent that it enhanced his own power, never as an end in itself. Historian Diego Bautista Urbaneja aptly summarized this neopatrimonial aspect of Gomecista state formation as "modernization at the service of personalism."[61] The simultaneous operation of bureaucratic and patrimonial logics created occasional tensions, especially in the army, but Gómez managed these disruptions, sometimes through the deployment of patronage, at other times through repression, and often by his shrewd selection of generals and cabinet ministers.

Historians of state formation have long viewed the treasury and military as key sites of political centralization. Scholars of European history have pointed to the creation of "fiscal-military" states as a classic pattern of state formation in which foreign wars triggered military professionalization, which in turn demanded greater fiscal resources that were secured through the bureaucratization of tax collection and treasury administration.[62] Historical sociologist Miguel Centeno found that this dynamic did not take hold in nineteenth-century Latin America.[63] Nevertheless, during the first decade of the Gómez regime a mutually reinforcing process of military and treasury reform unfolded that roughly paralleled the fiscal-military model, though it was shaped and limited by Gomecistas' demands for self-enrichment and by Gómez's recognition that bureaucratization, if it went too far, could curtail his personal authority.

Gómez's military reform of 1910–13 was clearly driven by his experience of narrowly defeating the Revolución Libertadora, a civil war rather than a foreign one as in the European model. The reform created the Venezuelan army of the twentieth century and paved the way for Gómez's consolidation of power over the regional caudillos. Historian Angel Ziems dates the beginning of the reform to January 11, 1910, when Gómez created the office of inspector general of the army to oversee the transformation. General Félix Galavís, a tachirense and one of Gómez's partners in the cattle trade since the Castro administration, was appointed to the new post. The military academy opened in July 1910 under the leadership of Colonel Samuel McGill, a Chilean officer contracted by Galavís. Cadets received instruction in artillery, engineering, tactics, administration, fortifications, and military history, topics virtually unknown in the caudillo armies of the past. The army purchased new equipment and weapons to standardize those used throughout the service. Enlisted men learned reading, writing, and hygiene along with their intensified training, and new barracks and military hospitals were built. Within a few years, the reform dramatically altered the army.[64]

The diplomatic community in Caracas, as well as the Venezuelan public, took notice. The US minister reported in January 1912 that "in the last six months there has been a noticeable improvement in the Venezuelan army," for which he credited Galavís.[65] The British minister likewise informed his government of the military's impressive progress, though he observed ominously that McGill was training troops "in the German manner."[66] Gómez and Galavís began to stage military reviews at the Hipódromo, a Caracas racetrack, on patriotic holidays with large audiences. Carlo Pietropaoli, the Vatican's representative in Caracas, attended the review on July 5, 1913, in which Gómez and his general staff rode across the parade ground to review 3,000 troops who marched and executed maneuvers. "The army is well organized, as in Europe," wrote the diplomat, noting that the troops performed "in a manner that cannot be criticized."[67] Like other rulers who oversaw military modernization in nations as diverse as France, Japan, and Egypt, Gómez grasped the power of military reviews to dramatize and convey the state's command of modern technologies of power.[68]

Nevertheless, Pietropaoli sent another dispatch the next day to make clear that this new professionalism was not the only factor shaping the armed forces. He wrote that Gómez, like previous Venezuelan rulers, "has not lost any time in accumulating wealth. He uses it, in large part, to maintain the loyalty of many men as avaricious as he, and in particular the military element on whom he relies and in whom he places his confidence."[69] Although Pietropaoli did not mention officers by name, by 1913 Gómez had established partnerships in the cattle business with several high-ranking military officers in addition to Galavís, such as Generals Pedro Murillo, Francisco Antonio Colmenares Pacheco, and José María García (the latter two were kinsmen of Gómez).[70] Like Gómez, they had won their military titles in Venezuela's civil wars. While they lacked the professional training of the younger officers educated at the new Academy, commanders such as these dominated the higher ranks, generating tensions with professionally trained officers who resented their subordination to men without such preparation.⁷¹ Galavís was well positioned to mediate between the two groups. The young officers respected his commitment to ongoing reform and professionalization, while the senior officers considered him one of their own, having fought side-by-side with him in Castro's 1899 invasion and against the Libertadora.

These divisions first came to a head in the succession crisis that unfolded in 1913–14. The constitution called for national elections in late 1913 and barred Gómez, as the incumbent president, from reelection. Gómez squashed one caudillo conspiracy to topple him in 1913. Then, in August, he suspended constitutional guarantees and led 6,000 troops on campaign, citing unfounded rumors that Castro planned to invade.⁷² With no rebels to fight, Gómez oversaw a period of intensive training of his troops on his estates near Maracay. According to McGill, young officers and cadets became outraged when they realized that Gómez had postponed elections and mobilized the army to perpetuate his hold on power. Their professional training taught them that their highest duty was to the constitution and the nation, not to Gómez. They hoped that Galavís would lead them in a rebellion to block Gómez's power grab, but the bonds of loyalty connecting Galavís and other generals of his generation to Gómez proved too strong.⁷³ Galavís and other high-ranking officers who had fought under Gómez—and in some instances were now his business partners—threw their support to him at this pivotal moment, allowing Gómez to consolidate his dictatorship.

The military reform came to an abrupt halt as Gómez reassigned Galavís to a state presidency and appointed his own kin to oversee the army. Gómez named his brother-in-law, Francisco Antonio Colmenares Pacheco, as the new inspector general in 1914. Colmenares Pacheco showed little interest in further reforms and harassed McGill until he resigned his post. Gómez appointed his son José Vicente Gómez to replace Colmenares Pacheco as inspector general in 1915. The younger officers viewed his unearned appointment as a denigration of their professionalism, but with Gómez as commander-in-chief and the higher ranks filled with his loyalists, they had nowhere to turn.⁷⁴ The partial modernization of the army proved sufficient to protect the regime against any caudillo uprising, and further professionalization was not in Gómez's interest. As Carlos Siso, a civilian functionary in the regime later noted, military reform never altered one essential reality: "It was Gómez's army."⁷⁵

Nothing demonstrated the subordination of the army to Gómez's personal interests more starkly than his use of military units as a personal workforce. With the onset of World War I in 1914 and the ensuing economic tensions in Venezuela, Gómez began to use army units as common laborers on his estates and those belonging to his allies, especially in the center-north.[76] Rank-and-file soldiers performing agricultural and ranching work for Gómez's benefit were supervised by junior officers. In 1917 Gómez established two new barracks in the vicinity of his extensive properties in Carabobo, near the town of Güigüe, to house troops working in his fields and pastures.[77] Exploitation of military forces to perform personal labor was not new in Venezuela; during the nineteenth century, militia commanders had occasionally utilized their men as unpaid workers.[78] But now the use of military units as ranch and farm peons clashed with the professional training and aspirations of the young officers charged with their supervision.[79] One academy-trained officer wrote in his memoirs, "As a career officer, I always felt a great indignation at the demeaning situation to which our Army was subjected when General Gómez kept troops working on his haciendas."[80] General Eleazar López Contreras, who spent most of his career in the military and would eventually become minister of defense in 1930 and then president from 1935 to 1941, warned Gómez that this use of military units damaged morale, but the dictator continued the practice.[81]

Gómez stationed the army's most professionalized units in Caracas and Maracay, leaving other, irregular forces to secure the interior. When a rebellion erupted outside the central-northern region, it was combated not by regular army units from the principal garrisons but by local forces mobilized by the state presidents. Some of these state-level troops were the local poor, press-ganged into service with little or no training, as the need arose. Others came from peasant or working-class families that received small stipends from the state presidents or the *jefes civiles* (district governors) in exchange for an obligation to defend the regime when summoned.[82] Despite their rag-tag nature, these forces knew the local terrain and population, valuable assets in combating a guerrilla-style uprising.[83] Officers from regular army units might be dispatched to the provinces to command irregular forces temporarily, but never with their professionally trained and outfitted units, which Gómez kept near Caracas and Maracay to defend his regime.

To maintain the loyalty of his military, Gómez gave officers a relatively free hand to engage in profiteering. Following long-established custom, officers serving on campaign commandeered livestock, foodstuffs, and other valuables from civilians to sustain their troops, but the distinction between legitimate provisioning and appropriating plunder for personal profit easily blurred. One example occurred in 1914–15 in the cacao-growing area of Los Caños in the eastern state of Sucre. In late 1914 rebels led by Horacio Ducharne sacked an estate belonging to Gómez and his former mistress, Dionisia Bello, reputedly with the acquiescence of local plantation owners. The US minister reported that Gómez dispatched sixty regular officers to Sucre. He explained, "But no regular troops have been assigned. The plan of conscripting privates in the towns and on the plantations continues, apparently because General Gómez intends that all of his trained forces shall remain in the proximity of the capital, for possible eventualities."[84] The officers camped their troops on haciendas in Los Caños for the next six months, harvesting and selling cacao and appropriating other resources. According to the British legation, which documented the episode because of abuses suffered by West Indian workers in the region, the officers passed some of their plunder to Gómez and Bello to compensate for the sacking of their estate. Another share went to Ezequiel Vivas, Gómez's personal secretary who oversaw the operation from Caracas, and the officers deployed to Sucre retained the rest.[85] This sharing of proceeds among the principal figures in an incident of profiteering typified the Gómez era, and it diagrams the cohesive bonds that corruption created within the regime.

Meanwhile, as Ducharne's rebels headed south, regular army officers and locally recruited fighters pursued them, commandeering livestock and other goods as they went. Government forces offered to sell some of this confiscated property to Cecil Meyerheim, a British businessman traveling through the region. The previous year, Meyerheim had witnessed similar actions in the state of Cojedes as government forces chasing rebels confiscated "a few thousand" head of livestock, many of which they delivered to a ranch belonging to Gómez. Meyerheim took photos of the rank-and-file troops pursuing rebels and shared them with the British minister, who contrasted their "ragged" appearance to that of the "regular troops at Caracas and Maracay."[86] The army officers who shuttled between Caracas or

Maracay and the interior, where they commanded state-level fighters when trouble arose, were crucial figures in the regime's "hybrid" military structure.[87] Their importance no doubt influenced Gómez to allow their profiteering during field operations.

Gómez's strategies to secure his officers' fealty—including periodic gifts of cash—were not foolproof. Academy-trained officers and cadets participated in conspiracies or revolts in 1918–19, 1921–22, and 1928, motivated largely by the cronyism and profiteering that they perceived as undermining the military's status. But the great majority of officers continued to serve Gómez to the end of his life.

The Neopatrimonial Treasury

Like the military, the treasury under Gómez underwent a process of professionalization and bureaucratization while retaining patrimonial features, thus reinforcing the neopatrimonial process of state formation. The disorder of national finances was evident when Gómez seized power in 1908, and the vulnerability it created had been demonstrated by European creditor nations' naval blockade six years earlier, during the Revolución Libertadora. Scholars Miriam Kornblith and Luken Quintana emphasize two weaknesses in pre-Gómez financial administration, each rooted in the colonial era but modified during the nineteenth century: first was the practice of dedicating revenues from specific sources to the payment of certain obligations, which prevented centralized control over the allocation of revenues; second was the practice of tax farming, which granted private individuals, usually regime favorites, the right to collect a specific tax and retain the revenues collected in return for the payment of a fixed sum to the treasury, which resulted in the state receiving less revenue than if salaried treasury personnel collected the taxes.[88] These procedures, along with antiquated accounting techniques and a lack of trained treasury personnel, prevented effective management of public finances and threatened Gómez's ability to fund military expansion, highway construction, and payments to foreign creditors. Two of Gómez's first treasury ministers, Abel Santos and Antonio Pimentel, proposed reforms, but major changes began with the appointment of Román Cárdenas in 1913.

Regarded by contemporaries and historians as one of Gómez's most able cabinet ministers, Cárdenas, like other Latin American technocrats of his era, was educated as an engineer.[89] He exuded the seriousness and methodical focus on results that Gómez prized in his collaborators; Cárdenas's identity as a tachirense probably added to the dictator's confidence in him. Gómez appointed him minister of public works in 1910 and he began work on a national system of highways but found that the disarray of the treasury undermined his efforts.[90] In 1912 Gómez offered Cárdenas the treasury portfolio, which he took up the following year after a trip to London to study public finance. Over the next decade, he zealously pursued the modernization of state finances as he drafted legislation to reorganize the treasury, centralized control over revenue collection and budgeting, introduced up-to-date accounting methods, and curtailed tax farming.[91] Cárdenas's reforms occasionally upended the profiteering of top Gomecistas, but the dictator backed him in intra-regime squabbles.[92] The scope and limits of reform once again reflected Gómez's personal interests.

One of Cárdenas's central objectives was to increase revenues from domestic taxes and thus reduce dependence on customs revenue, which typically provided 70 percent of government income when he took office. Customs receipts fluctuated with swings in the world market and in Venezuelan coffee harvests, and the drop in foreign trade following the outbreak of World War I in 1914 underscored the need for reform. That year, as Gómez extended his rule beyond his initial term as president, Cárdenas submitted an annual report to Congress that presented a withering criticism of the treasury's outdated methods, inefficiencies and *corruptelas* (corrupt practices). He singled out tax farming as especially damaging, due to its delegation of state authority to private individuals who routinely used their positions to control the production and trade of commodities they received the right to tax. Between mid-1914 and early 1916, Cárdenas shifted the levies on stamps, cigarettes, and salt away from the contract system to direct administration by treasury personnel. His attempt to end the farming-out of the liquor revenue, to be discussed in chapter 3, began in early 1915 and proved to be a years-long, back and forth process that nonetheless boosted revenue.[93]

Cárdenas's reforms produced a dramatic increase in domestic revenues just in time to offset the decline in customs receipts caused by the war. Internal revenue had totaled 12.96 million bolívares, or 19.8 percent of all federal revenue in 1912–13; by 1918–19, it had more than doubled to 29 million bolívares, or 50.9 percent of federal reve-

TABLE 1.1. Federal revenues and foreign debt, 1910–1923 (thousands of bolívares)

Year	Total Revenue	Internal Revenue*	Internal Revenue as % of Total	Revenue from Foreign Trade	Foreign Debt
1910–1911	62,939	13,249	21.1	44,809	197,518
1911–1912	76,171	13,936	18.3	52,683	194,418
1912–1913	65,438	12,962	19.8	49,622	118,511
1913–1914	60,371	12,523	20.7	42,516	114,853
1914–1915	50,598	18,088	35.7	29,521	110,993
1915–1916	65,674	22,739	34.6	39,328	111,284
1916–1917	72,127	24,582	34.1	43,301	105,457
1917–1918	53,253	25,325	47.6	23,507	101,101
1918–1919	57,102	29,038	50.9	22,467	96,457
1919–1920	101,134	35,169	34.8	52,704	89,296
1920–1921	81,561	29,529	36.2	42,460	84,004
1921–1922	70,927	29,794	42.0	26,394	78,210
1922–1923	87,691	31,727	36.2	41,127	69,919

*Includes revenues from stamps, cigarettes, salt, and liquor.

Sources: J. J. Bracho Sierra, "Cincuenta años de ingresos fiscales, 1910–1960," *Revista de Hacienda* no. 48 (1964): 39, 45; Miguel Izard, *Series estadísticas para la historia de Venezuela* (Mérida: Universidad de los Andes, 1970), 214. Percentage calculations by the author.

nue (see table 1.1). In these years before the onset of the oil boom in the mid-1920s, Cárdenas's reforms stabilized state finances.

Foreign observers praised these developments, sometimes upgrading their assessments of the dictator. British diplomats had alternated between lauding Gómez's imposition of political order and condemning his brutal and corrupt methods. "On the whole, however," concluded H. D. Beaumont, the British minister in Caracas in 1916, "it may be asserted that the rule of General Gómez is in the interests of the country, which has need of a strong hand. Considerable progress has been made during the last years. Peace and order prevail . . . and finance is on a sound basis, revenue exceeding expenditure."[94] Homer Brett, the US consul at La Guaira, specifically noted the rising contribution of domestic taxes to government income during the second half of 1917, "this being the first time that internal revenue has ever even approximately equaled customs revenue for any statistical period. Under direct governmental administration of the stamp, cigaret [sic] and liquor taxes and of the salt monopoly[,] revenue from these sources has greatly increased."[95] These trends allowed Venezuela to continue payments to foreign creditors despite declining exports, reducing the foreign debt from 114,853,071.61 bolívares in 1913–1914 to 96,456,796.52 bolívares in 1918–1919.[96] During this time, Gómez's pro-German sympathies raised concerns in London and Washington, but the orderly state of Venezuelan finances diminished any interventionist impulses. The modernization of the treasury, in sum, underwrote the domestic and international solidity of the regime at a critical juncture.

But Cárdenas's reforms, which were aimed primarily at advancing the bureaucratic *collection* of revenue, went hand-in-hand with the patrimonial *use* of public funds. A significant share of the money for Gómez's personal business investments came from the reformed public treasury rather than his own resources. In some cases, Gómez simply took large sums of money from public revenues. By 1917 it had reportedly become common for Gómez to appropriate several million bolívares from the treasury in the spring or summer of each year and to distribute some of it to cabinet members while keeping the bulk (up to 90 percent) for himself. *Caraqueños* (residents of Caracas) dubbed this pilfering "the annual spring drive upon the National Treasury."[97] The US minister in Caracas, Preston McGoodwin, reported that public employees whose salaries were cut during the war became especially "vehement" in their criticisms of the rumored embezzlement in 1917. At the same time, Gómez reportedly skimmed 4 percent from Venezuela's payments on its debt to Great Britain, which yielded him approximately 220,000 bolívares (US$44,000) a year and was carried out, in McGoodwin's view, with the knowledge of the treasury minister, Cárdenas.[98]

Funds collected by the reformed treasury underwrote Gómez's investments in other ways. The dictator repeatedly engineered favorable property transactions with the national government, buying state-owned properties at prices far below their value and selling land to the nation at inflated prices. Gómez acquired some of his largest properties in the plains—including La Candelaria, an enormous ranch in Apure encompassing some 200 leagues—through an exchange with the national government in 1915. The government, which had expropriated La Candelaria and five other rural estates from the exiled Cipriano Castro and his relatives, traded them to Gómez in exchange for various urban properties owned by the dictator and valued at 1,280,139 bolívares, far below the actual worth of the estates transferred to the dictator.[99]

Gómez's most notorious property deal with the national government occurred in 1926 and involved the ranches in Bolívar state known as Los Hatos del Caura. In cooperation with Colmenares Pacheco, his brother-in-law, business partner, and former inspector general of the army, Gómez began buying properties in the region in 1916, combining them into a large estate of 114 leagues.[100] Gómez then sold Los Hatos del Caura to the nation for 17 million bolívares, though he had paid only around a quarter of a million for the properties. Nevertheless, Gómez continued to use the land as his private property. He used the 17 million bolívares (approximately one-fourth of the treasury's reserves) as part of the 35 million he paid to Antonio Pimentel, his long-time friend and business partner, for the coffee estate El Trompillo and several other properties. Although the deal was "generally criticized" in Caracas, the criticism did not prevent future deals along similar lines.[101] In 1931 Gómez engaged the state in another lopsided transaction so that he could acquire ownership of a new cattle slaughterhouse, refrigerating plant, and several hydroelectric plants in Maracay and its environs, which had been built with government funds and, it was said, with "conscripted soldiers" providing much of the labor.[102] In exchange for these facilities, Gómez traded several properties reputed to be worth much less.[103] The properties he acquired became part of the last great cattle partnership that Gómez formed with his allies, as discussed in chapter 2.

State Presidents and Jefes Civiles

While the military and treasury played crucial roles in the consolidation of national power, these two institutions did not necessarily intrude into the daily experiences of many Venezuelans. Instead, the state presidents and jefes civiles were the representatives of the regime with whom most Venezuelans became familiar. As discussed above, these officials mobilized the regime's local security forces to combat uprisings in the interior. But their main function was to oversee day-to-day operations of the regime in their jurisdictions. Thus, they became crucial figures in the construction of relations between the state and society. Loyalty and cooperation among Gómez, state presidents, and jefes civiles played a fundamental role the integration of the national state. Cohesion among these three levels of administration often involved the coordination of profiteering and the sharing of profits.

As social scientist David Arellano-Gault has argued, people who engage in activities deemed corrupt by their fellow citizens rarely choose strangers as partners. Rather, individuals who share some previously established basis for trust and loyalty, and who are already enmeshed in long-term interactions of reciprocity, are the most likely to join together in profiteering networks.[104] The most common bases for such bonds among Gómez, his state presidents, and jefes civiles were kinship, regional identity grounded in Táchira, and shared military experience during Castro's uprising of 1899 or the Revolución Libertadora of 1901–3. Although personal bonds leading to political appointments could be formed at any time during the long course of the dictatorship, many of Gómez's choices for these offices reflected long-standing affinities, an example of the "homosocial capital" seen by political scientist Elin Bjarnegard as facilitating membership in corrupt masculine networks.[105]

The state presidents were crucial partners in the expansion and management of Gómez's economic empire, and in the process they often became wealthy themselves. Some state presidents had business dealings with Gómez—typically in the cattle trade—before he appointed them, as was the case with Generals Pedro Murillo (president of Táchira, 1910–13), Félix Galavís (Aragua, 1914; Yaracuy, 1929–35), and Argenis Azuaje (Falcón, 1924–29), to cite three examples. But as historian Elías Pino Iturrieta has noted, state presidents often spotted business opportunities in the areas they governed and then suggested to Gómez that they form a new partnership to exploit it, sometimes including other local business or political figures in the enterprise.[106] However the partnerships arose, state presidents often developed business ties to Gómez and managed their joint interests not only in the cattle trade, but in river transport, public utilities, railroads, and sugar production and processing. The insecurity of property rights in Venezuela had long motivated the politically powerful to band together to protect and expand their enterprises, but Gomecistas' penchant for cornering economic opportunities led to amplified criticism and accusations of corruption. The Vatican's representative observed this dynamic between official profiteering and public opinion in 1917 as he reported that "the great industries of this country are in the hands of the 'Supreme Chief' [Gómez] and of his favorites and those he needs to please. For this reason, while much wealth is gathered at the high levels [of the government], discontent is spreading with a muffled protest against the monopoly exercised by political functionaries over basic necessities."[107]

At the local level, resentment against Gomecista exploitation often focused on the jefe civil, the district governor who carried out a range of administrative duties, including road construction, forced recruitment into the army, and command of the police.[108] Like the state presidents, the jefes civiles often had military titles such as general or colonel, won in the civil wars around the turn of the century, and might be either outsiders or natives of the districts they governed. A few jefes civiles earned reputations for fairness, and some shielded their districts from the worst abuses of the regime.[109] The most widespread image of the district governor, however, was that of a heavy-handed ruffian whose corruption and exploitation of the local population was overt and persistent. The adage that Venezuelans attributed to corrupt political appointees—"I don't want them [my superiors] to give me [money], I want them to place me where there's money to be made"[110]—reflects the reputation of many Gomecista jefes civiles as grasping, predatory men-on-the-make.

Many jefes civiles worked smoothly with their state presidents. They often cooperated as managers of the cattle monopoly and, in many instances, as tax farmers who controlled local liquor markets. But other opportunities for mutual gain presented themselves as well. For example, in the state of Lara, district and state officials cooperated with the central government to privatize public lands occupied by small coffee farmers; men with political and economic influence gained title to large tracts of land, while the settlers who had brought the area under cultivation were reduced to rent-paying tenants.[111] Meanwhile, in many parts of the country, jefes civiles levied illegal taxes and fines on the local population. According to the British legation, state presidents expected to receive a cut of these illicit exactions from their jefes civiles.[112]

Some jefes civiles took their profiteering to such extremes that they provoked popular backlashes. State presidents then found themselves obliged to discipline or remove especially exploitative subordinates in order to preserve the stability of the system. Thus, the president of Apure state ordered a jefe civil arrested and tried for demanding hundreds of bolívares in cash, livestock, or other valuables from local couples seeking to register their marriages.[113] In Zulia, the state president and a jefe civil came into open conflict because the latter demanded that local families pay between 400 and 1,000 bolívares for the release of young men swept up in forced military recruiting drives; the state president believed that the jefe civil had also imposed illegal fines while regulating local food markets.[114] In Mérida a more nuanced case occurred in which a state president sought to restrain rather than remove an especially disruptive district governor. State president Amador Uzcátegui wrote to Gómez in 1918 to inform him that the jefe civil of Tovar, Anito Gutiérrez, had collected an unauthorized tax on salt, pocketed public funds allocated for road construction, extorted money from locals to release them from jail, and monopolized the local beef market, which led to complaints even from prominent families who usually avoided politics. Nevertheless, Uzcátegui chose to chastise Gutiérrez rather than replace him. "Apart from the defects that I've mentioned," he explained to Gómez, "Gutiérrez is good, because he's clearly a dedicated friend and doesn't lack the energy to govern."[115]

In sum, the chain of command linking Gómez, his state presidents, and jefes civiles contributed to the process of neopatrimonial state formation just as decisively as the reformed military and treasury. Gómez's ability to impose his loyalists as state and local governors across the country signaled the centralization of state power in his own hands, reinforcing the subjugation of caudillos by the new national army. His capacity to issue orders that would be executed throughout the nation signaled a critical milestone in the emergence of a modern state. But this centralized chain of command was constructed and maintained, in large part, through a shared understanding that at all levels of the regime—national, state, and local—public officials would be free to use their offices for private gain, often in coordination with one another, that they would share the fruits of these enterprises, and that they would act to curb abuses by their subordinates only when they generated enough outrage to foment unrest.

Gómez continued the patrimonial practices of caudillismo, in which there existed no meaningful distinction between public and private resources, and which since the 1870s included the distribution of de facto and de jure monopolies. These restrictive enterprises promoted solidarity among the leaders who profited from them, but many Venezuelans chafed under the cartels' predatory tendency to harm smaller entrepreneurs, workers, and consumers; some of these victims protested the cartels' violation of the constitutional ideal of economic freedom. Because Gómez and other public officials created and managed these monopolies, and because the dictator and political insiders often held shares in these enterprises, outcries against monopolies reflected the perception that officials used their positions for private benefit, to the detriment of the citizenry. While much research on the history of (anti)corruption focuses on the meanings that historical actors have attached to the word *corruption*,[116] in Venezuela protests against the abuse of public office for private gain most often decried the greed and predation associated with "monopolies."

As Gómez fulfilled his obligations to his clients by distributing opportunities for profiteering, he also built state capacity through the partial professionalization of the military and bureaucratization of the treasury. By the mid-1910s, the state rested on salaried tax collectors and modern military cadres to a greater extent than ever before. Political modernity, however, never became an end in itself; rather, it was selectively utilized to enhance Gómez's personal power and thus remained partial and uneven, resulting in a neopatrimonial dynamic that blended personalist and bureaucratic techniques of domination. These distinct forms of power and their ramifications are explored in the chapters that follow.

CHAPTER 2
THE GOMECISTA CATTLE MONOPOLY

A PATRIMONIAL ENTERPRISE

General Timoleón Omaña, president of the Andean state of Trujillo, clearly understood in mid-1914 that controlling the markets for cattle and beef would help him achieve his mission in the region: to break the power of Gómez's rivals and establish the authority of the central state among the people of Trujillo.[1] Gómez's chief opponent there was General Leopoldo Baptista, a caudillo and businessman who had fled Venezuela after turning against Gómez the previous year. Baptista's clan had dominated much of the state since the mid-nineteenth century; they were among the last remaining regional strongmen whose power Gómez had to dismantle in order to complete the dominance of the central state. Military forces under Omaña's command were now camped on estates owned by Baptista and his allies, harvesting the crops and livestock to supply themselves as they confiscated arms from Baptista's followers. But when Omaña wrote to Gómez in July, he explained that in order to "sustain" his officers he had also slaughtered some of Baptista's cattle for sale to the public, only to find that the people of Trujillo refused to buy the meat that came from their caudillo's herds without his consent and for the benefit of his enemies.

The people's refusal to consume this beef, Omaña understood, constituted a political act he could not ignore. It signaled resistance to the relations of power that organized the meat's production and sale, just as acquiescence in its consumption would signal grudging acceptance of the new authority he sought to impose. He explained to Gómez, "Such is the dread [*pavor*] inspired by the name Baptista, that no one wants to buy a product from those estates, much less the cattle that are offered for sale; therefore I have ordered that [the meat] be sold, and if they don't want to buy it, they will have to stop eating beef in the state."[2] Omaña's decision to treat the markets for cattle and beef as arenas for political subjugation came at a decisive moment. Two decades later, the local press still remembered the era when Omaña imposed the authority of the central state as "the tragic years [19]14 and '15 when the brave people of Trujillo were crucified on the cross of tyranny."[3] Omaña's attempt to oblige Baptista's followers to consume cattle seized from their defeated caudillo went hand in hand with his drive to disarm them. The coercive sale of meat illustrates how commonplace transactions could contribute to state formation in both material terms—by providing "sustenance" to Gomecista officers, whether Omaña's phrase referred to salaries, food, or profiteering—and symbolically, by integrating acts of submission into the routines of everyday life.

Over the twenty-seven years of his dictatorship, Gómez and his allies used their political power to establish control over markets for cattle and beef throughout much of Venezuela, creating monopolies that allowed them to reap profits and to insinuate the power of the central state into the lives of consumers and marginalized livestock producers who lost out in the forced transactions that came to characterize this sector of the economy. Gómez already controlled much of the Caracas market for cattle and beef when he seized power in 1908, and he expanded his monopoly across other regions of the nation thereafter. This geographical expansion mirrored and reinforced the centralization of political power that was the hallmark of the regime. Gómez's control over the markets for cattle and beef relied on the cooperation of government officials—especially state presidents and military commanders—who participated in the cartel through business partnerships with Gómez. The profits that flowed to top Gomecistas played a key role in consolidating alliances within the centralizing state. Meanwhile, the cartel's exclusive control over markets for cattle and beef made the power of the regime all too tangible in the lives of consumers forced to choose between buying meat to enrich their rulers or abstaining from a staple of the national diet. In sum, the cartel strengthened the two fundamental axes of state formation—the consolidation of alliances among political elites and their assertion of authority over those they ruled.

More than any other form of corruption, the cattle monopoly exemplified the patrimonial dimension of the Gómez regime. When Venezuelans and foreign observers remarked that Gómez governed Venezuela as though it were his personal property, they often specified that he managed the country as a landowner would manage his rural estate.[4] Venezuelans sometimes extended the metaphor to include the privileged members of the regime who accumulated wealth through the perquisites Gómez granted them. These favored clients of the dictator were said to be "in the pastureland [*potrero*],"[5] feeding on the verdant opportunities he provided. Such parallels between Gomecista rule and the management of the dictator's ranches, when considered alongside Omaña's understanding that controlling beef markets could reinforce new structures of political authority, highlight the significance that both rulers and citizens attributed to the power relations that made up the cattle economy.

Most importantly for the larger arguments of this book, the cattle monopoly illuminates why the Gómez era became a watershed in Venezuelans' experience and consciousness of corruption. As discussed in chapter 1, by the time Gómez seized power, Venezuelans had long deplored monopolies as a means by which government officials abused public authority for private enrichment. But the Gomecista cattle monopoly intruded more directly into the lived experience of people throughout the nation and was controlled more meticulously by the national ruler for a longer time than any previous monopoly Venezuelans had encountered. Their sense of corruption as a systemic national problem was deeply marked by their shared experience of the cattle monopoly, a cartel constructed in tandem with the advance of political centralization. No wonder, then, that when Venezuelans sought to describe the new state that dominated them, they created metaphors invoking livestock and landed estates. Even the oil boom of the 1920s, which transformed their nation in many ways, did not alter their habit of associating Gómez and his system of rule first and foremost with the cattle trade.

Cattle and Beef in the Venezuelan Context

The prominent role of the cattle monopoly in the consolidation of a *national* state reflected the nationwide importance of the cattle industry and the ubiquitous consumption of beef. Simply put, Venezuelans raised, sold, and consumed cattle throughout the national territory that the Gomecistas aspired to rule.[6] The *llanos* (plains) stretching across the central and southern regions had long constituted the nation's primary region for the raising of large cattle herds. The most lucrative markets, however, were hundreds of miles away in the central-northern cities of Caracas, Valencia, and Puerto Cabello (see fig. 2.1). To dominate cattle and beef sales in these urban markets, Gómez and his allies needed to own or control livestock herds and ranchlands in the plains as well as ensure the movement of livestock northward to cities where they could be slaughtered and sold, all while marginalizing rival producers. Because cattle arrived in the north worn and thin after the trek from the plains, they required at least two months' grazing and fattening before they could be profitably slaughtered. Ownership of prime grazing land near the major markets thus became another crucial choke point to enforce monopolistic control, and Gómez prioritized acquisition of land in the north-central states of Aragua and Carabobo. To supply cities outside the plains and north-central region, such as Maracaibo, a more localized network of cattle raising and marketing could suffice, but even cattle headed for these markets often moved across state boundaries. In sum, a nationwide system of political dominance could be intertwined with the far-flung business of raising and marketing livestock for slaughter and sale.

Venezuelan consumers of all social classes demanded a steady supply of beef, as meat occupied a central place in the national diet of the period. Historian Rafael Cartay undoubtedly exaggerated when he claimed that "all Venezuelans ate beef every day,"[7] but various sources indicate a high level of consumption. In 1899 Tulio Febres Cordero, a professor at the University of the Andes in Mérida and well-known public intellectual, published a cookbook titled *Cocina criolla o guia del ama de casa para disponer la comida diaria con prontitud y acierto* (Creole

THE GOMECISTA CATTLE MONOPOLY

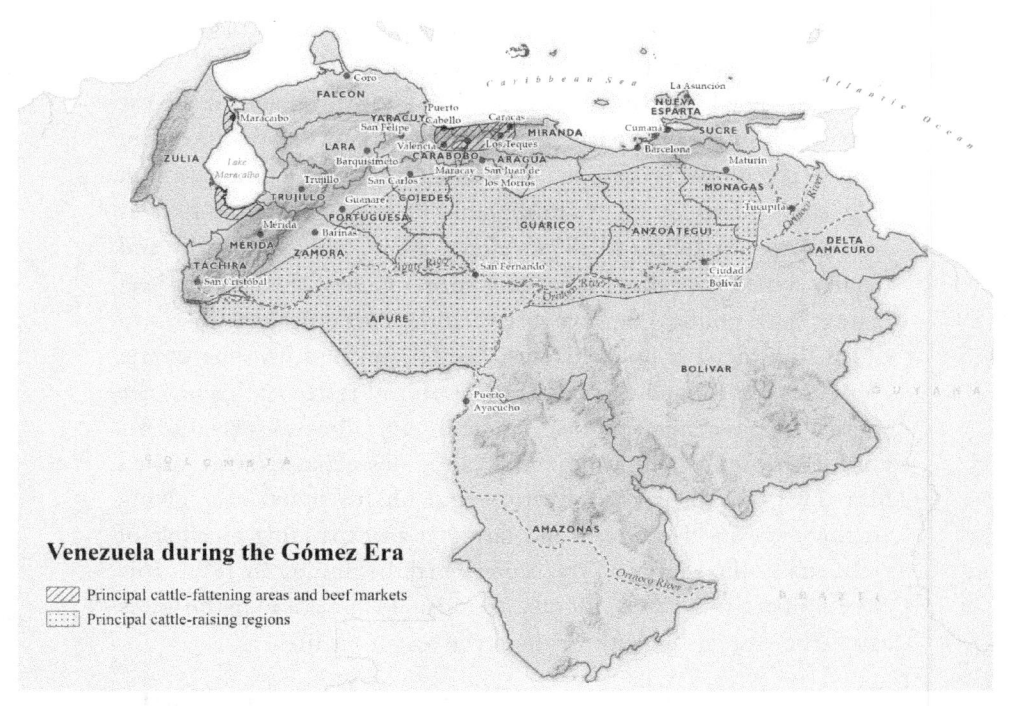

FIG 2.1. Venezuela During the Gómez Era. Credit: Madzie Boyles

cuisine, or a guide for the housewife to promptly and successfully provide daily food).[8] As Febres Cordero emphasized in his prologue, by focusing on "creole cuisine," or typical Venezuelan dishes rather than European recipes, he intended his book to be a reflection of local culture, a guide to the preparation of popular dishes. Significantly, the book featured dozens of recipes for beef dishes compared to only six for ham and poultry, signaling the centrality of beef in the national diet. Although Febres Cordero's intended audience was clearly literate and predominantly middle or upper class, the Venezuelan masses consumed large amounts of meat as well. The US consul in Maracaibo, Carl Sauer, noted that even "the poor people" of western Venezuela were "accustomed to eating much meat."[9] Similarly, public authorities considered it an "article of primary necessity."[10] One writer, Francisco Valeri, argued in a Mérida newspaper that Venezuelans ate so much beef that it caused health problems and advised his readers to eat less of it.[11] Although more difficult to document, beef's gendered meanings in Venezuela probably paralleled those in other nations where it was associated with masculine strength and, especially in times of scarcity, men's consumption would have been privileged over that of other household members.[12]

As discussed in chapter 1, Gómez's early involvement in the cattle business intersected with his political rise at several points before 1908. His regional success as a livestock trader in Táchira gave him the resources that led Castro to appoint him as quartermaster to their armed forces in 1892 and 1899. After Castro's 1899 victory, he and Gómez joined with other allies to control much of the Caracas beef market until political tensions between the two provoked Castro to end the partnership on terms intended to bankrupt his subordinate. Gómez's political and entrepreneurial survival rested on his partnerships with economic, political, and military elites—especially Antonio Pimentel, the caudillo and wealthy businessman who loaned him the funds to pay off Castro—and on his practice of giving employment on his ranches and farms to an expanding clientele of tachirenses who moved to the center-north beginning in 1899. This close connection between Gómez's political fortunes and his business as a cattleman persisted throughout the rest of his life.

The Cattle Monopoly in the Plains and the Center-North

Upon seizing power in 1908, Gómez continued the expansion of his cattle enterprises across the country. His acquisition of ever more property, even after he had become Venezuela's largest landowner, suggested to historian Domingo Alberto Rangel that Gómez's material sense of power implied a parallel between maximizing his political control of the nation and the ownership of ever more of its territory.[13] Many of Gómez's acquisitions, however, followed the geographical logic of the cattle industry explained above.

He came to own dozens of ranches in the plains, and his property acquisitions often relied on his political authority.[14] He acquired some of his most expansive estates in this region through lopsided property deals with the national government like those described in chapter 1. The properties seized by the government from Castro when he fell from power in 1908 included four large ranches in the states of Apure and Guárico; Gómez apparently took control of these properties soon after his coup, though Congress waited to transfer formal ownership to him, in exchange for some holdings of lesser value, until 1915, after he had ensconced himself in power.[15] In other instances, Gómez exerted political pressure on ranchers to sell their land to him at a low price, as when a woman who was negotiating the sale of her large ranch was forced to sell it to Gómez for a much lower sum after local authorities informed the dictator of the impending transaction.[16] Gómez used similar coercive tactics to add to the herds on his ranches. As early as 1913, ranchers in the region of San Fernando, Apure, who wished to sell livestock were reportedly required to give General Eulogio Moros, the manager of Gómez's estates in the region, the first option to buy their animals, at the price he dictated, or risk prison.[17] Two years later, a US consul visiting eastern Venezuelan reported similar tactics to force sales of cattle and land to Gómez in that region.[18]

Of equal importance to his monopoly, Gómez purchased extensive properties in the lowland areas of Venezuela's central coastal region. These properties, clustered largely between the cities of Maracay, Valencia, and Puerto Cabello, were perfectly situated for fattening cattle from the southern plains before they were slaughtered for sale in the region's urban markets, including Caracas, or exported from the coastal city of Puerto Cabello. Maracay, the small city sixty miles west of Caracas where Gómez had his primary residence from 1914 onward and which became the center of his cattle empire, was located at the natural entryway for livestock driven northward from the plains to the coastal region. To the west of Maracay lay Lake Valencia and its surrounding basin. These fertile lowlands stretched between Puerto Cabello, the site of a British-owned frozen meat plant that bought cattle from Gómez, and Valencia, the capital of Carabobo state and the second-largest city of the central coastal region after Caracas.[19]

Gómez began to purchase cattle properties near Puerto Cabello as early as 1903, and in 1905 he pooled his resources with two prominent politicians and entrepreneurs in Carabobo, Generals Antonio Pimentel and Manuel Corao, to buy properties with a combined value of 264,000 bolívares in Güigüe, on the south side of Lake Valencia.[20] Pimentel continued to cooperate with Gómez in the acquisition and running of cattle properties in the region after he seized power. In 1909, according to the British minister in Caracas, Gómez appointed Pimentel as his secretary general in order "that he might have him close at hand to consult in business matters, and especially in the management of the estates he is buying in the neighbourhood of Valencia and Puerto Cabello for the rearing of cattle on a large scale."[21] General Corao, meanwhile, became a major stockholder in several monopoly companies licensed by Gómez's government and in 1913 was named quartermaster general of the army.[22] By controlling access to strategically located pasturelands in the north-central region, Gómez and his allies laid the foundation for restricting other entrepreneurs' access to major beef markets.

Like some of his business partners—including Pimentel, Corao, and General Félix Galavís—Gómez often established his ranches in the central coastal region by acquiring agricultural land and converting it to pasture.[23] This practice resulted in dramatic transformations of the land surrounding Lake Valencia by the early 1910s. The British minister, after seeing the area in 1912, emphasized the social and environmental changes wrought by Gómez and his associates:

> It is regrettable that the President and his friends have acquired in one way or another large tracts of the fertile alluvial land adjoining the large Lake of Valencia, of which it originally formed a part. This is equal to any land in the world for sugar growing and formerly gave employment to a large number of families, but has now been fenced off for cattle enclosures, the land has reverted to prairie, and the population has disappeared[,] leaving little but scrub and tufts of coarse grass for which hardly one man to the square mile is required to tend it. A recent visit to this region confirms this description, and I attribute the decay of the town of Valencia to this change of culture.[24]

Gómez's acquisition of land in this region was so extensive that in 1921 he owned all the territory that could be seen from any point along the road connecting Maracay to Valencia, according to Carlos Siso, a loyal functionary of the regime who was nonetheless critical of the Gomecista cattle monopoly.[25] The environmental and social consequences of Gómez's conversion of agricultural fields to pasture in this region outlived the dictator and his regime: they were lamented in the national Congress in 1936 and in the press as late as 1946.[26]

Gómez's rapid expansion of his cattle interests relied on his business partnerships with military commanders, state presidents, and other officials. In most cases they were the strongmen of the regime, individuals who carried the titles of general or colonel from their action in the civil wars at the turn of the century, regardless of whether they held positions in the military after 1908. Their prominence in the Gomecista cattle monopoly reflected the logic of state-building through predatory profiteering. A cartel that relied on coercion, or the threat of it, required men who could command obedience, and these were also the men whose collaboration Gómez required to secure his regime. They often joined their capital and political influence with those of Gómez to buy land and livestock in their jurisdictions and then assumed responsibility for management of the enterprise in the regions where they held political or military positions.[27]

The ethos of patronage suffused these business partnerships. The strongmen sought to demonstrate their loyalty to Gómez by advancing his personal interests, hoping that he, in return, would grant them opportunities for profit. In one example, General José Antonio Baldó, president of Portuguesa state, wrote deferentially to Gómez in 1915: "There is a cattle deal here that I would venture to make [*que yo me atrevería a hacer*], investing my savings in it and giving it my full attention, if you would like to join me in it."[28] He outlined his plan to buy cattle in Apure state and bring them to Portuguesa, where grazing land was underutilized, and to turn a profit during the three years he assumed he would serve in his post. "You know the good and the bad of this business," Baldó continued, "and therefore I wait to hear your opinion, and above all to know if you would like to undertake it with me." In the meantime, Baldó wrote, he had already sent an agent to Maracay to buy breeding bulls from Gómez, who took pride in his efforts to improve the quality of Venezuelan cattle herds.

The president of Guárico, another state in the plains, General León Jurado (who had served under Gómez in suppressing the Libertadora rebellion) reported to Gómez in 1914 on the condition of the latter's lands and cattle there, while also warning him of the lax attitude of the manager of one his estates. Jurado's conscientious supervision of Gómez's properties apparently paid dividends. He thanked Gómez "for having preferred me in the purchase of the steamship 'Julia'" for which the Ministry of War paid Jurado 80,000 bolívares, and he asked Gómez to have the government buy another ship he owned, which he believed could be used for patrolling Venezuela's coasts.[29] While serving a second stint as president of Guárico a decade later, Jurado continued to report to Gómez on his cattle ranches in the state, as well as to propose partnerships in the grazing and breeding of cattle. Jurado later sold some of his properties in Guárico to Gómez before returning to the presidency of his home state of Falcón in 1929.[30]

Numerous generals and state presidents struck partnerships in the cattle business with Gómez similar to those already discussed for Baldó, Jurado, Galavís, Corao, and Pimentel. In 1917 the US minister in Caracas, Preston McGoodwin, forwarded to the US State Department a report by an American businessman in Venezuela that the legation deemed accurate. "The cattle business," wrote Charles Freeman, who represented various firms including W. R. Grace and Company, "is now completely monopolized by Gómez, through his agents in Caracas and the rest of the Republic (General Felix Galavís, Pérez Soto, Eustoquio Gómez, José Maria García, Manuel Sarmiento, [Isilio] Febres Cordero, Silverio González, etc., etc.), who are military men or Governors [sic] of States."[31]

The organization of the monopoly often extended to the jefes civiles at the district level, though some of these local officials were more tightly integrated into the cartel than others. In one case of explicit integration in early 1909, Gómez wrote to General Pedro Murillo, an important military commander, future state president, and occasional partner in cattle deals in their home state of Táchira, to say that he had just ordered state president General Jesús Velasco to appoint "General Eugenio Prato as jefe civil of Periquera, which I believe will be very favorable to your cattle business."[32] The dictator's support for Murillo apparently profited the latter, who was born a "modest son of the people" but died in 1916 with "a copious fortune amassed with the sweat of his brow," according to one newspaper.[33] In other districts, jefes civiles sought to establish such exclusive personal control over their local beef markets that their state presidents expressed frustration to Gómez, indicating that the close cooperation between Murillo and Prato provided by Gómez did not always occur.[34] In a further variation, in the Crespo district of Lara state, General Ramón Antonio Vásquez, a native of the district with solid Gomecista connections, supplied much of the cattle butchered at the public slaughterhouse while serving as jefe civil in the 1920s, but allowed other entrepreneurs to supply the rest.[35] In sum, the roles that jefes civiles played in the cartel varied substantially. Some, like Prato, acted directly as agents for more powerful Gomecista cattlemen, while others, like Vásquez, used their positions to claim a disproportionate share of the market for themselves but granted some access to other cattlemen. Still other district governors attempted such exclusive control that they had to be disciplined. But relatively few avoided the perception that they played some part in official profiteering from cattle and beef.[36]

The joint ventures between Gómez and his allies included the local transport of livestock in some areas. In 1916 General Vincencio Pérez Soto, the President of Apure state, invited Gómez to join him, Colonel Luis Felipe Torres, and Francisco Barbarito (a prominent Apure rancher) in establishing a business to ferry cattle, passengers, and cargo across the Apure River in modern barges and motorized boats. Gómez's role in the enterprise would be to arrange for the national Congress to grant the rights needed for a river transit business.[37] The operation was up and running two years later, and the following year Pérez Soto warned Gómez of an attempt to establish a rival ferry service that would harm "our enterprise."[38]

Another instance of blending public power and private interest involved Gómez's insistence that state presidents make extraordinary efforts to capture cattle thieves, an ironic initiative when juxtaposed to his own coercive tactics against rival ranchers. Beginning with a widely publicized telegram on July 29, 1915, Gómez repeatedly instructed state presidents to carry out a concerted campaign against cattle thieves.[39] To be sure, the theft of livestock had been a widely lamented scourge of the industry since colonial times. But the issue was also personal to Gómez, since some of his cattle had been stolen the previous year.[40] Officials and ranchers rushed to praise the dictator's directive and to keep him abreast of the ensuing arrests.[41] General José Antonio Baldó, the deferential president of Portuguesa state, informed Gómez that he intended to imprison the accomplice of a cattle thief even if, as he anticipated, the courts absolved the accomplice on a technicality.[42] Equally eager to demonstrate his zeal, General Julio Hidalgo, president of Aragua state, informed Gómez that fifty-pound leg irons (usually reserved for political prisoners) had been put on the cattle thieves captured in his jurisdiction, which included Maracay and many of Gómez's properties.[43] In the context of the Gomecista monopoly, cattle theft might be viewed as a political crime as well as a crime against property, and responses to the theft blurred the line between law enforcement and the protection of Gómez's personal interests.

As Gómez and his allies moved livestock across state borders, the selective application of taxes provided another opportunity to advance the interests of the cartel. State and local taxes on livestock crossing jurisdictional boundaries imposed heavy costs on cattlemen moving herds from the southern plains to northern markets, but officials did not collect the duties on animals belonging to Gómez and his partners.[44] Thus General Pérez Soto, as Apure president, wrote to Gómez in 1915 to assure him, "Here nothing is being charged on your cattle for the State or Municipal dues, nor are the Municipal dues being charged on your horses that enter [San Fernando de Apure], because this is what is just with me being in this office."[45] Similarly, General León Jurado, as president of Guárico, proposed a new cattle tax in 1924, but made it clear that it would be selectively enforced. Jurado explained to Gómez's secretary, "We understand that those [cattle] of our Chief and of some friends will remain exempt from this tax, but not those who speculate in this sector and take out large lots, it is just that they should pay a tax."[46] Jurado and Pérez Soto, both longtime allies and business partners of Gómez, presumably exempted their own herds from state and local taxes as well. The selective collection of state and local taxes, which could total one-fourth of the livestock's market value, created a substantial advantage for Gomecistas.[47]

To guarantee himself and his allies a privileged position in the next phase of cattle marketing, Gómez established control over the butchering of cattle in the public slaughterhouses of the major urban markets. Many cities and towns built or refurbished their slaughterhouses during the Gómez era, often inaugurating them on December 19, the holiday that celebrated Gómez's seizure of power, amid festivities that noted their modern and hygienic features, such as cement floors and metal roofs.[48] But these symbols of progress were also key sites in the patrimonial monopoly. Gómez appointed inspectors to the public slaughterhouses in the principal cities and instructed them to reject any cattle of "doubtful origin" and to accept only cattle that had been "properly fattened."[49] Such admonitions meant, in effect, that only cattle coming from pasturelands or ranches belonging to Gómez and his allies should be accepted for butchering. Gómez's domestic critics as well as foreign businessmen and diplomats believed that these inspectors even permitted the slaughter and sale of *diseased* cattle belonging to government officials.[50]

Gómez and his partners also restricted the slaughtering of cattle for sale in Venezuela's major cities through a system known as the *playa*, which had its roots in the colonial era. Municipal authorities throughout much of colonial Spanish America awarded monopoly contracts to ranchers and merchants to supply cities with cattle for slaughter and sale. These contracts served the public by assuring urban residents a reliable supply of meat while giving favored entrepreneurs a steady and predictable outlet for their cattle. After independence, republican governments in Spanish America tended to move away from such formal monopolies, but combinations of powerful businessmen still sought to control the supply of cattle to public slaughterhouses for their own benefit while shutting out rivals.[51] Gómez and his partners in the cattle business were not unique in Spanish America in their attempt to use political influence to control public meat supplies, but they were unusually successful in their ability to control markets in a number of cities scattered across the nation well into the fourth decade of the twentieth century.

Gómez's playa was essentially a system of quotas in which one or more ranchers supplied a certain quantity of cattle to a municipal slaughterhouse within a specified period of time. Sometimes the allotment was formalized in a contract, as in the western city of Maracaibo, discussed in more detail below. In other cases, quotas were managed on a more fluid basis by city officials with the understanding that Gómez could settle occasional disputes over market access. Manuel Sarmiento, the president of Guárico state in the plains south of Caracas, wrote to Gómez in 1923, hoping that the dictator could facilitate his access to the Caracas beef market. "Since I did not obtain the playa from the Governor [of Caracas] for the cattle that I have had in the pasture of La Hamaca for four and a half months, and since I presume I may lose out if I don't sell the cattle soon, I would like to propose to you, with the utmost respect, that you take charge of these cattle for me, since you can arrange their passage more easily."[52] Sarmiento, who owned important ranching operations in Guárico, hoped that Gómez would give him a good price for the 400 cattle because they were well fattened and ready for market.

Similarly, General Félix Galavís, Gómez's longtime business partner and leader of the military reform in 1910–13, asked the dictator repeatedly to grant him greater access to the Caracas market. Galavís wrote to Gómez in 1923, "[While in the past] you assigned me four days a month of the playa at 55 steers [per day, more recently] I have only been given two days per month, at a rate of 40 steers, and I have many fattened cattle and need funds to fulfill my commitments."[53] Appealing to Gómez's sense of obligation as a patron, Galavís added, "I hope that you, convinced of my unbreakable loyalty, will favor me as before with your trust [*confianza*]." But two years later Galavís was still frustrated. He wrote Gómez in 1925 to explain that his quota for the Caracas slaughterhouse continued to be forty steers a month, which was barely profitable since most of the cattle had to be transported from Urama, a coastal town east of the capital. Galavís requested that Gómez increase his allotment so that he could better cover his shipping costs; he also hoped that Gómez would grant his brother, Hely Galavís, "a monthly playa of 40 steers."[54] The following year, Galavís wrote Gómez yet again for assistance in marketing the cattle fattened on pasturelands in Urama, this time adopting a different approach. He invited Gómez to join him in a partnership to sell cattle from Urama to the Maracaibo market, which they could reach using Gómez's Venezuelan Navigation Company.[55] Galavís seemed to conclude that Gómez would not cede a greater share of the Caracas market, and that selling the cattle in Maracaibo depended upon Gómez receiving a share of the profits.

While members of the regime such as Sarmiento and Galavís faced occasional bottlenecks in slaughtering cattle for sale, ranchers without close connections to Gómez risked complete exclusion from major markets. Cattlemen outside the monopoly understood that their lack of access to these markets resulted in large part from the playa system and the discriminatory application of transit taxes, which could total from 5 to 25 bolívares per head of cattle, or up to a quarter of their value, as they went from the plains to northern cities.[56] The Caracas Chamber of Commerce, which included livestock investors, asked Gómez to abolish or relax these controls in 1922–23. In a rare act of confrontation, the chamber pointedly observed to Galavís that "in some states, the industry of slaughtering cattle is an exclusive business of the authorities."[57] Despite public assurances from Gómez that he would ease restrictions, the cattlemen gained no lasting concessions on the playa and only a limited reduction of transit taxes.[58] Even some officials within the regime acknowledged the economic hardship created by the Gomecista cartel. Carlos Siso, the faithful but not uncritical official who was secretary to two state presidents and also spent time among the dictator's entourage in Maracay observing the inner workings of the regime, singled out Gómez's cattle monopoly for censure. "General Gómez was a terrible competitor for the stock raisers [*criadores*] of the Republic, he caused them losses and in other respects was an obstacle to the progress of stock raising," wrote Siso in his study of Castro and Gómez. "Under a system called 'la playa,' the municipal authorities permitted only [Gómez] or the persons he favored to sell the cattle necessary for consumption in certain cities. This monopoly closed the principal markets to [other] stock raisers, who found themselves obliged to sell their cattle at a lower price; or to keep the cattle if they could not find a buyer, in which case the stock raisers missed the most opportune time to sell their cattle, according to the stock's fatness and age."[59] Clearly, Gómez's favor was necessary to prosper in the cattle trade, and he restricted opportunities largely to the strongmen whose support he needed for the regime's security and the enforcement of the monopoly.

A Regional Variation: The Cattle Monopoly in Zulia

Outside the central region of the country, Gómecistas formed more local or regionalized cattle monopolies in which Gómez still had a leading role, but he was less dominant than in the plains and north-central cities. In the western state of Zulia, Gómez and several associates established a cattle partnership that, in typical fashion, combined their financial capital with their political influence to form an exclusive and profitable enterprise. The partnership, organized in 1912 as Rincón & Compañía, included Onésimo Rincón, a merchant and rancher in Zulia; General Francisco Antonio Colmenares Pacheco, who was married to Gómez's sister Emilia and during the 1910s served as governor of the Federal District of Caracas and Inspector General of the Army; and General José María García, Gómez's cousin who served as military commander in Zulia in the early 1910s and, after a brief stint as president of the neighboring state of Trujillo, became president of Zulia in 1914. Gómez and these three associates were joined by a fifth partner when in 1915 Juan Crisóstomo ("Juancho") Gómez, the General's brother, paid 100,000 bolívares to join the enterprise. As described by historian Peter Linder, the company's primary purpose was to supply Zulia's capital, Maracaibo, with cattle for slaughter and sale to the public.[60] The enterprise began with the acquisition of a cattle hacienda in Encontrados, in the Sur del Lago region bordering Lake Maracaibo. Rincón managed the day-to-day operations of the company while García, as state president, provided oversight from Maracaibo on behalf of the other partners. Here, as in the region around Lake Valencia, some of the cattle estates were formed by purchasing agricultural land and converting cultivated fields to pasture. The operation also expanded through Rincón's acquisition of grants of thousands of hectares of public lands from the national government as well as municipal lands in Encontrados—acquisitions undoubtedly facilitated by the partners' political pull.[61] Rincón and his partners used much of the land they controlled to fatten cattle brought from outside Zulia for slaughter and sale in Maracaibo.

This regional Gomecista cartel monopolized access to the Maracaibo beef market, just as Gómez and his partners controlled markets in major cities farther east. During García's presidency of Zulia, Linder observes, Rincón received "exclusive contracts to supply steers to the Maracaibo slaughterhouse."[62] This control that Rincón, Gómez, and their associates exercised over the supply of beef in Maracaibo led to high prices and to complaints against the company in Maracaibo and Encontrados. (Resentment against the monopoly may have contributed to death threats against García and to a deadly riot against his leadership of the state in 1916.[63]) Eventually, in 1919, Gómez moved to loosen Rincón's domination of Zulia's cattle markets—as we have seen, Gomecistas occasionally restrained profiteering when it threatened political stability—but by that time Gómez and his associates had already realized substantial profits. For example, in 1916, García sent Gómez 14,368.89 bolívares as the dictator's share of the previous year's profits from the cattle enterprise in Encontrados managed by Rincón.[64] This was a modest sum in the context of Gómez's economic empire, but it represented a generous annual return on his initial investment of 40,000 bolívares.

The Cattle Monopoly and Anticorruption Sentiment

The Gomecista monopoly over the cattle trade and beef sales gave Venezuelans regular reminders of their rulers' power over, and profit from, important areas of their lives. The cartel of Gómez and lesser strongmen profoundly impacted ranchers' ability to make a living just as it impacted consumers' access to meat. Like the monopolies created by Venezuelan political leaders for their private benefit from the late nineteenth century through the Castro regime, the Gomecista cartel intruded into Venezuelans' livelihoods and their consumption of basic goods, provoking criticism and resistance. But Gómez's cattle monopoly was the first nationwide cartel created and managed by a national ruler for the enrichment of himself and his clique, and thus the first to provoke such widespread resentment over the predatory use of public power for private gain.

Ranchers and cattle traders who experienced economic loss or ruin due to their exclusion from the cartel reacted in different ways, but their resentment was nationwide. In Gómez's home state of Táchira, many cattlemen felt obliged to flee. Reporting on the numerous refugees who had crossed from Táchira into Colombia by early 1914, the US legation in Caracas observed that many were "cattle raisers, large and small, who claim to have been driven out of that industry by Generals [Juan Vicente] Gómez and [Félix] Galavís, who have an absolute monopoly on cattle raising and the sale of beef and all by-products."[65] US diplomats believed that Táchira had become "bitterly antagonistic" toward the regime and placed much of the blame on the cattle cartel. That same year, the British minister in Caracas attributed rising anti-Gómez sentiment in the north-central region to the cattle monopoly. He noted that "one of the many grievances of the population, apart from [Gómez's] unconstitutional and arbitrary acts, is his monopoly of the cattle trade. Practically no cattle can be sold or exported except by the President, and cattle raisers have to sell to him at his own price, a low one. This applies to a large area of territory extending from Caracas to Valencia, over 100 miles distant."[66] The monopoly had similar effects in the plains to the south. Emilio Arévalo Cedeño, who became a leading anti-Gómez rebel and is discussed at greater length in chapter 4, wrote of the anger and humiliation he experienced when in 1913 he was forced to trade horses and cattle with Gómez's representative in San Fernando de Apure. The low prices imposed on Arévalo Cedeño left him ruined. He claimed that he and other livestock traders had to confront the stark choice of whether to submit shamefully to the cartel or take up arms against Gómez to save their honor and "what little remained of our interests."[67]

Consumers of beef suffered from the monopoly less than did ranchers and cattle traders who lost their livelihoods, but for them as well formerly routine transactions became concrete reminders of their vulnerability to official exploitation. Gómez's beef monopoly kept retail prices artificially high. In Táchira, the monopoly meant that consumers paid twice as much for beef as consumers just across the border in Colombia.[68] In Caracas and other major cities, Gómez's representatives and inspectors controlled the weighing of meat and were said to give consumers only twelve ounces of beef while charging for a pound.[69] Consumers occasionally grumbled at the high prices or poor quality of the beef, leading meat retailers to complain about their inability to source meat outside the cartel to satisfy their customers. Gomecista officials usually met such complaints with little sympathy. In 1928 General Rafael María Velasco, the governor of the Federal District of Caracas, responded to complaints against the monopoly by stating that as long as he ran the city, consumers would eat beef from Gómez's ranches or they would eat no beef at all—an assertion that echoed Timoleón Omaña's determination to enforce political subjugation through control of the beef markets in Trujillo fourteen years earlier.[70]

Velasco's comment came during the most sustained anti-Gómez movement of the long dictatorship, as student protests against the regime in February 1928 inspired a military revolt led by young officers two months later, followed by several localized armed movements through 1929. The student protests have been remembered largely as a pro-democracy movement, but they were also motivated by a strong reaction against corruption, including critiques of the cattle monopoly. One anonymous broadsheet circulated in the capital in 1928 criticized the Gomecista monopoly of beef sales in Caracas markets as "extortion against free commerce and free industry, solely to benefit the personal interests" of the ruling clique.[71] Another clandestine publication in 1928 spoke directly to women who purchased meat: "Women of Caracas, what example do you give your daughters[?] . . . The Master [Gómez] sends meat, sometimes rotten, from Maracay, and you—the slaves [*vosotras—las esclavas*]—buy it with servility, without even an aloof, silent, dignified protest."[72] This criticism, while reflecting the beef monopoly's power to elicit widespread submission, overlooked the multifaceted contributions of women to the protests of 1928 (including their active participation in the clandestine press itself[73]) and may have overstated the "servility" of Caracas consumers more generally. Joaquín Gabaldón Márquez, a student leader who later joined the caudillo uprising against Gómez led by his father, General José Rafael Gabaldón, noted the wave of opposition against the beef monopoly in October 1928. He asserted that "a great many consumers now do without this item [beef], which results in considerable losses for the [retailers] who are obliged to buy it" from

Gómez's slaughterhouse in Maracay. Gabaldón Márquez emphasized consumers' dissatisfaction with the meat produced by the cartel, noting that "the beef that is sold is not of the quality that it should be."[74]

Throughout the dictatorship, popular resentment against the Gomecista beef monopoly intersected with concerns over the quality of meat, both in terms of its safety and its ability to satisfy consumer taste, issues that illuminate the experience of Venezuelans who bought—or, in Gabaldón Márquez's account, refused to buy—beef supplied by the monopoly. As mentioned earlier, suspicions had long circulated that Gomecistas slaughtered unhealthy cattle for public consumption. But colloquial references to "rotten" beef, as in the clandestine press's criticism of female consumers quoted above, also reflected popular distaste for the refrigerated meat that the monopoly began pushing onto the market on a large scale. Gómez introduced reluctant Venezuelan consumers to chilled beef following the inauguration of a new slaughterhouse in Maracay in July 1928. It was built with public resources, including materials supplied by the Ministry of Public Works and labor performed by conscripted soldiers, and was formally transferred to Gómez in 1931 along with a dairy, a refrigerating facility, and electrical plant, in exchange for some of the dictator's overvalued properties.[75] The following year the British minister reported that the main purpose of the operation was to

> supply the neighbouring country as far as Caracas with dairy products and meat. The meat is killed at Maracay and chilled and then shipped to Caracas in refrigerating vans. This chilling has the effect of improving the meat, making it more tender. This has been the cause of much dissatisfaction in the capital, where the taste is decidedly in favour of tough, freshly killed meat, and in the family circle the other variety is referred to as "carne podrida" ("rotten meat"). The residents, however, have no choice in the matter, and must either buy the meat supplied by the President or go without. In certain of the suburbs which lie outside the Caracas jurisdiction this freshly killed variety is obtainable, but the road is well watched to prevent any smuggling, and cars, both commercial and private, are frequently stopped and searched.[76]

Caracas consumers were far from unique in their preference for freshly slaughtered beef over the chilled variety. Consumers in Mexico and Colombia, for example, had similar tastes and acted to satisfy their preferences.[77] But beef-eaters in those nations never confronted a monopoly controlled so tightly, for so long, by one individual. In Caracas, by contrast, the simple act of buying and eating chilled meat had become an act of submission to the Gómez regime and its monopoly. The dictator's power intruded into the intimate space of "the family circle," perhaps humiliating household patriarchs by demonstrating their powerlessness to provide the food that their dependents, and they themselves, preferred. Even as the British minister composed his report on Venezuelans' distaste for chilled beef, however, one final permutation of the Gomecista cattle monopoly was about to unfold, imposing new frustrations on consumers and stock raisers alike.

The Compañía Ganadera Industrial Venezolana

In the last two years of his life, Gómez undertook an extensive restructuring of the cattle industry, seeking to defuse widespread anger over the cartel that he and his associates had maintained for a quarter-century. In early 1934 the government announced the formation of the Venezuelan Industrial Cattle Company (*Compañía Ganadera Industrial Venezolana*) for the production and sale of chilled, preserved, and fresh meats, presenting it as the salvation of the cattle industry (despite consumers' aversion to chilled beef). As the British legation reported, the initiative came "at an opportune moment, since it must be admitted that many [Venezuelan entrepreneurs] were beginning to lose their patience with the policy of the President and his friends, who have systematically smothered all enterprise in which they were not personally interested, and a certain murmuring had begun against them which had even become more or less public."[78] The reorganization of the industry promised stock raisers the free movement of herds, as well as opportunities to buy shares in the company and to sell cattle to Gómez's modern slaughterhouse at Maracay, now rented and administered by the company. But it was also apparent from the outset that the company would favor Gómez, the principal shareholder, and the state presidents, who also acquired shares in the company and would cooperate with the free transit of its livestock through their jurisdictions. The British report explained,

> The company is to guarantee the President an income of 11,000 bolívares per day, that is taking forty to forty-five beasts per diem at

the rate of 7 bolívares per arroba [11.5 kilograms], with which must be included certain minor additional fees. The remaining breeders may sell their stock, which is now to be granted free movement, to the company at 4 bolívares per arroba, the difference in price being partly accounted for by the fact that these cattle will not be classified as 'fattened stock' as are the general's, and partly, it may be said, to keep the general good. The company is to consist of various shareholders, including the President, the Governors of States (who thus will have a stake in the industry and will not wish to follow their previous policy of obstruction), and certain capitalists in the country who have interests in cattle. This scheme may, perhaps, be the saving of the cattle breeders, who, with the present policy of monopoly and suppression, are almost starving.[79]

That Gómez could organize the company so clearly for his own benefit and still have it be perceived as a concession to those who had suffered under the former version of monopoly underscores his domination of the cattle industry. At best, the company offered ranchers an outlet for some of their cattle and a more predictable, less arbitrary working environment. In granting Gómez and some state presidents control of the company, the arrangement reinforced the common knowledge that the Gomecista state operated largely as an enterprise for the enrichment of the governing clique.

The reduction in cattle taxes that coincided with the organization of the company may have reinvigorated the livestock trade, increased competition, and lowered consumer prices, at least in some urban centers. In San Fernando, the capital of Apure and a hub of the cattle trade, the retail price of meat fell from 1.5 or 2.0 bolívares per kilo to as low as 0.5 bolívares within months of the company's creation. Meanwhile, the number of steers processed at San Fernando's municipal slaughterhouse rose from two per day to six or seven as consumption rose.[80] In Valencia, where beef sales had been controlled by Santos Matute Gómez, the state president and a half-brother of the dictator, the competition introduced by the company's meat shops caused the price of beef to drop from 2.5 or 3 bolívares per kilo to 0.5 bolívares, which led to a tripling of consumption from fifteen head of cattle per day to forty-six.[81] Urban consumers presumably welcomed the lower prices, though now they understood how inflated previous meat prices had been. Meanwhile, the proliferation of stores belonging to the company provided a new symbol of the dictator's control over the sale of basic foodstuffs.

Despite its dominant position in the domestic meat market, the Venezuelan Industrial Cattle Company soon experienced serious managerial and financial problems. Its first general manager, a Uruguayan named Ramón Tabares, insisted that the company dedicate a substantial share of its production to salted and canned meats rather than the fresh meat Venezuelans preferred. An advertising campaign failed to alter consumers' tastes, and unsold cans of meat began to pile up in company warehouses. Even well-publicized telegrams from Gómez to the state presidents directing them to "stimulate the consumption" of company products in their jurisdictions failed to increase demand for canned meats and may have further alienated consumers.[82] Serious conflicts erupted between Tabares and other company officials who criticized him for poor management of day-to-day operations as well as his misreading of the Venezuelan market. It became apparent that a centralized national company, if not managed effectively, could create discord rather than cohesion within the regime. Gómez directed his minister of interior relations to ask Gumersindo Torres, the former cabinet minister considered to be one of the regime's most able and honest administrators, to step in as president of the company's board of directors. Torres accepted in March of 1934 and began to study the company's operations and devise solutions.[83]

Torres soon surmised that the company suffered from problems that went far beyond Tabares's poor decisions. The political insiders who held stock in the company had never paid the full price of their shares, leaving it undercapitalized despite government subsidies totaling 7.5 million bolívares. Moreover, some of the public funds received by the company had paid for upgrading the slaughterhouse at Maracay, which remained Gómez's private property and which he now rented to the company for 30,000 bolívares a month.[84] But most of the financial losses suffered by the company resulted from the high prices it paid for cattle. The rates of 4 to 7 bolivares per arroba, set in contracts with Gómez and other chief suppliers, did not reflect market conditions. To make matters worse, Gómez's cattle, for which the company paid the highest prices, were filled with large amounts of drinking water before weighing, "so that the Company paid for many kilograms of water," as Torres later recalled.[85] The company's fundamental problem was that it blatantly favored privileged cattlemen and stockholders at public expense.[86]

Torres's efforts to reorganize the company yielded mixed results. He hired more competent managers and insisted that the company purchase some of its livestock through a process of competitive pricing, though it continued to pay inflated prices to Gómez and a few of his closest associates. Unfortunately for the ranchers who hoped that the company would lead to a sustained liberalization of the cattle trade, most of the cattle it slaughtered at Maracay still came from the Gomecistas' herds, and less influential ranchers selling to the company often had to graze their livestock on Gómez's lands "at exorbitant charges," according to the British minister.[87] Other monopolistic practices persisted, especially outside the major urban centers. In some rural areas of Carabobo state, for example, Antonio Pimentel, Gómez's close friend and longtime business partner, continued to monopolize the sale of beef in country stores. He also forced local cattle breeders to sell him their livestock, which he then sold to the company for twice the price.[88]

In short, by late 1935, ranchers, consumers, and taxpayers all had reasons to deplore the company. Gómez's death in December 1935, less than two years after the company's founding, caught public resentment at its peak. In the upheaval that followed the dictator's demise, rioters sacked the company's offices and retail shops in Caracas and Valencia, intimidated company employees, and looted the company's meat trucks. As Gumersindo Torres watched one anti-company protest from the balcony outside his office, he lamented not only the destructive "savagery" of the rioters, but also their "crazed ingratitude."[89] Torres believed the public should have been grateful for the lower meat prices and increased consumption brought by the company. Despite his own battles against corruption within the regime, Torres failed to grasp the intensity of Venezuelans' accumulated rage against the most prominent Gomecista monopoly.

The success of Gómez and his allies in weaving together political and economic power in the cattle cartel, I have argued, advanced both their private economic interests and the formation of an effectively centralized national state. This predatory exercise of political authority at every stage of the livestock business, from the acquisition of ranchlands and cattle herds to the marketing of beef for public consumption, was crucial to the enterprise, and was evident for all to see. As a result, Venezuelans' long-standing resentment towards officially sanctioned monopolies as an abuse of public power for private gain was directed against the cattle cartel for much of the twenty-seven-year dictatorship. The national scope of the monopoly, and its effects on entrepreneurs and consumers alike, contributed to widespread perceptions of Gomecista corruption as it reached into the lives of Venezuelans across the nation.

This growing anticorruption sentiment—that is, the conviction that public officials should not use their positions to advance their private economic interests, regardless of whether such critiques used the word *corruption*—stood in stark contrast to the patrimonial attitudes exhibited by regime officials involved in the cartel. The Gomecistas, like previous national rulers, made little pretense of separating their public roles from their private interests. Although their instincts were sharp enough to lead them to curb their exploitation when excesses threatened their rule, for the most part Gómez and his allies showed little restraint in using their power to take control of land and cattle, to manipulate taxes and government inspectors to benefit themselves, and to engage in profiteering at the expense of consumers. The gulf between rulers' patrimonial attitudes and popular anticorruption sentiment was not new, but it became increasingly stark and widespread as the integration of the centralized state and the geographical reach of the cattle monopoly advanced in unison.

CHAPTER 3

BUREAUCRATIC REFORM AS ANTICORRUPTION

THE LIQUOR TAX AND NEOPATRIMONIALISM

The strongmen of the regime who featured prominently in the cattle cartel used their political pull to engage in other profitable ventures as well. Some acquired private title to public lands administered by the federal government, others used coercive tactics to monopolize local commodities ranging from heron plumes to goat dung, and many joined the hunt for petroleum concessions after World War I. But the formal economic perquisites most often held by the strongmen serving Gómez were contracts granted by the Venezuelan treasury allowing these officials, ostensibly in their capacity as private citizens, to collect the federal taxes on liquor in one or more states of the nation.

Under these agreements, the contractor paid the treasury a fee in exchange for the right to collect the tax and to keep all the revenue he collected, which provided one avenue to profit from the arrangement, provided that the revenue collected by the contractor exceeded his costs. The greater potential for profit, however, lay in contractors' ability to manipulate their legal powers as tax collectors to pursue the illicit goal of monopolizing regional liquor markets by driving out rival producers. The state-building dynamics of the liquor-tax contracts thus mirrored those of the cattle monopoly: Gómez distributed the concessions among his collaborators, many of whom were already his partners in the cattle cartel; these concessions contributed to the consolidation of alliances between the dictator and strongmen whose support he needed; and the rival producers forced out of business, as well as the consumers subjected to monopoly prices, endured economic exploitation at the hands of Gomecista officials. Tax farming, as historians refer to this type of contract system, thus played a role in state formation and came to be viewed by many Venezuelans as another instance of officials' corruption.[1] The system's inherent mixing of public and private interests, by organizing the collection of national tax in a way that allowed the individual enrichment of the tax farmer, rendered it one of the most prominent patrimonial features of the Gomecista regime.

Nevertheless, the place of the liquor tax in Gomecista corruption and state formation was more multifaceted than that of the cattle cartel. While the cattle monopoly persisted as a patrimonial enterprise until the dictator's death, the farming-out of the liquor tax (and other taxes) was challenged by Gomecista technocrats who believed that salaried federal bureaucrats should collect all taxes in order to maximize revenues for the treasury. Viewing the contract system as corrupt, archaic, and an obstacle to free markets and economic growth, the technocrats advocated for the reform of revenue collection as a means of modernizing the state. These reformers, led by Treasury Minister Román Cárdenas (1913–22), argued that replacing tax farmers with salaried federal tax collectors would shield the public interest in revenue collection from the intrusion of private interests, while also standardizing fiscal administration throughout the nation under legal-rational norms, thus creating a more uniform, predictable environment for entrepreneurs in the liquor industry.

Perhaps most importantly, Cárdenas argued that turning over the tax to a professional bureaucracy would increase state revenues as this sector of the economy was freed from the predation of tax farmers. The prospect of maximizing state revenues held substantial appeal for Gómez, who controlled the use of treasury funds and often treated them as his own, but he had to weigh this financial advantage against his allies' desire for the tax-farming contracts. The liquor tax became the last of several revenues to transition from the contract system to direct bureaucratic administration, with the final, definitive shift occurring only in 1931–32. The circuitous path of this transition reveals a good deal about the competing logics of patrimonialism and bureaucratization within the regime.

This chapter argues that both modes of administration—tax farming and the bureaucratic system that reformers advocated as an antidote to corruption—contributed to state formation. Gómez's oscillation between these two methods of revenue collection, his use of both patrimonial and bureaucratic modes of power, illustrates the neopatrimonial process of Gomecista state formation. Rather than choose between the two modes of administration, Gómez sought to utilize the advantages offered by each amid changing historical circumstances. Cárdenas's drive for direct administration of the liquor tax led to the gradual replacement of contactors by federal bureaucrats in most states before the post–World War I petroleum boom, contributing to the rise in revenues that, as we saw in chapter 1, allowed the regime to survive the disruption of the war while also investing in the military, road construction, and repayment of the foreign debt. A return to contracting out the liquor tax after Cárdenas's retirement in 1922 signaled the renewed treatment of the tax as a source of patronage, as rising petroleum revenues diminished the urgency to maximize liquor receipts. Only the fiscal crisis of the Great Depression led to the definitive transition to bureaucratic administration across the nation in the early 1930s. This meandering path toward bureaucratization of the liquor revenue was clearly not the linear transition toward fiscal modernity imagined by Cárdenas. Gómez's drive for personal power, rather than the abstract precepts of modern statecraft, shaped the transition in fiscal administration.

Aguardiente, Tax Farming, and Patronage, to ca. 1915

The widespread production and sale of alcoholic beverages had long made this sector of Venezuela's economy a promising source of tax revenue, but also presented challenges. Unlike customs revenues, which could be collected by a handful of officials in a few major ports, collection of liquor taxes required a nationwide administration. Aguardiente, the alcoholic beverage distilled from sugar cane juice without the filtering or aging associated with rum, was the most widely produced and consumed alcoholic beverage in Venezuela, though men reportedly consumed more than women.[2] Distilleries ranged in scale from large commercial firms to moderately sized operations on haciendas, to small household stills scattered across the countryside.

Cipriano Castro's government struggled fruitlessly to find the most advantageous way to tax aguardiente. Initially, municipal and state governments administered the liquor tax, but they squabbled over the revenues.[3] In 1904, as part of his drive to assert the supremacy of the central state over regional political bosses, Castro declared the liquor tax to be a national revenue and that, to compensate regional interests, 35 percent of the money collected would be distributed to the states.[4] The lack of a centralized bureaucracy to administer the tax, however, obliged the treasury to lease the collection rights to an entrepreneur for the sum of 4 million bolívares a year, with poor results.[5] When no one bid on the liquor revenue contract for 1907, the government attempted to administer the tax directly, without much success.[6] Such fiscal impasses were common throughout Latin America. During the century that followed independence, most governments in the region struggled to create fiscal regimes that would maximize revenue from domestic sources, reduce dependence on customs receipts, and strengthen the central state.[7]

By the early years of the Gómez regime, the federal government—having concluded that both direct bureaucratic administration and a single, nationwide tax farm were impractical—contracted the liquor revenue to powerful individuals allied with Gómez in each state and federal territory. Payments by the liquor tax farmers to the federal government in 1909 totaled 2.5 million bolívares, well below the figure of 4 million bolívares sought by Castro for the national contract a few years earlier. The meager taxes collected by customs officials on imported beverages brought total liquor revenues to a disappointing 2.8 million bolívares for the year.[8]

While receipts to the treasury remained low, tax farmers' potential profits—both legal and illegal—were substantial. Legal profits, in the form of revenues collected, were potentially high, due to the widespread production and sale of aguardiente. Illegal profits could be even higher as tax farmers established partnerships with selected distillers and merchants, denied licenses to rival distillers, invented taxes and fines to prevent the entry and sale of liquor from neighboring jurisdictions, and then raised prices.[9] Although their contracts with the treasury admonished tax farmers to respect freedom of commerce,[10] they routinely violated these provisions. In practice, commercial production and sales of aguardiente were shaped by political muscle, exercised in predatory fashion to ruin rival producers and squeeze consumers. Moreover, tax farmers' political connections to Gómez meant that Venezuelans experienced their coercive tactics as an integral aspect of state centralization.[11]

Tax farming, then, presented both risks and opportunities for the regime, even in the earliest years of Gómez's rule, before Cárdenas began his campaign to eliminate the contract system. On one hand, its abusive nature could destabilize the regime even as Gómez sought to consolidate power; on the other, its use as an instrument of patronage promised political advantages if the system were skillfully managed. The conflict that unfolded in the western state of Mérida in 1909 demonstrated both the risks and opportunities in using the liquor tax as a means of state-building. Its significance justifies a somewhat detailed narrative.

General José Eliseo Araujo, a prominent member of the Araujo-Baptista clan that had dominated politics in Trujillo and parts of Mérida since the 1860s, received the liquor-tax contract for Mérida in 1909. In June of that year, Araujo subcontracted the right to collect the liquor tax in Sucre district to four men, Manuel Uzcátegui, Gonzalo Rojas, Elpidio García, and José de Jesús Alvarez—all of whom he considered to be his faithful clients, apparently—in return for 1,000 bolívares a month.[12] In August, however, Gómez appointed General Esteban Chalbaud Cardona, an enemy of Araujo, as provisional president of Mérida state.[13] Cardona, as he was known, was a Liberal; Araujo and his family were historically allied with the Conservatives, though most Liberal presidents since the 1870s had reached accommodations with the clan, a strategy Gómez attempted to follow. In another effort to bring Andeans outside the Liberal party into his government, Gómez appointed Dr. Abel Santos, a tachirense affiliated with the Nationalist party and an ally of Araujo, to lead the Treasury Ministry in 1909.[14] Tensions soon erupted between Cardona and his Liberal allies, on one side, and Santos and Araujo on the other, threatening Gómez's attempt to include both groups in his regime.

In September, Cardona appointed Uzcátegui to the office of jefe civil of Sucre district, the same jurisdiction where Uzcátegui subcontracted a share of Araujo's liquor-tax contract. Araujo, angry that one of his clients had accepted an appointment in Cardona's government, revoked Uzcátegui's share of the subcontract. Uzcátegui countered that Araujo did not have the right to unilaterally void their agreement, and he continued to issue licenses and collect the liquor tax. Araujo contacted his ally Santos who, on October 15, sent Uzcátegui a pointed telegram saying, "You have no contract, according to documents presented to this Ministry, and if you continue perturbing the contractor [*rematador*, i.e., Araujo] by selling aguardiente without paying the tax and by stimulating rebellion among the merchants and distillers of Sucre district, an order for your imprisonment will be issued."[15] But Uzcátegui, under Cardona's protection and by virtue of his command of the district's police as jefe civil, continued to act as a subcontractor. Uzcátegui escalated the conflict by ordering his police to open fire on García, one of Araujo's loyal subcontractors, if he attempted to interfere with the men selling aguardiente under licenses issued by Uzcátegui.[16] Santos then informed state president Cardona that Araujo had suspended collection of the liquor tax because he did not have the protection of state officials. Furthermore, the ministry would withhold Mérida's share of the liquor revenue (the 35 percent apportioned to states) until further notice.[17] Prominent Liberals wrote to Gómez to denounce Santos's partisan conduct as treasury minister, and Cardona began proceedings to arrest Araujo.[18] Cardona also wrote to Gómez repeatedly in late 1909 to request the liquor-tax contract for himself or his son.[19]

Gómez sought to resolve the conflict and stabilize state politics by making concessions to both Cardona and Araujo. The liquor-tax contract for Mérida for the upcoming year, 1910, was awarded to a group of tax farmers allied with Cardona, signaling Gómez's conclusion that the contracts would contribute most to regime consolidation if they were used to cement the loyalty of top officeholders, especially state presidents like Cardona. In another win for the Liberals, Santos left the ministry for a diplomatic post in Colombia.[20] But Gómez upheld Araujo's rights through the end of his contract. In Sucre district, Gómez removed the rebellious Uzcátegui as jefe civil and the new jefe civil arrested José D'Elía, a merchant, for contraband production and sale of aguardiente.[21] D'Elía had mounted a substantial distilling operation under Uzcátegui's protection and never paid the requisite taxes, which—together with Santos's earlier order to Uzcátegui to stop "selling aguardiente without paying the tax"—suggests that Uzcátegui and D'Elía had cooperated to sell untaxed aguardiente while Uzcátegui taxed competing distillers, a tactic commonly used by tax farmers to monopolize local markets.

The rival groups in Mérida competed so fiercely for the right to administer the liquor tax because of its value in building patronage networks and generating private wealth. Similar conflicts sprouted across the country during the early years of the regime, as politically favored distillers and ambitious officials sought to capitalize on the system's opportunities for profiteering. León Santelli, a prominent distiller of aguardiente and rum in the eastern state of Sucre, sought the tax farm for his region so that he could maintain a captive market.[22] In Zulia, the tax contractors established a statewide monopoly in the early 1910s.[23] Other contractors, such as those in the state of Nueva Esparta, collected illegal taxes on liquor transported out of their jurisdictions.[24] Writing to Caracas from the Andean state of Trujillo, General Francisco María Vásquez, a loyal Gomecista, complained bitterly of the illegal fines, harassment, and forced sales of aguardiente carried out by the tax farmer, state president General Timoleón Omaña, whom Vásquez accused of sowing terror among the local population as he sought to maximize his returns.[25] The opportunities for profiteering that came with liquor-tax contracts were widely understood.

Enticed by the potential profits, Gómez's allies—such as Cardona—continually petitioned the dictator to award them the liquor-tax contracts.[26] And Gómez, in the aftermath of the upheaval in Mérida, granted contracts to powerful officeholders—state presidents or jefes civiles in important jurisdictions—or their close allies so that the patronage networks created by the liquor-tax contracts would reinforce the administrative hierarchy of the centralizing state. This use of liquor contracts to strengthen Gómez's ties to strongmen holding office at the state and district levels meant that the concessions were not always awarded to the individual who offered the highest payments to the treasury. For example, in 1910 General José Garbi, the jefe civil of Barquisimeto (the capital of Lara state) who had fought under Castro and Gómez against the Libertadora rebellion of 1901–3, asked Gómez to renew his contract for the liquor tax in the neighboring state of Yaracuy. Gómez responded that even though another

TABLE 3.1. Monthly payments by liquor tax farmers to treasury, 1914, 1929 (bolívares)

Jurisdiction	1914	1929	Change, 1914 to 1929
Anzoátegui	6,050	11,000	+4,950
Apure	4,800	1,750	-3,050
Aragua	18,000	20,000	+2,000
Bolívar	13,000	9,500	-3,500
Carabobo	31,000	30,000	-1,000
Cojedes	5,000	7,500	+2,500
Falcón	7,000	22,500	+15,500
Guárico	7,500	6,000	-1,500
Lara	23,000	58,000	+35,000
Mérida	8,000	16,000	+8,000
Miranda	24,000	50,000	+26,000
Monagas	3,500	9,500	+6,000
Nueva Esparta	6,000	5,000	-1,000
Portuguesa	3,000	5,000	+2,000
Sucre	27,000	40,500	+13,500
Táchira	16,000	18,000	+2,000
Trujillo	9,000	43,000	+34,000
Yaracuy	12,000	29,000	+17,000
Zamora	2,000	1,000	-1,000
Zulia	19,000	80,000	+61,000
Federal District (Caracas)	39,000	140,000	+101,000
Delta Amacuro Territory	1,000	2,500	+1,500
Totals	284,850	605,750	+320,900

Sources: Ministerio de Hacienda, *Memoria de hacienda correspondiente al año comprendido del 19 de marzo de 1913 al 19 de marzo de 1914* (Caracas: El Cojo, 1914), cxix; and *Memoria de hacienda presentada al congreso nacional en sus sesiones de 1930* (Caracas: Tipografía Americana, 1930), 362. Changes from 1914 to 1929 calculated by the author.

individual had offered to pay the treasury 2,000 bolívares more than Garbi, he would renew Garbi's contract "in consideration of our good friendship and because you have fulfilled your obligations."[27]

Recipients of statewide concessions often subcontracted the tax to their allies at the district level, as Araujo had attempted in Mérida, thus cultivating a wider network of clients. General Amador Uzcátegui, Cardona's successor as president of Mérida, had this in mind when he requested the liquor-tax contract for his state "so that I can distribute it here among various friends of ours who are very useful men and who it would be good to help because they are in need."[28] Similarly, General José María García, as president of Trujillo in 1913, asked Gómez for his state's liquor contract so that he could "fittingly remunerate persons of certain social and political significance whom I have employed in their respective localities."[29] The allocation of tax-farming rights went hand in hand with the development of Gómez's nationwide system of patronage.

This distribution of revenue contracts served Gómez's interests while he was initially consolidating his power. But once he survived the 1913–14 crisis at the end of his first presidential term, he could afford to reconsider the most advantageous system for administering the taxes that were farmed out, including the liquor tax. Moving to a system of direct administration had the potential to increase federal funds for the regime's state-building projects—and for Gómez's personal use. Even though liquor tax farmers paid 284,850 bolívares a month to the federal government in 1914 (see table 3.1), that year's report by the finance ministry concluded that the liquor tax "produces only a very small part of what it should for the Treasury."[30] The report argued that legislation governing the liquor tax "has not permitted the Government to reorganize the revenue through direct administration" and forced a reliance on "rental contracts" instead.[31] The solution was to reform liquor-tax legislation with the goal of maximizing revenues. Román Cárdenas, the treasury minister who oversaw the drafting of this opinion, would lead Gómez's effort to end tax farming, increase revenues, and create a modern fiscal system free of corruption, at least in the collection of revenue.

Cárdenas, Anticorruption, and Bureaucratization, 1913–22

In April 1914 Cárdenas presented to the Venezuelan legislature his plan for a sweeping reform of the fiscal system.[32] It called for an end to tax farming, an expansion and restructuring of the treasury bureaucracy, and increased collection of domestic revenues to end the long-standing reliance on customs receipts. In presenting the rationale for change, Cárdenas denounced current fiscal administration as backward, chaotic, riddled with corrupt practices (*corruptelas*), and harmful to Venezuela's economy. This was the strongest public criticism of existing administrative methods ever offered by a Gomecista official. Clearly the dictator had concluded that the financial benefits of reform outweighed the political costs of curtailing the patronage associated with revenue farming, which the treasury used to collect taxes on cigarettes, stamps, and salt, as well as liquor.

Cárdenas denounced the damage tax farming inflicted on economic development as well as on the state's financial and bureaucratic capacity. He lambasted the practice as an "atrocious system which tends to gradually become a regime that restricts the industry [that is taxed], with all the ruinous consequences of delegating the constrictive action of the Government to agents outside the [fiscal] Administration."[33] This emphasis on the corrosive effects of a tax system that, in practice, enabled contractors to restrict an industry for their own benefit reflected long-standing resentment of monopolies. "The pecuniary success obtained by the contractors," Cárdenas argued, "is extremely demoralizing" and undermined any legitimacy that taxation might enjoy among the public.[34] The result of these evils, he warned, was the degeneration of Venezuela's fiscal system. Not only did tax farming create "circumstances opposed to all progress in the evolution of the fiscal organism," it also led to the "atrophy of the energies, faculties, and activities of this organism" and even created the possibility that "the Nation might lose all [entrepreneurial] initiative in the end."[35] The system was inherently "pernicious."[36]

Cárdenas's attack on tax farming concluded with a sharp contrast between fiscal modernity and backwardness. "None of the national administrations of the modern civilized countries currently use a system of contracts for the leasing of revenues; this system finds itself relegated to countries where, because of the backwardness [*atraso*] of administrative evolution, there exist neither the means nor the effective legal instruments to collect public contributions through direct administration, the only acknowledged good system for this purpose."[37] Overall, Cárdenas's manifesto posited a dichotomy between backward fiscal regimes characterized by inefficiency, corruption, low revenues, and constraints on economic growth, on one hand, and more modern fiscal regimes characterized by efficiency, qualified personnel, increasing government revenues, and the promotion of economic growth, on the other. To be sure, Cárdenas included the caveat that Venezuela's adoption of "the great modern principles of financial legislation should be adapted to our circumstances and special conditions,"[38] but his dichotomy between fiscal modernity and backwardness remained.

Cárdenas's advocacy of direct federal administration supported Gómez's goal of centralizing power by promising to extend into every region of Venezuela the network of fiscal agents who, at least in theory, operated under federal control. Cárdenas's project echoed the perspective of early modern English excise tax administrators who, according to historical geographer Miles Ogborn, advocated "a rationally ordered, planned and territorially complete bureaucracy[,] ... an administrative framework that could operate effectively across the state's territory."[39] Because Venezuelan tax farmers and their allies monopolized regional markets and obstructed interstate commerce, they perpetuated the administrative and economic fragmentation of the nation. National integration required the spatial expansion of the federal bureaucracy's power at the expense of tax farmers. As Cárdenas argued, distillers could only become national entrepreneurs, producing for a unified Venezuelan market, when the federal government imposed a uniform system of taxation throughout the nation.[40] Fiscal modernity would advance the country's economic and administrative integration as well as boost revenues.

Cárdenas's proposals gained urgency as the outbreak of World War I in August 1914 led to a precipitous drop in customs revenue,[41] forcing a 50 percent reduction in the salaries of all federal employees.[42] Dependence on foreign trade, which typically generated around 70 percent of federal revenues,[43] pushed the regime toward crisis. An increase in domestic revenues became imperative, and Cárdenas's plan to replace tax farming with direct administration offered a solution. On January 1, 1915, the government established federal management of the liquor tax in the state of Zulia and in the Federal District of Caracas.[44] Later that same year, Congress approved Cárdenas's new liquor-tax law providing for direct administration of the liquor revenue throughout the nation.[45]

This ambitious 1915 legislation called for the establishment of regional offices, each headed by an administrator, to assess and collect the tax, which was primarily a levy on production. Distillers and wholesalers would be required to buy licenses, but the former would also pay a tax of 0.45 bolívares on each liter of liquor distilled, provided that the alcoholic content was 50 percent or less; stronger liquors would be taxed at higher rates. The base rate of 0.45 bolívares per liter represented an increase over earlier duties, but the law compensated Venezuelan distillers by raising taxes on imported liquors.[46] The legislation prohibited administrators and their staffs from having any financial interest in the liquor business, called for regular audits of their accounts, and established penalties for unlicensed production and smuggling.

But the government proved unable to implement immediately the system of national administration outlined in the 1915 law. Recruiting, training, and deploying new tax officials took time and necessitated a gradual shift toward bureaucratic administration.[47] By the end of 1915, the government had established direct administration only in the states of Zulia, Sucre, Lara, Miranda, and in the Federal District of Caracas.[48] All other jurisdictions continued temporarily under tax-farming contracts; such exemptions were authorized under article 127 of the law. Thus began an era of divided administration, in which federal officials collected the liquor tax in some states while tax farmers continued to operate in others. Throughout the remainder of his tenure in the Treasury Ministry, Cárdenas shifted more states from tax farming to direct administration. By his retirement in 1922, liquor tax farms remained in place in only four states (Táchira, Mérida, Aragua, and Carabobo).[49]

Cárdenas vigorously supervised the administrators and their staffs in the areas under federal management, insisting that they apply the law in a standardized, uniform manner, a clear contrast to the self-interested and unpredictable methods of tax farmers. He regularly wrote to liquor tax officials to remind them to follow established procedures,[50] to use the correct forms for submitting their reports,[51] to enforce the requirement that distillers clean their equipment,[52] and similar exhortations. No issue appeared too minute to escape Cárdenas's attention as he advanced the professionalization of liquor-tax administration, striving to make bureaucratic practice conform to the standards set in national legislation.

The shift toward direct administration yielded impressive results, as liquor revenues rose and vindicated Cárdenas's reforms (see table 3.2). The treasury's liquor-tax receipts doubled in the first few years of direct administration and continued to rise through the end of the decade. Significantly, these increases formed part of a broader trend.

TABLE 3.2. Federal revenue from liquor, foreign trade, and mining, 1910–36 (thousands of bolívares)

Fiscal year	Liquor revenue	Total federal revenue	Liquor revenue as % of total	Taxes on Foreign Trade	Mining, including oil	Mining as % of total federal revenue
1910–11	3,169	62,939	5.04	44,809	270	0.43
1911–12	3,355	76,171	4.40	52,683	466	0.61
1912–13	3,652	65,438	5.58	49,622	576	0.88
1913–14	3,694	60,371	6.12	42,516	579	0.96
1914–15	3,679	50,598	7.27	29,521	265	0.52
1915–16	6,566	65,674	10.00	39,328	543	0.83
1916–17	7,105	72,127	9.85	43,301	1,266	1.76
1917–18	7,438	53,254	13.97	23,507	838	1.57
1918–19	7,752	57,102	13.58	22,467	2,054	3.60
1919–20	9,617	101,134	9.51	52,704	2,811	2.78
1920–21	8,513	81,561	10.44	42,460	2,825	3.46
1921–22	8,000	70,927	11.28	26,394	2,766	3.90
1922–23	9,018	87,691	10.28	41,127	8,253	9.41
1923–24	9,095	102,249	8.89	49,355	5,158	5.04
1924–25	9,242	120,165	7.69	65,729	8,731	7.27
1925–26	10,868	172,098	6.32	86,825	25,416	14.77
1926–27	10,349	182,148	5.68	100,297	20,428	11.22
1927–28	10,851	186,752	5.81	89,524	35,110	18.80
1928–29	9,642	230,415	4.18	105,480	46,527	20.19
1929–30	9,405	255,445	3.68	115,664	54,325	21.27
1930–31	9,174	210,259	4.36	88,407	48,638	23.13
1931–32	11,582	185,096	6.26	70,366	51,011	27.56
1932–33	13,712	171,889	7.98	60,837	44,933	26.14
1933–34	12,248	171,829	7.13	59,494	47,519	27.65
1934–35	11,099	202,980	5.47	66,336	55,404	27.30
1935–36	11,376	189,125	6.02	65,267	57,222	30.26

Source: J. J. Bracho Sierra, "Cincuenta años de ingresos fiscales, 1910–1960," *Revista de Hacienda*, no. 48 (1964): 38, 39, 44, 45, 48, 49. Percentage calculations by the author.

Between July 1914 and January 1916, the treasury shifted several of the most important branches of internal revenue, including the sale of stamps and the taxes on salt and cigarettes, from private administration to direct federal management. Net revenues from these sources rose following the shift to direct administration, averting a fiscal crisis.

Reporting to Congress in 1917, Cárdenas trumpeted the success of his reforms. He reviewed his efforts to implement "the modern science of finances" since taking office in 1913.[53] "The first step," he argued, "had to be the replacement of tax farming [*arrendamiento*], which undermined revenue, with the direct administration of national taxes, [a system] which had been placed in oblivion and was almost unknown by previous [Venezuelan] regimes."[54] Rehearsing the evils of revenue-farming yet again, Cárdenas argued that it left taxpayers vulnerable to excessive charges, undermined public respect for legitimate taxation, discouraged investment by small entrepreneurs who lacked political protection, and—worst of all—favored the creation of monopolies. By contrast, he claimed expansively, "any possibility of monopoly disappeared under direct administration."[55] Cárdenas calculated that the shift toward direct administration of taxes on cigarettes, salt, stamps, and liquor had resulted in a combined net gain to the treasury of over 5.7 million bolívares per year after deducting new administrative costs. According to the minister, "direct administration of taxes that for many years were rented out has permitted the Government . . . to establish a public treasury capable of withstanding the universal crisis" of the war.[56] The regime's newspaper, *El Nuevo Diario*, praised the treasury's "modernización fiscal"[57] and informed readers that "the money that previously enriched the tax farmers [*arrendatarios*]" was now invested in highway construction and the military.[58] This discourse of fiscal modernity, which reflected decades of popular anger against de facto and de jure monopolies, framed the treasury reform as an instrument of national progress.

Foreign observers' enthusiasm for Cárdenas's policies, already strong, was redoubled. The British minister in Caracas, writing in 1917, pointed to the reform of the liquor tax as an example of the regime's sound financial management.[59] The following year, the US consul at La Guaira applauded the rise in domestic tax revenue and echoed Cárdenas as he assured Washington that "the objectionable conditions of private monopoly which prevailed when these revenues were farmed out have disappeared."[60] The advance of Cárdenas's program appeared to offer hope that Gomecista monopolies might be curtailed or overturned, at least in some circumstances.

Unión Destiladora and the Trials of Direct Administration

In early 1919 Cárdenas learned of a major failure in the federal administration of the liquor tax in the western state of Zulia, a failure which threatened to dissolve his neat contrast between the corrupt nature of tax farming and the modern system of bureaucratic administration. Four aguardiente distillers had combined to form Unión Destiladora, which created a de facto monopoly over production and sales in Zulia, a center of the distilling industry. Most alarming for Cárdenas, Unión Destiladora's monopoly had been consolidated in 1915, while the treasury administered the liquor tax in Zulia, and various government officials, including state president José María García (1914–18) and the federal administrator of the liquor tax in Zulia, José Antonio Calcaño, had colluded in the monopoly.[61] The complicity of the administrator undermined Cárdenas's premise that direct administration of taxes would end regional cartels, maximize revenues, and advance economic development.

Unión Destiladora and its political allies used their clout to drive competitors out of business and then raised prices. Under pre-monopoly conditions, with numerous distilleries supplying the market, aguardiente had sold for 1.00 bolívar per liter in Zulia, but after cornering the market Unión Destiladora charged 2.25 bolívares.[62] As prices rose, more consumers purchased or produced clandestine liquor, thus reducing the market for taxed liquor and driving down revenues.[63] It was this drop in regional tax receipts that prompted treasury officials to investigate the liquor trade in Zulia. The US consul in Maracaibo reported that local opponents of the monopoly had been too afraid to denounce it, because any criticism "might cause them serious inconvenience, and ultimately might deprive them of their liberty."[64]

Cárdenas's earlier claim that "any possibility of monopoly disappeared under direct administration" no doubt came back to haunt him. Once informed of Unión Destiladora's monopoly, he resolved to take action even though it would disrupt an enterprise from which García, a cousin of Gómez and one of his closest allies, profited. Cárdenas raised the issue of Unión Destiladora with Gómez in February 1919 and won his approval to dismantle the cartel. Cárdenas also urged Gómez to instruct the current president of Zulia, General Santos Matute Gómez, the dictator's half-brother, to "completely remove himself from all interest or participation, in any form whatsoever, in the aguardiente business,"[65] implying that he, too, probably had a stake in the monopoly. Cárdenas argued that government officials' divestment from the liquor industry was necessary to restore public confidence in the regime's commitment to free trade. Only then would investors who had withdrawn from the aguardiente business reinvest. He dispatched treasury officials to Zulia to break up Unión Destiladora[66] and then issued decrees closing the distilleries that made up the cartel, citing their efforts to restrict trade but making no mention of official complicity in the monopoly.[67] The federal government legally dissolved Unión Destiladora in July 1919 and the liquidation of its assets began.[68]

Treasury officials in Zulia reported that these actions led to both an expansion of the industry and increased tax revenue, redeeming Cárdenas's paradigm of fiscal modernity. Entrepreneurs who had abandoned the liquor industry rushed to fill the void created by the monopoly's demise. Over the following year, the number of licensed distilleries in Zulia rose from seven to eighteen; liquor processing establishments increased from four to twenty-two; and wholesalers increased from eleven to thirty-five.[69] Officials reported that, with greater competition among licensed producers and suppliers, prices declined and sales of taxed alcoholic beverages increased. From July through December 1919, liquor revenues in the state rose to 326,115.15 bolívares, an increase of 100,993.10 bolívares over the same six-month period in 1918.[70] Revenues continued to climb in 1920, when liquor receipts in Zulia rose by 406,629.12 bolívares over the previous year.[71] During this period the acting state president, General José de Jesús Gabaldón, guarded against the reemergence of the monopoly by discouraging a state official from going into business with Eduardo Leseur, a former partner in Unión Destiladora who sought to reenter the liquor trade. Gabaldón informed Cárdenas that he was cooperating with Zulia's new administrator to fulfill Cárdenas's agenda, which Gabaldón summarized as "liberty for the industry, consequent rise in revenue, and no manipulative intervention in this sector by agents of the Government."[72]

These developments bolstered treasury officials' faith in the maxim that freer competition boosted tax revenues. Treasury personnel in states under direct administration invoked this axiom when attempting to stamp out local monopolies, illustrating the diffusion of Cárdenas's vision within the fiscal bureaucracy.[73] Meanwhile, investors in the liquor business, long accustomed to the need for political protection to guarantee their access to local markets, continued to make overtures to political figures who could act as protectors or investors in their enterprises, but under Cárdenas the ministry attempted to steer the industry toward free trade.[74] His dream of fiscal modernity must have appeared progressively closer to realization. The major obstacle to its fulfillment was, of course, the continuation of liquor tax farming in states where the federal government still had not transitioned to direct administration. While this delay was publicly attributed to a lack of trained personnel,[75] political factors also played a role.

Issues of patronage and the personal interests of Gómez and his family prevented Cárdenas from ending the liquor tax farms in four states: Táchira, where the revenue contract went to state president General Eustoquio Gómez, the dictator's cousin who secured Venezuela's western border against dissident invasions; Mérida, where members of the influential Parra-Picón clan shared the contract with state president General Amador Uzcátegui; and Aragua and Carabobo, where Gómez, his family, and close allies owned extensive sugar haciendas that produced large quantities of aguardiente.[76] In these latter two states, business associates of Gómez held the tax farm throughout the period from 1915 to 1931. In Aragua, the liquor contract went to Roberto Ramírez, who was also employed by Gómez to manage his business enterprises and became a partner in the dictator's oil concession trading company.[77] In Carabobo the contract went to Ramón Ramos and General Antonio Pimentel, two of Gómez's partners in the Central Tacarigua, a large agro-industrial complex producing sugar and aguardiente.[78] (Pimentel, as discussed in chapter 2, was also a longtime partner of Gómez in the cattle trade.)

The imposition of direct administration in all other regions had increased revenues, but the shift to bureaucratic control came with political costs. In some states the arrival of treasury officials to administer the tax led to tensions with the strongmen who lost their contracts, illustrating the disruption that could accompany direct administration. In Trujillo, the state president and former tax farmer General Timoleón Omaña was reprimanded for not cooperating with the new administrator, and his jefes civiles had to be admonished not to become involved in the liquor trade and to enforce the treasury's policy of free commerce.[79] In Apure, where state president General Vincencio Pérez Soto lost his contract with the arrival of Tulio Carnevali Picón, the federal administrator, animosities aroused by the fiscal transition manifested themselves in a more indirect way. When, in February 1918, police arrested Carnevali Picón during a fight in a brothel, Pérez Soto refused the bureaucrat's demand to be released from jail, citing his reputation for scandalous behavior. He informed Gómez that the administrator had offended local sensibilities by driving around town with "a pale bird" (presumably a mistress or prostitute) at the same hour that townspeople, including Pérez Soto's family, customarily came out to socialize.[80] Pérez Soto had hesitated to hold Carnevali Picón accountable for this unsavory conduct because it might appear that he sought revenge for his lost contract. Now that he had jailed Carnevali Picón, Pérez Soto expected him to retaliate by seeking assistance from his powerful kinsmen, the Parra-Picón clan, who intermittently held the tax farm in Mérida.[81] In the end, Pérez Soto retained Gómez's confidence and Apure's liquor tax remained under federal administration, but the smooth running of a state where Gómez had extensive cattle interests had been jeopardized.

The spats in Trujillo and Apure exemplified the potential pitfalls of dispatching federal officials to collect a tax formerly controlled by state presidents. Adding to such tensions, liquor revenue officials in states under direct administration often took gratuitous swipes at the tax-farming system (and, by implication, insulted tax farmers) in their reports to Caracas, which the ministry then published for all to see.[82] Gómez, mindful of the need to maintain cohesion within his regime, had to weigh the financial benefits of direct administration against the potential disruption of imposing the new system.

These calculations of the trade-offs between maximizing revenue (via direct administration) and maintaining the perquisites available to powerful collaborators (via tax farming) changed around the time that Cárdenas retired as treasury minister in 1922. Not only did direct administration lose its most powerful advocate, but Venezuela's 1922 petroleum law heralded the birth of a new era that would fundamentally transform national finances. This legislation, highly favorable to foreign oil companies, attracted a rush of US and European investment.[83] In 1925 petroleum became Venezuela's leading export, surpassing coffee for the first time, and the oil industry became an increasingly important source of public revenues. Mining taxes, which provided only 3 percent of government revenues at the beginning of the 1920s, reached 21 percent of federal revenue by the end of the decade. The oil boom also stimulated foreign trade, boosting customs revenues. Liquor-tax receipts, relatively stable in absolute terms, slid from roughly 10 to 5 percent of all federal revenues. Treasury reserves, already at 35 million bolívares in 1922, reached 114 million in 1928.[84] In sum, oil made the fiscal rationale for direct administration of the liquor tax less pressing. Meanwhile, state presidents and other officials continued to seek tax-farming contracts.

Amid these trends, Gómez shifted away from direct administration and back toward tax farming. On August 16, 1922, less than two months after Cárdenas's retirement, the government contracted the rights to the liquor tax in Zulia, which had been under direct administration since 1915, to Ovidio Márquez, an associate of former state president García, the dictator's kinsman and former participant in the defunct Unión Destiladora.[85] In 1924 the Treasury Ministry rented the liquor tax in Trujillo, which had been under direct administration since 1917, to Pérez Soto, the newly appointed state president who had tangled with Carnevali Picón, the administrator in Apure, years before. In 1927, as oil exports boomed, the states of Miranda, Portuguesa, Lara, Yaracuy, and Cojedes were returned to the tax-farming system, accelerating the abandonment of direct administration.[86] On July 1, 1928, all states still under direct administration were turned over to liquor tax farmers, usually the state president.[87] For these initial years of the oil boom, then, Venezuela might appear to illustrate scholars' proposition that petrostates lack the incentive to fully develop the "extractive capacities" needed for domestic taxation.[88]

Tax Farming, 1915–31

This dismantling of direct administration, however, did not mean that the treasury lost all interest in maintaining its income from the liquor tax. The treasury demanded higher fees from tax farmers in selected states after passage of the 1915 liquor-tax law and imposed widespread fee increases from 1922 onward. As Gómez reintroduced liquor-tax contracts in the 1920s, therefore, the treasury required fees substantially higher than those of 1914, before direct administration had provided bureaucrats with direct knowledge of the liquor tax's potential (see table 3.1). For example, the monthly payment of 70,000 bolívares demanded by the ministry for the liquor-tax contract in Zulia in 1922 represented a dramatic increase over the 1914 rate of 19,000 bolívares.[89] The ministry noted that, having administered the tax directly in Zulia and other states, it now knew how much revenue could be collected and therefore how much contractors could truly afford to pay.[90]

In this way, the treasury benefited from its growing bureaucratic expertise even as it reverted to the patrimonial contract system. Some tax farmers—like General José Antonio Baldó, president of Portuguesa, who bore one of the earliest increases—initially resisted but ultimately accepted the changes, passing on the increases to subcontractors at the district level.[91] Thus Gómez's regime, like other centralizing states, successfully imposed more stringent contracts as it accumulated bureaucratic knowledge and strengthened its leverage vis-à-vis revenue farmers.[92] The treasury's "cognitive capacity," to use Laurence Whitehead's term for states' ability to gather and utilize information about the nation,[93] had clearly advanced since Castro. Significantly, Gómez's loyalists continued to request the liquor-tax concessions and to express gratitude when they received them, suggesting that tax farming remained an effective form of patronage despite the higher fees.[94] This modification of the patrimonial system of tax contracting through the application of bureaucratic knowledge exemplified the neopatrimonial dynamic of the regime.

Gómez, then, was not forced into a stark choice between the pursuit of increased liquor revenues and the distribution of perquisites to his most powerful collaborators. The strict dichotomy between fiscal modernity and tax farming originally posited by Cárdenas was eroded in other ways as well. The administrator of the liquor revenue in the state of Lara reported that most of the men who had worked for him as federal employees were subsequently employed by the new tax farmer and state president, General Pedro Lizarraga, when Lara was converted back to the tax-farming system in 1927.[95] Lizarraga's contract for Lara and the neighboring state of Yaracuy required him to pay the treasury 87,500 bolívares per month[96]—a hefty increase over the 1914 rate of 35,000 bolívares for the two states—but he could count on the expertise of former treasury bureaucrats to help him meet his quotas, pay expenses, and still turn a profit.

Regardless of the extent to which tax-farming operations became bureaucratized, Gómez and treasury officials understood that liquor tax farmers generated their profits through both legal and illicit means. During the period of rising fees, revenue farmers persisted in using their positions to monopolize local markets, levy illegal fines and taxes, and similar abuses[97] (strategies similar to those used by tax farmers across the globe[98]). The treasury all but condoned contractors' profiteering by ruling in 1915 that tax farmers and their employees, unlike federal revenue officials, could hold financial interests in the liquor business.[99] Contractual provisions requiring tax farmers to respect free trade[100] were difficult to enforce from Caracas; in reality, the government's decision to allow tax farmers to invest in liquor signaled its toleration of profiteering in the states where the tax was under contract. Indeed, the higher rental payments demanded by the treasury may have increased tax farmers' incentives to maximize their earnings through any available means.

Several examples illustrate tax farmers' continuation of illicit, monopolistic practices during the era of rising fees. One of the most dramatic cases of intimidation used to defend a regional cartel arose in Zulia. When, in 1922, the state was transferred from direct administration to the contract system, the treasury designated Ovidio Márquez as Zulia's new tax farmer. Márquez was an ally of General José María García, the former state president and partner in the dismantled Unión Destiladora monopoly, and the two men reportedly monopolized the liquor trade while Márquez held the contract (1922–30). Two independent distillers in Zulia, Audio Bozo and Ulises Fuenmayor, accused García and Márquez of coercing them and others to join a partnership that was structured to funnel profits to Márquez, García, and their allies at the expense of Bozo and Fuenmayor. The two men journeyed to Caracas in 1926 to present their grievances to Gómez. But García and his uncle José Rosario García, a confidant of Gómez, allegedly threatened to send them to one of the regime's infamous prisons if they complained to Gómez. Bozo and Fuenmayor gave in, but following Gómez's death in 1935 they filed a lawsuit against Márquez. He settled the case by paying the distillery owners 50,000 bolívares in compensation, though they claimed much higher losses.[101]

Similar coercive tactics led to the ruin of many distillers in the state of Yaracuy during the rule of General Félix Galavís, who had led the modernization of the military in 1910–13 and frequently partnered with Gómez in livestock deals. As state president and liquor tax farmer in the late 1920s and early 1930s, Galavís reportedly monopolized retail sales in Yaracuy by forcing distillers to sell their aguardiente to him at low prices and then selling it to the public at inflated prices—but only after diluting the booze with water to boost his profits even more. Distillery owners in the district of Nirgua who questioned Galavís's practices were summoned to meet him at the local police headquarters, where he berated them. One ruined distillery owner later declared that more than twenty of his colleagues went out of business because of Galavís's actions and the economic depression that coincided with his administration.[102]

Tax farmers also continued to guard their monopolies by discouraging merchants from importing liquor from other jurisdictions. The treasury received "constant" complaints that tax farmers invented a tax, referred to as a "valorization," charged on aguardiente brought into their states.[103] These unauthorized levies proved so onerous that many distillers stopped selling their product in neighboring states where tax farmers operated.[104] Francisco Santelli, who owned an important distillery in the eastern state of Sucre, complained that tax farmers "could always find pretexts to place obstacles" in the way of interstate trade.[105] At least one tax farmer claimed that such restrictions on trade were necessary for his contract to be viable. General Pérez Soto, as president and tax farmer of Trujillo state in 1924, informed Gómez that, after losing almost 11,000 bolívares administering the liquor tax over four months, he had created a partnership with various merchants and distillers that would, among other provisions, exclude imports from the neighboring state of Zulia. He asked for Gómez's understanding and reasoned, "You did not favor me with the contract so that I would lose [money]."[106] Pérez Soto's letter mentioned repeatedly the large sums he paid the treasury, implying that these fees required him to block Zulian imports.

Tax farmers' profits are difficult to calculate because these individuals reaped both licit and illicit earnings and because their expenses included overhead for collecting revenue and often for producing and selling liquor as well. Nevertheless, scattered evidence indicates that liquor-revenue contracts were quite lucrative (as they were in Colombia[107]), even with increased rental rates. US consul Emile Sauer learned from Eloy Montenegro that his patron, General Eustoquio Gómez, the president and tax farmer of Táchira state who monopolized aguardiente sales there, netted a profit of roughly 30,000 bolívares per month (or 360,000 bolívares annually) after deducting payments to the treasury and other expenses.[108] When, in 1946, the anticorruption tribunal prosecuted several liquor tax farmers from the Gómez era, investigators used a variety of sources to calculate profits from the contracts and arrived at estimates similar to those obtained by Sauer. They calculated that Márquez earned approximately 250,000 bolívares a year from the contract in Zulia in 1922–30, and that Galavís earned 400,000 bolívares a year in Yaracuy in 1929–31.[109] An especially cooperative defendant, General José Antonio Baldó, estimated that his periodic earnings from several liquor-tax contracts totaled 680,000 bolívares over the course of the dictatorship.[110] Roberto Ramírez, who was employed by Gómez to manage his economic enterprises, allegedly earned an average of 109,412 bolívares annually for the seventeen years that he held the contract in Aragua state and parts of neighboring Guárico, for a total of 1.86 million bolívares, much more than the 687,950 bolívares he apparently earned from his participation in petroleum concessions.[111] These admittedly rough figures suggest that liquor contracts were among the most lucrative perquisites that Gómez distributed to his allies.

The Transition to Direct Administration

The resurgence of tax farming lasted into the early 1930s, when the global depression struck Venezuela, threatened state finances, and drove Gómez to look for new revenues as he and Cárdenas had done in the mid-1910s. During the second half of 1930, as foreign trade and tax receipts plummeted, the treasury's cash reserves fell from roughly 100 million bolívares to 30 million.[112] Gómez, who had turned the presidency over to Dr. Juan Bautista Pérez in 1929 in order to devote time to his business empire and the army, was reportedly outraged by rumors that a significant part of the decline was due to embezzlement by members of Pérez's cabinet, such as the minister of public works.[113] This alleged malfeasance created a stir in diplomatic, government, and business circles in Caracas. The US minister noted that "certain American and English bankers in the city . . . with years of experience" in Latin America found the level of embezzlement during the Pérez administration to be surprisingly high.[114] Gómez demanded Pérez's resignation, returned as president in July 1931, and directed major budgetary decisions, determined to preserve his reputation for fiscal discipline.[115]

The crisis persuaded Gómez to abandon the liquor-tax contracts and establish direct government control in hopes of increasing revenue, even though it would hurt his allies. After months of planning, he decreed in December 1931 that treasury personnel would administer the liquor tax throughout Venezuela.[116] As of January 1, 1932, the farming of the liquor tax—the only federal revenue under contract—would end. The regime's newspaper, *El Nuevo Diario*, announced the appointment of a new "special commissioner for organization of the liquor revenue," with a headline emphasizing that his jurisdiction encompassed "all the national territory."[117]

Gómez's attempt to restore national finances and faith in his administration yielded results within months, even before the oil industry began to recover. "The government's program of economy outlined in the budget is being adhered to in a fairly satisfactory manner," reported the US minister in February 1932. "The government's tendency to look for further sources of income within the country," he added, "was clearly reflected in the Decree placing the control of the liquor traffic in the hands of Federal authorities."[118] In May 1932 he reported that the Venezuelan government's cash reserves had increased steadily since Gómez reassumed the presidency and now totaled more than 60 million bolívares, a notable upturn since Pérez's departure.[119] US diplomats continued to report favorably on Gómez's fiscal management, contributing to American support in his final years.[120] Although total revenues under Gómez never returned to pre-1930 levels, the regime partially offset trade-related losses by reducing expenditures and increasing receipts from domestic taxes. Liquor revenue rose from 9.17 million bolívares in 1930–31 to an all-time high of 13.71 million bolívares in 1932–33 following the shift to direct administration (see table 3.2). The increase resulted not only from the change to bureaucratic administration, but also from a 50 percent increase in liquor-tax rates.

This return to bureaucratic administration did not eliminate clientelistic or patrimonial practices. Some of Gómez's allies, including former tax farmers Antonio Pimentel and Ramón Ramos, continued in the aguardiente business and received favored treatment under the new tax regime.[121] Gómez also continued to claim privileges for himself and his family. Between 1932 and 1935, over 3.5 million bolívares of taxes on aguardiente produced on estates belonging to the dictator and his relatives were paid out of the presidential slush fund in the Ministry of Interior Relations; these liquor "revenues" represented nothing more than funds transferred from one ministry to another.[122] Thus the imagined dichotomy between "modern" fiscal administration and "backward" tax farming continued to be blurred in reality. Just as growing bureaucratic expertise had informed the treasury's supervision of the tax-farming system during the period of increasing fees, so, too, patrimonial practices persisted into the new era of federal administration.

The history of the liquor tax under Gómez illustrates the interweaving of bureaucratic and patrimonial forms of rule within a process of neopatrimonial state formation. The practice of contracting the liquor tax to Gómez's clients ceded them control over a sector of their regional economies, allowing them to reap private profits. This exercise of patrimonial power was deplored by Cárdenas and by disadvantaged distillers, merchants, and consumers, who all had ample reason to view tax farmers' monopolies as an abuse of public authority for private gain. Gómez, though not overly troubled by tax farmers' corruption, periodically and selectively embraced bureaucratic administration when he needed the additional revenue this system produced. Cárdenas, the architect and most able administrator of bureaucratic taxation, articulated his ideals of efficiency, economic progress, and modernity within a framework of anticorruption, while knowing that some of the revenue generated by his reforms would be channeled into the regime's patrimonial practices.

Each of the two revenue systems offered Gómez a means to consolidate his power, and so he used each one as circumstances indicated. The result was a winding, contingent fiscal transition stretching over decades in which bureaucratic practice impacted tax farming and patrimonial practices shaped bureaucratic administration. To be sure, fiscal management drew closer to Cárdenas's bureaucratic ideals over the course of the dictatorship; it was Cardenas's reforms, not the oil boom, that initially stabilized state finances. But, in the end, corruption and anticorruption both left their mark on the treasury.

Before turning to the issue of honor and anticorruption in the next chapter, it is important to highlight the centrality of predatory corruption associated with cattle and liquor in Gomecista state formation, especially during the years before the post–World War I oil boom. As I have argued, the cattle cartel and regional liquor monopolies shared similar dynamics, especially as they strengthened bonds among Gomecistas while subjecting Venezuelans to coercive exchanges that wove the power of the central state into their lives. My emphasis on cattle and liquor in the consolidation of the Gomecista state is somewhat novel; it contradicts those scholars who associate the regime's consolidation with the rise of the petroleum economy. A focus on cattle and liquor, two ubiquitous commodities, calls attention to the importance of everyday exchanges both among state officials and between officials and those they sought to rule. It assumes that Gomecistas constructed their political authority first and foremost at the grass roots of society.

Oil, in contrast, was far removed from the daily lives of the great majority of Venezuelans, so much so that Fernando Coronil referred to the state's apparent "magic" as it transformed subterranean petroleum deposits into a source of wealth and power.[123] By the time oil contributed significantly to public finances in the early 1920s, however, state-building was already advanced—and the political stability sought by oil investors was already in place—thanks largely to the political networks consolidated through control over more mundane and familiar commodities. Petroleum's impact on Venezuela is, of course, undeniable. But before the state discovered the magic of petroleum, it was already being built on a foundation of beef and booze.

CHAPTER 4

OPPONENTS AND PRISONERS

MIDDLE-CLASS HONOR AND ANTICORRUPTION

What was it like to live under the predatory corruption of the Gómez regime? In previous chapters, we have glimpsed the economic losses suffered by merchants, ranchers, and distillery owners who fell afoul of the regime's profiteering, and we have seen how consumers were gouged by the regime's monopolistic practices. But an approach to corruption and state formation that focuses on material exchanges offers only a partial view of life under Gomecista profiteering. For many Venezuelans, especially middle-class men, submission to Gomecismo's predatory practices produced intense emotions of humiliation and dishonor; meanwhile, defending one's honor by resisting official predation risked death or confinement in the regime's dreaded prisons. This chapter argues that the cultural values and emotions associated with honor were often central to middle-class Venezuelans' understanding of what it meant to resist or submit to the corrupt practices of the Gomecista state. The discussion of bourgeois honor and the related themes of humiliation and dignity provides a window into the affective dimension of state formation and corruption while also laying a foundation for understanding the virulent backlash against Gomecismo that erupted following the dictator's death in 1935.[1]

The expansion of the middle class in the early twentieth century formed a crucial part of the context in which Venezuelans experienced predatory corruption and forged common understandings of Gomecista profiteering. Middle-class status rested on two criteria, both of which were vulnerable to predatory corruption.[2] First, the middle class occupied an intermediate economic position between the wealthy elite and the poor. In Venezuela, as in the rest of Latin America, the financial situation of middle-class families (whether professionals, civil servants, junior military officers, or small-time entrepreneurs) was almost always tenuous.[3] The untimely death of a family patriarch or, under Gómez, the intrusion of predatory corruption could jeopardize the household economy and, along with it, the social standing of its members. Second, middle-class families claimed status as *gente decente* (decent people), a culturally defined category that required adherence to evolving standards of male and female honor.[4] Middle-class honor is discussed in greater detail below, but what bears emphasis here is the way that economic losses imposed through predatory corruption undercut families' ability to meet the cultural criteria for honorable conduct. A middle-class man lost honor if he was shown to be powerless to protect his family's livelihood from predatory corruption (or other threats); and, at least through the 1920s, a middle-class woman (and her male relatives, her putative protectors) risked a loss of honor if her family's economic misfortune obliged her to seek employment outside the home. These interconnections between material and cultural criteria for middle-class status meant that economic loss could lead directly to an emotional experience of humiliation, shame, and dishonor. In many instances, then, middle-class opposition to predatory corruption was not a political tactic employed by an ambitious class on the rise but rather the defensive reaction of a nascent (and still vaguely defined) segment of society whose claims to respectability were made all the more precarious by Gomecista profiteering.

Scholars writing on the cultural context of corruption usually focus on the different understandings or definitions of corruption across societies. They note, for example, that officials who dispense government jobs and other favors to their friends and family may face greater or lesser censure in different cultures, or at different points in history as a nation's political culture changes over time.[5] In short, such studies examine how cultural values distinguish between corruption and acceptable practices. By contrast, research into how culture shapes the experiences of people obliged to live under systemic corruption remains relatively sparse.[6] A promising avenue for exploring how culture informs the experience of corruption is to follow scholars who have begun to examine historical actors' emotional responses to corruption.[7] If we view emotions as feelings processed and articulated through cultural values that are historically contingent,[8] then attention to Venezuelans' shame, humiliation, indignation, and fear in the face of predatory corruption can inform our understanding of how honor and dishonor shaped the experience of living under Gomecismo.

The historiography of emotions, still a relatively young field of study, provides two concepts useful for an examination of honor-based anticorruption under Gómez. Ute Frevert, a leading historian in this field who treats honor as embedded in the history of emotions because of its inextricable relation to humiliation and shame, encourages scholars to consider the "historical economy of emotions"—a concept that views emotions as "dynamic and mobile, both enacting and reacting to cultural, social, economic, and political challenges."[9] Second, since no nation is an emotive monolith, scholars in this field also call attention to distinct "emotional communities," each one composed of individuals whose shared emotional responses to particular historical events and processes set them apart from others.[10]

This chapter suggests that many middle-class Venezuelans who experienced the predatory corruption of Gomecismo formed an emotional community, one that evaluated submission to such profiteering through a shared discourse of humiliation, shame, and (dis)honor. Their memoirs and other writings provide insight into an emotional economy of anticorruption in which victimization at the hands of Gomecistas was equated with humiliation and dishonor, which could only be remedied through acts of resistance, whether physical or rhetorical. This emotional community included Venezuelans who experienced predatory corruption in the form of Gomecista monopolies as well as political prisoners and their families subjected to profiteering by prison officials. Moreover, these middle-class opponents articulated a critique of Gómez's official image, in which Gomecista propagandists presented the dictator as the personification of bourgeois honor. In the aftermath of the student protests of 1928, some young anti-Gomecistas moved beyond this debate over honor and corruption. They sought instead to harness anticorruption sentiment to the pragmatic goal of recruiting the alienated middle class into a broad-based opposition movement—an early attempt to integrate class analysis explicitly into anti-Gomecista strategies. The visceral reaction against Gomecista corruption nonetheless remained, and it burst forth in the protests after Gómez's death.

The State, Masculine Honor, and the Ideal of the "Hombre de Trabajo"

Scholars of Latin America have integrated honor, understood as "the value of a person in [their] own eyes, but also in the eyes of society,"[11] into their examination of the social, cultural, and political history of the region from the colonial era onward. Emphasizing the emotional dimension of honor in colonial Latin America, Lyman Johnson and Sonya Lipsett-Rivera introduced an influential collection of essays by citing William Ian Miller's assertion that "honor is above all the keen sensitivity to the experience of humiliation and shame," a perspective useful in understanding honor's role in social and political conflict and relations of power.[12] In the colonial era, the crown distributed individual honors and prized its role as the ultimate arbiter of disputes over social precedence, contributing to imperial hegemony over a divided colonial society.[13] The interweaving of honor and state power continued in postcolonial Latin America. Ideologies of republicanism included new, more egalitarian notions of male dignity in which citizens' individual virtue and accomplishments began to outweigh the attributes of birth and race that were privileged under colonialism.[14] In the century following independence, popular responses to state initiatives could hinge on whether citizens believed they respected or undermined the honor of patriarchal households.[15]

Studies of republican honor in post-independence Spanish America call attention to the heightened value attached to individual economic achievement and work discipline. As the colonial emphasis on family lineage declined, honor was increasingly claimed by men of any class who engaged in productive labor and demonstrated a strong work ethic. As one historian notes, the new republican understanding of honor "blend[ed] traditional expectations of patriarchs as providers and a rising liberal emphasis on labor discipline."[16] In his study of nineteenth-century Venezuela, historian Reuben Zahler confirms the emergence of these new precepts, arguing that "individual economic productivity became increasingly important as a marker of social decency, honor, and status."[17] To be sure, postcolonial attitudes continued to prize some qualities associated with older notions of male honor, such as assertions of personal autonomy and the exercise of patriarchal control over female and younger male relatives.[18] In another sign of continuity, the middle and upper classes only grudgingly and partially relaxed their association of honor with the racial hierarchy of the colonial era.[19] But the increasing linkage to economic productivity, bourgeois values, and virtuous citizenship nevertheless adapted male honor to liberal visions of progress. This extension of honor to male heads of household outside the elite, however, restrained changes in legal and social definitions of female honor, which continued to revolve around women's acceptance of patriarchal authority and adherence to colonial norms of chastity.[20]

Gómez, a mestizo and a member of the rising provincial bourgeoisie, was well positioned to claim status within the republican ethos that incorporated more egalitarian, merit-based notions of virtue in Venezuela, especially as his economic fortune expanded. As historian and anthropologist Julie Skurski has argued, Gómez maintained his rule for twenty-seven years in part through the projection of a masculine style that emphasized his military skill, virility, personal autonomy, and dedication to work, all of which resonated within the culture of republican male honor.[21] When Gómez and his supporters claimed that he personified the ideal of the "hombre de trabajo" (hardworking man), they drew on the postcolonial formulation of male respectability to legitimate his rule. As historian Arlene Díaz observes, Venezuela's positivist philosophers, as they searched for the key to the nation's elusive material progress, condemned most nineteenth-century caudillos as men who sought wealth and status through force of arms rather than productive labor. Positivists concluded that for Venezuela to advance, "bourgeois masculine values" centered on economic production had to supersede "aristocratic and military ideas of honor."[22] Gómez's propagandists portrayed him as the embodiment of bourgeois honor, the ideal man to guide Venezuela toward a more modern, industrious future, a portrayal that mirrored Gómez's image of himself.[23] He purportedly sought power not for any personal benefit, but only to guarantee a stable environment in which hardworking men could prosper.[24]

This drive for legitimation led a succession of propagandists to visit Gómez's ranches and other enterprises near Maracay and to praise him as the exemplar of national progress. One such writer, reviewing the General's efforts to breed cattle that would thrive in Venezuela, informed readers that before Gómez "no one had dedicated such an intense effort or such systematic and steady attention, nor [had anyone] obtained such a useful result" as the national strongman. The journalist reported that ranchers throughout the nation followed Gómez's example "with the greatest enthusiasm." The dictator had "inaugurated the era of work, which redounds to the benefit of the individual and the public good."[25] In a similar vein, the official press asserted that all hardworking men supported Gómez and placed themselves at his command.[26] He was the "Chief of the Army of Work"[27] and his supporters were "the soldiers of work,"[28] metaphors that gained resonance as the annual military reviews showcased the discipline, precision, and obedience of Gómez's armed forces.

Readers of official propaganda may have been relatively few, but celebrations of newly completed public works allowed the regime to reach a wider audience. As Gómez toured newly improved highways in 1916, for example, the archways erected for the event featured inscriptions declaring him "the hero of work" and the "apostle of work"; others sported variations on the regime's slogan of "peace, union, and work"; and a poem composed for the occasion argued unambiguously that "the hardworking man is the best ruler."[29] More ominously, Gómez labeled his political opponents as men who did not want to exercise an honorable profession and therefore needed to be eliminated, or imprisoned and subjected to forced labor so they would learn how to work.[30] In the discourse of the regime, then, Gómez's success in building his business empire and fomenting national development confirmed his republican virtue and his fitness to rule over—and to discipline—a population that had not fully absorbed the values associated with productive labor.

"The Hardworking Man Would Transform Himself into a Warrior": Masculine Honor and Corruption in the Opposition Discourse of Emilio Arévalo Cedeño

Gómez's middle-class opponents, as the remainder of this chapter will demonstrate, turned the tables on the dictator by invoking the ideal of work in their critiques of his regime's corruption. In their accounts, Gómez's "success" as a businessman—that is, the rapid expansion of his enterprises—resulted from his abuse of public power rather than hard work, thrift, or business acumen. By using his political clout to drive out competitors, they charged, he made it impossible for most of the bourgeoisie to engage in honorable (i.e., independent) work or to enjoy the fruits of their labor. Gómez therefore prevented them from living as honorable patriarchs. Similarly, the prisons did not teach inmates how to work but rather subjected productive citizens to an especially raw form of profiteering designed to enrich prison officials while humiliating and impoverishing detainees and their families. For middle-class opponents and prisoners, the deeply ingrained values of republican honor provided a powerful framework for articulating resistance to a corrupt regime even if, by the end of the Gómez era, honor-based critiques of corruption failed to satisfy a rising generation of young activists.

Emilio Arévalo Cedeño, one of the most famous middle-class rebels to take up arms against the regime, justified his resistance first and foremost as a defense of honor. Following his initial uprising in 1914, he led six armed invasions of Venezuela aimed at toppling Gómez and survived to publish his memoirs in 1936. Unlike many of the regime's leading adversaries, he was not an established political figure of the pre-Gómez era. Instead, he was a typical member of the lower reaches of the bourgeoisie in the plains of Venezuela. Moving among jobs in journalism, commerce, and telegraphy, he occasionally scraped together enough capital to open a store or buy some livestock, until he ran afoul of Gómez's monopolies.[31] His memoirs refer only briefly to his desire to build a democratic state in Venezuela. By contrast, his concern with masculine honor and humiliation permeates the entire text, guiding his comments on work, corruption, family, and the alleged feminization of men who submitted to the Gómez regime. His articulation of these themes resonated with the emotional economy of anticorruption, which equated submission to official predation with humiliation, indignation, and a loss of honor, and posited resistance as the only path to honor's recovery.

In the first pages of his memoir, Arévalo Cedeño's justification for taking up arms against Gómez establishes the dynamic linking corruption, honor, and opposition to tyranny. He claims that early in the regime he was forced to "pay tribute to the voracity and plundering" of Colonel Paulino Torres, who oversaw "the cattle monopoly in Cúa [Miranda state] . . . as an agent of Gómez."[32] By 1913 life had become increasingly difficult for "us, the men of work, who went wherever we could, day and night, searching for business wherever we might find it, in order to save ourselves from ruin and satisfy our necessities, pay our creditors and save our reputation as men of honor and dignity."[33] Matters came to a head when Arévalo Cedeño attempted to sell some horses in the state of Apure. Ranchers there told him that Gómez had ordered that the only man permitted to buy livestock in the region was General Eulogio Moros, the administrator of La Candelaria, one of the dictator's ranches. Moros offered to buy Arévalo Cedeño's horses at a ridiculously low price and to pay him in bulls at inflated prices. Even though Arévalo Cedeño knew it meant "ruin and bankruptcy,"[34] he accepted the deal.

Acquiescing to these transactions no doubt filled Arévalo Cedeño with shame for, as explained below, he associated submission to Gómez with a loss of masculine identity. He assured his readers that his only motivation was to avoid arrest and prison, which implied a permanent state of subjugation, so that he could launch a rebellion. Arévalo Cedeño explained:

> Refusing to hand over my horses [to Moros] would have meant going to jail, and because I know how to protest against tyranny with a rifle in my hand, and I was not born to be a slave but rather a free man, I resolved to accept the *brilliant* transaction that General Moros proposed to me; but from that moment I swore in silence and on the memory of my father, that I would abandon home, wife, and everything to go to war. . . . The hardworking man would transform himself into a warrior, pledging never to give up his status as a worthy citizen, to stand up with a rifle in his hand to confront an offensive tyranny rather than kneel or bow down before it like conquered

slaves, as did . . . the majority of my countrymen during the twenty-seven years that covered the Venezuelan home with sorrow.[35]

Rebellion had become the only honorable course of action. Armed resistance was necessary to save "our homes and what little remained of our interests."[36] Moreover, Arévalo Cedeño's references to submissive victims of corruption as "slaves" implied his fear that passivity would signify an association with Venezuelans of African ancestry.[37]

Arévalo Cedeño's defense of his reputation as a virtuous worker took on particular importance in light of the regime's attempt to define all rebellious opponents as thieves and bandits. Government officials regularly painted rebels as men who sought to avoid work by choosing a life of armed vagrancy in which they seized food, livestock, and other supplies from productive citizens.[38] Perhaps in anticipation of this assault on his character, Arévalo Cedeño sought to define Gómez as the real thief in Venezuela. In an open letter to Gómez in 1914, he referred to the dictator as "the insatiable robber, who has usurped all our businesses, who has stolen all our cattle."[39] As he composed his memoirs years later, Arévalo Cedeño still thought it necessary to call out the hypocrisy of Gomecista attempts to portray him as a bandit. "It is well known," he wrote, "that the flatterers of the tyrant Gómez, who were thieves and murderers like him, were in the habit of labeling as thieves, rustlers, and bandits, the free and honorable men who, like I, never consented to kill our honor in order to be a slave of that miserable coward and criminal named Juan Vicente Gómez, who was worshipped by the corrupt Venezuelan of the epoch."[40] Gomecista profiteering had made it impossible for honorable entrepreneurs to survive. Arévalo Cedeño's most succinct justification of rebellion was his declaration, referring to the conditions prevailing in 1913–14, "We could not work then."[41]

Nevertheless, Arévalo Cedeño found few recruits to take up arms during his seven revolts. To him, this widespread acquiescence to Gomecista profiteering signaled the feminization of Venezuelan men and the degeneration of the national population. He introduced the theme in the first chapter of his memoir, unleashing a diatribe against his countrymen too afraid to fight the dictatorship: "Venezuelan men renounced their sex in order to be transformed into women!! Venezuelans felt pleasure and pride in being slaves of Gómez and his tribe, who alone could tyrannize the Venezuelan of the epoch, [and were made] unthinking by fear and degenerate by vice!!"[42] This gendering and racializing of dominant and submissive roles appears throughout the narrative (and in other anti-Gomecista writing as well[43]). In a similar vein, Arévalo Cedeño impugned the honor of "whining exiles" who found excuses not to take up arms against Gómez even as they denounced his tyranny. In a well-worn phrase, Arévalo Cedeño accused them of "crying like women over what they could not defend as men."[44] These opponents of the regime, he charged, "felt themselves disqualified as men" when they could not match his bold actions. They criticized his failed uprisings only because of their own "impotence and fear."[45]

Like other writers in Europe and the Americas during the late nineteenth and early twentieth centuries who perceived a loss of manliness among their compatriots, Arévalo Cedeño warned of national degeneration.[46] Nevertheless, Arévalo Cedeño stood apart from many such writers in his insistence that degeneration and emasculation resulted from submission to tyranny and exploitation.[47] The most remarkable example of this discourse came during his 1921 campaign in his native state of Guárico, located in the central plains and a focal point of Gómez's cattle monopoly. As Arévalo Cedeño and his troops passed through the town of Zaraza, women threw flowers in their path, but the men of the town kept their distance, refusing to join the rebel forces "as duty required them to do."[48] Arévalo Cedeño claimed that the men of Zaraza would curse Gómez in the privacy of their "domestic gatherings" (i.e., in spaces gendered as feminine), but their cowardice when given the chance to rebel demonstrated that such curses were in truth "the cry of impotence of [those] who did not choose to be masculine."[49] So, he told the young women of Zaraza not to marry men from the town, "because slaves cannot produce children who are free citizens of the homeland, but rather servants of the tyrant Gómez."[50] Arévalo Cedeño's denigration of passive victims of Gomecismo once again revealed his own fear of losing honor if he accepted humiliation at the hands of the regime.

Arévalo Cedeño was not alone in asserting that widespread submission to Gómez signaled a crisis of Venezuelan masculinity. Jacinto López, another regime opponent, lamented in 1922 that Gómez—"the king of plunder"—had destroyed Venezuelan manhood and asked rhetorically, "How can we explain Gómez, if not by the utter lack of men in Venezuela?"[51] Similarly, Magda Portal, a Peruvian poet and political activist who supported Gómez's opponents, pondered why opposition to the dictator was not more widespread, and asked, "Is it because Venezuela has died, [because] its ability to produce manly men has atrophied after it produced the Liberator of America [i.e., Simón Bolívar]?"[52] Arévalo Cedeño's remedy was for Venezuelan men to recover their masculine identity as he did, by "confronting the tyrant with a rifle in our hand, the only redemptive formula for washing away our dishonor as an enslaved and degenerate people."[53] Only then could bourgeois males reestablish themselves as patriarchs of honorable households sustained by their own independent labor.

"One Pays for Masculinity": Prisons, Corruption, and Masculine Honor

The themes of corruption and masculine honor that emerged so powerfully in Arévalo Cedeño's memoir also featured prominently in accounts written by Gómez's middle-class opponents who survived confinement in the regime's notorious prisons. Thousands of his opponents suffered imprisonment without trial for offenses ranging from outright rebellion to careless remarks made in the street and interpreted as hostile to the regime. These political prisoners endured starvation diets, abysmal sanitary conditions, leg irons weighing up to sixty pounds riveted around their ankles, and gruesome tortures, some of which were physically emasculating. Many died under torture or from illnesses brought on by the harsh conditions, while others were killed by prison officials who placed poison or finely ground glass in inmates' food. Officials extorted substantial sums of money from prisoners' families with the promise—often unfulfilled—that the payments would be used to provide their loved ones with more and better food than the usual prison rations. Occasionally, prisoners were released alive, and stories of prison conditions circulated throughout Venezuela and abroad.[54]

Prisons not only played an important role in the everyday exercise of power and profiteering by the regime, they also became a pervasive symbol of the dictatorship, both domestically and internationally. José Rafael Pocaterra, perhaps the most famous memoirist of Gómez's jails, asserted that life inside Caracas's La Rotunda mirrored many aspects of life throughout the nation, suggesting that the prison became a microcosm of Venezuela.[55] The image of Gomecista prisons created by inmates' families, rumor, and survivors' accounts incorporated the same themes of corruption and (dis)honor that pervade Arévalo Cedeño's memoir, underscoring the shared sentiments and common understanding of corruption among the community of the regime's victims.

The metaphorical emasculation of men who submitted to Gomecista corruption, as imagined by Arévalo Cedeño and others, no doubt resonated with Venezuelans in part because of the regime's notorious practice of physically emasculating some of its prisoners.[56] Beginning as early as 1912–13 and continuing through the end of the regime, stories circulated of male prisoners hoisted by ropes tied around their genitals and similar tortures. In January 1913, Carmen Vallenilla de Aguirre wrote to Gómez from the eastern city of Carúpano to inform him that her husband Juan Aguirre had been arrested the previous month by local officials who, after tying his hands, "tied a rope around his parts [i.e., genitals] and hung him shamefully until his flesh tore."[57] Vallenilla de Aguirre wrote to Gómez confident that he would not condone such barbarous acts, but this method of torture only became more widespread.

Pocaterra, in his memoir of La Rotunda, Caracas's main prison, recounted that one fellow inmate told him "that as the result of the tortures he has endured, the skin of his genital organs has been torn off and the pain is spreading through his lower abdomen and kidneys."[58] Pocaterra reported that Gomecistas inflicted emasculating tortures on political prisoners in several of the cells at La Rotunda and at the army barracks of San Carlos; he lived in fear of being subjected to such barbarity himself.[59] It was rumored that dissident military officers and others implicated in a failed 1919 movement against Gómez suffered this form of torment in the courtyard of Villa Zoila, a home formerly owned by Cipriano Castro and used as a temporary interrogation center. The US legation reported that many neighbors in the fashionable district heard the screams of the victims.[60] As late as the early 1930s, two citizens of the British West Indies (a small-scale farmer and a mechanic) who had migrated to Venezuela and were detained in the regime's counteroffensive against rebels in the late 1920s, testified that their Venezuelan captors threatened them with suspension by their genitals during interrogations.[61] Both men had heard rumors of such torture during their years living in rural Venezuela, attesting to its notoriety.

Jorge Luciani, who published a memoir of his confinement as a political prisoner in La Rotunda from 1919 to 1921, combined the themes of corruption, honor, and emasculation in his denunciations of the Gómez regime. Luciani labeled Gómez "the emasculator" and "a thief without equal among the dictators of Latin America,"[62] and (like Arévalo Cedeño) he questioned the honor of men who complained of the dictator's abuse without actively opposing it.[63] Luciani alleged that corrupt Gomecistas, in order to quell opposition to their profiteering, purposefully sought to "subdue manly instincts, cut the virile organs, [and] brutally extirpate manliness. In Venezuela, one pays for masculinity [i.e., active opposition to the regime] at the cost of one's life. . . . The dictatorial decree has ordered an effective emasculation. The national organism is thereby intended to become docile to every yoke, the supreme ideal of the herdsman."[64] In this way, Luciani constructed a parallel between Gómez's management of his livestock and the regime's subjugation of male citizens, arguing that the dictator carried out "the task of Venezuelan castration"[65]—understood as both the literal and symbolic emasculation of opponents—as a strategy of political control. As Luciani informed his readers, Gómez's assault on Venezuelan masculinity had become so notorious that the dictator felt compelled to address the issue in a 1927 book titled *Venezuela y su gobernante* (English edition, *Venezuela and Its Ruler*), written by a pro-Gómez Mexican journalist, Nemesio García Naranjo.

García Naranjo's book was clearly an effort to respond to the international circulation of stories about the regime's barbarism. An admirer of Mexican strongman Porfirio Díaz (in power 1876–1911), García Naranjo was brought to Venezuela by the regime to interview Gómez, and his book praising the Venezuelan dictator was published in both Spanish and English, indicating the breadth of its intended audience. García Naranjo criticized the "passionate propaganda" spread by the regime's enemies who claimed that the dictatorship had broken Venezuelans' spirit. He reassured his readers that Venezuelan men remained in full possession of their "virility." But he also emphasized that, in contrast to previous eras of Venezuelan history, when this virile spirit led to unending rebellion and civil war, under Gómez it "has been nobly [re]directed into works of progress and construction."[66]

During an interview at one of the dictator's ranches outside Maracay, Gómez shared with García Naranjo a parable to illustrate his success in imposing order without resorting to emasculation. Gómez began by pointing out some bulls pulling a cart. "Calling my attention to the size and strength of those animals," García Naranjo wrote, "he made me notice also that they were not castrated. 'There has been no need to mutilate them to make them work,' [Gómez] said to me with satisfaction, and then added, 'At the beginning they resisted but after working a little with them, they finally pulled the carts peacefully.'"[67] García Naranjo considered this to be an "admirable allegory," and he made sure his readers understood the point. "As with the bulls," he wrote, "so he did with the human multitudes. He has not mutilated them but has only stopped them from using their heroic impulses and powerful energies to destroy one another. He has not killed virility in Venezuela."[68] Despite these remarkable declarations, the regime and its propagandists failed to quell the association between Gomecista rule and emasculation.

Prisons performed several functions in the regime's systematic profiteering. Venezuelans submitted to the coercion of the Gomecista cattle monopoly and other economic rackets because, as Arévalo Cedeño noted, the threat of prison and torture lay behind every forced transaction. The US consul at La Guaira wrote in 1915 that "men who have refused to sell their farms to the President elect [Gómez] or his friends at prices offered by them have been sent to prison as political offenders."[69] Similarly, the British legation in Caracas reported in 1917 that when owners of factories, sugar mills, or other businesses refused to sell out to Gómez, they were imprisoned until they agreed to Gómez's offer, which typically represented "a quarter or a fifth of the real value" of the enterprise.[70] Property owners accepted these ruinous and humiliating transactions because they found the threat of prison, whether implicit or explicit, so horrifying.

But the most direct connection between profiteering and the prison system involved the internal administration of the jails themselves. Officials at Venezuela's most infamous prisons—La Rotunda in Caracas and the Castillo in Puerto Cabello—imposed daily routines to extort money, labor, and other resources from political inmates and their families. Most political prisoners came from the middle and upper classes. Lists of those detained as regime opponents, who were usually segregated from common criminals, referred to them as journalists, lawyers, bureaucrats, poets, business owners, members of the clergy, students, military officers, and property owners (*propietarios*).[71] These men not only endured the physical hardships of prison, they also lived under a system of coerced transactions even more pervasive than the one that prevailed outside the prison walls.

Corrupt prison administrators—like their counterparts in other regions of the world—found that the management of inmates' food rations provided ample opportunities for profiteering.[72] Gomecista prison officials enjoyed two sources of private income connected to prisoners' food supply: they pilfered government funds allocated for inmates' rations and they extorted money from prisoners and their families for "extra" food. The two schemes were intertwined. Spending only a fraction of the funds budgeted for prisoners' rations, the governors bought cheap, often poor quality food, such as rancid meat and spoiled beans and vegetables, which were served in meager portions.[73] One disgruntled employee at La Rotunda reported that the prison governor pocketed 36 bolívares out of the 115 allocated for daily food purchases for the inmates in 1913, which would produce an annual income of 13,140 bolívares (or roughly US$2,500 at that year's exchange rate).[74] This diversion of funds resulted in food that bourgeois prisoners found disgusting and which they associated with their social inferiors. "The few political prisoners who have lived to describe their experiences," reported the US minister to Venezuela, "declare they were given the most miserable peon fare, consisting of food which was decayed and filthy."[75]

Thus, inmates who had the means would pay exorbitant sums for better or additional food, providing a second source of illicit income for prison officials. Families of political prisoners would visit periodically to leave money with the governor of the jail to be spent, at a prisoner's discretion, on supplemental food.[76] Prisoners believed that in the harsh conditions of the jails, where many died of disease or simply wasted away, these extra rations could make the difference between life and death. Prison officials' periodic termination of extra rations was one of the harshest measures they could impose on prisoners.[77] When José Garbi Sánchez, a follower of Arévalo Cedeño imprisoned in Puerto Cabello, lost his supplemental rations, he became so debilitated that he could no longer remember his own name. A comrade helped him scratch it into the wall of his cell so that he could remember who he was.[78] Inmates saw the purchase of food as a necessary, though exploitative, transaction.

Prison officials charged inmates different amounts for supplemental rations based on their ability to pay. Families of wealthy prisoners typically paid up to 50 bolívares per day, though the family of General Román Delgado Chalbaud, a wealthy and implacable enemy of the regime, was charged several times that amount early in his confinement.[79] Prisoners buying extra food reported paying between two and three and half times the street prices for what they received, and sometimes the officials simply pocketed all the money left by relatives.[80] Like the Gomecista monopolies outside the prisons, the sale of extra rations became a routine transaction that reproduced relationships of subordination and exploitation. As one prisoner in Puerto Cabello summarized officials' sale of food to inmates, "The robbery was shameless and daily."[81] The profits garnered from sales to political prisoners probably dwarfed the sums that officials pilfered from the government funds. The well-known Venezuelan adage describing the attitude of officials engaged in profiteering—that they preferred appointment to a position with opportunities for graft, rather than a monetary gift from their patron[82]—apparently held true.

At the Castillo during the early 1920s, prisoners' need for money to buy extra food became tied to a degrading system of coerced labor. Garbi Sánchez, captured during Arévalo Cedeño's 1921 revolt, wrote in his memoir that prison officials in Puerto Cabello supplied the inmates with tortoise shell from which to fashion elegant combs which were then sold to passengers on ships in the harbor. Prisoners who made the combs were paid on a piecework basis at a rate that allowed efficient laborers to buy daily arepas, the cornmeal griddle cakes that formed a basic part of the national diet but were not included in the ordinary rations. The arepas arrived stale, had to be soaked to be made edible, and came at an exorbitant price. Nevertheless, the lure of extra food spurred workers to produce the combs, even though they knew their captors sold them at prices far above what they paid the inmates to produce them. Garbi Sánchez and his comrades spent their days in a web of coerced transactions, in which both their production of combs and their purchase of supplemental food enriched the men who confined and exploited them.[83]

Particularly striking is the way that Garbi Sánchez's indignation over exploitation is mixed with his pride in the craftsmanship needed to fashion the stylish combs, a pride that reverberates with the bourgeois ideal of the "hombre de trabajo." Because the work of making the combs was difficult, his mastery of it became a source of pride. When the prisoners received the rough pieces of tortoise shell, they were also given Seville-style combs as models, as well as instructions on how to replicate them using a crude tool made by sharpening one end of an iron hoop to grind the shell into the proper shape, and charcoal to smooth and polish it. "It was hard for us to perfect those tasks," wrote Garbi Sánchez, "but we managed to establish a beautiful yet small industry, such that from the boats arriving in the port people asked to buy the combs made in the Castillo in order to sell them in Spain and other parts of Europe."[84]

This pride, however, coexisted with the shame and outrage that resulted from the knowledge that the fruit of his labor went almost entirely to his jailers. The inmates received 4 bolívares for each comb, the product of eight days' labor, but each one was sold "for 100 bolívares or more, according to the beauty of the engravings and polish" achieved by the prisoner-craftsmen.[85] Garbi Sánchez fumed, "The exploitation that the [prison] officials imposed on us by selling these hard-to-make handicrafts seemed to us to be a bare-faced robbery, with the added insult that those scoundrels were taking advantage and profiting from the work of defenseless and destitute persons, for we, racked with hunger, had no way of defending ourselves and were obliged to receive the insignificant price that they paid us."[86] The combination of hunger and coercion placed bourgeois prisoners in an exploited position they found unfamiliar and humiliating.

Adding insult to injury, prison officials subjected inmates to rhetoric that denigrated them as "vagos" or "vagabundos" (lazy tramps) who needed the regime's tutelage to instill a sense of discipline and a love of work. According to an affidavit submitted to a US congressman by a former political prisoner at the Castillo, officials referred to detainees arrested in 1913 as "vagos," using the word broadly (and repeatedly) as an epithet for "all men upon whom the Dictator looked askance."[87] Such epithets echoed the regime's assertions that anti-Gomecistas, regardless of their social and economic status, lacked a work ethic and needed to follow the dictator's example to learn to work.[88]

Prisoners defended themselves against such insults, both through their behavior in prison and by later shaping their memoirs to highlight their honorable conduct in the dehumanizing conditions of confinement. The procurement and distribution of scarce food, which had the potential to turn prisoners against one another in a struggle for survival, instead became a focus of solidarity and self-sacrifice as the inmates voluntarily shared among themselves. When wardens placed individual inmates on starvation diets, other prisoners would smuggle some of their own scant rations to the victims. Inmates at La Rotunda secreted some of their food to Delgado Chalbaud when his rations were cut, and later to officers imprisoned after the failed military conspiracy of 1919, even though the warden threatened to starve anyone caught making unauthorized transfers of food.[89]

In an especially telling anecdote, Garbi Sánchez highlighted the honorable nature of his fellow prisoners by recounting their virtuous conduct in the face of hunger and hardship. A prisoner, Juan Carabaño, managed to obtain a dozen bananas, which he left in a corner of his cell to ripen. Since prisoners were allowed to leave their cells for part of the day—a situation that gave them the opportunity to enter each other's cells unnoticed—Carabaño's nonchalance with his prized fruit demonstrated his trust in his fellow inmates, which proved entirely justified. Garbi Sánchez observed, "This shows the quality of men that the Gómez regime considered to be highly dangerous, that in that atmosphere of hunger and misery no one was capable of stealing a banana from don Juan."[90] While Gomecistas profited from the marketing of food and the exploitation of captive labor, prisoners' conduct remained honorable, allowing them to transcend the degrading conditions imposed upon them.[91] Such contrasts demonstrated who the real vagos were.

"It Was Painful to See Her Work in the Street": Prisoners' Families and the Costs of Corruption

Inmates, then, could spar with the prison regime in an effort to guard their dignity. But as long as they were confined, prisoners remained powerless to fulfill some of the fundamental duties of honorable bourgeois males, such as providing economic security to their families and guarding the chastity of their female kin.[92] The precarious economic state of prisoners' families, as well as their tenuous hold on respectability, emerges as a major theme in the memoir of Cecilia Pimentel, the daughter of a prominent Caracas family. From 1919 onward, four of her brothers, Francisco (a noted journalist and humorist), Luis Rafael (a captain in the Venezuelan army), Clemente, and Tancredo, were arrested repeatedly and imprisoned for years at a time. Cecilia's father had already died, so her brothers were the family's primary breadwinners. Deprived of a reliable income whenever the brothers were incarcerated, the family faced the added burden of making monetary payments to prison officials for the brothers' food. Cecilia, her mother, sister, and younger brothers often ate only one meal a day and occasionally had to ask friends for loans to pay for the extra rations needed by the Pimentel men. They realized that prison officials pocketed much of the money, making only a fraction available to the inmates for the purchase of food. They also knew that Luis, as one of the leaders of the failed military conspiracy of 1919, went for long periods without the right to buy extra rations, but they felt obliged to continue sending money to prison officials because they feared for his well-being if they halted the payments.[93]

This constant financial drain to satisfy corrupt Gomecistas left the Pimentels unable to afford the affluent lifestyle they had previously enjoyed. When they could no longer pay rent on their house, the owner threatened legal action to evict them and sell their belongings at auction. Indignant, Cecilia's mother responded that the owner knew the circumstances that had caused the lapse in rental payments. Cecilia recalled her mother's angry confrontation with the landlord's lawyer: "My mother answered him that he should go ahead and throw her and her daughters into the street, but that he should remember that her sons were not dead and that one day they would avenge this outrage."[94] Eventually, the family had to abandon their home and move to "a small house, with a roof made of cane" in the town of El Valle, then just outside Caracas.[95]

Financial hardship obliged Cecilia and her younger sister, Clara, to seek salaried work in Caracas, another blow to the family's status. When a relative of Cecilia's mother used her connections to secure Cecilia a job interview at the Casa Blohm, a major commercial firm, Cecilia's brothers Vicente and Clemente (her only two brothers not in prison) objected. "In those times hardly any women worked in the street," wrote Cecilia, using a telling phrase to refer to female office jobs, "and they [her brothers] said that for them it was a stigma [*desdoro*] that one of their sisters had to do it."[96] When Vicente saw that Cecilia remained determined to go to the interview, he insisted on escorting her. But "when we went out into the street, he could not contain his tears."[97] Cecilia accepted the job even though it meant a long commute, usually unaccompanied, and the pay—200 bolívares a month—was only half the salary of the male worker she replaced. Cecilia found that the men in the office treated her poorly. They gave her orders, she wrote, "with greater or lesser surliness and even rudeness, [which] caused in me a dread, a shock, to which I never grew accustomed."[98] When Cecilia lost her job, her younger sister Clara felt obliged to accept employment as an accounting assistant at Venezuela Drugg, which paid only 150 bolívares a month. Cecilia remembered that "it was painful to see her . . . work in the street, a girl accustomed to other surroundings."[99] The deterioration of the Pimentels' economic status, caused in part by prison officials' predatory profiteering, imperiled their social standing and self-regard.

Cecilia's references to her and Clara's jobs as work "in the street" invoked a widely shared Latin American phrase referring to female employment outside the home, especially in settings where women mixed with men. Until the mid-twentieth century, such work posed risks for women's reputations and thus jeopardized both their honor and that of their putative male protectors (hence Vicente's tears).[100] As historian Susie Porter notes in her study of female office work and middle-class identity in Mexico, such references to "street work" (*trabajo callejero*) implied a parallel to prostitution due to the supposed risks to women's chastity.[101] Nevertheless, women working in such jobs were expected to meet the standards of female dress and education associated with the *gente decente*, and they claimed middle-class status for themselves, illustrating the contradictory, ambiguous, and contested intersection of gender and middle-class identity. Women striving to rise into the middle class might see office work as an opportunity, but for women in more well-to-do families like the Pimentels, accepting these jobs out of necessity could signal an emotionally fraught loss of status and identity.

But perhaps the greatest threat to Cecilia's honor came when she found herself in a compromising situation with General Paulino Camero, the governor of the Castillo in Puerto Cabello, where her brothers Luis and Tancredo were imprisoned in 1930. As contemporary observers remarked, the visits of female relatives who brought food payments and other necessities to prison administrators for the sake of their confined relatives rendered them vulnerable to rumors of sexual impropriety.[102] Presumably this was the concern that led the Pimentels to send one of their dependents—a trusted, long-time domestic worker named Ruperta—to deliver their weekly payments to officials at La Rotunda when their men were imprisoned in Caracas.[103] But when Luis and Tancredo were jailed in Puerto Cabello, Cecilia decided to journey there with three other women who also had male relatives confined in the Castillo so that they could deliver food and other items at Christmas time.

Upon arriving in Puerto Cabello, Cecilia and Josefina Juliac went in search of Camero, the allegedly corrupt prison governor who, aside from the usual profiteering from food rations, occasionally used prison labor to work his landed estate.[104] They eventually found him traveling about the city in his car. "We shouted to him," Cecilia later recalled, "and he invited us to get into his car to return to his house. We had no choice but to go with him, Josefina in front and I at his side, and when along the route we passed some policemen[105] who, upon seeing us, cleared their throats [i.e., suggestively], he smiled with joy. Conquests of Camero! Anything for our prisoners, even appearing to be conquests of Paulino Camero."[106] At his house, Camero accepted the articles brought by Cecilia and Josefina and agreed to pass news of their families to the prisoners. The visit ended without further incident. The episode illustrated how the predatory corruption of the prison system threatened the sexual as well as economic dimensions of female honor as women sought to maintain their reputations as *gente decente* while aiding their male kin.[107]

"We are Not a People of Feminine Men": Anticorruption in 1928 and Beyond

The student-led protests against the Gómez regime that erupted in Caracas in early 1928 hold a privileged place in many histories of twentieth-century Venezuela, not only because of their immediate impact but also because of the later prominence of some individuals within the "generation of '28." Many of the young men and women who participated in the 1928 anti-Gómez movement—including Rómulo Betancourt, Raúl Leoni, Jóvito Villalba, Antonia Palacios, Cecilia Nuñez Sucre, Miguel Otero Silva, and Joaquín Gabaldón Márquez—went on to play prominent roles in the public life of the country over the next half century. They were widely credited with initiating a new phase of Venezuelan politics in which caudillismo gave way to the modern era of mass politics, multi-class political parties, and political ideas (including social democracy and Marxism) that had been banned under Gómez. But historians have overlooked or minimized anticorruption's significance in the movement. From 1928 to Gómez's death in 1935, the anticorruption discourse of young activists incorporated elements already developed by others, such as a concern with masculine dignity and a rejection of Gómez's claim to be the ideal hombre de trabajo, but in the early 1930s activists also explored the usefulness of anticorruption sentiment for a new era of mass mobilization.

The protests began during a week of social and cultural celebrations in early February 1928, organized through the Venezuelan Student Federation at the Central University. Speeches by Villalba and Betancourt included criticisms of Gómez, as did poetry composed for the occasion. The regime responded by jailing the perpetrators.[108] To the surprise of many, large protests broke out in Caracas and other cities, including Valencia, Maracaibo, and La Guaira, in support of the detained youths. Over 200 students, acting in solidarity, presented themselves at the regime's jails and were incarcerated; dozens of other protesters were jailed as demonstrations spread beyond the student population. Significantly, many of those protesting in support of the students came from the middle class. Telegrams to Gómez emphasized the leading roles of white-collar employees (*empleados*) from banks and commercial companies, as well as middle- and upper-class women (*damas, señoras,* and *señoritas*).[109]

Opposition to corruption as well as a desire for civil liberties motivated the protestors. The US legation commented in early March on "the surprising promptness and spontaneous sympathy with which the business elements made common cause with the students." By way of explanation, the legation pointed to Gomecistas' practice of establishing "virtual monopolies of the principal resources of the country" and muscling their way into every "lucrative" sector of economic activity. "This has caused heavy losses to private business enterprises," the report concluded, "and the latter were evidently glad to seize an opportunity of challenging the despotism of the Government."[110] Similarly, British diplomats explained the protests as a reaction against "the oppressiveness of the Gómez regime and the acquisitiveness of the President and his family."[111] Gómez relented and released the prisoners.

Once free, Betancourt and other students established contact with dissident members of the military led by young, professionalized officers. These officers resented the continued predominance of Gomecista officers with no formal military training, and they felt demeaned when they were assigned to oversee troops ordered to work on farms and ranches belonging to top Gomecistas.[112] Dissident military units in Caracas and their civilian allies rose in revolt on April 7, 1928, but were defeated in counterattacks led by General Eleazar López Contreras. The captured officers and students were imprisoned and some suffered torture. Betancourt evaded arrest and fled into exile.

Gómez sentenced many of the arrested students to work on the highways in the southern plains under horrible conditions. In a public statement infused with patriarchal presumption and the regime's ideology of work, Gómez declared that he had decided to treat the detained youths "as a severe father would" and that "since they do not wish to study" he had sent them to the road crews where they would "learn to work."[113] The regime touted the highway network as a signal achievement to advance the economy, but men forced to labor on the roads claimed that the routes were designed to benefit estates belonging to prominent officials.[114] In their view, Gomecistas' celebration of the highways was merely another instance of the regime manipulating the rhetoric of work and progress to obscure corruption. Meanwhile, young women detained by the authorities for dissident activities during 1928 were confined in an asylum for the mentally ill outside Caracas in Catia, a move that Miguel Febres Cordero, a former treasury official from a prominent Mérida family, cruelly described in a private letter as "full of amusing irony."[115]

In the weeks following the failed rebellion of April 7, anonymous flyers appeared in Caracas and other major cities calling for continued resistance. These broadsheets highlight the significance of anticorruption sentiment in fueling unrest. The flyers accused Gómez of using public funds to finance his business enterprises and converting "the nation into the personal feudal domain of the Gómez family," culminating with a call to "every honorable citizen . . . every patriot" to bring down the government.[116] One especially detailed broadsheet reviewed the markets in Caracas that Gomecistas had monopolized for "twenty years." It criticized the beef monopoly as "extortion against free commerce and free industry, solely to benefit personal interests," while also alleging that José Vicente Gómez, the dictator's son, gained 600 bolívares a day by controlling the Caracas food market; similarly, it criticized the contracting of the liquor tax in the capital to a member of Gómez's clan.[117] Another flyer warned working-class men that they could be pressed into military service and put to work on Gomecistas' estates, laboring as "slaves" on lands usurped from the people.[118] A similar leaflet reminded army officers and soldiers that they had been "reduced to the absurd and sad condition of peons and slaves" laboring on the estates of Gomecista officials.[119] A notice calling for a protest on April 19, 1928, the anniversary of beginning of Venezuela's independence movement, declared that "the day has arrived for us to prove to the world that we are not a people of feminine men (*que no somos un pueblo de afeminados*), but rather the contrary."[120]

Together, the flyers appealed to numerous segments of the population—consumers, business owners, workers, military personnel, and anyone humiliated by the regime's predatory practices. The authors of these manifestos not only referenced the material impact of corruption; by invoking the humiliation and indignation associated with submission to corruption, and the recovery of honor inherent in resistance, they also tapped into the emotional economy of anticorruption that had developed over the past two decades. If the broadly based reaction against the regime in 1928 signaled the birth of modern democratic politics in Venezuela, as is often claimed,[121] then anticorruption sentiment was part of the new politics from the beginning.

The years after 1928 became a period of ideological experimentation and maturation for the former students. They struggled to integrate anticorruption into a vision of Venezuela's future in ways that transcended the rhetoric of their elders. In 1928, for example, Gabaldón Márquez synthesized anti-Gomecistas' critique of the regime's rhetoric of work by deconstructing the "inverted dictionary" that Gomecista propagandists used to praise the dictator's work ethic and obfuscate the issue of corruption.[122] But Gabaldón Márquez offered no strategy for combating corruption other than replacing Gomez with "honorable and conscientious men."[123] The following year, Betancourt and Otero Silva declared the hope that Gómez's "domestic policy of embezzlement [*peculado*] and monopoly might be replaced with one of honesty and free competition,"[124] but such formulas, as the regime entered its third decade, sounded no different than those of Gómez's ageing caudillo opponents. In the early 1930s, however, some of the young exiles shifted away from denunciations of corruption based on honor and morality and initiated an analysis of anticorruption's potential for building a multi-class coalition capable of overturning the structures that undergirded Gomecismo.

Betancourt exemplified the exiles' intellectual evolution as he articulated the need for a multi-class party to lead a revolutionary transformation of Venezuela. He was the primary author of the Plan of Barranquilla, signed in Colombia on March 22, 1931, by a group of twelve exiles. It analyzed Gomecismo as an alliance between the Venezuelan traditions of personalist politics and latifundia (large landholdings) and the international forces of corporate capitalism based in the United States and Europe.[125] The linchpin of this alliance was the tacit agreement that the domestic economy fell under the "personal monopoly"[126] of Gómez and his allies while foreign companies such as Standard Oil and Royal Dutch Shell controlled the nation's natural resources. In keeping with their structuralist critique of Gomecismo, the signatories of the Plan reiterated their distance from well-worn anti-Gomecista formulas. They dismissed the slogan "Put honorable men in power and Venezuela will be saved"[127] as naive.

The mechanism for transcending outdated opposition strategies, Betancourt insisted, would be a broadly based political party, distinct from the coalitions of caudillos and economic elites of the past. By the early 1930s, he and his collaborators were calling for labor rights and land reform (including the distribution of land from Gómez's estates) to attract urban and rural workers. Meanwhile, in his private correspondence Betancourt expressed his conviction that Gomecistas' predatory corruption created opportunities to recruit the middle class. Writing to a colleague in August 1931, Betancourt argued that "the middle classes, meaning the small merchants and small manufacturers ruined by monopolies,"[128] would join the revolutionary project. Distinguishing himself from more orthodox leftists, he insisted that the middle class was, for political purposes, part of "the great mass of the Venezuelan population" that had been marginalized by the political economy of Gomecismo. "The larger part of our middle class," he insisted, "has knocked on the doors of pauperism, of proletarianization."[129]

In a pamphlet published the following year, Betancourt addressed the issue of whether the regime's "private monopolies" had inflicted enough damage on the upper echelons of the national bourgeoisie for them to break with the regime. He concluded that Venezuela's wealthiest elites, on the whole, would continue to support Gomecismo because, despite the regime's encroachment on their economic interests, it provided elites "impunity in the peaceful enjoyment of the benefits produced by their salaried slaves."[130] Examining the middle sectors of society, Betancourt confirmed his belief that "the small merchant . . . the small property owner . . . the school teacher and other proletarianized intellectuals . . . together with the subordinate public employee" constituted a "class" that suffered exploitation along with rural and urban workers.[131] This call for a multi-class party to transform Venezuela was innovative and historically consequential, to be sure, but Betancourt's class-based analysis should not obscure his continuity with earlier Venezuelan thought. The young activist's belief that monopolies designed to enrich public officials contributed to the impoverishment of Venezuela's middle class echoed grievances dating back to the Nationalists and disaffected Liberals of the previous century.

Anticorruption discourse, then, showed signs of both continuity and evolution over the course of the dictatorship. From the early years of the regime, many middle-class Venezuelans found that Gomecista predation posed a threat that was both economic and emotional. Attached to a sense of self that emphasized their autonomous pursuit of profit in the marketplace and their families' right to the fruits of their work, middle-class men and women objected that officials' profiteering threatened the honorable identities they held dear. The material exchanges vividly recalled in anti-Gomecista memoirs—such as Arévalo Cedeño's ruinous sale of animals to the managers of Gómez's cattle monopoly, Garbi Sánchez's purchase of arepas with the miserly wages earned by fashioning Seville combs for the profit of his captors, and the Pimentels' handing-over to prison officials of money painfully earned and saved—shaped the emotional experience of living under a dictatorship that undermined its victims' claims to bourgeois respectability. Predatory profiteering made the dishonoring of middle-class individuals and families an intrinsic, rather than an incidental, aspect of Gomecista state formation.

The emotional economy of anticorruption that equated humiliation, emasculation, and dishonor with life under Gómez, and that framed resistance to the dictatorship as a defense of male honor, was clearly a masculinist trope that glossed over corruption's multifaceted impact on women, including the female kin of political prisoners. The oppositionist discourse of bourgeois men, with its persistent focus on male honor, reflected the patriarchal character of Venezuelan society no less than the patrimonial assumptions of the dictator and his allies did. The regime's assertion that Gómez deserved power over the nation because he personified the ideal of the hardworking man, like the opposition response that the regime was illegitimate because it undercut the honor of male heads of households, posited national politics as a contest over masculine honor. As Cecilia Pimentel's memoir illustrates, however, Gomecismo's impact on women was no less tangible, even if their stories were sometimes framed by notions of female respectability that echoed society's patriarchal foundations.

The decades-long discussion of honor by middle-class Venezuelans who suffered predatory corruption illustrates the cultural and emotional dimensions of their experiences. As this chapter has argued, these experiences were firmly rooted in a particular time and place. Indeed, it may be that the young exiles led by Betancourt were able to step back from their compatriots' association of corruption, economic loss, and dishonor, and to focus instead on the strategic opportunities created by middle-class opposition to Gomecista profiteering, precisely because they were removed from the degradation of daily life in Venezuela. But, as we will see in subsequent chapters, the relationships among corruption, humiliation, gender, and the middle class could at times be more ambiguous and multifaceted than either the young exiles or the victims of Gomecista predation claimed.

CHAPTER 5

OIL MONEY

PETROLEUM CONCESSIONS, CHAPTER VII PAYMENTS, AND AMBIGUOUS CORRUPTION

Unlike cattle, liquor, and political prisons, petroleum did not play a central role in Gomecista state formation from the early years of the dictatorship. Only after World War I did oil become the new foundation of the national economy. The wealth generated by petroleum circulated in two ways that some Venezuelans, during and after the dictatorship, considered corrupt. First, the government granted concessions to explore and exploit oil fields to its favorites, who then sold their rights to foreign companies. Second, as the oil economy produced rising tax revenues, Gómez oversaw the distribution of millions of bolívares to regime insiders and to ordinary Venezuelans through the discretionary fund designated as Chapter VII of the budget of the Ministry of Interior Relations.

By dispensing petroleum concessions and Chapter VII payments to an increasingly wide circle of recipients, Gómez acted as a generous patron to an expanding clientele. Of course, to some Venezuelans—including those already alienated by Gomecista profiteering in other areas of the economy—Gómez's selective generosity smacked of corruption. But because a portion of the middle class and elite benefited from Chapter VII and petroleum concessions, the distribution of oil money ameliorated some anti-Gomecista sentiment. Significantly, Gómez's two modes of spreading the nation's oil wealth did not involve the appropriation of resources directly from the Venezuelan population, in contrast to the predatory forms of corruption analyzed in previous chapters. The divided and ambivalent reactions to Gómez's distribution of the nation's newfound bounty places both petroleum concessions and Chapter VII payments in the category of ambiguous corruption.

The arguments advanced in this chapter diverge from two prominent assertions about petroleum and corruption that permeate scholarly writing on Venezuela. First, scholars often portray oil wealth as the root cause of Venezuela's rent-seeking political culture in which citizens view connections to the state as the surest path to economic security and affluence.[1] The transformations associated with the petroleum economy, in this view, are the fundamental cause of widespread corruption from the Gómez era onward. This position either slights or ignores the profiteering that was already central to state formation before the petroleum wealth began to flow. As we have seen, patrimonial practices characterized the Gómez regime from the start. The cattle and liquor monopolies provided much of the glue that held the centralizing state together even before the post–World War I oil boom. Corrupt practices facilitated by petroleum, while departing from the predatory character of other Gomecista rackets, obeyed the clientelist logic already entrenched in Gomez's coalition and much of society. Oil certainly accentuated rent-seeking proclivities, but it did not create them.

Second, scholars who have discussed petroleum-related corruption in the Gomez era have focused overwhelmingly on the oil concessions granted to the dictator's relatives, friends, and political allies, who often made fortunes as they sold these rights to foreign companies. But these concessions are only part of the story. The Chapter VII payments discussed in the last third of this chapter, funded largely by the petroleum bonanza, need to be understood as "oil money" along with the profits from concessions. The beneficiaries of Chapter VII became much more numerous than the recipients of oil rights and included Venezuelans throughout the nation—male and female, military and civilian, urban and rural, the famous and the obscure. If oil did extend a rent-seeking culture beyond the ranks of statemakers into the bulk of Venezuelan society, encouraging average citizens to expect their share of petroleum's bounty from a paternalistic state, then Chapter VII played a leading role in that process. Gómez and his supporters used payments from Chapter VII, even more than the granting of oil concessions, to fortify his image as a stern yet benevolent patriarch who extended his protection and favor to worthy members of the Venezuelan family. This justification of Chapter VII lent legitimacy to rulers' personal discretion over state resources, at least in the eyes of some.

The Early History of Petroleum and Foreign Investment under Gómez

The development of Venezuela's petroleum industry progressed gradually during the first decade or so of the Gómez regime.[2] Castro's government had granted some rights for oil exploration to private citizens who lacked the capacity to make use of them, and these concessions as well as others granted under Gómez were duly acquired by foreign companies. The first commercially successful oil well did not enter production until 1914, and then only to supply the small domestic market. Venezuelan petroleum exports began in 1917 and reached significant levels in the early 1920s. The Royal Dutch Shell corporation controlled virtually all Venezuelan oil exports during this early period,[3] but Standard Oil and Gulf Oil (as well as smaller, often transient companies) bought concessions after World War I and increased their share of exports beginning in the mid-1920s.

As these companies entered Venezuela and established operations, they interacted with a range of Venezuelan officials, including some who owned or controlled concessions despite a legal prohibition against high-ranking officials receiving petroleum concessions.[4] Violations of this prohibition, as well as the overt favoritism in granting concessions, created an occasional air of impropriety around the concession system. Moreover, bribery of Venezuelan officials by foreign corporations seeking access to oil became a common feature of the industry. This corruption, however, was not necessarily more prevalent in the oil sector than in other areas of foreign investment. A brief discussion of corruption and foreign investment in Venezuela will provide a broader context for analysis of profiteering related to oil.

Foreign companies that invested in Venezuela under Gómez routinely faced demands from regime officials for payoffs in a variety of forms. The British legation in Caracas reported in 1914 that virtually every government official involved in any project demanded a "consideration" from British investors. Rumor had it that Dr. Ezequiel Vivas, Gómez's secretary, used his control over access to Gómez to extort investors. Vivas allegedly "refused to allow two British capitalists to see the President unless they first bought from him gold-mining claims of doubtful value. They refused and were not admitted."[5] Investors who pressed ahead with negotiations were often asked to hand over stock in their enterprises to the officials who approved their projects.[6] In other cases Venezuelan officials reportedly extorted cash rather than stock; for example, Gómez demanded that the British firm J. G. White and Company pay him 200,000 pounds for the right to invest 800,000 pounds in the construction of a water system for Caracas.[7] "In general," according to the legation, "the enormous 'commissions' demanded by General Gómez, and in a lesser degree by the Ministers concerned, the Secretary General [of the President], and the President's relatives are enough to make any company hesitate before signing a contract."[8]

Nevertheless, over the course of the dictatorship many companies decided to make the necessary payoffs in cash or stock. The Venezuelan Telephone Company, having run their enterprise for forty years, found that a renewal of the concession would require payment of "a consideration" to a Venezuelan intermediary. The government would not grant the new concession to the company, but rather to "someone in the President's entourage" who would then sell it to the company. After some grumbling to the British legation, the company decided to make the payment. The company's chief concerns were "to fix the price [of the payment] as low as possible, [and] to guard against a competitor obtaining the concession instead of them."[9] In this matter-of-fact approach, foreign companies regarded such payments as illicit, but saw them as a necessary cost of operating in Venezuela and merely tried to minimize the amount. The oil companies often found themselves in similar situations and in general adopted a similar attitude. Meanwhile, the Venezuelan officials who extracted such payments followed the etiquette of corruption described in previous chapters, which held that the benefits from corrupt operations should be shared. The granting of concessions to regime favorites, rather than directly to the companies that operated them, provided one means of spreading such benefits. The variety of cabinet ministers and other officials with opportunities to demand payments widened the circle of beneficiaries still further.[10]

Petroleum Concessions during the Gómez Regime

Venezuelan law, reflecting legal principals from the colonial era, established the national state as the arbiter of subsoil mineral rights. In general, even petroleum under privately owned lands fell under state control. Exploration for hydrocarbon deposits and the exploitation of oil fields thus required a concession. Concessions were, essentially, contracts with the state specifying the terms under which the recipient could carry out exploration and production within a particular geographical area. The concession trade—in which individuals or companies received concessions from the state and then sold them—became crucial to the development of Venezuela's oil industry and to the profits that state officials and their clients extracted from it. According to historian Brian McBeth, the Gómez regime granted 4,875 oil concessions to individuals and 1,354 to Venezuelan and foreign companies, including both concession-trading companies and foreign production companies.[11] A concession could change hands several times before being acquired by a production company that would develop the fields. Although only three companies—Shell, Standard, and Gulf—produced almost all Venezuelan oil under Gómez, their dominance rested on their acquisition of thousands of concessions, most of which the state had originally granted to individuals, many of them regime insiders or their front men. The concession trade involved payments of hundreds of millions of bolívares to private individuals and companies for rights to natural resources that in theory formed part of the national patrimony.[12]

Of course, the national state extracted some revenue from the oil industry in the form of taxes. The legislation governing petroleum changed several times under Gómez through 1922, but, as historian Edwin Lieuwen observes, it maintained certain broad features established just before Gómez seized power: "A limited exploration period, a surface tax, an exploitation tax, exemption from import duties, disputes subject only to domestic courts—all these became permanent features of Venezuelan petroleum law."[13] The gradual development of the oil industry during the first half of the Gómez regime produced relatively little tax revenue. As of 1921, the oil sector accounted for only 3 percent of annual federal income.[14] But soon thereafter, oil production rose strongly due to Venezuela's 1922 oil legislation, which favored the foreign companies (it was written with their advice), and revenues from oil dramatically increased. The boom in production was also fueled by competition among US and European companies and their governments, eager to control the petroleum supplies that were now crucial to economic and military power.[15] Oil surpassed coffee as Venezuela's leading export in 1925 and accounted directly for 14.2 percent of government revenues; by 1928 taxes on oil provided 22.5 percent of all federal revenue.[16] Climbing oil exports also financed the expansion of imports and thus boosted customs receipts, increasing oil's importance to the national treasury.

Despite these national financial benefits, several prominent members of the Gómez regime pointed out that the concessions needlessly permitted private individuals and companies to reap substantial profits from selling concessions. Vicente Lecuna, an advisor to Gómez who headed the Caracas Chamber of Commerce and the Banco de Venezuela, believed the government should sell concessions directly to oil companies so that the proceeds went to the national treasury rather than concession dealers.[17] Gumersindo Torres, who tried to increase Venezuela's share of the oil wealth during his two stints as development minister, also attempted to persuade Gómez not to use concessions to reward his favorites. In his memoirs, Torres went much further in criticizing the rampant profiteering from concessions.[18] General Eleazar López Contreras also disapproved of the concessions trade but may not have shared his misgivings with Gómez, and certainly refrained from publicly denouncing concessions during Gómez's lifetime.[19] By contrast, denunciations of corrupt exchanges among Gómez, concessionaires, and the oil companies became a staple of opposition discourse, especially following the 1928 protests.[20]

The dictator's extended family and close associates controlled a significant portion of the concession trade. Members of the presidential clan who received concessions from the government, either in their own names or through front men, and who often bought and sold concessions, included Gómez's brother, Juan Crisóstomo Gómez, governor of the Federal District of Caracas and First Vice-President of the republic; Gómez's son, José Vicente Gómez, inspector general of the army and Second Vice-President of the republic; and two of Gómez's sons-in-law, Julio Méndez and Carlos Delfino. José Vicente and Delfino both served on a committee in the Chamber of Deputies that dealt with concessions and thus had privileged information regarding the oil industry, in addition to the influence they derived from their family connections.[21] Relatives of the dictator sometimes received and traded concessions using the names of friends, business associates, or private secretaries, either because of the legal provision against high-ranking government officials receiving concessions or to avoid publicizing the extent of their clan's enrichment through the traffic in national resources. McBeth concludes that José Vicente Gómez may have outpaced all his relatives in seeking oil concessions for his friends and associates. In 1921–22 he requested that the Ministry of Development award 115 concessions to twenty individuals, and the contracts were duly issued; it is not clear how many of the twenty recipients truly held the concessions themselves and how many were strawmen, but the anticorruption investigation in 1945–46 found that José Vicente often used front men (*testaferros*) to obtain concessions.[22] Méndez, who acquired a fortune through the concession trade, received some concessions in his own name but also used front men even though his minor diplomatic appointments did not legally bar him from holding petroleum contracts.[23]

Pedro Tinoco, a lawyer who served as an intermediary between the Gómez family and Standard Oil, eventually married into the clan and reportedly controlled the granting of many concessions during the regime's final years. Tinoco was a legal adviser and business manager for José Vicente Gómez and also worked as a legal counsel for Standard Oil.[24] Following José Vicente's exile and death, Tinoco married his widow, Josefina Revenga de Gómez. He became minister of interior relations in 1931 but was understood to exercise much broader influence, especially over financial matters and petroleum concessions.[25] By the time of Gómez's death, Tinoco was said to have parlayed his control over concessions into "a large fortune."[26] According to the British legation, allegations swirled around Tinoco's relation with Standard during the anti-Gomecista reaction of early 1936: "The company, in order to obtain their last concessions, are alleged to have paid Dr. Tinoco, the late Minister of the Interior, a bribe of 20 million bolivares."[27]

Outside Gómez's family, other regime insiders also reaped substantial profits from concessions. Dr. Victorino Márquez Bustillos, who served as provisional president of the republic from 1915 to 1922, received permission from Gómez to intervene in issues relating to oil concessions and used this authority for his own financial benefit, according to Gumersindo Torres, the minister of development responsible for processing concession requests from 1917 to 1922. Torres wrote in his memoirs that recipients of concessions informed him that, in order for their concessions to be approved by Márquez Bustillos, they had to agree to pay him 25 percent of whatever amount they later received from their sales to foreign companies.[28] Torres also indicated that Márquez Bustillos offered him a share of these proceeds, but he declined. The US legation in Caracas reported in 1921 that Márquez Bustillos and his general secretary were "the actual owners" of extensive oil concessions (implying that they acquired the grants through front men), even though they were barred from receiving concessions under existing law.[29] As discussed below, some observers believed that Márquez Bustillos managed the revision of petroleum legislation in the early 1920s to facilitate the sale of his concessions to foreign companies, which would lift national production but also benefit him personally.

Perhaps the regime insider outside Gómez's family who profited most handsomely from the concession trade was Dr. Adolfo Bueno. A physician, Bueno treated Gómez for a prostate infection that threatened his life in 1921. In gratitude, Gómez arranged for Bueno to receive petroleum concessions and named him private secretary when he resumed the presidency the following year. The contracts awarded to Bueno turned out to hold extraordinarily rich deposits of petroleum. Torres noted that the tracts proved so lucrative that "some elements near to General Gómez . . . thought of trying to find a way to take the concession from Bueno."[30] Bueno maintained control of the concessions but, in keeping with Gomecista etiquette, he shared the wealth. McBeth recounts the financial history of Bueno's concessions and how the profits were divided with one man who lent his name to the concessions and two other associates who presumably helped find buyers for the contracts: "On 14 June 1922 he [Bueno] requested Gómez to grant Gustavo Escobar Llamozas three oil concessions, which were later transferred to the British Equatorial Oil Co.

for a 5 per cent production royalty to be divided as follows: Adolfo Bueno, 65 per cent; Gustavo Escobar Llamozas, 20 per cent; Tomás Duarte P., 10 per cent; and Carlos Heny, 5 per cent. Bueno received Bs. 2 million in royalty payments before the Falcón Petroleum Corp. (an American company) on 20 July 1928 procured the 5 per cent production royalty for Bs. 14,040,000 of which Bueno's share was Bs. 9,126,000."[31] Aside from making Bueno wealthy, these concessions provided several million bolívares to those who assisted with the deal.

The profits generated by Bueno's concessions were unusually high, but the distribution of profits to multiple recipients was a common feature of the system. Many concessions benefited not only the formal recipients, who often sold their contracts within days to prearranged buyers, but also a combination of front men, well connected fixers who helped grease the wheels of the concession-granting bureaucracy, and intermediaries (both Venezuelan and foreign) who specialized in connecting concession holders with oil companies interested in acquiring their rights. Even members of the regime's inner circle used such assistance.[32] One apparent intermediary was Dr. Isaac Capriles, a physician identified by the British legation as the son-in-law of General Joaquín Crespo (national president in 1884–86 and 1892–98).[33] Capriles had directed the postal service, housed in the Ministry of Development (which also oversaw petroleum concessions), and in 1928 he became the private secretary of Gonzalo Gómez, one of the dictator's sons who eschewed politics in favor of business.[34] Capriles received ninety-four concessions from the Ministry of Development, covering just over one million hectares in the state of Zamora (present-day Barinas), as announced in a special issue of the *Gaceta Oficial* on March 3, 1928. The US legation reported that two small oil companies, "both belonging to the Sinclair interests," had already arranged to purchase the concessions.[35] Since there was no reason for the regime to favor Capriles alone with such largesse, he may have acted as a representative of other individuals whose names did not appear in the official record.

How much was the concession trade ultimately worth? No precise answer is possible, because many owners sold their grants for a combination of cash, stock in the company that purchased the concession, and/or a royalty payment (usually between 2.5 percent and 5 percent) to be paid on the value of the oil produced under the grant. The Ministry of Development published a summary of all concession sales

TABLE 5.1. Value of petroleum concessions sold (in bolívares), 1920–35.

Year	Payments in cash	Payments in stock	Total payments
1920	8,625,334	847,189	9,472,523
1921	5,023,498	4,859,856	9,883,354
1922	885,961	1,488,000	2,373,961
1923	3,965,141	1,757,659	5,722,800
1924	15,035,900	2,086,100	17,122,000
1925	10,660,638	5,936,148	16,596,786
1926	13,825,802	4,813,575	18,639,377
1927	15,828,601	3,169,250	18,997,851
1928	29,090,170	0	29,090,170
1929	13,012,965	949,400	13,962,365
1930	16,773,936	1,260,000	18,033,936
1931	3,629,123	1,770,000	5,399,123
1932	867,848	10,000	877,848
1933	4,676,075	10,000	4,686,075
1934	1,772,311	1,149,225	2,921,536
1935	20,611,581	0	20,611,581
Totals	164,284,884	30,106,402	194,391,286

Source: Gonzalo Trujillo, "Resumen de los documentos de traspaso de concesiones de hidrocarburos, del año 1920 al 1938 inclusive," *Revista del Ministerio de Fomento* 2, no. 8, (January 1939): 274.

from 1920 to 1938 listing the price of each in terms of the cash and value of stock received by the seller, as well as the percentage royalty, but not the amount eventually paid in royalties to the seller.[36] While some concessions never yielded any oil and thus no royalties, others yielded a fortune in such payments. Table 5.1, above, shows the value of concessions sold each year from 1920 through 1935. During these sixteen years of the Gómez era, the value of the concession trade averaged 12.15 million bolívares annually, not including royalty payments to the sellers.

The concession trade, then, contributed to the consolidation of Gomecista patronage networks in a manner similar to the cattle monopoly and the farming-out of the liquor tax. It reinforced Gómez's position as the distributor of opportunities for enrichment, with some opportunities paying larger returns than others, depending in part on the entrepreneurial ability (and the luck) of the recipient. And, in the petroleum sector as in cattle and liquor, a successful operation required cooperation and the sharing of profits, encouraging cohesion among regime members and sympathizers. To be sure, competition and envy, such as the resentment over the wealth of Bueno's concessions, could occasionally undermine this integrative tendency, but individuals disappointed by any single event could always hope to be favored in the next round of grants. There was plenty of money to go around, most of it supplied by foreign investors.

The social profiles of the concession beneficiaries, however, point to an important contrast with the Gomecistas who dominated the cattle and liquor monopolies. The most numerous participants in the concession trade came from the urban professional classes. They were often well educated and usually lacked military experience, in clear contrast to the strongmen of the regime who figured so prominently in the cattle and liquor monopolies. As we have seen, this latter category of Gomecistas played a pivotal role in the formation of the state because they exercised its coercive power. Certainly, they were not excluded entirely from the concession trade. Generals Vincencio Pérez Soto, Félix Galavís, José María García, and David Gimón—all of whom served as state presidents—participated in the concession trade[37]; and José Vicente Gómez served as vice president of the nation and inspector general of the army. In contrast, military officers who never held political posts rarely participated in the concession trade. Colonel José Murillo, who served as a military aide to Gómez and as the army's inspector general of arms and services, received twenty-eight petroleum concessions, but he was an exception.[38] The strongmen who claimed shares of the oil wealth were far outnumbered by the civilian professionals who received grants or served as intermediaries, front men, and legal advisors in the market for oil rights. They represented the professional, more formally educated wing of the Gomecista alliance rooted in commerce, law, and upper echelons of the bureaucracy.

This class had been reluctant to embrace the Gomecistas when they seized power in 1908, but state control of the oil wealth contributed to their eventual integration into the regime. As late as 1913–14, the British minister observed that the Gómez clan and most top Gomecistas, despite their political clout and growing fortunes, remained "a class apart" from the upper echelons of Caracas society. Established families did not mix socially with Gomecistas and privately told jokes that cast them as "peons" from the Andes.[39] Gómez's survival of the 1913–14 succession crisis encouraged pragmatic members of the elite to relax their social prejudices, but the postwar acceleration of the concession trade provided the most powerful incentive for the affluent urban classes to lay aside their reservations and incorporate themselves into Gomecista networks. Eloy Pérez, who worked as a lawyer for José Vicente Gómez, painted a vivid picture of the elite's integration into the concession trade during the provisional presidency of Márquez Bustillos (1915–22), himself a lawyer. Pérez later recalled that a petroleum concession

> was offered to me by Dr. Márquez Bustillo's secretary, Dr. Elías Rodríguez, who was a good friend of mine, as was President Márquez Bustillos. I remember very well that Dr. Rodríguez—who, I repeat was an intimate friend—while in the rooms of the Club Venezuela offered to obtain for me a parcel [i.e., a concession] for the production of petroleum, since all my friends already had parcels, but not me. . . . I remember that the parcel was granted to me around the same time Gustavo Escobar acquired one, though I can't remember if he acquired it in his own name or in the name of Dr. Adolfo Bueno, but in the Club Venezuela we commented on the possibilities for the parcels that had been granted us.[40]

Thus an elite social venue where denigrating comments about Andean "peons" may well have been uttered into the early 1910s became a place where affluent men breezily discussed the profits they hoped to reap through their ties to the regime. Clearly by this time—probably the early 1920s—many of the well-to-do had overcome their aversion to mixing with the Gomecistas, thanks to the lure of petroleum.

Private Interests in the Making of the 1922 Oil Law

The oil boom that began in the mid-1920s resulted, in part, from the rewriting of Venezuela's petroleum legislation. As Daniel Yergin notes in his history of the global oil industry, the future of petroleum production in Venezuela remained uncertain at the beginning of the decade, despite Shell's initial success there.[41] Many of the promising oil fields lay in areas of the Lake Maracaibo basin that lacked roads and were infested with insects and disease, casting doubt on the feasibility and profitability of production. Moreover, the shallow entrance at the mouth of the lake required the use of small tankers that rode no more than eleven feet deep in the water.[42] Venezuela's rise as a major oil producer was by no means foreordained, even though the decline of Mexican oilfields and growing international demand created incentives to invest there. US companies and their agents purchased concessions to avoid being shut out by competitors, but they limited investments in production due to concerns that Venezuela's petroleum legislation was not favorable enough to outweigh the environmental obstacles. In the end, the 1922 oil law resolved companies' concerns and unleashed the boom. Yet this milestone legislation came into being through a process shaped by the private interests of Gomecista concession holders and—if allegations by British diplomats were true—due to the bribing of Venezuelan legislators by a representative of US companies.

Venezuela first created legislation tailored specifically to the oil industry (rather than mining in general) in 1918, but its failure to satisfy the companies led to a battle over revising the law. Development minister Gumersindo Torres pushed for legislation that would allow the national treasury to reap a larger share of the oil wealth, but the companies and concession holders pushed for provisions that incentivized production. Torres believed that as the economies of the US and Europe began a postwar expansion, their need for ever more petroleum would provide Venezuela with leverage to impose higher taxes and greater control over the industry. Under his influence, legislation passed in June 1920 that increased taxes, restricted the area of concessions to 10,000 hectares (down from 15,000), and introduced provisions to pressure the companies to accelerate production, despite the companies' claims of logistical obstacles.[43] The 1920 law also maintained the broad outlines of the 1918 system of national reserves, lands presumably containing oil but which the companies would have to turn back to the nation once the exploration period in their concessions expired. After the two-year exploration period, companies would retain only half the area of their concessions; this retained area would be divided into production blocks of 200 hectares that would be arranged to alternate with blocks of national reserve lands to be returned to the state.[44] This provision seemed to guarantee that if a company developed a concession into a productive oilfield, the half that reverted to the nation would increase in value due to its presumptive oil deposits and the roads and other infrastructure built during exploration. The legislation allowed the government to auction rights to exploit national reserve fields to the highest bidders.[45]

US companies, however, objected to the 1920 law and hesitated to buy new concessions. Torres had overplayed Venezuela's leverage. The US minister in Caracas, Preston McGoodwin, organized a series of meetings among "the attorneys for and representatives of all the American companies" to draw up a list of recommended changes to the legislation.[46] McGoodwin then met with Gómez at the dictator's retreat in San Juan de los Morros over a period of six days to discuss "the necessary changes" to Venezuelan law, as McGoodwin reported to Washington. Gómez was receptive to the US minister's suggestions and said he would have his brother, Juan Crisótomo Gómez (who, McGoodwin must have known, was deeply involved in the concessions trade) speak to legislators about modifying the law. McGoodwin received assurances from congressional leaders and provisional president Victorino Márquez Bustillos that the oil legislation would be changed along the lines that he and the companies desired.

According to McGoodwin, however, President Márquez Bustillos and others had a personal financial stake in the outcome of these revisions to the petroleum law. "It is well known," he wrote, "that Doctor Márquez Bustillos himself, his Secretary General Doctor Elías Rodríguez and various members of his family are the actual owners of vast areas of prospective petroleum territory [i.e., concessions] which they have been unable to sell under the existing law. One of the most prominent representatives of American companies, who is on terms of intimacy with him, has just informed me that he told the Provisional President quite frankly . . . that until the several objectionable features are repealed [from the legislation] he need have no hope of disposing of his holdings."[47] The companies demanded a lengthening of the thirty-year life of concessions, lower taxes, a relaxation of provisions to accelerate drilling, and guarantees for companies holding concessions that had not yet entered production, along with other changes.[48] A revision of the law to satisfy the companies would allow the Gomecistas to sell their concessions, but it would weaken or eliminate the nationalistic elements Torres had won in the 1920 legislation. Torres agreed that new legislation was necessary but resisted the companies' demands.

Márquez Bustillos tried to overcome Torres' resistance but found that "there is no way to convince him" to cooperate with some of the changes.[49] Writing to Enrique Urdaneta Maya, Gómez's secretary, Márquez Bustillos reviewed the situation and outlined his plan to circumvent Torres and secure passage of legislation that would facilitate the sale of concessions. He lamented that Torres's stubbornness might lead to "the loss of all the contracts [that have been] celebrated." This would suppress government revenue, Márquez Bustillos observed, but "also as regards our interests, we [concession holders] will not earn that which correctly, and with positive benefit to the Nation, we were going to earn."[50] He concluded that the best strategy was to work with Congress, rather than with Torres, to alleviate the companies' concerns.

Despite Márquez Bustillos's efforts, the 1921 legislation did not meet with the approval of the companies. While it included lower taxes as well as larger concession areas, and eased pressures to speed production, the changes did not go far enough to satisfy foreign investors; in addition, provisions they found confusing had crept into the text.[51] The companies balked at buying concessions until the legislation was modified yet again. "According to American oil men," wrote McGoodwin, "the reason for this state of affairs is that the Venezuelan law is ambiguous on many important points and was drafted less with a view to the interests of practical oil operators than to the native concession holders who naturally hope to derive the maximum profit for their leases from foreign purchasers."[52] This frank assessment of the opposing forces at play reflected the extent to which Torres's nationalist concerns had been marginalized in favor of the competing interests of concession holders and foreign companies.

The British legation believed that a North American involved in the concession trade, with rumored ties to Standard Oil, may have bribed some Venezuelan legislators to assure that the new legislation proposed and passed in 1922 would satisfy the companies. As early as 1919, the British minister in Caracas, Cecil Dormer, had criticized the "backstairs intrigue and bribes" employed by American businessmen seeking concessions.[53] In June 1920 Dormer reported that a certain Mr. McKay had established himself as "the most prominent American" in the concession trading circles of Caracas and that he "figures very prominently in local society."[54] McKay had business dealings with Julio Méndez and Juan Crisóstomo Gómez, two members of the Gómez clan active in the concession trade, and sold numerous grants to companies controlled by Standard. A year later, McKay had become the "representative of an important group" of US oil companies and exercised "a considerable share" of US influence over Venezuelan oil policy.[55] H. D. Beaumont, Dormer's successor, noted that McKay was "liberally supplied with funds" by the companies he represented to use in advancing their interests. When Beaumont explained McKay's role in shaping the 1922 oil legislation, he asserted that the American "has again been active in influential quarters by methods which, tactfully employed, appeal with special force to South American legislators."[56] But Beaumont also noted the fundamental impetus behind the new oil legislation: "Under the conditions imposed by the laws of 1920 and 1921, holders of the very numerous oil concessions recently granted had found it almost impossible to dispose of them." With these factors at work to ensure favorable treatment of foreign companies, Beaumont concluded that it was not necessary to use the influence of the British legation to shape the new law.

The 1922 legislation contained important revisions to placate foreign interests. Companies would have three years rather than two to explore the territory in concessions they acquired, and the contracts would run for forty years rather than thirty. In addition, as McBeth writes, under the 1922 legislation the companies received "a very significant reduction in the overall surface tax rate, something which was of considerable importance to those operators who were expecting to develop the oilfields on a long-term basis."[57] Nevertheless, the 1922 law also included provisions designed to safeguard national interests. The government retained the right to cancel a concession if the holder sought diplomatic intervention in a dispute with the state. In addition, concessions could not be held by oil companies that were owned or controlled by a foreign state. This specification stymied repeated efforts by Britain's Anglo-Persian Oil Company to enter the Venezuelan market between 1926 and 1934;[58] however, this provision posed no threat to the US companies or Shell.

The 1922 legislation—published in the *Gaceta Oficial* on June 13—finally provided the companies with the guarantees they sought. They now felt assured that investments could be profitable despite the transportation difficulties, disease environment, and other conditions that had concerned them. The US consul in Caracas summarized their reactions: "Representatives of petroleum interests in Caracas freely express opinions that . . . this law is the best that has been put in force in any Latin American republic."[59] Later the same year, in mid-December, Venezuela Oil Concessions, a Shell company, brought in the richest oil well yet in Venezuela, at their La Rosa field near Lake Maracaibo.[60] With the wealth of the country's oil deposits now confirmed and favorable legislation in place, the boom was on.

Gómez's Company: The Compañía Venezolana de Petróleo

Gómez followed developments in the petroleum sector during his first decade in power but refrained from establishing a large financial interest in the industry. During this early period, Gómez occasionally discussed petroleum matters with his advisors (especially the ministers of development); he kept abreast of concessions (although he gave Márquez Bustillos considerable leeway in granting them during the latter's provisional presidency); and he met with representatives of foreign oil companies, just as he met with other investors. But Gómez's knowledge of and interest in oil remained limited compared to the enterprises that he knew best. Historian José Miguel Medrano has even suggested that Shell owed its early dominance in Venezuelan oil to William T. S. Doyle, a former State Department official who became the chief representative of Shell interests in the country and who drew on his rural childhood to chat knowledgably with Gómez about cattle and thus enter his good graces.[61] Only as the possibility of the industry's postwar expansion came into view did Gómez take a more active interest in oil matters. But he still waited until after the 1922 law and the gusher at La Rosa to make his decisive move into the oil sector.

In June 1923 the formation of the Compañía Venezolana de Petróleo (CVP; Venezuelan Petroleum Company) was announced. The official notice identified the principal investors only as Venezuelan capitalists, but rumors immediately spread that Gómez, who was president again, controlled the company and that its purpose was to receive and sell concessions on behalf of the dictator, his family, and his close associates.[62] Due to the legal prohibition against the president's receiving concessions, Gómez's involvement in the CVP was not officially stated. Nevertheless, the company's publicity enticed potential clients by playing on the perception of its unrivaled political influence. The local press informed readers that the CVP would "facilitate commercial transactions by offering to the public effective advantages which need not be enumerated."[63] The following year, Gómez issued a special invitation to foreign diplomats in Caracas to encourage investors from their home nations to "present themselves" to the CVP.[64] As details of the company became known, they confirmed the CVP's links to the regime. The president and manager of the company was Roberto Ramírez, who oversaw many of Gómez's businesses from an office in Maracay; the CVP's Caracas office was in a building owned by the national government; important CVP contracts were drawn up at Gómez's home in Maracay; and the company offered its clients concessions it had not yet received from the government, indicating that it could secure the grants it desired.[65]

The establishment of the CVP posed a dilemma for the oil companies. On the one hand, the CVP appeared ready to control the most promising concessions, including the valuable national reserve lands.[66] Foreign companies wishing to expand their operations would need to do business with the CVP. On the other hand, the US legation and some US businessmen believed that any concessions sold by the CVP would be vulnerable to legal challenge under a future regime. Gómez appeared healthy, but he had narrowly survived his health crisis in 1921, and he turned sixty-six years old soon after the CVP opened. Gulf's representative in Caracas, R. E. Hardwicke, wrote to the company's general counsel in Pittsburgh to explain that buying concessions from the CVP ran a "first class risk of having the purchase nullified for reasons which will readily occur to you. Under present conditions the title would be safe but what will happen five or ten years from now is another matter. Of course, the answer to this argument is that when one buys, these things are considered and labelled as nothing more than a hazard of doing business. Just the same, the situation is a most awkward one."[67] Meanwhile, State Department officials in Washington, anxious for US companies to expand in Venezuela, sought to overcome these concerns.[68] Analysts at State pointed out that while Venezuelan legislation prohibited the president from receiving and selling oil concessions, it established no such prohibition against a company in which the president owned stock, as in the case of the CVP.[69] The legation remained skeptical.

As US companies and officials pondered these questions in early 1924, Gómez prodded investors to deal with the CVP. He opened negotiations with German interests controlled by Hugo Stinnes and his family to create a new company in Venezuela to purchase concessions from the CVP.⁷⁰ The US legation received reports that if this deal were made, the Germans could dominate promising concessions in the future.⁷¹ This would lock US companies out of new oilfields, including the national reserves, estimated to total 3 million hectares in mid-1924.⁷² US companies held many of the current exploration contracts; if the Stinnes group acquired the national reserves that reverted to the government from those concessions, it would capitalize on the exploration and infrastructure financed by US firms.⁷³ The longer that US companies hesitated to buy concessions from the CVP, the greater the risk that Stinnes would seize the advantage.

Standard Oil proved unwilling to risk exclusion from new concessions. Its companies decided by May 1924 to do business with the CVP, despite the uncertain future of these concessions. Around the same time, the US legation received word that the Stinnes group had ended its negotiations with the Venezuelan government. "It is felt by many," reported the legation, "that this German scare was purposely arranged so as to stimulate other petroleum interests' activity in Venezuela."⁷⁴ Historian Stephen Rabe echoes this theory that the rumored partnership with Stinnes was a "ruse" by Gómez and his allies to persuade reluctant US investors to purchase concessions from the CVP.⁷⁵ McBeth, by contrast, argues that Gómez would have welcomed German investment as a counterweight to US and Anglo-Dutch interests, and finds it plausible that Stinnes withdrew from negotiations for financial reasons.⁷⁶ On the whole, the numerous reports of negotiations between the regime and Stinnes indicate that Gómez and the Germans engaged in serious talks before the latter decided to withdraw.⁷⁷ Gómez and his partners in the CVP most likely used the interest expressed by Stinnes as a convenient opportunity to encourage reluctant investors to buy the company's concessions.

Whatever the truth of the Stinnes episode, the CVP produced large profits for Gómez and his associates once foreign companies did business with it. According to McBeth, the CVP received 177 concessions for national reserves from 1924 to 1929.⁷⁸ Even though this figure represents just under half the national-reserve concessions granted during these years, the CVP seemed to receive a disproportionate share of the most promising parcels. The US legation noted that the CVP commanded high prices for the concessions it sold.⁷⁹

Thus the establishment of national reserves—a system ostensibly designed to increase the nation's control over its oil wealth—in practice added to the personal wealth of Gómez and those connected to the CVP. Historian Tomás Polanco Alcántara concludes that Gómez netted between Bs. 10 and 20 million from the CVP, roughly 10 percent of his fortune.[80] McBeth deems even the upper figure of Bs. 20 million "far too conservative," because it does not include royalties and other payments to Gómez linked to CVP transactions.[81] The profits of other CVP stakeholders were much lower but still substantial. Roberto Ramírez, the CVP's manager, made Bs. 647,950 from the company, according to the anticorruption investigation in 1945–46, while the other CVP directors, Dr. Lucio Baldó and Dr. Rafael González Rincones, reportedly made Bs. 485,962 each.[82] The investigation also found that some of Gómez's allies and business associates received substantial payments from CVP accounts.[83] These may have been outright gifts from the dictator or transfers to cover his business expenses outside of oil. For example, Ramón Ramos, who dealt with Gómez in sugar and aguardiente over many years, received Bs. 200,000 from CVP funds.[84] In late 1930 the British minister believed that Gómez had stepped back from CVP affairs, allowing roughly half the company's concessions to be controlled by a group led by Dr. José Gil Fortoul, a lawyer, intellectual, diplomat, and advisor to Gómez.[85] Although the CVP was known as Gómez's company, the profits it reaped from trafficking in Venezuela's natural resources benefited his circle of adherents as well.

Chapter VII: Gómez as the "Providing Father"

The boom in oil production that began in the mid-1920s transformed government finances. Taxes on the industry, and on the expanded imports financed by oil, led to a tripling of federal revenues over the course of the 1920s. Even the onset of the Great Depression did not return government income to pre-boom levels. This fiscal expansion during the second half of his rule allowed Gómez to increase spending on public works and the military, expand the civilian bureaucracy, and complete repayment of Venezuela's foreign debt in 1930 to honor the centenary of Bolívar's death. Most significantly for the history of corruption, some of the additional funds flowing into the national treasury went into Chapter VII of the budget of the Ministry of Interior Relations, the section of the budget dedicated to meeting unplanned government expenses. Tens of millions of bolívares flowed through Chapter VII each year by the early 1920s, much of it in payments to Gómez's officials and allies. Formally designated as a contingency fund to be spent at the president's discretion, Chapter VII functioned as the regime's slush fund.

Over time, expenditures from Chapter VII became immensely controversial. Critics of the regime claimed that many payments from this account were nothing more than transfers of public funds into the private accounts of regime officials and sympathizers, a view that led to several anticorruption prosecutions beginning in 1936 and many more in the corruption trials of 1946. Meanwhile, defenders of Chapter VII payments emphasized that the law allowed presidential discretion in the use of the fund, and that payments were approved by the congress or cabinet, as legally required.

These controversies became heated in part because Chapter VII expenditures ran into the hundreds of millions of bolívares, and in part because the poor documentation of the purpose of these payments left their legitimacy open to divergent interpretations. According to Juan José Abreu, the attorney general (*procurador general*) who in 1936 launched the first prosecutions for private enrichment through Chapter VII, the Gómez regime spent Bs. 289.6 million from the controversial account between June 1924 and November 1935, for an average of Bs. 25.2 million per year during the period that oil enriched the regime. (As a point of comparison, the trade in oil concessions averaged Bs. 12.41 million during this time, not including royalties.) Any definitive accounting of Chapter VII expenditures was complicated, however, by the regime's practice of listing relatively modest sums for this account in the formal budget and then adding much greater sums over the course of the fiscal year in the form of "additional credits." Abreu's investigation found that only Bs. 36 million was assigned to Chapter VII through the normal budgeting process in 1924–35, while additional credits were roughly seven times greater, totaling Bs. 253.6 million.[86] In response to Abreu's accusation that almost half of the expenditures had gone to illicit purposes, former interior minister Pedro Manuel Arcaya (1925–29) published his accounting of Chapter VII expenditures during his four years and three months managing the fund. His total of Bs. 134.6 million for this period translates into an annual average of nearly Bs. 31.7 million for these prosperous years after the onset of the oil boom and before the global economic slump.[87]

Both Arcaya's and Abreu's figures are impressive when viewed in a larger fiscal context. The annual average of Chapter VII payments reported by Abreu represents approximately 13 percent of federal revenues for 1924–35, and Arcaya's annual average of Chapter VII expenditures is equal to approximately 16 percent of the average annual federal revenues during his tenure, 1925–29. The two men differed dramatically, however, in their evaluation of the legitimacy of these payments. Abreu alleged that Bs. 131.2 million, or roughly 45 percent of the payments from Chapter VII in 1924–35, was spent for purposes that "could not remotely be considered public services and had no legitimate reason whatsoever for an expenditure by the Treasury."[88] Arcaya resolutely maintained that all Chapter VII expenditures were legal because the fund was managed in accordance with the law.[89] Since the government had adhered to legal procedures in dispersing the money, he reasoned, the expenditures were beyond reproach. Each of these perspectives on Chapter VII found adherents over the years, turning the discretionary payments into the regime's clearest example of ambiguous corruption, a practice condemned by some Venezuelans but defended (or tolerated) by others.

This sharp divergence of opinion reflected, in part, two competing visions of government. Arcaya embraced a patrimonial view that blurred distinctions between public and private interests and thus maximized presidents' discretionary authority, which he saw as necessary for the imposition of political order. In contrast, Abreu advocated for a clearer division between public and private interests as a means of overcoming Venezuela's tradition of personalist rulers. Poor documentation of the purpose of most Chapter VII expenditures reinforced these disagreements. Typical disbursement orders listed only the amount to be paid, the recipient, and a notation stating "by order of the General" to indicate Gómez's approval, omitting any other justification or purpose.[90] Adding to the murkiness that supported divergent interpretations, the persons listed as recipients were often only intermediaries who received the cash at the treasury office and then delivered it to the intended beneficiaries or spent it for a purpose that was communicated verbally. Because the payment orders did not indicate whether the recipient listed was an intermediary or the final beneficiary, it was often impossible to determine whether any payment enriched a specific individual.

Information culled from these debates and prosecutions—all of which occurred after Gómez's death—as well as from memoirs of the period, indicates that a variety of licit and illicit payments were made from Chapter VII and from smaller, similar funds in other ministries. Certainly, Gómez's use of Chapter VII and similar funds exemplified his patrimonial conception of the state and its resources, in which he made no distinction between his personal or family expenses and the public expenses that he authorized in his role as a public official, much like monarchs from an earlier age who mixed the revenues and expenses of the royal household with those of government.[91] The Chapter VII expenditures that can be documented include some that support Gomecistas' justifications of discretionary payments, others that support anti-Gomecistas' accusations of malfeasance, and many that fall into an ambiguous, intermediate zone.

To place the issue in context, discretionary presidential payments decried as corrupt did not begin in Venezuela with Gómez. President Juan Crisóstomo Falcón (1863–68) allegedly began the practice of widespread payments to friends and followers from the national treasury, and President Francisco Linares Alcántara (1877–78), despite his brief time in office, also stood out for excessive generosity.[92] Nor was misuse of funds from the national treasury necessarily limited to the chief executive. Antonio Pimentel, the business partner and confidant of Gómez who served as treasury minister during his first presidential term, reportedly paid some of his business expenses out of public funds. The British legation noted in 1912 that "the present Minister of Finance [Pimentel], a very wealthy coffee planter, pays the railway freight of the coffee exported by him by orders on the Treasury under the heading of 'Unforeseen Expenses.'"[93] Gómez's innovation was to gather the majority of such discretionary expenditures into one section of the budget, a change included in Treasury Minister Román Cárdenas's fiscal reforms. Under Cárdenas's 1914 legislation to centralize fiscal management, Chapter XXXII of the budget of the Ministry of Interior Relations was designated for "Commissions, Temporary Assignments and other similar expenditures" (*Comisiones, Asignaciones eventuales y otros gastos semejantes*), and a second reorganization of the ministry's accounts in 1919 designated this contingency fund as Chapter VII, the heading it retained until its abolition soon after the coup of October 18, 1945.[94] The creation of Chapter VII as part of Cárdenas's drive to rationalize the administration of the treasury reinforces the argument, presented in chapters 1 and 3, that Venezuela's fiscal system exemplified a process of neopatrimonial state formation, in which the selective modernization of segments of the state served to reinforce Gómez's personal power.

A significant share of the expenditures from Chapter VII were for purposes of such clear public interest that they were rarely, if ever, questioned. Natural disasters and public-health emergencies sometimes required an immediate response with resources beyond those in the annual budget. Government buildings needed repairs, situations arose that required the hiring of new personnel, and ministers sometimes found that their departments' expenditures exceeded those foreseen in the budgeting process. When Venezuela's diplomatic representatives were appointed to overseas posts, sometimes on short notice following the resignation or death of previous officials, their travel expenses (and sometimes their salaries) were paid out of Chapter VII. Expenditures such as these demonstrated the necessity of a contingency fund.[95] Even Abreu, the highly critical attorney general who reviewed Chapter VII payments from 1924 to 1935, declared, at the height of the anti-Gómez reaction in early 1936, that over half the expenditures from the account were legitimate.

At the other end of the spectrum, some payments from Chapter VII clearly served private rather than public interests. Those benefiting Gómez and his family were especially egregious. These included payments to Gómez's personal lawyer for work on the dictator's business affairs; payments for improvements to Gómez's agricultural estates; a payment of Bs. 1.53 million to settle a lawsuit against one of Gómez's daughters for an automobile accident during a contest in Paris; and the payment of over Bs. 3.5 million in taxes owed by Gómez and his sons for aguardiente produced on their estates.[96] Expenditures such as these were obviously for the personal benefit of the dictator and his family.

Other expenditures combined personal and political motivations and seemed designed to bolster Gómez's image as a generous patron who rewarded his friends and allies. Arcaya claimed that it was completely appropriate for Gómez to spend almost Bs. 200,000 a year on jewelry that he gave as gifts. The dictator ordered jewelry for "the great number of marriages and baptisms in which General Gómez was named a Godfather and was obliged to provide gifts to the couples and the godchildren. Both politics and courtesy required this."[97] The numerous requests to serve as a godparent at baptisms and weddings came, of course, from Gómez's friends and political followers. Arcaya maintained that Gómez, as head of state, had an "inherent" obligation to accept these invitations and to provide appropriate gifts;[98] in his view, such purchases of jewelry constituted a legitimate government expenditure. Similarly, when a town named Gómez a patron of the annual festival to celebrate its saint, he used Chapter VII funds to make a donation for the food, drink, music, and fireworks that the townspeople expected.[99] The fact that these gifts came from public funds rather than Gómez's private resources did not alter the reality that they were given entirely at Gómez's discretion and thus represented his personal favor.

Carlos Siso, the bureaucrat who wrote a sympathetic but not uncritical account of the regime, agreed with Arcaya that such benevolence was crucial to Gómez's leadership, especially within the military. He emphasized that Gómez "was generous and attentive to the needs of the officers. . . . He never neglected to satisfy the need of an officer, and always rewarded the deserving ones; in this way he came to know how to capture the respect of his Army."[100] This patronage, Siso believed, constituted part of Gómez's "gift for command" (*don de mando*). Many of these cash payments were unsolicited; by anticipating the needs of his officers, Gómez spared them the embarrassment of requesting aid. Siso wrote that "when [Gómez] knew that some military man had a sick person [in his household] or that his wife was about to give birth, he always took care to send a gift, which was necessary to compensate for the lack of social programs at that time."[101]

But not all of Gómez's generosity to military officers arose from the lack of social welfare programs. General López Contreras recounts that in 1931, during his tenure as minister of war, a colonel came to Maracay, like countless others, to pay his respects. Gómez told López Contreras that he and the colonel had been partners in a cattle deal in which they both lost money (a rarity for the dictator), and that the colonel seemed to harbor resentment. Gómez casually instructed López Contreras to establish a "pension" (i.e., a long-term payment order) of 400 bolívares a month for the colonel to compensate for his losses and, by implication, to keep him loyal.[102] Many other officers, either retired or in active service, received similar payments from Chapter VII. By Arcaya's count, 794 military officers ranging in rank from sub-lieutenant to general (and one priest working as a military chaplain) received payments from Chapter VII totaling over 11 million bolívares during his four years as minister of interior relations.[103]

To the junior officers, payments from Chapter VII aided in maintaining a respectable middle-class lifestyle rather than providing a source of enrichment. Cadets entering the military academy came predominantly from lower-middle-class families in the Andes, and once commissioned as junior officers most still faced the economic precarity typical of the middle class.[104] Their pay was notoriously low, and promotions could be painfully slow. Some academy graduates spent a decade as lieutenants, despite their professional qualifications, and even future president Isaías Medina Angarita spent ten years (1917–27) at the rank of captain.[105] Some gained extra income by seizing opportunities for profiteering (for example, from the money budgeted for their troops' rations), but higher-ranking officers often guarded such opportunities for themselves.[106] In sum, the household finances of young officers, like those of other middle-class families, could be upended by an unexpected illness or other difficulties. Young officers and their spouses must have faced agonizing choices when confronted with economic challenges. At a time when female employment outside the home could undermine a family's respectability, extra income of even a few hundred bolívares from Chapter VII could safeguard the dignity of both spouses by providing material assistance.

While assuring the military's loyalty was undoubtedly a priority for Gómez, he did not neglect the needs and desires of his civilian supporters, including (again) many from the middle class. When Gómez or his cabinet ministers heard that civil servants, their widows, or other deserving individuals lacked the resources to make a house payment or pay for medical care, they often provided assistance through Chapter VII.[107] For example, Rómulo Gallegos, the famous novelist, school teacher, and future president who served in Gómez's congress before breaking with the regime, received funds from Chapter VII to facilitate medical treatment for his wife, Teotiste, in Italy.[108] In addition to ad hoc payments made as circumstances arose, Gómez also paid public employees' traditional Christmas bonuses, the *aguinaldos*, from Chapter VII. Arcaya reported that the amount spent on aguinaldos in the second half of the 1920s averaged Bs. 3.1 million per year. The largest expenditure on these year-end bonuses (almost

Bs. 4.6 million) came in 1928, following the anti-Gómez protests of that year.[109]

Arcaya highlighted the fact that 1,650 Venezuelan women received Chapter VII funds totaling Bs. 5.25 million (including one-time payments and long-term pensions) during his four years as minister of interior. Many of these female beneficiaries, according to Arcaya, were "descendants of the leaders of Independence, including some from the very family of the Liberator [Simón Bolívar]; widows and daughters of distinguished public men of Venezuela, [such as] Presidents of the Republic, cabinet ministers, [and] State Presidents who left their families in poverty, exposed to malevolent public opinion which believed they were wealthy; widows and daughters of many military men killed in our civil wars; and all of them, in sum, with the title of being Venezuelan women worthy of the protection of the Chief of the country, who is seen in the psychology of our people as a providing Father."[110] As this phrasing suggests, Arcaya (and probably Gómez) assumed that widows and daughters of prominent men had a particular claim on long-term assistance (or "protection") from Gómez in his role as the nation's "providing Father" following the death of their patriarchs—an assumption that highlights the connections between Gomecista patrimonialism and patriarchy. Arcaya's comments also make clear that these payments safeguarded both the material well-being and the honor of recipients by preventing their slide into "poverty," understood as downward social and economic mobility that would jeopardize their standing as *gente decente*.

But many Venezuelans—male and female—received Chapter VII funds at the discretion of high-ranking officials without specific approval from Gómez. Cabinet ministers, state presidents, and other top bureaucrats received unusually large stipends (ranging up to a few thousand bolívares a month) and onetime payments (for tens or even hundreds of thousands of bolívares) from Chapter VII.[111] (Some of the largest recipients were prominent officials related to Gómez by blood or marriage.)[112] Such officials claimed that they or their assistants used these funds to support worthy individuals who needed economic assistance—a common government practice before the establishment of institutionalized forms of public assistance—or to cover other legitimate expenditures.[113] Although later investigators argued that in some cases these funds contributed to the officials' illicit enrichment, it is also clear that some monies were used for payments to individuals in need. Anecdotal evidence gives a sense of how high-ranking officials used their allotments of discretionary funds to spread the benefits of Chapter VII beyond the thousands of beneficiaries named in Arcaya's lists.

One woman considered worthy of a cabinet minister's assistance was Dolores Meaño Escalante de Blanco, the widow of Dr. Luis Felipe Blanco, a physician, hospital administrator, and professor. He dedicated much of his career to caring for children and patients suffering from leprosy, often not charging for his services. Blanco was also the friend and personal physician of two prominent Gomecistas, Victorino Márquez Bustillos and Melchor Centeno, who served as treasury minister (1922–29) and minister of public works (1932) under Gómez. Blanco died in February 1927, and Centeno (then treasury minister) offered to pay the funeral expenses. Soon thereafter, he arranged for Dolores to receive 160 bolívares every two weeks from Chapter VII, saying that she deserved this pension as the widow of a distinguished and generous public figure. Dolores, whose children were unable to offer her economic support and whose precarious finances left her unable to pay the mortgage on the house she had shared with Luis Felipe, accepted the pension. The stipend continued even when her son, the famed poet and political activist Andrés Eloy Blanco, was arrested following the 1928 protests and spent several years in prison. As he later wrote, the "modest pension" did not make his mother wealthy by any means, but it did allow her to maintain a dignified life, a telling acknowledgment from a prominent anti-Gomecista.[114]

The family of Cecilia Pimentel received onetime financial assistance, rather than a pension (which could have spared Cecilia and her sister, Clara, from seeking work outside the home), but the single payment came at an especially difficult moment. Cecilia's younger brother Vicente died in the spring of 1925 of typhoid fever, possibly the result of the family's declining economic fortunes, which had obliged them to move to a cheaper house—one without sewers—as they sacrificed to make payments to prison officials on behalf her older brothers. Francisco Baptista Galindo, a relative of the family who was Gómez's general secretary and a former minister of interior relations, approached the Pimentels through an intermediary and offered to pay the funeral expenses. While Cecilia does not specify the source of these funds, it was certainly the type of payment that a regime official—especially a former minister of interior relations—would use Chapter VII to make.[115] Cecilia's recounting of the episode emphasizes the care that Baptista took to respect the family's dignity. The morning after Vicente died, Cecelia, writes, "a young man presented himself [at the Pimentel home] and asked to speak with *mamá* on behalf of Dr. Francisco Baptista Galindo, to tell her that he, as our relative and in the absence of my brothers, had taken the liberty of arranging for Vicente's burial and he hoped she would not refuse. *Mamá* accepted that offer made in such a personal and delicate manner, since she knew that otherwise we would not have gone along with it. . . . But she asked that [the funeral] be as unadorned as possible, and so it was."[116] As with the support provided by the regime to other women, Baptista Galindo and the Pimentels framed the aid as appropriate due to "the absence" of male household members, even as they understood the need for discretion to spare the family the embarrassment of state assistance. The payments in favor of the Pimentels and Dolores Meaño Escalante de Blanco also demonstrate the importance of personal connections to high-ranking Gomecistas, which not all families in similar circumstances enjoyed but which would have been more common among the middle class than the working class.

In sum, Chapter VII payments spanned a broad range from the clearly legitimate to the clearly illicit, with many falling into an expansive ambiguous area in between, setting the stage for future debates over the rectitude of these transactions. But at least two aspects of Chapter VII emerge from accounts provided by Gomecista sympathizers and critics alike. First, a significant portion of the funds went to middle-class families when they faced challenges to maintaining their standing as *gente decente*. Second, the discretionary payments distributed by Gómez and his ministers were often framed by considerations that mixed political loyalty, friendship, kinship, interests of state, and a culturally informed assessment of the worthiness of the recipients. Chapter VII reinforced the patriarchal nature of the regime by demonstrating the generosity that Gómez, either directly or through his officials, could choose to bestow. The "severe father" who condemned his opponents to prison or forced labor on the highways was also the "providing father" who saw to the material needs of families deemed deserving and honorable. This paternalistic discretion to reward or punish was an integral aspect of state-society relations before Gómez, but the flood of oil revenues multiplied the number of those receiving the state's largesse, whether they were grateful to the regime or resentful of their implied dependency. Clearly, the sheer number of Chapter VII beneficiaries reflected the state's growing penetration of society, especially the middle class, but the variety of circumstances in which the payments occurred would problematize future efforts to distinguish between corrupt and legitimate uses of these public funds.

Gómez's distribution of oil concessions and Chapter VII payments gave him substantial control over Venezuela's oil money during the second half of his regime. Venezuelans' ability to gain access to this new source of wealth depended largely on the regime's favor. In theory, subsoil deposits and the public revenues they produced belonged to the nation, but in practice Gómez and his ministers exercised personal discretion over these resources and used them to strengthen their position as patrons upon whom Venezuelans depended. If Fernando Coronil is correct in his argument that oil gave rise to a "magical state" in which Venezuelans expected their government to convert petroleum into a source of riches for many, if not all, of its citizens, then clearly Chapter VII payments, as well as the granting of oil concessions, played a role in its emergence. Together, these two modes of distributing oil money spread hundreds of millions of bolívares among thousands of beneficiaries, reinforcing the regime's consolidation.

While recipients obviously welcomed this distribution of petroleum's bounty, the inherent selectivity and favoritism provoked accusations of corruption. Both Chapter VII payments and oil concessions stand as examples of ambiguous corruption, condemned by some Venezuelans but defended or grudgingly tolerated by others. Moreover, while some concessions and payments clearly followed the law, others just as clearly contributed to Gómez's self-enrichment and—especially in the case of the CVP—raised legal concerns even before the dictator's death allowed a fuller examination of questionable transactions. These divided and ambivalent reactions to the ambiguous corruption associated with oil money may be viewed as paralleling the process of neopatrimonial state formation, which featured both personalist and legal-rational forms of power. Arcaya spoke for many Venezuelans when he argued that Gómez's absolute discretion over public resources was necessary to impose political stability, even as many other Venezuelans believed the country should leave behind the personalist rule Gómez exemplified.

Finally, the ambiguous status of oil concessions and Chapter VII reflected important contrasts with other, overtly coercive modes of Gomecista corruption. The social dynamics of oil money's circulation differed markedly from the predatory practices I have discussed in previous chapters. Gomecista profiteering from cattle, liquor, and political prisons extracted wealth directly from Venezuelans living under the regime—from consumers, entrepreneurs excluded from Gomecista monopolies, and prisoners' families—and gave rise to what I have called the emotional economy of anticorruption, in which victims of the regime's exploitation experienced humiliation and dishonor. Oil money, by contrast, was not extracted from Venezuelans but rather from the global market and the foreign companies, with the state mediating its distribution. In contrast to predatory corruption, which threatened the status of *gente decente*, the circulation of oil money often protected the status of middle-class households. As I argue in the two remaining chapters, this distinction between the ambiguous corruption associated with the discretionary distribution of state resources, and the widely condemned predatory corruption of the Gómez era, rippled through Venezuelan politics for years after the dictator's demise.

CHAPTER 6
TRANSITION, 1935-45

Juan Vicente Gómez died of natural causes shortly before midnight on December 17, 1935, at the age of seventy-eight. He had fallen ill a month before, touching off increasingly dire rumors of his decline. Many Venezuelans had long feared that the General's death, whenever it came, would lead to widespread unrest, perhaps even a return to the civil wars that plagued the country before he consolidated power. Gomecista officials and their allies, many of whom had gathered in Maracay as the dictator lay dying, went about their business well-armed, fearing personal attacks or a general outbreak of violence.[1] When Gómez slipped into a coma on December 15, the cabinet voted to designate minister of war General Eleazar López Contreras as acting president so that there would be no vacuum of power when Gómez died.[2]

During the day and a half between Gómez's death and his funeral in Maracay on December 19, the nation remained generally peaceful but on edge. Gumersindo Torres, the head of the Venezuelan Industrial Cattle Company and former development minister, visited the chapel in Maracay where Gómez's body lay for viewing on the night of December 18–19. As Torres arrived, a group of mourners, some in tears, were departing the chapel, having paid their respects, but afterwards there were few visitors other than the guards. Rather than leave the body in solitude, Torres, along with Dr. Manuel Gimón Itriago (the son of General David Gimón, a former state president) remained in the chapel, "providing company to the man who in life was never alone," as Torres later wrote.[3] He remarked bitterly that neither Gómez's relatives nor the officials of his regime who had gathered in Maracay visited "the cadaver that night, when the most elemental notion of duty required them to pass those hours accompanying the dead man to whom they owed everything—their renown, honors and riches."[4] The funeral on December 19—the anniversary of Gómez's seizure of power which the regime had celebrated for over two decades—was well attended, but the air of foreboding was pervasive. "Once the last bouquet of fresh flowers was put down, the absolute majority in attendance bid a definitive farewell to [Gómez] and began to set aside his memory."[5] When Torres returned to Caracas later that day, riots and looting of Gomecista properties had already begun.

A broad-based reaction against Gomecista corruption, and debates over its continuity and consequences, marked much of the politics of the next decade, during which Venezuela was ruled by two men from Gómez's army who were elected president under a highly restrictive voting system: López Contreras (1936–41) and General Isaías Medina Angarita (1941–45), both from Castro's and Gómez's home state of Táchira. The attacks on Gomecistas' properties that began on December 19 and continued for weeks were widely interpreted as a reaction against the regime's corruption and political repression. Moreover, the attacks influenced López Contreras's decisions to allow the nationalization of Gómez's vast fortune and to end the worst forms of predatory profiteering associated with his regime. Under López Contreras, corruption no longer provided the central logic of the state, and submission to state authority no longer required a humiliating endurance of official predation. Nevertheless, neither López Contreras's reforms nor Medina Angarita's 1943 oil law, which ended petroleum concessions to private citizens, convinced their critics that corruption ceased to be an issue. Opponents of López Contreras and Medina Angarita argued that the two presidents' ongoing use of Chapter VII to reward their loyalists perpetuated a personalist system of rule and obstructed the establishment of a modern democratic state. This discursive dichotomy between modernity and corruption reached an ever-wider audience in the more open political climate of the post-Gómez transition, especially under Medina Angarita. Perhaps most significantly, it resonated with the junior military officers who overthrew Medina Angarita in 1945.

Historians of the post-Gómez transition of 1935–45 have long debated whether the governments headed by López Contreras and Medina Angarita represented a true break with Gomecismo or a continuation of the "Gómez system." Scholars who take the latter view include US historian Judith Ewell and numerous Venezuelan authors, many with ties to Acción Democrática (AD), the party founded by Betancourt and others in 1941.[6] For evidence of continuity during the post-Gómez decade, they point to the ongoing power wielded by some (but by no means all) of the Andeans who had served Gómez, to the political influence of the army, and to limitations on voting rights. Moreover, they observe, the two transition presidents opted to maintain generally cooperative relations with foreign oil companies instead of seeking to change Venezuela's subordinate role in the global economy. By contrast, other scholars, often referred to as revisionists, argue that López Contreras and Medina Angarita eliminated the most oppressive elements of Gomecismo and led the creation of more democratic institutions, a necessarily gradual process in a nation with no democratic experience prior to 1935.[7] While scholars in the first camp implicitly or explicitly justify the coup of 1945, those in the second group believe that the overthrow of Medina Angarita and the imposition of a self-styled revolutionary government in 1945 derailed the organic evolution of democracy begun by Gómez's two successors.[8] Rather than take sides in this controversy, this chapter contends that the post-Gómez transition was marked by a curtailment of predatory corruption, the onset of public debate over alleged corruption in Chapter VII payments, and changes that refined rather than ended the neopatrimonial process of state formation.

Before exploring these aspects of the post-Gómez transition, it is useful to outline the political context of the first year and a half after the dictator's death, when the parameters of the new political system were contested and established.[9] It was a time of intensive political mobilization. As anti-Gómez protests broke out across the country in late 1935, political exiles returned and added their voices to calls for far-reaching change. Facing a new wave of protests in February 1936, López Contreras announced his plan of government, popularly known as the February Program, in which he detailed his intention to "root out gradually the vices of the past" by promoting labor rights, education, honest management of public funds, the modernization of agriculture, and economic development. The program even raised the possibility of land redistribution.[10] Rómulo Betancourt and other middle-class survivors of the 1928 student protests, having moved increasingly to the Left in exile, returned to Venezuela and established the Movimiento de Organización Venezolano (ORVE; Venezuelan Organizing Movement), while members of the banned communist movement created the Partido Republicano Progresista (PRP; Progressive Republican Party). Both groups, encouraged by López Contreras's initial respect for civil liberties and his moves to retire the most hated members of the old regime, called on him to implement the reforms in the February Program. They also hoped that a new constitution promised by López Contreras would establish a democratic order in which they could harness popular sentiment to pursue more fundamental changes to Venezuela's political, economic, and social structures.

López Contreras entered the presidency with valuable political capital. His popularity within the army rested on his long-standing support for the professionalization of the institution, which placed him among those Gomecistas who, like Torres and treasury minister Román Cárdenas, had sought to modernize segments of the national state. Similarly, López Contreras had avoided association with the abusive practices of the past regime and was considered one of the most honest of top Gomecistas. As he assumed the presidency, his most pressing challenge was to move the country past the horrors of the Gómez era by responding to pent-up demands for change, while holding more reactionary Gomecistas in check. López Contreras's political instincts and view of the state were largely those of a nineteenth-century liberal, but as Venezuela became more open to the ideologies circulating internationally in the mid-1930s, the divisions within the country increasingly fed into a polarization between the political Left and Right.

On the Left, both the PRP and ORVE denounced corruption

in their founding documents, but ORVE went further. The PRP's program called for an end to Gomecista monopolies and peculation;[11] ORVE's program, though briefer, offered a more robust contrast between Gomecista corruption and the party's vision of political modernity. ORVE denounced "the personalist state of Gómez and his clientele" which had "made the administration [of the state] an instrument of public plunder," and called for the transformation of Venezuela's government into a "modern state" with expanded suffrage that would provide "justice, protection, and efficiency to all Venezuelans."[12] This change, ORVE indicated, would depend on the expertise of professions associated with the middle class. Thus it called for the creation of "technically proficient teaching staffs in primary, secondary, and normal education," "the modernization of the armed forces" with "institutes of military training," and "the establishment of administrative careers in all public services [with] statutes and an administrative ladder [and] laws for retirement and pensions."[13] This modernist vision of a merit-based bureaucratic state was not uncommon among the middle classes of Latin America by the mid-1930s, but its contrast to systemic Gomecista corruption gave it particular resonance in Venezuela. ORVE drew support from recently organized middle-class groups representing white-collar employees, teachers, professionals, and women, as well as worker and peasant groups attracted by its populist economic proposals.[14]

The most effective challenge to ORVE and the PRP came from moderate conservatives who supported López Contreras against both the Left and hardline Gomecistas. These moderate conservatives found an unexpected spokesperson in Rafael Caldera, a young law student and graduate of a Jesuit secondary school. Caldera had publicly broken with progressive student groups when they backed educational reforms aimed at restricting church schools. Adhering to Catholic social doctrine, he called on the new government to carry out moderate reforms from above while holding firm against left-wing demands. Caldera's Unión Nacional Estudiantil (UNE; National Student Union) was well positioned to take advantage of middle- and upper-class suspicions that Betancourt, who had collaborated with the Costa Rican Communist Party during his years of exile, held aspirations more radical than those in ORVE's formal pronouncements. Caldera developed a following not only among Catholic students but also among men and women who longed for change but viewed the

PRP and ORVE as too radical.[15] Despite these differences among the UNE, ORVE, and PRP, however, all three broadly agreed with López Contreras's call to end "the vices of the past." Diehard Gomecistas found themselves an isolated minority.

After several months of political liberalization and moderate reform, López Contreras moved to suppress the Left and limit structural change.[16] He was pulled to the Right by his own political disposition and by domestic and international developments. The Left had accepted Congress's election of López Contreras to a five-year term as president in April 1936, citing the need to adhere to constitutional rule, but reacted strongly against new legislation, supported by López Contreras, that aimed to restrict political activity. ORVE and the PRP backed a general strike in protest in June, raising fears of mass violence and alienating many of their potential supporters. Congress then issued a new constitution which restricted voting rights to literate males over the age of twenty-one and maintained congressional election of the president, dashing the Left's hopes of electoral gains. The constitution's ban on communist activity, it was understood, gave the government the means to repress the Left. The outbreak of civil war in Spain in July 1936 led Venezuelans on both the Right and Left to draw parallels between the political polarization in Europe and at home; this growing fear of disorder led many to unite around López Contreras rather than embrace the Left. A last-ditch effort to rally popular sentiment against the government's crackdown failed when López Contreras broke an oil workers' strike backed by ORVE and the PRP. López Contreras's government then delivered the final blows in early 1937 by outlawing the PRP, ORVE, and other left-wing political and labor organizations, and by ordering the exile of dozens of leftist leaders, including Betancourt, accusing them of subversion. Despite López Contreras's repression and his failure to vigorously pursue the reforms in his February Program, he nonetheless enjoyed widespread support among many Venezuelans eager to move beyond the degrading confines of the Gómez era. Developments related to the issue of corruption help to explain this paradox.

The Protests of 1935–36 and the Curtailment of Predatory Corruption

The protests that swept across Venezuela soon after Gómez's death were a spontaneous expression of outrage at the tyranny, corruption, and humiliation of the old regime, and they pushed López Contreras to end the most predatory practices of previous decades. As early as December 18, 1935, the day after Gómez's death, university students and other groups circulated manifestos in Caracas. They called for freedom of commerce and an end to Gomecista monopolies, as well as demanding the restoration of civil liberties, the release of political prisoners, an end to military press gangs, and the appointment of "the most competent and honorable [men]" to government positions.[17] As demonstrations turned violent the next day, rioters targeted properties belonging to officials with reputations for profiteering, demonstrating anger at officials' self-enrichment. The cattle and meat company formed by Gómez and many of his state presidents was an early target, as crowds in Caracas and Valencia sacked the company's butcher shops and seized meat from the company's trucks.[18] Crowds attacked mansions in Caracas belonging to Gómez, his family, and top collaborators, including Antonio Pimentel and Rafael María Velasco. Protestors carried off the mansions' furniture and fixtures, destroyed the interiors, and in some cases set fire to the structures.[19] Two Caracas cinemas belonging to Pimentel were also sacked, as were the offices of *El Nuevo Diario*, the regime's newspaper. The US embassy in Caracas reported that "the Jefe Civil of [nearby] Sabana Grande has fled and his properties destroyed. He has long been notorious for his sequestration of private properties in his district and the villagers have taken complete revenge."[20] Protesters looted and burned the house of the jefe civil in the La Pastora neighborhood and cornered the official himself, pulling down his trousers and chasing him through the streets as they turned the tables of degradation on their tormentor. The protesters' discipline in selecting their targets amidst the carnivalesque atmosphere impressed the British consul as he rode through the city to observe the unrest: "It is greatly to the credit of the mob that there was no general looting, their operations being confined to the property of those from whose tyranny they had suffered so long. There was a spirit of hilarity and good humour about the business that was almost attractive."[21]

In other parts of the country, as in Caracas, protesters generally took aim at targets that symbolized Gomecista abuses and ill-gotten wealth. In the city of Valencia and its hinterland, a center of sugar and aguardiente production, stockpiles of these two commodities belonging to Ramón Ramos were destroyed, as were sugar stockpiles and vehicles at estates belonging to Félix Galavís—as we saw in chapter 3, both men had profited handsomely from regional monopolies in the liquor trade under Gómez.[22] Across wide swaths of rural Venezuela, peasants and workers attacked ranches and farms belonging to Gómez and his allies—including such reviled figures as Vincencio Pérez Soto, president of various states during the dictatorship, and Paulino Camero, director of the Castillo prison—burning crops, killing or stealing livestock, destroying fences and invading estate lands.[23] In the Crespo district north of Barquisimeto, where local Gomecistas in the 1910s and '20s had used their political connections to seize public lands and appropriate coffee groves planted by peasant settlers, protestors attacked local Gomecistas' estates and petitioned López Contreras to grant them title to their lost farms.[24] At Puerto Cabello, a crowd prevented the minister of public works, in whose department an unexplained deficit of 40 million bolívares had been discovered, from boarding a ship to leave the country; his luggage was also destroyed.[25] In late February, workers destroyed 60,000 bags of coffee on El Trompillo, a plantation that Gómez bought with funds he received from the national treasury in a notoriously fraudulent transaction.[26] In sum, the protests of late 1935 and early 1936 revealed the geographical breadth and emotional depth of popular resentment against Gomecista profiteering. As Betancourt recalled years later, they resulted from decades of "oppression and humiliation."[27]

López Contreras responded to the protests with restraint, fueling hopes that he sought to break with the past rather than defend the old order. According to the British consul, the police and army in Caracas made no real effort to prevent attacks on Gomecista properties or to arrest the looters during the worst of the disturbances on December 19–21. The looters, meanwhile, often shouted cheers for López Contreras and the army. Martial law was declared late on the twenty-first, following the death of Eustoquio Gómez, who was shot earlier that day while making a desperate grab for power in hopes of maintaining his clan in power. "By this time, however," the consul explained, "practically all the property of the adherents of the old regime [in Caracas] had been destroyed and the mob were ready to suspend their operations."[28] In rural areas, the government response was in the hands of the jefes civiles, some of whom fled as soon as unrest broke out; others made brief, violent attempts to suppress the protests before being forced to flee. In some of these contested areas,

López Contreras and the new state presidents he appointed tried to restore calm by naming jefes civiles who sympathized with local demands for change.[29] The only extensive use of force to quell the unrest of December 1935 and January 1936 occurred in Maracaibo and the oilfields of Zulia, where attacks on the oil companies, looting of businesses, a short-lived labor strike, and clashes between the local army garrison and the police of Maracaibo resulted in some 200 deaths before López Contreras dispatched outside security forces to the region. Some of the dead in Maracaibo and the oil camps were striking workers, looters, or abusive employees of the oil companies, but here too the targets of popular violence included predatory Gomecistas.[30]

Significantly, López Contreras moved decisively to end the predatory practices that had marked the relationship between the Gomecista state and society. By December 30, 1935, the new government had announced that the old regime's cattle company would be reorganized in the public interest, the monopoly on supplying Caracas with fresh fish was ended, and the administration of the lottery was removed from Gómez's son Gonzalo, with future proceeds to go to medical facilities and the Red Cross. US minister Meredith Nicholson reported that "the cancellation of [these] monopolies has done much to enhance the belief that [López Contreras] is firm in his intention to furnish honest government."[31] López Contreras even moved to curtail corruption among military officers by eliminating their "illegal perquisites" as part of his "brave attempt to abolish corruption,"[32] according to the British legation. Specifically, López Contreras curtailed payments to military commanders to be used to buy food for their men, from which officers often skimmed a large percentage. This reform provoked grumbling among some officers, but López Contreras maintained his military support by implementing pay raises and ending the use of soldiers as laborers on the estates of political insiders, a significant source of military grievance under Gómez.[33] Gumersindo Torres stated in his memoirs that within a few months of Gómez's death López Contreras had ended the Gomecista monopolies and the widespread abuse of political power to manipulate business dealings.[34] These changes solidified López Contreras's support among politically conservative anti-Gomecistas like Emilio Arévalo Cedeño, who praised López Contreras in May 1936 for putting an end to the corruption (*corrupción* and *peculado*) of the Gómez era.[35]

López Contreras further signaled his willingness to break with the old regime by dismantling—at least for the moment—the Gomecista system of political prisons, which were infamous as sites not only of torture and political repression, but also of predatory corruption. Political prisoners were released soon after Gómez's death, and prison officials and their properties were attacked by crowds, but popular sentiment demanded more. On January 2, 1936, the government announced that La Rotunda, the main political prison in Caracas, would be torn down.[36] Before its demolition, authorities allowed the public to enter and see the dreaded facility for themselves. A month later, López Contreras authorized a ceremony at the equally notorious Castillo prison in Puerto Cabello. Fifteen tons of chains, leg irons, and instruments of torture were loaded onto a barge, taken away from shore, and thrown into the sea. Hundreds of people watched from shore, where Andrés Eloy Blanco, the poet and former political prisoner, made a speech to mark the occasion.[37] The significance of these acts went beyond the destruction of hated instruments of state power. Venezuelans' fear of imprisonment had loomed so large in Gómez's psychological hold over the population that López Contreras's apparent repudiation of this aspect of Gomecismo added to the sense of a rupture with the past.

López Contreras was slower to comply with popular sentiment in favor of nationalizing Gómez's fortune, though in the end he reluctantly agreed. Calls for the confiscation of the late dictator's wealth became widespread after his death, but López Contreras initially balked at the measure, partly because he hesitated to label his former chief as corrupt but also due to fear of a backlash from Gómez's clan. He allowed more than ninety of the General's relatives to leave Venezuela soon after his death, despite objections that the wealth they took with them rightfully belonged to the nation.[38] Venezuelan diplomats in London informed their hosts that some of the Gómez clan fled to avoid financial claims made against them by victims of Gómez's predatory practices.[39] Indeed, one of the arguments in favor of confiscating the late dictator's properties was that a portion of the wealth should be used to settle claims against the dictator by those seeking compensation for unjust imprisonment, torture, and economic harm inflicted through predatory practices. Initially, the government steered these claims into the courts to be adjudicated as individual cases.[40] But throughout the first half of 1936, calls for confiscation continued. ORVE and the PRP called for confiscation not only because Gómez had abused public office to build his fortune, but also in hopes that his estates could be parceled out to peasant cultivators in a land reform program to advance social justice and economic modernization.[41] When, in July and August 1936, López Contreras relented and approved the nationalization of Gómez's assets passed by a Congress packed with former Gomecistas, it was widely understood that he had yielded to public opinion, perhaps to gain additional breathing space as he sparred with the Left.[42] The government would now sell, rent out, or manage the operation of the confiscated properties, and one quarter of their value was set aside to compensate victims of the dictatorship.[43]

By the second half of 1936, then, López Contreras appeared to many Venezuelans to have distanced his government from the corruption of the Gómez era. Not only had he suppressed predatory practices, he also appeared ready to move against the misappropriation of government revenues. His February Program had called for "the scrupulous management of public funds,"[44] and in May 1936 López Contreras allowed his chief prosecutor to initiate legal proceedings against Pedro Manuel Arcaya and other former interior ministers for misuse of Chapter VII funds. In the face of López Contreras's anticorruption initiatives, Betancourt's ORVE and other opposition groups struggled to find political traction against the new president. They found it politically advantageous, especially following his shift to repression in mid-1936, to label his government a continuation of Gomecismo, but López Contreras's moves to curtail Gomecista corruption complicated such critiques.

An editorial published in late November 1936 in *ORVE*, the party's official paper, revealed the opposition's frustration over López Contreras's adroit handling of corruption while he simultaneously declined to advance the deeper economic, political, and social reforms called for by Betancourt and other leaders of the Left. The editorial acknowledged that under López Contreras "the most virulent aspects [of Gomecismo] have disappeared" but asserted that this development had merely resulted in "a kind of innocuous Gomecismo" that left other structures untouched.[45] The editorial ruefully asserted that in a country "where the terms ruler and thief are interchangeable in the popular lexicon" citizens' expectations for their rulers were too low. "There persists in the spirit of every Venezuelan a complex which is difficult to root out, which leads him to adopt an almost thankful attitude toward a ruler for the mere fact that the latter does not take advantage of his power to exploit or abuse. Likewise, the simple occurrence that the national administration has ceased to be an organization dedicated to pillage and peculation is enough to make many [Venezuelans] feel satisfied with the more-or-less normal management of public resources."[46] As the country approached the first anniversary of Gómez's death, many saw López Contreras's reforms as a welcome relief from the relentless predations of the old regime, undercutting support for the Left's larger agenda.

It was only after Lopez Contreras's exile of ORVE and PRP leaders in March 1937 that the Left began to criticize him persistently for corruption, and they did so by focusing on Chapter VII, reinvigorating a debate over the discretionary fund that would continue for more than a decade. Public denunciations of Chapter VII began, as mentioned in the previous chapter, soon after Gómez died—but these early condemnations were directed at the old regime, not López Contreras. For example, an article published in the Caracas newspaper *La Esfera* on January 22, 1936 identified "the famous Chapter VII" as one of the means through which "[a] great and permanent embezzlement of millions of bolivares was made at the expense of the National Treasury in favor of . . . high officials, agents, favorites and hangers-on of the late [Gómez] regime."[47] Similarly, in May 1936, ORVE charged that the dictatorship had spent more through "the famous Chapter VII of Interior Relations, with which Gómez rewarded his buffoons, lackeys, and concubines," than it had on education.[48]

Initially, it appeared that López Contreras's government might reform Chapter VII. The chief prosecutor in the new government, Juan José Abreu, brought a lawsuit in May 1936 against Gómez's heirs, former president Juan Bautista Pérez, and former ministers of interior relations and of the treasury, charging that they had made or received illicit expenditures from Chapter VII totaling over 131 million bolívares during the final ten years of the dictatorship. But hopes that the lawsuit would result in the reform or abolition of Chapter VII fizzled out. The portion of the case targeting Gómez's heirs became mute when the General's fortune was nationalized; José María García, a cousin of Gómez who served as treasury minister, negotiated a settlement in which he forfeited some property; and proceedings against the remaining defendants became bogged down in legal wrangling, providing no definitive verdict on Chapter VII. In 1938, despite López Contreras's shift to the Right, Abreu launched a new lawsuit against Pedro Manuel Arcaya, former minister of interior relations, and Melchor Centeno, former minister of the treasury, for illicit expenditures from Chapter VII under Gómez.[49] Amid this renewed attention to the discretionary fund, the clandestine leftist groups jumped on López Contreras's own use of Chapter VII to argue that he continued this form of Gomecista corruption.

The Partido Democrático Nacional (PDN), an alliance of ORVE and other proscribed groups, attacked López Contreras for using Chapter VII for purposes allegedly indistinguishable from those of the Gómez era. A September 1938 editorial titled "Chapter VII: Udder of Parasites," published in the PDN's periodical, *Izquierdas*, expressed support for Abreu's new suit against Arcaya and Centeno but argued that López Contreras's government continued to make unjustified payments from Chapter VII to its allies. "Between the embezzlement [peculado] of Arcaya and that which we are denouncing [i.e., payments by López Contreras's government]," the editorial asserted, "there is no substantial difference."[50] To support this claim, the editors listed current monthly payments from Chapter VII to various individuals, including former office holders from the Gómez era, journalists (presumably for favorable coverage of López Contreras's government), current members of the Senate and Chamber of Deputies, and a member of the Caracas city council. Various publications by the PDN made briefer references to other forms of alleged corruption in the López Contreras government, including embezzlement of funds in the Ministry of Public Works, bribes paid in exchange for government positions and favors, and local transportation monopolies allegedly created by officials in López Contreras's government and old Gomecistas.[51]

Public attention to Chapter VII grew during the remaining years of López Contreras's presidency, thanks in part to Arcaya's writings on the subject. Although the new suit against him by Abreu was dismissed in 1939 on procedural grounds, Arcaya, a prolific scholar, published two books on Chapter VII during the López Contreras administration (and a third in 1945). One goal of these books was to expose what Arcaya saw as López Contreras's hypocrisy in allowing Abreu to bring charges against him related to Chapter VII. Arcaya noted that López Contreras had received funds from Chapter

VII during the Gómez regime; that López Contreras served in the cabinet when it approved expenditures by the Ministry of Interior Relations, including those from Chapter VII; that Congress had approved Arcaya's accounts; and that López Contreras's administration continued to spend Chapter VII funds in the same ways and for the same purposes as Gómez had done. Moreover, Arcaya argued that even though the amount of money spent through Chapter VII declined under López Contreras, this was only because his administration shifted some expenditures to other accounts. Arcaya charged that López Contreras allowed Abreu to initiate legal proceedings against him for practices that López Contreras perpetuated.[52]

Ironically, the PDN and Arcaya—writing from opposite ends of the political spectrum—agreed that López Contreras continued to practice the same types of discretionary spending as Gómez. But they differed on the question of whether these practices were improper, exemplifying the divided opinions that would swirl around Chapter VII for years. The PDN portrayed López Contreras's expenditures from Chapter VII as illicit gifts of public funds to "parasites" who served him politically in exchange.[53] Similarly, Jóvito Villalba, a leader of the 1928 student protests who was more moderate than the communists or Betancourt and moved in and out of the PDN, opined in 1940 that while López Contreras had greatly curtailed Gomecista corruption, "our famous Chapter VII" was a clear example of ongoing official malfeasance.[54] Arcaya, by contrast, argued that Venezuelan law authorized the president (whether Gómez or López Contreras) to spend discretionary funds however he liked, and that as long as the budgets and expenditures were approved by Congress, they were legal. He claimed that since he had followed Gómez's instructions regarding Chapter VII expenditures, his actions were immune to legal challenge. Arcaya, unlike the PDN and Villalba, saw nothing illicit in López Contreras's use of discretionary funds; rather, he objected to what he saw as López Contreras's cynical inconsistency in allowing his administration to bring charges against him for practices that López Contreras continued.[55]

In truth, López Contreras's use of Chapter VII represented a mix of continuity and real change. He clearly used Chapter VII to funnel government funds to his supporters both inside and outside of government, as well as to many ordinary Venezuelans who approached his administration for personal assistance.[56] His use of the fund to build and maintain a personal political following was not fundamentally different than under Gómez. On the other hand, Gómez's blatant use of Chapter VII to pay his personal and family expenses had no documented parallel under López Contreras. Moreover, López Contreras's administration modified the management of Chapter VII with the goal of limiting abuses. When he received requests for financial assistance, a special section of the government telegraph office investigated petitioners' financial status to gauge their neediness—a new application of bureaucratic surveillance to inform the president's paternalistic benevolence, illustrating the ongoing process of neopatrimonial governance.[57]

In a similar vein, López Contreras's government created a new office in 1938 to audit public expenditures but exempted certain accounts, including Chapter VII, from oversight. The Contraloría General de la Nación (General Comptrollership of the Nation) was intended to implement López Contreras's promise, in his February Program, to prevent illicit uses of government funds. Nevertheless, the legislation that created the Contraloría severely limited its oversight of accounts in the Ministry of War as well as accounts related to national security and "extraordinary expenditures" in the Ministry of Interior Relations, a clear reference to Chapter VII.[58] (Chile's Contraloría, by contrast, was given broader powers when it was established a decade earlier, in 1927.)[59] Gumersindo Torres served as the first director of the new agency and upon taking office he denounced Venezuelan rulers' long tradition of administering the national treasury as though it were their personal estate.[60] But Torres's experience at the Contraloría led to disillusionment. He expressed reservations concerning the types of expenditures exempted from review by his office, the opaque nature of extra salary payments to some government officials, and the lack of resources budgeted for the Contraloría. He found that López Contreras, Medina Angarita (as minister of war under López Contreras), and other officials responded to his office with limited cooperation or passive resistance.[61] Thus while some types of government spending came under enhanced bureaucratic scrutiny, the president retained personal control over expenditures from Chapter VII and similar discretionary accounts, marking another permutation of neopatrimonialism.

In sum, while López Contreras received widespread credit for dismantling *predatory* corruption (public officials' abusive extraction of resources directly from those they governed), the accusations of malfeasance (or of lax anticorruption efforts) in his government centered on *financial* corruption, the misuse of public resources. This distinction between predatory and financial corruption is crucial to understanding López Contreras's political success and stature during the transition. His initiatives against predatory corruption meant that Venezuelans were spared the humiliating submission to monopolies, seizures of properties, and other rapacious hallmarks of the Gómez era. Although accusations of financial malfeasance circulated, they never conveyed the same emotive force as the outcries against predatory corruption under the old regime. As I argued in chapter 4, the emotional economy of anticorruption emerged specifically in response to Gomecista predation. While López Contreras reaped large political gains by curbing predatory corruption, he suffered comparatively little in the court of public opinion from accusations of financial corruption leveled by his opponents.

As a consequence, many Venezuelans experienced López Contreras's rule as a welcome relief from the day-to-day degradation of the Gómez era, despite his crackdown on the Left and his failure to implement much of his February Program. López Contreras referred to this shift in the relationship between the state and society when he reviewed his presidency at the end of his term in 1941. "I have upheld the dignity of the Republic and that of my fellow citizens," he asserted in his farewell address. "I take pride in declaring that passion has never led me to harm the lives, the honor, or the material interests of my countrymen."[62] Some of Gómez's most implacable foes argued more directly that López Contreras's ending of ubiquitous predation had rescued the nation from humiliation. Rufino Blanco Fombona, a prominent anti-Gómez intellectual, praised López Contreras in the press as he left office, reminding readers that the Gómez dictatorship had been a "horrifying regime of blood and peculation" during which Venezuelans were "humiliated by our nationality. . . . Everything was at the mercy of the dictator." He believed López Contreras "returned to us our confiscated dignity, our trampled rights, our freedom of opinion and our right to look other men in the eyes without lowering our gaze."[63] This trope of López Contreras restoring dignity to a nation degraded by Gómez became ingrained in Venezuelan public discourse, often overshadowing his moves to limit political participation and social reform. In his narrative of Venezuelan political history published in 1999, former president Rafael Caldera, after reviewing the corruption and oppression of the Gómez era, credited López Contreras with leading Venezuela from its "humiliating situation" in 1935 toward "modernity."[64]

Medina Angarita, 1941–45

Public discussion of corruption, already more open under López Contreras than under Gómez, became even freer under the former's handpicked successor. Isaías Medina Angarita's presidency was marked by an expansion of political and civil liberties, reflecting the enthusiasm for democracy in much of the Americas during World War II. The new administration allowed opposition parties, including Betancourt's Acción Democrática (AD; Democratic Action), to organize. Medina Angarita even cooperated with the communists, and eventually permitted the creation of the Partido Comunista de Venezuela (PCV; Venezuelan Communist Party), alienating many of his conservative supporters, including López Contreras. The press enjoyed considerable freedom and Congress became a site for debating sensitive issues, including corruption. The new president's cultivation of a populist political style, as he connected with the public through radio and public events across the country, raised hopes for fundamental changes in the political system. Indeed, Medina Angarita achieved some significant reforms, including the nation's first income tax and, most notably, a new petroleum law that aimed both to ensure the Venezuelan state a 50 percent share of annual oil profits and to put a definitive end to the granting of concessions to private individuals, which López Contreras had suspended in 1938.[65] Despite these reforms, however, the bedrock structures of political power remained largely unaltered. Authority was still concentrated in the hands of the president, voting in national elections continued to be restricted to literate males, and the constitution dictated that presidents were chosen by Congress rather than directly by voters, which virtually permitted the incumbent executive to select his successor.

Medina Angarita faced challenges from three groups who objected to his perpetuation of a personalist system of power that impeded the establishment of a more modern state based on universal suffrage and bureaucratic principles of technical expertise and individual merit. The first of these groups was AD, founded in 1941 by Betancourt, the novelist Rómulo Gallegos, and other predominantly middle-class reformers, many of them veterans of ORVE. The second group were young military officers whose careers, despite their technocratic abilities, were still obstructed by the lingering influence of Gomecista officers without professional training. A third group of critics were the journalists at *La Esfera*, led by editor Ramón David León, an independent conservative whose critique of Medina Angarita increasingly resembled AD's and circulated widely among the middle and upper classes. Betancourt and other AD leaders pioneered the anticorruption discourse directed at Medina Angarita, but by 1944 dissident military officers and *La Esfera* had come to share AD's view that the president used corruption to maintain a personalist political system. The spread of this discourse denouncing corruption as an entrenched obstacle to modernity contributed to the 1945 coup and to AD's belief that holding Andean officials accountable for corruption would pay political dividends.

Medina Angarita came to the presidency in 1941 with the support of many of the same young officers he would eventually disappoint, who initially saw him as a supporter of their hopes to modernize the army and Venezuela's political institutions.[66] Medina Angarita had graduated from the military academy in 1914 and became minister of war under López Contreras. Among the groups López Contreras consulted when choosing his successor to be elected by Congress, Medina Angarita emerged as a compromise choice. His military record and his identity as a native of Táchira placated Gomecistas, while his professionalism, youth, and reputedly liberal disposition relative to other possible candidates fed the hopes of those who, like the younger officers, longed to accelerate the pace of change. In his speech upon taking office, Medina Angarita promised to advance the creation of a "modern state," to "conquer definitively all the norms of true democracy," and to end corruption. Addressing the need for "administrative probity" in fiscal management, the new president promised that "peculation will not occur in Venezuela because I am determined to apply the inflexible rigor of the Law to those charged with such an opprobrious crime."[67] Medina Angarita's detractors rarely missed an opportunity to remind their audiences of this early pledge.

As under López Contreras, critics of corruption viewed Chapter VII as a perpetuation of Gomecista malfeasance. A congressional debate in late May 1941, shortly after Medina Angarita's inauguration, encapsulated opposing views of the discretionary fund.[68] When the

Chamber of Deputies considered the government's spending request for Chapter VII of the budget of the Ministry of Interior Relations, opposition deputy Ricardo Montilla of Guárico (a future AD official[69]) proposed cutting half the funds proposed and using them to aid the livestock industry instead. Montilla and his allies refrained from explicit accusations of corruption and instead advocated for cuts by criticizing the absence of any specified purpose for the Chapter VII funds, which they noted had customarily been used to pay "political pensions."[70] The legislators maintained a genteel tone, but both supporters and critics of Montilla's proposal referred to Medina Angarita's promise to end "peculation," a clear indication of the stakes in the debate. In opposing Montilla's proposal and defending the discretionary nature of Chapter VII, deputy Manuel Vicente Tinoco argued that Venezuela could not be ruled effectively without a presidential discretionary fund because, he claimed, "We Venezuelans all have Chapter VII in our blood," a reference to what Tinoco saw as an ingrained clientelistic political culture.[71] Presenting Chapter VII as necessary to political stability, Tinoco concluded that Congress should trust Medina Angarita's recent pledge to administer public funds honestly. Montilla countered by noting that the president's promise to end peculation was one of the most loudly applauded sections of his inauguration speech, suggesting that this sentiment justified trimming Chapter VII. In a humorous jab at Tinoco's pronouncement, Montilla quipped that while all Venezuelans might have Chapter VII in their blood, only some were fortunate enough to have it in their pockets.[72] Despite the witticism, Montilla's proposal to cut Chapter VII was defeated, and Congress approved the requested funding without change.[73]

AD continued its relentless attacks on Chapter VII. Speaking at the party's founding ceremony in September 1941, Betancourt declared that in order to "moralize and sanitize administrative practice" in Venezuela it was imperative that "Chapter VII should pass to the category of a frightening dream, an unpleasant recollection in the popular memory."[74] Such condemnations of the discretionary fund reflected AD leaders' desire to position their party as the national leader in fighting corruption. In August 1942, while applauding Medina Angarita for prosecuting one of his own officials for embezzling 85,000 bolívares, AD's newspaper reminded readers that *adecos* (AD members) were the ones who "have been clamoring inflexibly against peculation in all its forms; who have opened public judgment against Chapter VII and other administrative leakages [of money]; who have repeatedly affirmed that moralizing the management of national, state, and municipal funds is the starting point for any government project to achieve widespread change."[75] The new party never tired of calling attention to Chapter VII. Even while cooperating with Medina Angarita to draft legislation establishing the nation's first income tax, AD noted its dilemma in providing increased revenue to a government that used Chapter VII.[76] More typically, AD rhetoric offered full-throated condemnations of the slush fund, as when in 1944 Betancourt accused Medina Angarita's newly organized party, the Partido Democrático Venezolano (PDV), of using "that inexhaustible vein of gold, that clinking money-box [*alcancía tintineante*] of bolívares, which is called Chapter VII" to fund its partisan electoral campaigns and maintain Andeans' grip on power.[77] Such broad denunciations of Chapter VII made no distinctions between licit and illicit uses of the fund and ignored past payments to some AD members and their families.

The most meaningful change in public anticorruption discourse under Medina Angarita was the emergence of a critique of official malfeasance from the political Right which, by mid-1945, closely paralleled AD's criticisms. *La Esfera*, the conservative anti–Medina Angarita newspaper, was eventually credited with contributing to the downfall of his government.[78] Ramón David León, who served as editor of the paper from its founding in 1927 until 1957, may have initially become disenchanted with Medina Angarita because he allowed the Communist Party to organize and operate openly, but *La Esfera*'s widely read editorials, which León wrote or supervised, increasingly decried the government's financial corruption. León also exercised significant influence through his frequent conversations with young military officers. According to Ana Mercedes Pérez, a pioneering journalist at *La Esfera*, the officers regularly visited the paper's headquarters, seeking León's political guidance.[79]

La Esfera informed its readers that government corruption had become entrenched in Venezuela around the middle of the nineteenth century but intensified around 1900 as the Andeans led by Castro and Gómez settled into power.[80] Although López Contreras "humanized" and "dignified"[81] the government, corruption remained a widespread problem about which "men of good will" constantly complained, and which the Contraloría and the Ministry of the Treasury seemed unable to halt.[82] *La Esfera* argued that officials in Medina Angarita's government engaged in a variety of forms of financial malfeasance, including overpayments for public works and other contracts; the sale of properties confiscated from Gómez at low prices, presumably to political insiders; the payment of salaries for nonexistent government personnel; and—in an apparent reference to Chapter VII—"the subterranean channeling of national riches to private coffers."[83] Suggesting that Venezuela's political system "facilitates robbery," *La Esfera* called for "heroic remedies."[84] Like AD, *La Esfera* linked corruption to personalism and to Venezuela's limited democracy: "We have constantly preached against personalist influence in our government, which converts the Nation into a fiefdom for the benefit of men in the high levels of the Executive [branch of government]; . . . against the shameful graft that provides us with the surprising spectacle of those favored by Chapter VII suddenly converted into powerful individuals; [and] against the political-military dominance of a group that has wrongfully converted the Presidency of the Republic into a regional monopoly."[85]

Linkages among personalism, limited democracy, and corruption emerged most powerfully in condemnations of Medina Angarita's use of presidential patronage to maintain his control over Congress. AD and *La Esfera* condemned Medina Angarita for giving salaried government jobs to members of the legislature who did his bidding, thus undermining the separation of powers. As a remedy, they supported legislation to establish the principle of "incompatibility," which would ban members of the national legislature from holding additional public positions throughout their term of office. AD, which had raised the issue of incompatibility as early as 1942, charged in 1944 that Medina Angarita's use of government jobs and Chapter VII payments to reward obedient legislators at the end of each congressional session constituted a "corrupting practice" (*práctica corruptora*).[86]

Condemnations of Medina Angarita's personal hold over legislators came to a head in mid-1945 when the president's loyalists blocked passage of the Law Against the Illicit Enrichment of Public Functionaries and Employees. This anticorruption legislation, drawn up by a commission that included AD deputy Andrés Eloy Blanco, was endorsed by the conservative *La Esfera*. Its front-page editorial on July 10 argued that the proposal reflected "the opinion of the national community: it is urgent to end embezzlement [peculado]."[87] Nevertheless, the legislation was defeated when on July 16, 1945, the presiding officer in the Senate declared that a majority of senators voted against it. Opposition lawmakers and journalists in the gallery responded with raucous cries that a majority of senators physically present had voted *in favor* of the law. *La Esfera* published a lengthy article detailing the procedural chicanery used by senators belonging to Medina Angarita's PDV to defeat the law.[88] The following day, it ran an editorial charging that the anticorruption measure failed to win approval because "the majority of senators and deputies are at the same time employees of the executive branch of the regime due to the 'compatibility' defended by the PDV."[89] *La Esfera*'s coverage, no less than AD's denunciations, portrayed Medina Angarita's administration as perpetuating personalist control over the state behind a veneer of gradual political liberalization.

Junior military officers conspiring to overthrow Medina Angarita had already reached similar conclusions. The officers who formed the secret Unión Patriótica Militar (UPM; Patriotic Military Union) believed that both their promotions and the modernization of the armed forces were delayed by the continuing influence of Gomecista military leaders whom Medina Angarita had declined to dislodge. Moreover, the young officers' economic circumstances continued to deteriorate. Consumer prices shot up 50 percent under Medina Angarita, but officers' salaries rose only 12 percent, obliging some to live with their parents or to use the free medical clinic sponsored by *La Esfera* as a community service.[90] Adding to their frustration, they believed their commanders garnered extra income by skimming money from their budgets or by receiving special stipends, similar to Chapter VII payments, through the Ministry of War, which remained exempt from oversight by the Contraloría.[91]

Resentment over their economic situation compared to that of their less-deserving superiors meshed with the young officers' view of the government as a whole. The UPM's founding document declared the officers' commitment to "put an end to the incompetence, the peculation, and the bad faith that guide the actions of our government." The formula for achieving this was to establish "a government based upon the universal and direct vote of the Venezuelan citizenry, a constitutional reform that expresses the national will, and the creation of a truly professional army . . . [in sum] all the political and administrative measures that redound to the progress of our homeland."[92] Even before this document became public, the US ambassador to Venezuela reported that the young officers were "disgusted with [the] peculation of [the] Medina Angarita Government."[93] The UPM's critique of the nation's problems, and its prescription to solve them, aligned with those of AD; the logic of a possible alliance with AD was reinforced by the party's nationwide organization and growing popular base.[94] The leaders of the UPM decided to approach AD leaders to propose that they cooperate in a coup against Medina Angarita, to be followed by a provisional government led by Betancourt that would oversee Venezuela's first direct election of a president based on universal suffrage.

But when the officers met with Betancourt on July 6, 1945, to negotiate AD's participation in a coup, he did not accept.[95] AD leaders hoped that they could reach an accord with Medina Angarita that would lead to the democratic reforms they desired. This seemed achievable when Medina Angarita endorsed Diógenes Escalante, the Venezuelan ambassador to the United States and long-time public servant, as the official candidate for president. AD believed that Escalante would introduce reforms to establish universal adult suffrage, the secret ballot, and direct election of the president, and then step aside after new elections.[96] AD and many others—including the young officers and independent conservatives at *La Esfera*—believed that the establishment of the "universal, direct, and secret vote"[97] was not only the key to democratizing the state but also the precondition for solving a myriad of national problems. Ramón Velásquez, a journalist in the 1940s who later became a leading historian of twentieth-century Venezuela and an AD member of Congress, recalled in the mid-1970s that "all Venezuelans in 1945 . . . thought that once the vote of the majority was respected, Venezuela would do away with all the traditional evils of nepotism, cronyism (*amiguismo*), peculation, the traffic of influences, deceit, and the farce that we attributed exclusively to the oligarchical origin of the successive regimes that had exercised power."[98] This hopeful scenario—which Velásquez, with hindsight, referred to as "beautifully ingenuous"—collapsed when Escalante suffered a health crisis in August 1945.

Escalante's exit from the election created a political opening that appeared to increase the possibility of López Contreras's returning to the presidency. As the only staunch conservative with a realistic opportunity to win election by Congress, López Contreras had gained popularity among many of Medina Angarita's right-wing critics. Even hardline Gomecistas who had clashed with López Contreras during his own limited liberalization in 1935–36 now joined the former president in asserting that Medina Angarita's liberalization, especially his cooperation with the Communists, had gone too far.[99] Medina Angarita, alarmed by López Contreras's momentum, announced that he would use all the means at his disposal to block López Contreras's election by Congress.[100] Then, following weeks of speculation about a new PDV candidate, Medina Angarita chose little-known Ángel Biaggini, his Minister of Agriculture. Biaggini lacked the national reputation and stature expected of a future president and, if elected by Congress, would owe his position entirely to Medina Angarita, allowing the outgoing president to perpetuate his control.[101] In response, rumors of an imminent coup by López Contreras intensified. Medina Angarita and his former mentor appeared to be locked in a personal struggle for power, not unlike the caudillos of a supposedly bygone age.[102] With hopes for peaceful democratization in tatters, AD joined the conspiracy with officers in the UPM to overthrow Medina Angarita before Congress could elect his successor.

Betancourt underscored the theme of corruption when he addressed a rally of supporters on the evening of October 17, 1945. Privately aware that the coup was imminent, he told his audience that official malfeasance constituted a major obstacle to realizing the nation's democratic aspirations. After a brief but biting reference to Chapter VII—which drew applause—he asserted that "the flourishing of peculation, which has characterized the administration of Medina Angarita," was one cause of the crisis enveloping national politics.[103] As he concluded his speech, Betancourt reiterated AD's promise to build a modern state free of corruption: "We will struggle in favor of the technical expertise and morality of public administration, against peculation, against the illicit enrichment of public functionaries, against the use of political influence for personal ends."[104] This was, in effect, AD's closing argument against Medina Angarita's government.

The next day, October 18, 1945, military units led by junior officers and supported by AD overthrew Medina Angarita. The coup was far from bloodless, with approximately 400 casualties, but the struggle was surprisingly brief in comparison to Venezuela's previous violent changes of government. Medina Angarita, considered a popular president for much of his term, surrendered only twenty-four hours after the uprising began. The forty-six-year era in which Venezuela was ruled by military men from Táchira had come to a sudden end.[105]

Gomecismo's distinct legacies of widely condemned predatory corruption and ambiguous financial corruption shaped the post-Gómez transition. The popular protests of late 1935 and early 1936, fueled by humiliation and outrage against the dictatorship's predation, constituted the most dramatic, widespread rejection of corruption in the nation's history. They provided leverage for López Contreras to marginalize Gomecista strongmen and end their hated monopolies, and also paved the way for the nationalization of Gómez's properties. Taken together, the protests and López Contreras's reforms marked corruption as a terrain for the negotiation of rule by reshaping the relationship between the state and society. Although López Contreras's political liberalization proved to be decidedly limited as he cracked down on the Left in 1936–37, his moves to end predatory corruption contributed to many Venezuelans' sense that his presidency represented a meaningful rupture with the past rather than a continuation of Gomecismo. López Contreras's suspension of petroleum concessions to private individuals, and the end of such concessions in Medina Angarita's 1943 oil legislation, signaled another step away from the profiteering of the Gómez era.

In contrast to these changes, both López Contreras and Medina Angarita continued to distribute large sums of money through Chapter VII and similar accounts. Betancourt and AD led the way in criticizing Chapter VII during the post-Gómez decade, and under Medina Angarita *La Esfera* and the young officers joined in sketching a dichotomy between financial corruption and political modernity. Thus, Chapter VII became a widely recognized—though still contested—symbol of personalism and financial malfeasance. For the opponents of López Contreras and Medina Angarita who sought to portray them as perpetuators of an inherently corrupt system of Gomecista rule, criticism of Chapter VII was not only convenient but necessary, since other prominent forms of Gomecista corruption had been curtailed or eliminated.

Both the end of endemic predatory corruption and the continuation of Chapter VII payments shaped the politics of the decade, but the divergent effects of these developments illuminate Venezuelans' distinct evaluations of these two forms of malfeasance. The goodwill generated by López Contreras's willingness to dismantle monopolies and political prisons allowed him to negotiate a path through the political minefield of the early post-Gómez transition despite his continued use of Chapter VII. Simply put, the new president's moves against predatory corruption in 1935–36 did more to legitimize his rule than the continuation of financial malfeasance through Chapter VII did to undermine it. Criticisms of Chapter VII never included the visceral outcries that characterized opposition to predatory corruption. Similarly, the presidential discretionary fund, unlike Gomecista predation, never lacked defenders. Attacks on Chapter VII only gathered political momentum when Medina Angarita's mishandling of the political transition in 1945 demonstrated the limits of personalist politics and his opponents seized the opportunity to tie Chapter VII to a broader critique of his regime. The extent to which opposition to financial corruption, in and of itself, had undermined support for Medina Angarita among the wider public was by no means certain. But such caveats did not weigh heavily, if at all, on AD leaders and the young officers as they basked in their victory over Medina Angarita and López Contreras in October 1945. At that moment, the modernist ideal of building a democratic state free of corruption—a project that encompassed both heartfelt idealism and political calculation—inspired them as they set about the task.

CHAPTER 7
THE CORRUPTION TRIALS, PUBLIC OPINION, AND THE MIDDLE CLASS

The young officers who led the 1945 coup installed Rómulo Betancourt as president of a revolutionary junta that would govern until elections could be held under a new constitution to be drafted by an elected assembly. While some positions in this interim government went to military officers, political independents, and others outside AD, it was an AD-dominated regime, organized to pursue the party's reformist agenda. The junta's earliest proclamations announced its intention to establish a new democracy based on universal suffrage and direct elections; to create a modern bureaucratic state free of personalism and corruption; and to develop the economy for the benefit of all Venezuelans. To underscore their dedication to national advancement rather than personal ambition, Betancourt and the other junta members pledged that none of them would seek the presidency in the first elections to be held under a new charter.[1]

The government moved quickly to apply revolutionary justice to officials deemed to have engaged in corruption during the regimes of Gómez, López Contreras, and Medina Angarita. On October 22, only four days after the uprising against Medina Angarita, the junta announced the creation of a commission to decide which former officials would have their financial assets frozen pending trials for improper enrichment.[2] A week later, President Betancourt laid out the justification for corruption trials in a speech that reiterated the themes he and other AD leaders had articulated for years. López Contreras, Medina Angarita, and their allies, he charged, had perpetuated Gómez's "personalist" regime; they had "persisted in considering Venezuela their fiefdom"; and they had betrayed the public trust by "enriching themselves illicitly and trafficking with the collective patrimony."[3] Just as corruption had contributed to AD's indictment of the old regime before the coup, punishment of past malfeasance was now considered essential to the establishment of a democratic state. "The basic goal of our movement," Betancourt announced, "is to liquidate, once and for all, the vices of administration, the corruption [*peculado*], and the system of personalist and autocratic imposition" that characterized the past four decades. To this end, former officials would be obliged to explain the origin of their fortunes to a special tribunal organized by "the Government of the People" and suffer confiscation of their property if they were found to have used public office for private gain.[4] The provisional government established new measures to prevent and punish future malfeasance,[5] but throughout the three-year period of AD rule known as the *trienio* (1945–48) public discussion of corruption focused on the 167 trials of former officials from governments led by Gómez, López Contreras, and Medina Angarita.

The corruption trials garnered extensive and often enthusiastic support early in the trienio, and some *adecos* (AD members) never wavered in their defense of the proceedings. By the end of March 1946, however, public opinion had swung so decisively against the trials that they contributed to the November 1948 overthrow of AD's government. What caused this dramatic reversal of public support for AD's campaign to punish official malfeasance? Historians have argued that the shift to public disapproval resulted from the partisanship and arbitrary actions of the anticorruption tribunal.[6] But these factors provide only a partial explanation. An examination of the specific controversies aroused by the prosecution of different types of corruption yields additional insights into how and why AD's anticorruption campaign ran afoul of Venezuelan attitudes toward the use of public office for private gain during this era of rapid political and social change.

This chapter argues that the distinction between widely condemned predatory corruption and ambiguous financial corruption—both of which were prosecuted in the trials—shaped reactions to the proceedings. Significantly, convictions for predatory corruption were applauded and accepted as valid throughout the trienio, while prosecutions for mishandling public financial assets provoked the most strident opposition to the trials. The broad acceptance of convictions for predatory corruption signaled that Venezuelans had not forgotten the humiliation and hardship imposed through the abusive profiteering of the Gómez regime, which, as we have seen, constituted an especially salient aspect of middle-class experience during the dictatorship. In contrast, numerous convictions for making or receiving payments from Chapter VII proved extremely controversial. Indeed, prosecutions related to Chapter VII—the fund that had provided a safety net to some middle-class families—led to ever more outcries against the trials. Especially damaging to AD were criticisms that some prosecutions, especially those related to Chapter VII, intruded grievously into the private sphere of the family. The ensuing erosion of support for the trials appeared to be concentrated within the middle class. AD's claim that ending corruption would usher in political modernity had been tailor-made to appeal to this group's aspirations and self-image, so this loss of middle-class approval dealt a devasting blow to the party's anticorruption campaign.

Changes in the Venezuelan middle class around the time of the trienio, and the rising contestation of proper boundaries between the public and private spheres, provide vital context for understanding the controversies aroused by the trials. The middle class stood at the nexus of social and political transformations that, taken together, called into question traditional conceptions of appropriate boundaries between the public and private spheres, complicating consensus on issues of corruption, which relied on a common understanding of the division between public and private interests. AD's anticorruption campaign required agreement regarding the public-private divide for two purposes central to building public support for the prosecution of official malfeasance. First, a broad consensus regarding the line between the two spheres was necessary for agreement on the identification of corrupt actions that deserved punishment, since corruption involved the use of public power for private benefit. As this chapter demonstrates, debates over public-private boundaries plagued the trials, especially by provoking disagreement over whether certain uses of Chapter VII served public or private interests.

Second, as historian Benjamin Smith has argued in the context of Mexico during the mid-twentieth century, investigations of corruption could easily become fraught with difficulties because they required intrusion into the private sphere of home and family, a space culturally defined as feminine and therefore outside the traditional realm of politics.[7] The corruption trials of the trienio, however, occurred as Venezuelan women gained the right to vote and hold public office and as the stigma on middle-class women working outside the home began to relax, developments that challenged but by no means ended the customary, highly gendered division between public and private spheres. AD's drive to prosecute corruption reflected party leaders' belief that public opinion would tolerate a degree of intrusion across this formerly sacrosanct boundary for the sake of ending official malfeasance. But as the trials unfolded, the perceived trespass of investigators and prosecutors into the private domain of the family, which often impinged upon defendants' female kin, gave rise to protests that the anticorruption campaign came at too high a cost and was driven by AD's hatred of its foes. Moreover, most intrusions into the realm of home and family occurred in prosecutions for Chapter VII payments, undermining AD's attempt to persuade the public that this form of ambiguous corruption truly deserved punishment. An understanding of Venezuelans' divided and shifting reactions to the trials, therefore, requires consideration of the social changes that lay behind the increasing contestation of public-private boundaries.

Changes in gender roles were concentrated in the middle class and inextricably intertwined with diverging opinions regarding the division between the two spheres. The middle class grew significantly from the mid-1920s onward as oil wealth expanded white collar jobs in the public bureaucracy and the commercial sector.[8] It was only after the death of Gómez, however, that changes in women's lives began to challenge assumptions about the division between a supposedly masculine public sphere and a private, more feminine sphere of the home and family. The stigma experienced by women who engaged in paid labor outside the home began to recede in the late 1930s and through the 1940s, as both the state and large commercial firms needed women's labor and as World War II–era inflation squeezed family finances.[9] Along with secretarial and clerical jobs, women moved into higher-paid professions, such as medicine, architecture, and journalism, in increasing numbers. One law student interviewed in the 1940s declared that she and other boundary-crossing women began to "invade" the national university in 1937 as a means of achieving "intellectual and economic liberation."[10] Middle-class women mobilized for voting rights in the 1930s, and Medina Angarita permitted literate women to vote in local elections, but only with a decree by Betancourt in 1946 did all women and men over the age of eighteen gain the right to vote in national elections, a right confirmed in the 1947 constitution.[11] AD included some prominent female organizers and activists, but political leadership and office-holding remained overwhelmingly male. Alterations to Venezuela's patriarchal society remained limited, but shifts were tangible enough to reveal growing disagreements over traditional ideas of putatively separate public and private spheres.

Some of the most publicized controversies touching on the gendered nature of this divide had no direct connection to the corruption trials but nonetheless shed light on the divided attitudes toward social change that conditioned reactions to AD's anticorruption campaign. In a 1948 cause célèbre, for example, public opinion split over the trial of middle-class office worker Ligia Parra Jahn, who was put on trial for murdering her lover after he reneged on a promise of marriage and abandoned her and their unborn child. No one doubted that Parra Jahn committed the murder, for she shot the man in front of witnesses in the office where she and he had met. The controversy centered instead on the question of whether men alone should have the right to defend family honor, as the law (which dated from the 1870s) said, or whether women (now more active in the public sphere) should have that right as well.[12] Such debates reflected disagreement over the broader question of whether women's increasing participation in the public world of business and government had rendered traditional gender roles obsolete along with the old understandings of private and public domains to which they were joined.

Diverging attitudes toward the proper boundary between public and private spheres also revealed themselves in response to AD policies that granted greater prerogatives to the state as it pursued social and economic modernization. One of the most controversial of AD's initiatives was a 1946 decree to increase regulation of private schools, which were almost all Catholic. AD's opponents claimed that the decree violated the rights of parents to raise their children—to educate them and to shape their values—as they wished. The defenders of private schools, including middle-class families who viewed these institutions as markers of social status, won a temporary victory when Catholic opposition obliged Betancourt to suspend the decree.[13] Such developments suggested that many in the middle class did not unequivocally accept AD's claim that the pursuit of modernity justified state intrusion into matters long considered to be within the private domain of the family.[14] Contestation of the boundary between the state and the family during an era of dramatic social and political change added to the potential pitfalls in AD's crusade to punish corruption.

Early Reaction to the Anticorruption Campaign: Broad Support and Underlying Apprehension

In their reporting and commentary on the trials, Venezuelan newspapers often claimed to articulate "public opinion," but in a society with a literacy rate of 44 percent in 1946, we may assume that journalism both reflected and influenced opinion primarily among the middle class.[15] Walter Dupouy, a public intellectual who completed a report on the Venezuelan middle class for the Pan-American Union in 1949, posited a significant association between middle-class identity and newspaper readership. He claimed that in 1946 seventeen newspapers in eight Venezuelan cities produced a combined daily run of 242,750 copies, a number that he took into account in his calculation of the size of the nation's middle class, which he assumed constituted much of the market.[16] Not only was the middle class an important consumer of printed news and commentary, it also played a disproportionate role in its production, as journalism was a largely middle-class profession.[17]

The two papers that provided the most consistent coverage and commentary on the trials, *El Universal* and *La Esfera*, provide much of the documentary basis for this chapter. Both were Caracas dailies that circulated across the country. The moderately conservative *El Universal*, with the largest daily run of any Venezuelan paper at 35,000 copies, provided "the most balanced" coverage of trienio politics, according to one leading scholar of the history of Venezuelan journalism.[18] *La Esfera* published only 5,000 copies a day but enjoyed outsized influence due to its widely read editorials, which were written or supervised by its editor, Ramón David León, the independent conservative who crafted the paper's attacks on corruption in Medina Angarita's government. León was popular among the young, middle-class officers who carried out the 1945 coup, some of whom would have supported him for president had he chosen to run.[19] According to the journalist and author Ana Mercedes Pérez, who worked at *La Esfera* in the 1940s, many of the officers frequented the newspaper's office and often conversed with León.[20] Both of these influential dailies shifted from endorsing the corruption trials to severely criticizing them, matching the decline in public support documented in other sources.

The government's announcement of its intention to hold corruption trials garnered strong endorsements in the press, even while the rules to be followed in the proceedings remained uncertain. As early as October 24, 1945, an editorial in *La Esfera* denounced "the orgy of peculation" that it said had characterized Venezuela's government for many years, and welcomed the prospect of prosecuting not only high-ranking officials guilty of corruption but also the intermediaries and underlings who facilitated the higher-ups' enrichment.[21] Only six days later, it published an opinion column that congratulated the government on its willingness to prosecute corruption, which it described as "that cancer which has always corroded the public treasury" and "the bloodiest scourge that has lashed Venezuela."[22] Readers of *El Universal* found similar endorsements, including the sweeping claim that AD's intention to hold trials "has the unanimous backing of the people because the struggle against corruption [peculado] constitutes one of their most sincere longings."[23]

The move to prosecute corruption received a major boost when, in early November, Rafael Caldera agreed to join the government as attorney general (*procurador general*) and endorsed the proposed trials.[24] Caldera, who had entered politics in 1936 as a Catholic student leader and established the moderately conservative National Action Party, enjoyed a national reputation as an expert on legal matters. His decision to join the government was especially noteworthy because of his past rivalry with Betancourt and his allies. But in late 1945 and into early 1946 (i.e., before AD's decree on education), he endorsed the goals of the new government and called on his followers to join in achieving them. Caldera's backing of the revolution of 1945 and the corruption trials signaled support from the moderately conservative middle class early in the trienio and probably reflected the belief (or at least the hope) that the officers who had placed AD in power would prevent any initiatives driven by excessive sectarianism or ideological zeal.

Upon joining the government in November 1945, Caldera explained to the press why he believed the corruption trials should be held in a special tribunal not bound by existing laws or rules of judicial procedure.[25] The idea of such an ad hoc tribunal, which had been discussed for days in government circles and the press,[26] reflected the belief that self-interested members of the old regime had crafted laws to shield themselves from prosecution. For example, Gómez-era constitutions had granted government officials broad powers to seize private property or violate other rights whenever they deemed it necessary for "the conservation or reestablishment of peace,"[27] which could protect defendants from prosecution for predatory profiteering. Similarly, existing laws established a ten-year statute of limitations on prosecutions for embezzling public funds.[28] Caldera explained that such provisions created unacceptable obstacles to punishing corruption in ordinary legal proceedings. He also voiced support for reversing the burden of proof; that is, those accused of corruption would have to explain the legal origin of their wealth, and failure to do so could contribute to a conviction. Caldera's endorsement of an extraordinary tribunal coincided, perhaps by design, with the government's announcement of its intention to organize the corruption trials on this basis.[29] Moreover, following these announcements, other men deemed to be political moderates or conservatives accepted positions in the government,[30] suggesting that they, too, found AD's aggressive approach to corruption to be acceptable. Caldera's declaration that "No one can deny the necessity of punishing acts of corruption [peculado]"[31] conveyed a sense that, even outside AD, there was broad agreement that the extent of official malfeasance justified extraordinary measures to prosecute it.

Engagement with these issues extended beyond governing elites. During those heady days of November 1945, corruption became the talk of the town, at least in Caracas, but probably elsewhere as well. According to *El Universal*, "in the press, in the street, and in many public hallways, everything related to embezzlement [of public funds] is being discussed and debated with great interest and zeal."[32] Some of this interest was probably nervous apprehension. One former official who had taken a stand against financial corruption in the López Contreras administration confided to US diplomats that "the network of graft and special privilege in Venezuela [before the coup] had been such that ninety per cent of those who had had any connection with the Government would be affected if an attempt were made to prosecute everybody who is tainted in any way."[33] Journalists stoked popular interest and anxiety surrounding the trials by insisting that the government publicize its lists of individuals who had received payments from Chapter VII.

These demands from journalists should not have come as a surprise to the government as it organized the trials, because AD leaders had continued to denounce Chapter VII since taking power. Soon after the coup, as Betancourt moved into the presidential office, he found in Medina Angarita's desk several orders for Chapter VII funds to be given to military officers, including Medina Angarita's nephew, and he instinctively interpreted these as evidence of corruption, according to the US ambassador.[34] Days later, in his speech of October 30, Betancourt announced that the government had abolished Chapter VII and similar discretionary funds. In his usual pugnacious style, Betancourt referred to these accounts as "hidden drains through which many millions of bolívares flowed into the private patrimony of the friends and beneficiaries [*usufructuarios*] of the regime."[35] The new government, he pledged, would teach the nation "how one can administer the public treasury without confusing it with private wealth." Missing from such sharp dichotomies was any recognition that some Chapter VII funds had gone to middle class or needy families in moments of financial stress, rather than to wealthy regime insiders.

Valmore Rodríguez, the new minister of interior relations and an experienced journalist himself, responded skillfully to newspapers' demands. Nevertheless, he also acknowledged that Chapter VII had a decidedly more nuanced history than Betancourt implied. The ministry allowed journalists to review the lists of Chapter VII recipients but warned that they would be liable if they used the information in a way "that harms the reputation of honorable persons," a characterization of some recipients that seemed at odds with Betancourt's rhetoric. The ministry's rationale was that "alongside the many beneficiaries who evidently received illicit disbursements from this account, there appear many names of honorable persons, of old and meritorious servants of the State, of widows, orphans and poor students, on whose reputations it would be unjust for any suspicion of wrongdoing to fall."[36] This balance between the public's right to information and the government's duty to protect families' dignity won some praise in the press. *El Universal* editorialized that while "we all hope justice will be done" in prosecuting corruption, it would be unacceptable for "the shortcomings, errors, necessities and weaknesses of thousands of citizens and their families to be brought to light publicly for the morbid delight of others who have nothing to lose."[37] Chapter VII and similar accounts "belong to an era that we all long to see liquidated once and for all," the paper reasoned, but the deserving recipients of these funds should not be punished for "the imperfect organization of social assistance" that prevailed at the time. The ministry and the country's largest newspaper, then, agreed that some Chapter VII payments were (probably) illicit while other payments had gone to worthy recipients—individuals whose honorable character, it seemed to be agreed, would be evident to any reasonable observer.

As the government moved ahead with its organization of the trials, public discussion continued to focus on Chapter VII and new controversies emerged. On November 10, the government announced an initial list (later expanded) of 127 individuals under suspicion of malfeasance whose assets were frozen, and on November 17 another decree ordered the suspects to submit declarations of their assets within fifteen days. Any property omitted from the declarations would be subject to confiscation.[38] Moreover, the second decree created a Substantiating Commission with far-reaching powers to investigate the veracity of the asset declarations as well as the culpability of the accused and anyone "intimately connected" to them.[39] Pedro Manuel Arcaya, who had served as minister of interior relations under Gómez and had vigorously defended his expenditures from Chapter VII, was among those named in these decrees. His son responded by publishing an open letter defending the legality of Chapter VII payments and asking why certain AD leaders, who were rumored to have received payments from the fund, were not under investigation by the commission.[40] The letter gave voice to a question already circulating in Caracas. Many in the capital suspected that the ministry of interior relations' call for discretion in handling the lists of Chapter VII payments had been motivated, in part, by the presence of prominent adecos among the recipients.[41]

One AD leader rumored to be a Chapter VII beneficiary was Andrés Eloy Blanco. He responded by publishing a series of articles in *El Universal* denying that he profited personally from the discretionary fund and recounting the story of his mother's payments from the account. Following the death of Blanco's father (a revered community doctor), a family friend who was a minister in Gómez's cabinet had arranged for Blanco's mother to receive a modest pension to meet basic living expenses.[42] This was precisely the kind of family circumstance that, in the minds of many, justified a Chapter VII pension, and would normally be treated with discretion. Amid the tensions generated by the upcoming trials, however, Blanco felt obliged to disclose the intimate details of his mother's hardship.

Blanco was not alone in feeling compelled to explain his family's association with Chapter VII. Authorities involved in the anticorruption campaign received 724 letters from beneficiaries of the discretionary fund explaining how their personal circumstances qualified them for assistance. In response, investigators were sent to the beneficiaries' homes to ascertain whether their situations justified public support.[43] It was increasingly clear that Venezuelans' perspectives regarding the proper boundary between the public and private realms would influence not only how they understood corruption but also how they would assess whether authorities' investigations of possible malfeasance demonstrated sufficient respect for this boundary. Such questions would swirl around the corruption trials, and especially around cases involving Chapter VII—the epitome of ambiguous corruption—for the remainder of the trienio.

On November 27, the government formally announced the creation of the Jury of Civil and Administrative Responsibility (Jurado de Responsabilidad Civil y Administrativa) and confirmed that it would operate as an ad hoc tribunal. The jury, free from the restraints of ordinary legal proceedings and existing laws, was designed to deliver swift justice. Once it received a report from the Substantiating Commission detailing the assets of one of the accused, the jury would have less than three weeks to carry out its investigation, to hear "explanations and observations"[44] from the accused, and to render a verdict, which required only a simple majority of the seven members. The jury would decide, based on its members' sense of "justice and equity," whether each defendant had committed "acts or deeds" that manipulated the powers or influence of public office for private enrichment.[45] Because the referral of a case to the jury from the Substantiating Commission "established a presumption of illicit enrichment to the detriment of the Nation," the burden of proof would be on the accused.[46] In the event of a conviction, the jury could seize property belonging to defendants or their heirs up to the amount obtained through corrupt means. The confiscations could include any property the defendant had transferred to another owner in an attempt to conceal it from authorities. The jury, however, could not impose prison sentences on those it convicted; rather, its goals were to recover national wealth lost through corruption and to "establish administrative morality."[47] The individuals named to the jury included two little-known lawyers, one of whom would preside, two junior military officers, a priest, and two others, all men.[48]

The Trials Begin, January–March 1946

The jury handed down its first verdicts on January 3, 1946, amid intense public interest in the trials.[49] Support for the jury remained widespread well into February, despite the undercurrents of unease described above. This early sentiment in favor of the trials was probably buoyed in part by the jury's acquittal of roughly one-third of the defendants it tried through mid-February, which may have projected an image of balance and fairness. But the jury also benefited from its convictions of notorious officials believed to have engaged in predatory, abusive practices for personal profit under Gómez. For example, on January 12 it announced the conviction of Hugo Fonseca Rivas, the former jefe civil of Maracay, who had allegedly imprisoned men without justification so that he could force them to work without pay on public sanitation projects while he pocketed the money budgeted to hire workers for the task.[50] Like the wardens of political prisoners, Fonseca Rivas also appropriated funds intended for prisoners' food, according to the jury.

By far the most anticipated and celebrated verdict during this early period was the conviction of General Vincencio Pérez Soto. Referred to as "the hated strongman [caudillo] of the Gómez dictatorship" by one newspaper, Pérez Soto had served as state president of Portuguesa, Apure, Bolívar, Trujillo, and Zulia and was widely believed to have amassed a large fortune.[51] Public interest in the case was so high that the jury's reading of its findings and verdict, lasting two hours, was broadcast live on national radio. The jury found that Pérez Soto had received 342,528 bolívares in unjustified payments from Chapter VII, but its judgment focused largely on more predatory actions. According to the verdict, the strongman had "abused his influence as a public functionary and imposed monopolies, such as a cattle monopoly in the states of Apure and Zulia, which our constitution and laws prohibit,"[52] a reference to the legal guarantees of freedom of industry trampled upon by the Gomecistas. Similarly, Pérez Soto had used his position as state president in Zulia to appropriate public lands and sell them to foreign oil companies, in violation of the rights of Venezuelans who lived and worked on the land.[53] The jury calculated that Pérez Soto's official salaries—that is, his legitimate income—had totaled a little over 900,000 bolívares, but that his total wealth, most of which he had attempted to hide, amounted to well over 15 million bolívares based on the properties' original purchase prices. The jury ordered the confiscation of all Pérez Soto's assets, noting that their current value might be close to 20 million bolívares.[54] The audience packing the jury's chamber interrupted the final verdict twice with prolonged applause, after which "numerous persons warmly embraced the judges [i.e., jury members]" to express their appreciation, according to *El Heraldo*, a Caracas daily.[55]

In the afterglow of this decision, the press continued to provide backing for the trials but, increasingly, the support came with caveats. On February 20, *El Universal* published an opinion column that offered a decidedly positive review of developments since the overthrow of Medina Angarita and claimed broad approval for the new government and for the jury in particular, noting that the corruption trials "absorbed virtually all public attention."[56] But the very next day, the paper published an editorial expressing reservations about some of the jury's work. It granted that "the majority of Venezuelans" still approved of "the mission" of the jury—i.e., the goal of combating corruption—but expressed concern that the jury had decided to pursue prosecutions against some deceased officials from the Gómez era.[57] In the event of a guilty verdict, properties now belonging to the heirs would be confiscated. The prospect of seizing wealth from individuals who had not been convicted of any wrongdoing suggested that the jury might be pursuing "revenge" rather than justice. The editorial implored the jury to reject such a course. "Public opinion," it claimed, "desires that [the jury] should demonstrate the qualities of humanity, reasonableness, and good faith" in the administration of justice. Such a correction would contribute to "national understanding" and the "harmonious advancement" of the country. Implicitly, the editors posited that seizing property from a defendant's innocent heirs would constitute an unjustified intrusion into the realm of the family, a punishment based on ties of kinship.

Two days later, *La Esfera* published an editorial congratulating *El Universal* for capturing the sentiments "that today pulsate in the national soul."[58] The conservative daily agreed that the jury was at risk of giving in to "the pleasure of revenge" by confiscating property belonging to the heirs of corrupt officials. It endorsed prosecutions against living defendants who had used public office to enrich themselves "at the expense of the community's misery," but to punish spouses and children who had lived honorable lives would violate "the collective conscience" and taint the jury's work. Although neither newspaper named specific heirs, the jury had frozen assets belonging to the heirs of Juan Vicente Gómez and his son José Vicente Gómez, as well as the heirs of two deceased Gomecista strongmen, Generals Antonio Pimentel and Félix Galavís. All four were widely regarded to have abused public power for private gain, but the confiscation of property now belonging to their kin would clearly be divisive.

Public approval for the trials had already softened when, in March and April, a series of events rapidly unfolded that swung many observers against AD's anticorruption campaign. These developments amplified misgivings about the jury that were already circulating: that prosecutions for Chapter VII payments might in some cases be unjust; that perhaps the jury intruded too far into the private realm of the home and family; and that the jury might be driven by a thirst for vengeance rather than AD's professed aim of building a modern state based on the principles of bureaucratic expertise and efficiency. Despite the jury's attempt to focus outrage on the misdeeds of past officials, public debate related to corruption was increasingly consumed by the question of whether AD's crusade to punish malfeasance was itself an abuse of power.

Public Opinion Turns Against the Trials

On March 15, 1946, the jury convicted former president Eleazar López Contreras and ordered him to repay the nation 13.4 million bolívares. This sum represented the total amount of funds which, in the jury's view, he had either embezzled for his personal enrichment or otherwise misused for his personal benefit. Of the verdicts issued by the jury through mid-March, the decision against López Contreras stood out for two reasons that went beyond the amount of money he was ordered to repay. First, it proceeded from a stringent view of the distinction between legitimate and illegitimate expenditures from Chapter VII and similar discretionary funds, payments at the heart of disputes over ambiguous financial corruption. Second, and of equal importance to public opinion, the jury and its agents committed what many perceived as affronts against his wife, María Teresa Nuñez de López Contreras, and their daughters.

The judgment against López Contreras rested primarily on the payments from Chapter VII and similar accounts that he, María Teresa, and her secretary received during López Contreras's presidency. López Contreras, like other officials charged with making or receiving improper payments from Chapter VII, claimed that he used the money for legitimate government expenses, including pensions and onetime payments to needy citizens who appealed to him for assistance, and that the first lady and her secretary had likewise used their Chapter VII funds for expenses tied to their official roles. The jury disagreed. It condemned López Contreras's use of Chapter VII to buy presents for prominent families who asked him to serve as godfather at their weddings and baptisms. The jury concluded that these gifts (often expensive jewelry), along with López Contreras's assistance to needy citizens, were intended to build his personal political base, an allegedly private benefit. The jury condemned the former president for "granting gifts that no law authorizes, with the purpose of attracting supporters and sympathizers who would guarantee his continuation in power. . . . The President does not have the authority to take funds from the Public Treasury for the private aims of political propaganda."[59] Along with penalizing López Contreras for making improper payments from Chapter VII, it censured him for receiving a gift of 100,000 bolívares from Gómez.

López Contreras responded to the jury's conviction in a public letter, written from exile, in which he invoked the familiar defense that presidential charity was essential to preserving the legitimacy of the state. "Everyone in Venezuela knows," he wrote, "that thousands of people filed through Miraflores [the presidential palace] to solicit resources to attend to urgent necessities: the purchase of medicines, medical treatment, money for students, pensions for widows, orphans, invalids, the extremely poor, etc., etc., and that there they received monetary assistance when their situation justified it. These are widely known facts. I would have provoked inflamed protests if I had withheld the protection of the State from so many indigent people."[60] It had been especially important to meet the paternalistic obligations of the state during the prolonged uncertainty of the post-Gómez transition. Many Venezuelans still admired López Contreras for stabilizing politics during the transition, avoiding civil war, and ending the worst abuses of the Gómez regime. Moreover, many junior military officers continued to respect the former president for his contributions to military professionalization. They were familiar with López Contreras's administrative practices and the gift he had received from Gómez, and their esteem for him remained undiminished.[61] As the US ambassador noted when he first learned that AD intended to try López Contreras for corruption, even the former president's "worst enemies" usually refrained from questioning his personal honesty.[62]

López Contreras's conviction might be put down to politics, but the treatment of María Teresa and their daughters appeared more scandalous, illustrating again how prosecutions for corruption could lead to unseemly intrusions into the private realm of the family. The first controversy erupted even before López Contreras's trial, as the three women passed through the airport to fly into exile in December 1945. Officials searched their luggage to ensure that they were not taking any of López Contreras's frozen assets out of the country. They confiscated a pair of diamond earrings found in the former first lady's luggage; the Substantiating Commission valued the jewelry at 59,000 bolívares in its inventory of López Contreras's property.[63] The authorities' assumption that the earrings should be considered López Contreras's property and evidence of corruption, rather than simply María Teresa's property, reflected the long-standing criticism that presidents used Chapter VII to buy lavish jewelry as a means of enriching regime insiders. But even Betancourt, who had done more than anyone to fan indignation over Chapter VII, realized that this treatment of a former first lady would cause an outcry. He later recalled that when the minister of interior relations showed him the confiscated jewelry in the presidential office, he exploded with anger.

"Why has this outrage been committed? Get this away from me!" he shouted.[64] López Contreras's lawyer confided to the US ambassador that the incident had created such intense outrage that it might contribute to a coup against Betancourt's government.[65]

The episode clearly breached social norms, and the former first couple jumped at the opportunity to appeal to traditional notions of propriety. María Teresa sent two public letters to *La Esfera* protesting that the authorities at the airport had treated her and her daughters "like vulgar smugglers," failed to respect "my condition as a woman," and inflicted "moral damage" on her family.[66] But the jury was not deterred. When it issued its finding against López Contreras in March 1946, it not only treated the now-famous earrings as López Contreras's property, it also insisted that the Chapter VII payments received by María Teresa and her secretary were corrupt. Perhaps most damaging of all, it confiscated several properties that the family treated as belonging to the two daughters and María Teresa. After reviewing the bank accounts of each member of López Contreras's family, the jury asserted that these properties had been purchased with money from López Contreras's allegedly embezzled funds, though the evidence appeared open to interpretation.[67]

López Contreras responded to the jury's verdict in April 1946 with a statement published in both *El Universal* and *La Esfera*. He pointed out that political opponents usually refrained from attacking each other's wives but, he charged, the current government's "thirst for vengeance" had led it to ignore "the traditional respect" for women.[68] Of course, this was not the first time that Venezuelan conservatives had argued that the rough and tumble of politics needed to remain an exclusively masculine affair. In his 1941 defense of his use of Chapter VII, Pedro Manuel Arcaya had denounced some critics of the discretionary account for their willingness to besmirch the reputations of female recipients of pensions by questioning the assistance they received. He proudly recounted how, even in 1928, as women joined the mostly male students in protests against the regime, leading Gomecistas (including the reviled Eustoquio Gómez) had refused to order sweeping arrests of female dissidents, choosing instead to adhere to the traditional principle "against men, anything, but against women, nothing."[69] Despite growing female participation in the public realm of politics and business, the former first couple clearly believed that their traditionally gendered view of the boundary between the state and the private realm of home and family would resonate with the newspaper-reading public.

Only five days after the jury announced its verdict against López Contreras, another controversy erupted over AD's anticorruption campaign. On March 20, Baldomero Uzcátegui, a prominent member of the Caracas elite, committed suicide while under investigation by the jury. As the US embassy explained to Washington, the news sent shock waves through the upper class because Uzcátgui was a popular figure, having been "recently reelected President of the Country Club of Caracas."[70] The jury had scrutinized Uzcátegui because of his decades-long association with the Gómez family. Uzcátegui had assisted with the management of the gambling monopolies held by the dictator's son José Vicente Gómez and served as an intermediary in José Vicente's acquisition of petroleum concessions, while also making large investments of his own in agriculture and cattle. He had been so closely linked to José Vicente that when, following the 1928 unrest, the dictator ordered his son to leave the country, Uzcátegui was instructed to go with him.[71] Following José Vicente's death in 1930, Uzcátegui served as a financial advisor to his widow, Josefina Revenga, and by early 1946 he regretted recommending that she keep most of her wealth in Venezuela, which left her properties exposed to confiscation once she, along with José Vicente's other heirs, was identified as a defendant in the trials. But the principal motive for Uzcátegui to end his life appeared to be that the jury had interrogated him "rather roughly," leading him to conclude that its members would find him guilty of receiving illicit payments from Chapter VII.[72]

According to the narrative that spread among the capital's well-to-do, Uzcátegui had been concerned to protect his family's good name in the face of the jury's unjustified persecution of him. The US embassy reported the story, which it accepted as true, that Uzcátegui "left a note to his adolescent son" stating, "'My name is not and cannot be stained.'"[73] In reporting his death, the press portrayed Uzcátegui as an honorable patriarch who had dedicated himself to the support and protection of his family. *La Esfera* praised the deceased for his "spirit of work," for being "an exemplary father of a family [*padre de familia*]," and for having "fostered an environment of warm affection in his house and with all those around him."[74] *El Universal* began its front-page coverage by offering similar praise for Uzcátegui as "a man completely dedicated to work and entirely consecrated to the elevation of a virtuous home."[75] But the usually restrained editors then went further and all but blamed AD's anticorruption campaign for his suicide. "The circumstances in which Señor Uzcátegui's death occurred are truly lamentable, because they are a product of the present situation in which many compatriots suffer intense and unnecessary persecution. . . . It is not possible, in the case of Señor Uzcátegui, to silence the motives that led to his death because they are patent in all our [social] sectors and constitute, without any doubt, clear proof that a climate of harmony among all Venezuelans . . . cannot be achieved through means that are governed by violence and hatred."[76] Uzcátegui's funeral, according to the Spanish legation, turned into an "extraordinary demonstration that . . . was interpreted as a vindication of his honor [*honorabilidad*] and a patent critique of the Government's handling of the question of peculation."[77] The sanctity of honorable families, which had framed much of the resistance to predatory corruption under Gómez, now became an effective frame for critiques of AD's anticorruption crusade.

Lawyers representing Uzcátegui touched on similar themes as they presented his defense before the jury and in the press in early April. Reiterating the trope of the honorable patriarch, they insisted that Uzcátegui had not been driven to suicide by fear of the financial penalties the jury could impose. Instead, they explained, "it was the horror of seeing himself defamed, it was the pain of a moral penalty to which he had been subjected, that unbalanced his nerves and brought him to the tragic resolution that deprives his family of their strongest support and deprives the Fatherland . . . of a useful man and exemplary citizen."[78] The lawyers sought to demonstrate that Uzcátegui had not profited from any of the Chapter VII payments he received. One payment of 1,440 bolívares had covered his expenses as a Venezuelan consul in Germany in 1923. Uzcátegui had received a second payment, for 25,000 bolívares, in early 1928 to cover a donation made by Juan Vicente Gómez when he was named the patron of the annual celebration of Our Lady of Candelaria in the village of Turmero, near his residence in Maracay. Uzcátegui received these funds because he led the committee that organized the festivities. He received the third payment of 50,000 bolívares in exchange for a field of sugar cane he had to abandon when Gómez sent him into exile in 1928. His lawyers emphasized that he had no choice but to accept the payment as he hurriedly settled his affairs in time to leave

Venezuela as Gómez ordered. The jury acquitted Uzcátegui two and a half months later, in June. It accepted his lawyers' explanations of the Chapter VII payments and concluded that he had not profited personally from his role in administering José Vicente Gómez's gambling concession, but the jury made no mention of Uzcátegui's death and expressed no regret for its investigation of him.

The final episode that began in March 1946 and undercut support for the jury was the case of Arturo Uslar Pietri. Like the investigations of López Contreras and Uzcátegui, Uslar Pietri's case revolved around Chapter VII and touched on themes of family and honor. But the most damaging aspect of Uslar Pietri's trial was that it provoked him to pen a devastating critique of AD's anticorruption initiative—one that synthesized the misgivings already amplified by the other two cases.

Uslar Pietri, a member of the elite who had grown up as a friend of the Gómez family and held a variety of political appointments since 1929, had become the most prominent member of Medina Angarita's administrative team.[79] The jury found him guilty of misusing or appropriating 1,157,200 bolívares from Chapter VII and similar accounts.[80] From his exile in New York, he wrote a public letter to Betancourt, dated March 26, in which he defended his use of public funds, accused AD and the jury of a hateful campaign against their rivals and their rivals' families, and asserted that Betancourt and other adecos lacked the necessary temperament and experience to lead a government. The letter, written in a tone dripping with scorn and condescension, remains one of the most famous polemics of twentieth-century Venezuelan politics.

Uslar Pietri argued that his conviction revealed the jury's ignorance of the inner workings of government. His early payments from Chapter VII, between 1929 and 1933, were salary and moving expenses following his appointment to a diplomatic post in France, a legitimate and common use of the fund. His largest payments from Chapter VII came during his service as Medina Angarita's secretary, and Uslar Pietri stated that he used these funds to provide pensions and payments to needy individuals, a practice that he (like Arcaya, López Contreras, and others) defended as "inherent in the paternalistic character of our Governments."[81] For the jury to assume, he wrote, "that I may have unduly appropriated these funds, is mere nonsense." Uslar Pietri believed that his conviction was so riddled with "whopping errors and falsehoods" that it demonstrated the jury's "bad faith" and desire for "political revenge."

But he directed his most vituperative attacks at Betancourt. He accused the AD leader of organizing the jury to ensure convictions, so that it functioned as "the grotesque guillotine of your revolution." The provisional president, derided by Uslar Pietri as an unqualified upstart, had recklessly inflicted harm on the patrician's family: "Drunk with gratuitous hatred and rancor, you have forcibly taken from me the legitimate patrimony of my children, though my conscience and honor remain unscathed." Moreover, Betancourt's tribunal had confiscated property belonging to Uslar Pietri's wife, wrongfully treating it as belonging to him, and its verdict implied that a pension paid to his father was corrupt. Betancourt's spiteful persecution of his political opponents, according to Uslar Pietri, had "driven good and useful men to suicide"—an obvious reference to Uzcátegui—and had "managed in only five months to divide the nation with an impassable pit of mortal hatred." Uslar Pietri belittled Betancourt as "nothing more than a demagogue" who had "fabricated the image of a cultivated man." Writing from his privileged position as an internationally recognized intellectual, Uslar Pietri judged the AD leader to be hopelessly ill-prepared to create a modern state: "You are not familiar with even the general outline of the great juridical and social monument of administrative science."

The publication of the letter in two papers, *El Heraldo* and *La Esfera*, provoked a bumbling response from the government that, over the course of three excruciating days, seemed to confirm Uslar Pietri's accusation of partisan overreach and ineptitude. The government ordered the detention of the editors of both papers; one was arrested and the other went into hiding. The police detained a prominent kinsman of Uslar Pietri for distributing the letter. Amid the predictable outcry against censorship, the authorities released the two detained men but at the same time appeared to double down on press restrictions by cautioning against expressions of "virulent disrespect" for the government.[82]

The press ignored the warning and had a field day. Manuel Vicente Tinoco, who had defended Chapter VII in the 1941 congressional debate, published a column in *El Universal* that echoed Uslar Pietri's disdain for adeco leaders who allegedly rose above their natural station in life: "Perhaps through reading and close contact with our public men who are seasoned in the delicate experience of command, you could acquire, over time, a better sense of the responsibility of Government."[83] From the opposite side of the political spectrum, Miguel Otero Silva, an independent communist and cofounder of the moderately progressive *El Nacional*, joined in chiding Betancourt, his former comrade in the 1928 student protests. Otero Silva observed, with his trademark combination of humor and cutting irony, that AD's overreaction to the letter had achieved a remarkable, but clearly unintended, outcome: "There does not remain a single Venezuelan who has not read Uslar Pietri's letter."[84] *La Esfera* summarized the clumsy attempt at censorship by quoting the aphorism "It is worse than a crime, because it is an act of foolishness."[85] The US ambassador reported that the government's handling of the episode "has served to alienate, at least temporarily, much of the press and many political independents who have been friendly or open-minded toward it."[86]

The erosion of support for AD's government and for the trials was in fact already underway. Rafael Caldera, the social Christian leader who had accepted the post of attorney general and supported the jury's organization as an ad hoc tribunal, resigned on April 13, midway between Uslar Pietri's conviction in March and the publication of his letter in early May. The event that triggered Caldera's resignation was AD harassment of his followers in the western state of Táchira, which contributed to Caldera's growing sense that AD sought to suppress all opposition.[87] His departure from the government signaled a serious decline of support among conservative-leaning members of the middle class. As leader of the newly organized Christian democratic party, COPEI, which drew much of its support from the middle class,[88] Caldera never denied his initial endorsement of the corruption trials; rather, he argued that AD's campaign against profiteering had begun as a noble effort but was derailed by adecos' determination to punish their political enemies. Campaigning in elections for the constituent assembly in October 1946, he reiterated what had become his familiar narrative: "I accept my responsibility in history" for endorsing the jury, "but that which could have been the most glorious work of the Revolution of October—how it became stained by hatred!—lost its strength in the conscience of Venezuelans."[89] By the time Caldera made this speech, his audience had ample time to consider the trials, which had concluded several months previously, in July 1946. The jury had convicted 118 individuals of illicit enrichment and absolved 49 others.[90]

Financial versus Predatory Corruption in the Trials

The partisanship decried by Caldera certainly played a role in undermining public approval for the trials. The rushed proceedings, the jury's propensity to dismiss defendants' explanations of poorly documented financial transactions, and the failure to investigate AD members involved in Chapter VII payments all suggested that political bias tainted the proceedings. And yet, the trials' overwhelming focus on Chapter VII as a source of corruption clearly amplified these concerns as the trials unfolded, contributing to the loss of support over time. A comparison of prosecutions for financial corruption (i.e., the misappropriation of public resources) with prosecutions for predatory corruption (the use of public power to extract wealth directly from the citizenry) yields additional insight into controversies surrounding the trials.

As we have seen, Venezuelans' opinions regarding Chapter VII had remained sharply divided for a decade by 1946, ever since Gómez's death opened a space for public debate. Venezuelans' clear-cut rejection of predatory corruption stood in contrast to their divided and ambivalent assessments of discretionary payments through Chapter VII, rendering the latter a classic example of ambiguous corruption. In hindsight, therefore, it is remarkable that the jury made Chapter VII the centerpiece of the trials. Of the 167 individuals tried by the jury, 104 (62 percent) were investigated for making or receiving payments from Chapter VII or similar accounts, with 84 of these (81 percent) convicted specifically for these transactions. Both investigations and convictions for Chapter VII malfeasance far outnumbered those for other types of corruption (which included mishandling funds from the Ministries of Public Works and War and Marine, as well as the predatory corruption discussed below). Why had the jury chosen to focus so heavily on Chapter VII "corruption" when the public had such divergent evaluations of it? Why attack corruption so persistently at its most ambiguous point?

Politics clearly played a role. AD leaders had denounced Chapter VII as corrupt for years, and the case for overthrowing Medina Angarita relied in part on these accusations, making prosecutions related to Chapter VII politically necessary. Practical considerations must have also shaped prosecutors' decisions. Of all the types of alleged corruption during the past four decades, Chapter VII transactions were perhaps the easiest to document. The published proceedings of the trials demonstrate that the jury had extensive records of payments from the fund. These records listed the recipient of each payment but often did not include a rationale for the outlay. The rhetoric employed in the verdicts demonstrates that a majority of the jury shared adeco leaders' assumptions that many Chapter VII payments were corrupt and that officials' payments to needy supplicants served some nefarious purpose. One verdict described Chapter VII as "the secret drainpipe through which the People's money flowed in a capricious and arbitrary manner . . . from which the favorites of the regime obtained special remunerations."[91] Similarly, the jury convicted former minister of interior relations Tulio Chiossone (1941–42) by arguing that "public functionaries cannot dispense money that is not theirs to demonstrate their generosity to people who come to them asking for aid."[92] In convicting Juan Penzini Hernández, Chiossone's successor as minister (1943), the jury declared, "It is not licit for a public functionary, at his whim, to dispense money from the budget to help private individuals."[93] Assertions like these, repeated throughout the trials, pointed to the jury's hope that the public would be persuaded to share its negative view of the discretionary fund and reject state paternalism.

To be sure, the jury presented evidence of widespread irregularities in Chapter VII expenditures to defend its suspicions regarding the fund. For example, it found that top Gomecistas routinely used Chapter VII to pay import taxes on personal goods they brought into the country.[94] The jury also demonstrated that high-ranking officials (such as cabinet ministers and members of the president's staff) often listed their low- or mid-level subordinates as recipients on payment orders for Chapter VII and other discretionary accounts, and that these underlings were instructed to deliver the money to a superior, thus creating a paper trail that failed to show any money going to the official who actually spent (or kept) the funds.[95] In two cases, the jury declared that cabinet ministers under Gómez made large deposits into their private bank accounts shortly after they or a relative received Chapter VII payments for amounts congruent with the deposits.[96]

But the jury lacked such compelling evidence of personal enrichment in many convictions related to Chapter VII. According to the published summaries of the trials, the jury often convicted defendants solely because they had not proven the legitimacy of the Chapter VII payments they received or authorized—a dramatic demonstration of the effect of shifting the burden of proof to defendants and of the compressed timeline for the ad hoc proceedings. Defendants who had been imprisoned or exiled following the 1945 coup simply did not have the opportunity to assemble evidence of their proper handling of funds, sometimes years in the past.[97] The inconsistent standards the jury used to determine defendants' guilt also undermined confidence in the verdicts. For example, the tribunal was fickle when deciding whether Chapter VII defendants should be convicted only for enriching themselves from public funds or if the use of payments for other forms of personal benefit constituted sufficient grounds for conviction. The jury *acquitted* some defendants because it found no evidence that they had illicitly enriched themselves, even though it was clear the defendants had not spent all the funds appropriately.[98] In contrast, it *convicted* several high-profile defendants—including Medina Angarita, López Contreras, and former ministers of interior relations Luis Gerónimo Pietri (1938–41), Tulio Chiossone, and Juan Penzini Hernández—for distributing money and gifts to followers and needy supplicants even though it acknowledged they had not profited financially from such transactions.[99] The jury's obvious waffling on the question of whether a finding of personal financial gain was necessary for a Chapter VII conviction—in short, its failure to apply a consistent definition of corruption—added to the sense that decisions reflected bias against some defendants.[100]

Significantly, the prosecutorial inconsistencies and ambiguities that characterized many Chapter VII convictions were largely absent in cases that targeted predatory corruption. These latter cases were much fewer in number than Chapter VII prosecutions and generated considerably less controversy. Among all the cases brought before the jury, only two involved the exploitation of political prisoners and their families, three involved the cattle monopoly, and twelve involved the contract system of administering the liquor tax. All these alleged offenses occurred under Gómez, and, notably, the individuals tried for predatory types of corruption were all convicted. In justifying convictions for the cattle and liquor cartels, the jury played to Venezuelans' long-standing condemnation of government officials who used their position to create and profit from "monopolies," a term that the jury invoked repeatedly in these cases, often along with references to the constitutional guarantee of freedom of industry that was violated by monopolistic practices.[101] When convictions for predatory corruption did provoke controversy, it was usually over the jury's confiscation of goods belonging to the heirs of a deceased official found to have engaged in corruption.[102] No one publicly defended monopolistic practices per se, in contrast to the ongoing debate over officials' discretionary use of Chapter VII funds to aid needy individuals. The broad condemnation of predatory corruption continued to stand in contrast to the divided responses to allegations of financial corruption.

The only significant exception to this distinction was one that, I would argue, supports the broader rule. The jury convicted all defendants who held high positions in, or were paid a share of the profits from, the Compañía Venezolana de Petróleo (CVP), the company Gómez established to receive petroleum concessions.[103] The uniform outcome of cases involving the CVP would appear to indicate that some types of financial malfeasance were as uniformly condemned as predatory corruption. However, the jury pointedly criticized the CVP for its cartel-like control over access to the most profitable oil concessions, noting that "thanks to the unrestricted support of the dictator Gómez, [the CVP] could monopolize the concessions in the most advantageous locations in the Republic,"[104] an exclusive advantage that, as the jury noted, most concession recipients did not enjoy. In short, the jury justified its conviction of defendants in CVP cases by invoking popular resentment against monopolies, as in its verdicts against predatory corruption. Similarly, of the thousands of individuals who received oil concessions, the only ones brought before the jury and convicted were those who received especially lucrative or numerous concessions through their personal ties to Gómez.[105] The aversion to monopolistic practices, then, informed the jury's intolerance of some forms of financial corruption, in contrast to its acquittals in 19 percent of Chapter VII cases.

The Review of the Jury's Verdicts and the 1948 Coup

As the final trials were held in July 1946, newspapers called for the jury's convictions to be reviewed and, in some cases, overturned. The editors at *El Universal* and *La Esfera* made it clear that while they agreed with some of the guilty verdicts, they found others to be unacceptable. On July 18, the latter paper published an editorial stating that "all honest Venezuelans" applauded the punishment of those whose guilt had been demonstrated, but that the jury had also committed "excesses, acts of vengeance, or injustices."[106] As a result, "honest families have been reduced to poverty for no other fault than that of having legitimate ties of family and of friendship with former officials." The next day, editors at *El Universal* likewise lauded AD's original intention to end corruption but criticized the conduct of the trials, including the confiscation of property belonging to the heirs of officials deemed to have engaged in corruption. They, too, indicated that such "unjust" acts reflected the jury's "hatred" of those affected and had created "nine months of anxiety."[107] "In our view," they concluded, "it is the government's duty . . . to look for a corrective, a review [of the verdicts]" in order to restore "strict justice and the most objective fairness."

Criticism of the trials reached such an intensity that even Betancourt began to consider a review of the jury's verdicts. On July 19, 1946, the same day that *El Universal* published the editorial cited above, the US embassy learned that he was contemplating the creation of a review process, largely in the hope of defusing a rumored counterrevolution led by López Contreras.[108] But there was persistent opposition within AD, especially from the party's left wing. Writing in AD's *El País*, Domingo Alberto Rangel, an adeco intellectual, reiterated the argument that the convictions would facilitate Venezuela's transition from "the personalism of the caudillo" to a "liberal state" with a "modern constitutional organization."[109] Perhaps more tellingly, he also argued that the confiscations ordered by the jury were necessary to break the financial power of AD's hardline opponents and advance revolutionary change.

The debate over reviewing the verdicts was settled by the military. Defense minister Major Carlos Delgado Chalbaud, a leader of the 1945 coup who presumably spoke for others in the armed forces, privately voiced support for a review of the jury's findings in November 1946.[110] Military concern over the trials was no doubt heightened by the jury's investigation of fifty-three current and former officers, thirty-seven of whom were convicted.[111] In October 1947 the government decreed that a commission drawn from the elected, AD-dominated national constituent assembly would review the convictions and sentences of any defendants who submitted an appeal. The commission completed its work in January 1948.[112]

During the three months that the review process was underway, numerous individuals both inside and outside the government attempted to utilize personal relationships to overturn the convictions of friends and relatives. Lieutenant Colonel José Elio Vargas, the commander of the military garrison in Táchira and brother of Lieutenant Colonel Mario Vargas, a leader of the 1945 coup and member of the governing junta, wrote to Betancourt on behalf of Julio González Cárdenas, "a friend I hold in the highest regard," who had been convicted for Chapter VII corruption. Although Betancourt had no formal role in the review, Vargas asked him to "do whatever may be within your capacity so that the case of my friend González Cárdenas is favorably resolved."[113] Josefina Revenga, the widow of José Vicente Gómez, wrote to Betancourt at the suggestion of her friend Alberto Ravell, a prominent figure in AD, to request a favorable review of her son's case, while also reminding Betancourt that in 1928 she had used her influence to soften the treatment of students arrested in the protests that year.[114] Meanwhile, Rómulo Gallegos, the AD nominee for president who won election in 1947 in a landslide, privately encouraged Tulio Chiossone, a former minister of interior relations convicted for Chapter VII expenditures, to submit an appeal.[115] Despite AD's professed goal of eliminating personalism from politics as it built a modern bureaucratic state, such relationships clearly remained part of political practice. In stark contrast to these efforts by regime insiders (Vargas, Ravell, and Gallegos) to rectify some verdicts, union leaders affiliated with AD called for all the jury's convictions to be upheld.[116] The trials not only failed to unify public opinion regarding corruption, but also provoked divergent responses within AD.

The decisions of the review commission altered dozens of verdicts but did not ameliorate the bitter disputes over the trials. The commission received 117 appeals for the return of confiscated property from those convicted by the jury and from their relatives and heirs. In thirteen of these cases, the commission ordered the return of all confiscated property to the defendants, in effect overturning their convictions.[117] Six of the thirteen exonerated were military officers. Thirty-six other petitions resulted in the return of some properties confiscated from defendants, their relatives, and heirs, in effect modifying the jury's decisions without completely overturning defendants' convictions. The commission rejected sixty-eight petitions. Some high-profile defendants, including Uslar Pietri and former presidents Medina Angarita and López Contreras, did not request reviews of their convictions because they believed such petitions would imply their legitimization of the government and its procedures. Nevertheless, critics of the trials denounced the review, claiming that more convictions should have been overturned.[118]

Although the review commission did not publicize the criteria it used in its deliberations, its decisions made clear that it was most open to revising convictions for financial corruption and to appeals from defendants' heirs and relatives. All thirteen convictions that were completely overturned involved types of financial corruption: seven for misuse of Chapter VII funds only; four for misuse of funds from Chapter VII and either the Ministry of Public Works or the Ministry of War and Marine; one for misuse of funds from the Ministry of War and Marine only; and one for misuse of funds from Chapter VII, the Ministry of War and Marine, and the CVP.[119] The reversal of these convictions demonstrated that the commission differed from the jury in its evaluation of financial malfeasance, confirming once again its status as ambiguous corruption. Moreover, none of the thirteen defendants whose convictions were overturned had been convicted for predatory types of corruption. In keeping with this pattern, the commission rejected appeals from several living defendants who had been convicted of predatory practices, confirming the broad disapprobation of this type of abuse. Finally, the commission returned properties belonging to relatives and heirs of men the jury deemed guilty of all types of corruption, demonstrating the commission's sensitivity to charges that the jury had gone too far in confiscating property belonging to the families of defendants.

In other especially revealing decisions, the commission overturned convictions in which the jury had condemned defendants' discretionary payments to needy supplicants as corrupt. The jury had convicted former ministers of interior relations Tulio Chiossone and Juan Penzini Hernández explicitly for using Chapter VII funds to provide such assistance, but the review commission concluded that they should not be punished for these acts. Similarly, the commission overturned the conviction of Manuel Silveira, Medina Angarita's minister of public works, whom the jury had convicted for improper use of over 900,000 bolívares from his ministry's budget. Silveira had defended himself with arguments similar to those made by López Contreras, Uslar Pietri, and others who sought to justify their use of Chapter VII funds. Silveira's defense, published in *El Universal*, claimed that the payments the jury deemed unacceptable were in reality "an authentic system of charity" in which money was given directly to supplicants or, more often, to officials who then gave the money to recipients who had lost their jobs or needed funds for medical care, a family burial, or similar expenses.[120] Silveira claimed he used such intermediaries "with the merciful goal of preventing the embarrassment of the humble person in need," by delivering the money discretely and sparing the recipient the need to collect it at a government office. The commission's overturning of these three cases signaled a tacit toleration of state paternalism, in contrast to the jury, which had taken a tougher stand against the discretionary use of public funds to relieve private hardship. In its attempt to mollify public opinion, the commission seemed to signal that the government's attack on personalism had gone too far.

But the concessions enacted by the review commission failed to satisfy AD's critics. By early 1948, objections to the adecos' anticorruption campaign had become inextricably woven into opposition narratives charging that the party was dangerously partisan and intolerant of its adversaries. Even the election and inauguration of Gallegos, the revered novelist generally considered to be far less partisan than other AD leaders, failed to alleviate opposition concerns that his allies aimed to create a one-party state. The developments that supported this narrative included AD's renewed push to regulate Catholic schools, its land reform program, and its drive to incorporate the growing labor movement into the party.[121] The drumbeat of critics decrying the jury's procedures and calling for more verdicts to be overturned fit neatly into the accusation of AD exclusivity. In the end, it made no difference that the party had acknowledged and corrected some errors committed by the jury, or that convictions of especially abusive members of the Gómez regime were widely accepted as just.

The armed forces overthrew President Gallegos on November 24, 1948, initiating a military government that eventually devolved into the personal dictatorship of Marcos Pérez Jimenez, which lasted until January 1958. In September 1949, the government ordered the return of all properties seized during the corruption trials, in effect overturning all the jury's convictions.[122] The most prescient response to this decision came from Rafael Caldera, the social Christian leader who had initially supported the trials, joined the government, and accepted many of the verdicts, but then turned against AD after concluding that its policies, including the trials, were irredeemably tarnished by sectarian rancor. Writing in his party's newspaper, *El Gráfico*, Caldera disapproved of the decision to overturn all the convictions. Without a case-by-case review, he lamented, "it will never be known which individuals were responsible for public theft. . . . Now the danger is that peculation of public funds will be regarded as a crime without punishment."[123] Caldera's shifting yet politically astute responses to the trials and their aftermath reflected the difficulties inherent in defining and punishing corruption, especially the financial wrongdoing he alluded to in his column.

Public reaction to the trials confirms the importance of distinguishing between ambiguous financial corruption and widely condemned predatory corruption. The shift from broad public support for the ad hoc tribunal to growing disapproval occurred as the jury's emphasis on Chapter VII became clear and as high-profile cases concentrated attention on flaws in the prosecution of alleged financial malfeasance. Significantly, however, objections to the jury's procedures did not prevent public approval of the convictions of living officials who had engaged in predatory corruption; rather, the rushed procedures and insufficient investigations attributed to the jury only became controversial in prosecutions of alleged financial corruption, especially Chapter VII. AD's fundamental error may have been its decision to prosecute such distinct types of corruption under the same harsh procedures of revolutionary justice.

Declining public support also reflected the growing realization that the prosecutions involved new state intrusions into the private sphere of the family. Investigators scrutinized the property holdings and bank accounts of defendants' male and female relatives, and the jury frequently seized properties that officials' kin claimed as their own, including properties inherited from deceased officials. The intensity of controversies sparked by the harm experienced by families—and especially the sense that Maria Teresa Nuñez de López Contreras, her daughters, and Baldomero Uzcátegui had been treated unjustly—indicated that the rapid social change of the era had not produced a fundamental shift in many Venezuelans' understanding of the proper boundary between the state and the patriarchal household. Just as the defense of honorable families provided the foundation for condemnations of Gomecista predation, so, too, it became a crucial criterion in evaluating AD's anticorruption campaign, at least in the minds of many observers.

In sum, while the initial support for AD's anticorruption crusade may be read as backing for the modernist ideal of anticorruption, with its strict division between public and private interests, the decline in support reflected a growing realization of the costs incurred in pursuit of that abstraction. Studies of the middle classes in other Latin American nations have found similarly ambivalent attitudes toward state practices built upon bureaucratic ideals. Middling social sectors in the twentieth century often endorsed the precepts associated with a modern bureaucratic state while relying on personalist (or what may also be called patrimonial) practices as a means of safeguarding their status and interests.[124] In the case of Venezuela, this ambivalence between adherence to the principles of bureaucratic rationality and acceptance of the benefits of patrimonialism reflected the process of neopatrimonial state formation in which both forms of power were deployed in the creation of a centralized state under Gómez and then continued in modified form under López Contreras and Medina Angarita. The status of Chapter VII payments as ambiguous corruption—condemned by some and condoned by others, even within AD—was confirmed by reactions to the trials, dashing any hope of building a consensus that such discretionary perquisites should be purged from state practice. Members of the middle class might endorse the abstraction of an impersonal state as part of their self-image as modernizers, but in the end many recoiled from such a leap into the unknown.

CONCLUSION

TWENTIETH-CENTURY VENEZUELA AND THE HISTORICAL STUDY OF (ANTI)CORRUPTION

The conflicts over corruption that rocked the trienio reverberated through Venezuelan politics for several decades. Just as opinions regarding the trials were divided at the moment of the 1948 coup, later memories of AD's anticorruption crusade were highly polarized. If we follow scholars who view historical memory as the meanings that are attached to individual and collective experiences over time,[1] then it becomes clear that the significance of the trials was not confined to the trienio itself. Rather, struggles to shape Venezuelans' memories of the trials became a touchstone in debates over corruption and anticorruption for another half century. While critics of the Jury of Civil and Administrative Responsibility continued to condemn its procedures and to present it as a cautionary tale of the weaponization of corruption for political advantage, some AD partisans defended the trials by emphasizing their noble intentions, with neither side exploring the complex questions raised by the proceedings. These contested recollections of the nation's first attempt to confront widespread malfeasance hindered efforts to curb corruption during the second half of the twentieth century.

Rómulo Betancourt remained a prominent but divisive figure, and his uncompromising defense of the trials shaped the battles over their memory. His influential *Venezuela: política y petróleo* (English edition, *Venezuela: Oil and Politics*), a combination of contemporary history, memoir, and passionate defense of his trienio policies published in 1956, presented AD's anticorruption crusade as a laudable effort to end official profiteering. Occasionally acknowledging flaws in the jury's conduct, he nevertheless maintained that any shortcomings paled in comparison to the many justified verdicts that had recovered, he claimed, "over 400 million bolívares" in corrupt wealth before the military government nullified the jury's sentences.[2]

Political leaders remained leery of returning to the polarization of the trienio, however, and during the transition to democracy following the end of the Pérez Jiménez dictatorship in 1958, Betancourt and others were cautious not to repeat the controversial policies of the past. As historian Judith Ewell has argued, this included a determination to avoid the controversies provoked by the jury.[3] It was generally agreed that Pérez Jiménez, who had headed the military government from 1950 until his overthrow in 1958, had presided over an extremely corrupt administration, but the caretaker government led by Admiral Wolfgang Larrazábal (1958–59) avoided aggressive retribution. He began efforts to extradite Pérez Jiménez from his refuge in the United States but showed no appetite for mass prosecutions of corruption mirroring those of the trienio. Once elected and inaugurated as president, Betancourt (1959–64) continued the drive to prosecute Pérez Jiménez but was otherwise circumspect regarding the prosecution of former officials for malfeasance. Pérez Jiménez was successfully returned to Venezuela for trial and, following numerous delays, in 1968 was convicted of improperly profiting from public office by Venezuela's Supreme Court, not an ad hoc tribunal like the jury. The court ordered the confiscation of his properties in Venezuela and sentenced Pérez Jiménez to four years in prison, which he had already served by the time of the verdict, allowing him to depart for a comfortable exile in Francisco Franco's Spain. In dissent, a five-justice minority argued that Pérez Jiménez should have been convicted of a broader array of financial crimes and sentenced to a longer prison term.[4] Others who had engaged in embezzlement, bribery, and profiteering during the dictatorship were in some cases spared prosecution altogether for the sake of stabilizing the new democracy. While the successful extradition and conviction of a former head of state for financial crimes set a significant precedent, on balance the prosecution of corruption was decidedly less far-reaching than during the trienio.

The desire to avoid another military coup led Betancourt, COPEI's Rafael Caldera, and Jóvito Villalba, the 1928 student activist who now headed the centrist Unión Republicana Democrática (URD, Democratic Republican Union), to make an agreement known as the Pact of Punto Fijo to consolidate the post-1958 democracy.[5] This "pacted democracy" committed the signatories to respect electoral outcomes and refrain from attempts to concentrate power in the hands of any single party, a promise with the potential to discourage or complicate future accusations of malfeasance by any of the three parties against others in the pact. Betancourt and his two successors as president—AD's Raúl Leoni and COPEI's Caldera—all enjoyed reputations for personal honesty, but corruption continued to be widespread in the bureaucracy and was not uncommon in the judiciary. President Betancourt expressed frustration at endemic public-sector malfeasance despite his attempts to enforce the 1948 Law against the Illicit Enrichment of Public Functionaries or Employees, which the 1961 constitution had strengthened.[6] One of the prosecutors in the Pérez Jiménez trial, José Díaz Andara, lamented not only the pervasive nature of corruption but also what he saw as Venezuelans' indifference. "Today," he wrote in 1965, "people follow the Spanish proverb which says, 'Who steals from the public robs no one.'"[7] A team of social scientists that conducted extensive interviews with middle-class public employees in the 1960s found that they readily espoused ideals conforming to bureaucratic, merit-based norms but that political clientelism and personalism more often characterized the functioning of the public sector.[8]

The mid-1970s were a watershed in the history of corruption during the era of pacted democracy due to transformations in the oil economy. Venezuela received a massive influx of petrodollars following the 1973 price increase engineered by the Organization of Petroleum Exporting Countries (OPEC) and the nationalization of Venezuelan oil in 1976. Leaders across the political spectrum, along with journalists and academics, agreed that the sudden flood of money into state coffers triggered an upsurge in diverse forms of corruption, including bribery, illegal commissions on government contracts, and outright embezzlement. A slew of books published in the 1970s decried corruption as systemic throughout most state institutions, bemoaned society's apparent indifference to official malfeasance, and expressed despair at existing institutions' inability to resolve the problem.[9] The long-standing hope, dating back to the post-Gómez transition, that corruption could be ended through the consolidation of a democratic government, appeared illusory. Venezuela's pacted democracy may have guarded against a return to military dictatorship in the short term, but by the 1970s the system had allowed AD and COPEI to entrench themselves in power so thoroughly that the parties could now guard themselves from accountability.[10]

Betancourt, nearing seventy years of age, dedicated much of 1976 and 1977 to issuing urgent calls for more vigorous anticorruption measures in Venezuela and internationally. In his keynote speech at the May 1976 meeting of Political Leaders of Europe and Latin America in Favor of International Democratic Solidarity, the elder statesman touted AD's past struggles against official malfeasance, including the trials of the trienio, and called for greater transnational cooperation to prevent corrupt politicians from fleeing abroad with their ill-gotten wealth, a problem he saw as being worldwide.[11] Speaking to an AD gathering in Caracas the following year, Betancourt endorsed Luis Piñerúa as the party's presidential nominee in the 1978 elections by lauding him as the most credible anticorruption candidate. Betancourt posited that corruption had become so widespread that it threatened Venezuelan democracy, a pointed observation because the current president, AD's Carlos Andrés Pérez, was his former protégé. In the speech's most dramatic turn, Betancourt called for the creation of a special anticorruption tribunal, which he called a "jury," unabashedly evoking parallels to the controversial tribunal of the trienio. The proposed jury would investigate high-level corruption during each presidential administration since the return to democracy, including Betancourt's government (1959–64) and the current Pérez administration.[12] In calling for COPEI to support a new anticorruption jury, Betancourt noted that during the early months of the trienio Rafael Caldera had publicly endorsed the formation of an ad hoc tribunal, not bound by existing legislation, as necessary for the effective prosecution of corruption. The implication inherent in

Betancourt's proposal—that the democratic system to which he had dedicated his life had become so corrupt that it required countermeasures similar to those used against the Andean regime overthrown in 1945—sent shock waves through the political elite and media.

The responses from prominent figures were often paradoxical. They agreed that corruption was pulling Venezuelan democracy toward crisis but they rejected Betancourt's proposal, often citing the trials of the trienio as a negative precedent, without offering feasible solutions of their own. Caldera, the only political leader whose stature approached that of Betancourt, responded to the proposal for a new jury in two interviews, one of which was included in a series of articles on corruption in *El Nacional* following the AD leader's speech. The COPEI chief reviewed what he saw as the arbitrary actions of the jury during the trienio, warned against using accusations of corruption for political gain, and suggested that instead of creating a new jury, AD and COPEI should pass a law requiring political parties to disclose the source of their funds—a measure that, even if successful, would not address other forms of corruption.[13] Emphasizing the disillusionment created by the controversies surrounding the trienio's jury, Caldera argued that if the new tribunal proposed by Betancount resulted in another high-profile failure, public cynicism toward all future anticorruption efforts would become insurmountable.[14]

Arturo Uslar Pietri, whose polemical letter to Betancourt denouncing his conviction for Chapter VII payments had caused such a stir in 1946, was even more vehement in condemning the jury as a harmful precedent for a new anticorruption campaign. Uslar Pietri once again protested his treatment during the trienio—and stated inaccurately that there had been no opportunity to appeal the jury's decisions.[15] Joining the chorus, Jóvito Villaba, still a notable voice in national politics despite the poor electoral performance of his URD party, publicly rejected Betancourt's call for a new jury and likewise pointed to the injustices inflicted during the trienio as his rationale.[16] Only a few, generally less prominent figures voiced support for Betancourt's proposal, such as ex-comptroller Manuel Vicente Ledezma, who had held office under Betancourt in the 1960s.[17] But thoughtful readers of Ledezma's interview in *El Nacional* must have wondered whether his endorsement of the need for a special tribunal merely confirmed the long-term failure of the comptroller's office, established by López Contreras four decades ago to ensure the proper handling of public funds. In the end, Betancourt's proposal for a new jury went nowhere, signaling a victory for his critics and their narrative of the trienio's jury as a negative precedent.

Corruption continued to eat away at political institutions and at the legitimacy of the democratic system in the years that followed.[18] Attempts to reform the system and save it from collapse proved fruitless. The 1982 Organic Law to Safeguard the Public Patrimony, designed to tighten the anticorruption controls already in place, left enforcement in the hands of judicial bodies controlled by AD and COPEI.[19] As with previous measures, it led to occasional convictions of low-level offenders but failed to pierce the de facto immunity of prominent individuals. Even the explosive RECADI scandal involving corruption in the multi-tiered foreign exchange system of the 1980s failed to provoke many prosecutions, despite the loss of billions of dollars to elites who fraudulently obtained hard currency at below-market rates created to stimulate productive investments.[20] It seemed to many Venezuelans that the only part of the bureaucracy that functioned with relative efficiency and rewarded merit was the national oil company, Petróleos de Venezuela, or PDVSA.[21] But like the reformed treasury under Román Cárdenas, PDVSA delivered revenue to a neopatrimonial state riddled with graft, even if it was now political parties rather than a dictator and his inner circle that used public funds to advance their own narrow interests.

The government's financial reserves had almost run out when in early 1989 Carlos Andrés Pérez took office as president the second time, forcing him to impose painful measures of economic austerity. As subsidies and social services were cut and real wages fell, outraged Venezuelans demanded to know why such hardship was necessary. Where had the nation's famous oil wealth gone? Two coup attempts against Pérez in 1992 reflected this popular anger over the imposition of austerity by a political elite widely seen as corrupt. The manifesto issued by Hugo Chávez and other leaders of the first coup attempt justified the uprising by pointing to endemic corruption, a stance that elicited considerable sympathy for the defeated rebels.[22] When Pérez was removed from office the following year by Congress and the Supreme Court over corruption allegations, many Venezuelans interpreted the move as a desperate attempt by a moribund political establishment to save itself by sacrificing Pérez.

Regardless of whether Pérez was guilty of the alleged malfeasance or merely a scapegoat after decades of impunity, corruption clearly contributed to the collapse of pacted democracy and Venezuelans' embrace of the alternative embodied by Chávez.[23] Mirtha Rivero's journalistic examination of the complex political, economic, and personal tensions that culminated in Pérez's downfall, *La rebelión de los náufragos* (The rebellion of the shipwrecked), makes clear that some root causes of the collapse stretched back to the trienio. The political and economic elites she interviewed alluded to the jury's proceedings as a significant episode in the long-term accumulation of pressures that reached a crescendo in the 1990s. Whether they referenced the corruption trials of the trienio as a source of animosities still festering among prominent individuals, or as an example of the harmful politicization of corruption accusations, Rivero's interviewees treated the jury as a shared point of reference whose consequences through time were assumed to be detrimental.[24] Betancourt, who had died in 1981, clearly lost his battle to define the trials in different terms, as a principled and at least fleetingly successful effort to hold corrupt elites to account.

The struggle over public memory of the trials—a struggle that Betancourt himself had played a leading role in initiating and polarizing—ended with the widespread conclusion that Venezuela's most extensive anticorruption prosecutions in the twentieth century constituted a political and moral failure and should not be repeated. This winner-take-all contest to define the past, however, never examined the trials as a historical episode that might reveal deeper insights into the dynamic interaction of corruption and anticorruption over time. With the benefit of historical hindsight, and in dialogue with scholarly studies in the growing field of corruption studies, this book has pursued a more complex and nuanced understanding of the past by exploring the experiences and perspectives of Venezuelans whose lives were touched by official malfeasance and the struggles against it during the first half of the twentieth century. Five methodological precepts derived from recent interdisciplinary analyses of (anti)corruption provide a useful framework for reviewing this book's findings and illuminating their significance. These precepts underline the desirability of adopting an emic definition of corruption; distinguishing among different types of corruption; recognizing anticorruption as a historical phenomenon as significant as corruption; incorporating cultural context, including social constructs of gender, into the study of (anti)corruption; and examining each nation's unique history of corruption and anticorruption.

First, I have followed scholars who adopt an emic, constructivist approach to corruption that privileges the viewpoints of historical actors.[25] Indeed, this entire study has been shaped by my choice to define corruption as the use of public office and other public resources for private benefit in ways that were condemned by significant segments of Venezuelan public opinion. An alternative definition of corruption as merely "the abuse of entrusted power for private gain"— the definition used by Transparency International (TI) and widely adopted in the international arena—avoids the issue of diverse understandings of corruption across (and within) cultures and historical eras.[26] TI's definition implies a universally shared understanding of the boundary between malfeasance and acceptable conduct that recent scholarship indicates does not exist.[27] The choice of an emic approach to corruption in Venezuelan history requires close attention to the popular reaction against monopolies that loomed so large in Venezuelans' perception of official wrongdoing. By the early twentieth century, Venezuelans believed that political elites who abused public office for personal enrichment most often did so by creating monopolies over essential consumer goods or natural resources. The former type of monopoly aroused particular opposition because it forced consumers to contribute directly to the enrichment of predatory rulers. This popular rejection of monopolies endured through 1948. Even during the controversies provoked by the anticorruption trials of the trienio, Venezuelans remained in broad agreement that the use of political power to create monopolies was an unacceptable manipulation of public office and deserved punishment.

This constructivist approach to the history of Venezuelan (anti) corruption highlights the importance of attention to variations among societies' use of language to describe corruption. Historians often seek to reconstruct past attitudes toward the abuse of public office by tracing historical actors' use of the word *corruption*.[28] This study, by contrast, points to the utility of considering other keywords that critics have used to describe the abuse of public office for private gain. Venezuelans' infrequent use of the word *corruption* did not mean that they were indifferent to official malfeasance; rather, it reflected their particular experience with officials' self-enrichment, which since colonial times had centered on the creation of monopolies. Moreover,

CONCLUSION

this heighted sensitivity to the detrimental effects of monopolies may have contributed to ambivalence regarding alternative forms of malfeasance, including the forms that I have labeled "financial corruption." In contrast to the predatory corruption of monopolies, the diversion of public resources to private use was widely tolerated as a victimless form of maladministration, at least until the unprecedented economic crisis and widespread hardship of the late twentieth century. In sum, an emic approach to corruption, by emphasizing historical actors' experience with corruption and the language they used to describe it, can illuminate paradoxes in a society's attempts to control official malfeasance.

Second, this book offers strong support to recent calls for scholars to "disaggregate" corruption into different types of malfeasance.[29] In the present study, I have not only contrasted predatory and financial corruption, I have also distinguished among different forms of malfeasance within each of these two categories. To understand corrupt practices during the Gómez regime, and to understand Venezuelans' reactions to corruption, this book has examined the cattle monopoly, the state-level liquor monopolies, profiteering in prisons, the distribution of oil concessions, and Chapter VII payments as separate issues. The state-level liquor monopolies, for example, became the only type of corruption effectively opposed from within the regime due to Treasury Minister Román Cárdenas's ability to frame them as drains on government revenue during a period of fiscal crisis. Gómez was thus persuaded to allow the curtailment of tax farming in favor of bureaucratic administration. By contrast, the cattle monopoly, another form of predatory corruption, did not generate such effective pushback from within the regime, partly because the same trade-offs between patronage and maximizing government revenue were not in play, and partly because Gómez's personal involvement in the cattle monopoly was greater than his involvement in the liquor economy. Attention to the differences between the cattle and liquor monopolies allows us to understand why the patrimonial cattle monopoly continued throughout the dictatorship even as the liquor tax shifted to bureaucratic administration (albeit in a halting, circuitous manner), a contrast that highlights the neopatrimonial nature of the regime.

Disaggregating corruption also reveals the logic in Venezuelans' different reactions to different types of corruption. Men and women victimized by predatory corruption experienced humiliation within the gendered culture of honor, a misfortune that could threaten their claim to middle-class status. But that same concern with preserving honor led to more ambivalent responses to Chapter VII payments, which never threatened honor and sometimes rescued families' social standing. As a consequence, predatory monopolies were widely condemned, while Chapter VII became a prime example of ambiguous financial corruption. Any discussion of corruption or anticorruption during the Gómez era that lumps together varieties of malfeasance would distort both the logic of the regime and the experiences of Venezuelans living under it. More broadly, an analysis of corruption, anticorruption, and state formation requires the disaggregation of corruption for any precise understanding of the interactions among rulers or between rulers and those they dominated, two principal axes of state formation.

Unpacking different types of corruption, then, is closely related to a third precept that emerges from recent scholarship: corruption and anticorruption need to be studied together.[30] Phrased another way, anticorruption needs to be analyzed as a phenomenon in its own right, but it can only be understood in relation to the specific types of corruption it opposes. Corruption and anticorruption were closely related not only during the Gómez dictatorship, but also during the post-Gómez transition. The protests of 1935–36 that targeted symbols of predatory corruption, together with López Contreras's predisposition to end such abusive profiteering and Congress's decision to confiscate Gómez's property, led to a dramatic shift in the relationship between the state and society as monopolies collapsed or were dismantled and Gomecista strongmen lost political clout. But the continuation of Chapter VII's ambiguous corruption provided a target for regime critics eager to claim malfeasance by López Contreras and Medina Angarita. The result was increasingly sharp (and often exaggerated) rhetoric that painted Chapter VII as nothing more than a nefarious slush fund. This shift in anticorruption discourse from visceral denunciations of predatory corruption, which reflected many Venezuelans' lived experience under Gómez, to occasionally hyperbolic critiques of Chapter VII after 1935, had concrete consequences. AD's attempt to create an equivalency between predatory monopolies and Chapter VII payments by denouncing both as corrupt, and by subjecting those accused of these distinct activities to the same ad hoc procedures in the 1946 trials, lost credibility with many Venezuelans, including, apparently, many of AD's middle-class supporters. The history of Venezuelan anticorruption from 1908 to 1948, then, is complex and consequential enough that it demands to be analyzed as carefully as corruption itself. Anticorruption can only be understood in light of the range of activities that were labeled—and contested— as corrupt.

Fourth, this work points to the insights that can be gained by integrating cultural context, including considerations from gender studies, into the history of Latin American corruption and anticorruption.[31] In Venezuela, at least during the four decades contemplated here, the constellation of masculinity, honor, paternalism, and patrimonialism proved to be particularly potent in shaping the history of both corruption and anticorruption. The concept of patrimonialism, as mentioned in previous chapters, has been reinvigorated by emphasizing its patriarchal foundations, including the discretion of the patrimonial ruler to reward or punish, a key element in paternalism, whether in Latin America or elsewhere.[32] In treating Venezuela as his landed estate, Gómez exercised great discretion in parceling out its resources, including petroleum concessions, Chapter VII payments, shares in the cattle and liquor monopolies, and positions in the military and the administration of prisons with opportunities for graft. He could be the generous patron and beneficent father to those he chose to favor, just as surely as he could punish and ruin many who failed to please him.

While Gómez's supporters cast him as the father of the national family, many of his male opponents also operated in a cultural field that was explicitly patriarchal. They critiqued corruption by framing its impact as emasculation, a rhetorical strategy with such strong cultural resonance that, as we saw in chapter 4, Gómez felt compelled to respond. But by treating the struggle against corruption as a contest over masculine honor, anti-Gomecistas not only marginalized female experiences of corruption (experiences for which I wish I had uncovered more sources), they also chose to confront Gómez on an ideological field that the dictator was already making his own. The thousands of middle-class families that received assistance through Chapter VII found that the "personalism" decried by anti-Gomecistas into the 1940s could safeguard the honor of their households, including those that were otherwise without masculine protection. To be sure, the emotive force of the opposition's critique of predatory corruption contributed to the demise of this form of malfeasance after Gómez's death, but by centering honor in the evaluation of corruption, opponents left unchallenged some of the cultural ideals that critics of the corruption trials would mobilize with great effect a decade later. The defense of discretionary payments as appropriate aid to honorable families by López Contreras, Arcaya, and others, as well as the criticisms of the anticorruption trials as intrusions into the realm of the family, attests to the continuity of patriarchal values and their power to thwart anticorruption. It is difficult to resist the conclusion that anti-Gomecistas' emphasis on the sanctity of the patriarchal household played some role in buttressing a cultural ideal that later contributed to the unraveling of AD's anticorruption campaign in the trienio. To neglect cultural context—a potential pitfall in cross-national studies of corruption—would obstruct our understanding of corruption, anticorruption, and the dynamics between them over the course of a nation's history.

Finally, this book lends support to the proposition that attempts to control corruption in any nation will be affected by that nation's unique history of corruption *and* anticorruption.[33] Despite the often-productive turn toward transnational analysis in historical studies and the emphasis on transnational and comparative studies of (anti)corruption in the social sciences, national-level historical studies remain indispensable. Venezuelans' particular experiences of corruption and anticorruption—as well as their memories of these phenomena—loomed over debates about possible remedies to corruption into the decisive decade of the 1970s and beyond. The history of (anti)corruption, in other words, provides a through line for understanding key processes in Venezuela during the twentieth century. The connections between Gomecista corruption, the controversies surrounding the anticorruption efforts of the trienio, and the disastrous stalemate over anticorruption measures in the last quarter of the twentieth century create a narrative thread linking major developments in national politics up to the dawn of the Chávez era.

This book, then, has engaged with recent studies of corruption in order to deepen our understanding of Venezuela and to advance historians' methodologies for researching and analyzing corruption. Nevertheless, one may reasonably ask whether such historical studies written within a national frame can claim much present-day relevance. After all, the world of the twenty-first century is much changed from the period emphasized here. Today, both corruption and anticorruption have become truly globalized, as nefarious elites launder their wealth through offshore shell companies and foreign real estate transactions, and as anticorruption entities reach across national borders in a frenzied and technically complex pursuit. As efforts to prevent and punish corruption become ever more global, the insistence on a "universal" definition of corruption and on one-size-fits-all solutions acquires a certain logic, at least in some powerful corners of the world. But many of the dynamics between corruption and anticorruption continue to unfold in contexts that are driven largely by each nation's particular circumstances. Individuals and networks that engage in corruption and those that fight to end it will always bring multifaceted legacies to their work, legacies shaped by experiences, memories, and individual and collective identities that have been molded and contested through time. Regardless of the homogenizing tendency of transnational forces, the unique configuration of each nation's history of (anti)corruption will continue to shape the present.

NOTES

Introduction: Approaching Corruption and Anticorruption in Venezuela, 1908–48

1. Torres, *Memorias*, 50, 87, 121–24, 179–80.
2. Torres, *Memorias*, 127–39.
3. Torres, *Memorias*, 135–36. A literal translation of "no han comulgado con esa hostia" is "they have not taken communion with that host." Like the English phrase "have not played that game," Torres's words are an idiomatic expression referring to a conscious decision not to engage in a common practice.
4. Cartay Ramírez, *Caldera y Betancourt*, 92, 111; and Luzardo, *Notas histórico-económicas*, 158.
5. For recent corruption scandals and anticorruption measures in Latin America, see Arellano-Gault, *Corruption in Latin America*, 107–207; Goldstein and Drybread, "Social Life of Corruption"; and Pozsgai-Alvarez, *Politics of Anti-Corruption Agencies*.
6. For a synthesis of recent corruption issues in Venezuela, see López Maya, "Populism, 21st-century Socialism, and Corruption." For Transparency International's 2022 ranking, see "Corruption Perception Index, 2022," Transparency International, accessed May 23, 2023, https://www.transparency.org/en/cpi/2022.
7. Important works on corruption in colonial Latin America include Rosenmüller, *Corruption and Justice in Colonial Mexico*; Rosenmüller, *Corruption in the Iberian Empires*; McFarlane, "Political Corruption and Reform"; and Myrup, *Power and Corruption*.
8. Holmes, *Corruption*, 1–17; and Johnston, "Definitions Debate."
9. Mungiu-Pippidi, *Quest for Good Governance*, 11.
10. Katzarova, *Social Construction of Global Corruption*.
11. Shore and Haller, "Sharp Practice"; Pierce, *Moral Economies of Corruption*, 1–23; and Kroeze, Vitória and Geltner, "Introduction: Debating Corruption."

12. This method is followed in Knights, *Trust and Distrust*.

13. De Graaf, Wagenaar, and Hoenderboom, "Constructing Corruption," 100.

14. Johnston, "Search for Definitions," 333.

15. Kerkhoff et al., "Dutch Political Corruption," 447.

16. Kerkhoff et al., "Dutch Political Corruption," 466.

17. Cromwell, *Smugglers' World*.

18. Rosenmüller and Ruderer, "Introducción," 11–12; Rosenmüller, *Corruption and Justice*, 53–91; Kroeze, Vitória, and Geltner, "Introduction," 2, 15; Buchan and Hill, *Intellectual History*; and Kerkhoff, Kroeze, and Wagenaar, "Corruption and the Rise of Modern Politics."

19. Johnston, "Search for Definitions," 321–35.

20. Engels, "Corruption and Anticorruption."

21. An earlier generation of scholars referred to such malfeasance as "black corruption." Heidenheimer, "Perspectives on the Perception of Corruption."

22. What I call "ambiguous corruption" parallels what earlier scholars termed "gray corruption." Heidenheimer, "Perspectives on the Perception of Corruption." Heidenheimer's essay, reflecting the assumptions of modernization theory, posited that over time societies would become increasingly intolerant of gray corruption as they embraced bureaucratic norms. By contrast, I see ambiguous corruption as an enduring feature of Venezuela's neopatrimonial state.

23. The best sympathetic biography is Polanco Alcántara, *Juan Vicente Gómez*. For an older example of this approach, see Lavin, *Halo for Gómez*. Ramón Velásquez attempts to capture Gómez's worldview in *Confidencias imaginarias*. Brian S. McBeth argues that Gómez demonstrated considerable skill in fending off political adversaries and extracting increased taxes and compensation for environmental damage from foreign oil companies; see McBeth, *Juan Vicente Gómez*; and McBeth, *Dictatorship and Politics*.

24. Ellner, "Venezuelan Revisionist Political History," 95–100. An example of dependency school writing is Rodríguez, *Gómez*. The most influential criticism of Gómez and his political heirs was Betancourt, *Venezuela*. The English edition's forward by Arthur Schlesinger and its introduction by Franklin Tugwell indicate Betancourt's influence among mid-century US intellectuals.

25. On the concept of neopatrimonialism, see Bach, "Patrimonialism and Neopatrimonialism"; and Erdmann and Engel, "Neopatrimonialism Reconsidered." Historical studies of Latin America have noted the tension between patronage or patrimonial power, on one hand, and the expansion of bureaucratic power, on the other. Examples include Salvatore, "Between Empleomanía and the Common Good"; and Herrera and Ferraro, "Friends' Tax."

26. My inclusion of predatory, corrupt practices in this paragraph is in line with the more extreme forms of patrimonialism sometimes referred to as sultanism. See Chehabi and Linz, "Theory of Sultanism," 4–7. While the term *sultanism* has been applied to Gómez (as the authors note on page 5), and a case could be made that *neosultanism* is likewise applicable, I prefer the term *neopatrimonial* for two reasons. First, *sultanism* might strike readers as exoticizing Gómez (and Venezuela), while *neopatrimonialism* emphasizes the continuity between his regime and other, later regimes across the globe. Second, *neopatrimonialism* focuses attention on the interplay between patrimonial and bureaucratic forms of rule, rather than focusing narrowly on the power exercised by one individual, and thus offers greater insight into the regime as a whole.

27. Similarly, it was the perception of excessive patrimonialism that gave rise to complaints of corruption in eighteenth-century England, according to Woodfine, "Tempters or Tempted?"

28. The term *peculado*, despite its literal meaning of "embezzlement," was often used to refer to all forms of corruption, including what I have labeled as predatory corruption.

29. Yarrington, "Tax Farming," 246–47.

30. Siso, *Castro y Gómez*, 384–85.

31. López Contreras, *Proceso político social*, 17; and López Contreras, *Páginas para la historia*, 241–42.

32. Ziems, *El gomecismo*.

33. Yarrington, "Tax Farming," 246–62.

34. Ministerio de Hacienda, "Introducción," in *Memoria de Hacienda* (1916), b (this page is lettered, not numbered).

35. The changing nature of neopatrimonialism after the death of Gómez may be conceptualized as movement along a spectrum from "predatory neopatrimonialism" towards "regulated neopatrimonialism," following the typologies in Bach, "Patrimonialism and Neopatrimonialism."

36. Coronil, *Magical State*. Coronil's conceptualization of the Gómez regime (see especially 68–69, 76–86) is largely consistent with mine, but he focuses primarily on the post-Gómez era. Moreover, in contrast to my analysis, he does not devote attention to the regime's involvement in cattle, liquor, or Chapter VII payments, nor does he discuss the corruption trials in detail.

37. López Maya, *El ocaso del chavismo*, 47–52; López Maya, "Populism, 21st-century Socialism, and Corruption," 69–71; and Giraudy et al., "Impact of Neopatrimonialism."

38. Even Alfonso Quiroz's magisterial history of malfeasance and its detrimental effects on economic development in Peru does not offer a sustained analysis of anticorruption. Quiroz, *Corrupt Circles*. Similarly, Niblo, *Mexico in the 1940s*, offers little analysis of anticorruption.

39. Muir and Gupta, "Rethinking the Anthropology of Corruption"; Kroeze, Vitória, and Geltner, *Anticorruption in History*.

40. Kroeze, Vitória, and Geltner, "Introduction," 6; see also Knights, *Trust and Distrust*.

41. For the importance of affect in the study of (anti)corruption, see Muir and Gupta, "Rethinking the Anthropology of Corruption," S10–S11.

42. Cristóbal Kay notes that modernization theory "was largely absorbed uncritically [beginning in the 1950s] by social scientists and policy makers in Latin America." Kay, "Modernization and Dependency Theory," 15.

43. For diverse approaches to state formation, see Centeno and Ferraro, *State and Nation Making*; Centeno, *Blood and Debt*; Derby, *Dictator's Seduction*; and Graham, *Patronage and Politics*.

44. Joseph and Nugent, *Everyday Forms of State Formation*.

45. McBeth, *Dictatorship and Politics*; and Martz, *Acción Democrática*. There was significant overlap between the young democratic reformers and the radical Left; see Sosa A. and Lengrand, *Del garibaldismo estudiantil*.

46. McBeth, *Juan Vicente Gómez*.

47. Owensby, *Intimate Ironies*, 72–99; and Owensby, "Middle Class Politics."

48. López and Weinstein, "Introduction: We Shall Be All."

49. Engels, "Corruption and Anticorruption"; and Bratsis, "Construction of Corruption." For a critique of teleological assumptions in some works utilizing concepts of patrimonialism and neopatrimonialism, see Pierce, *Moral Economies of Corruption*.

Chapter 1: The Formation of a Neopatrimonial State, to 1935

1. Cook to Department of State (hereafter, DS), May 11, 1925, 831.00/1269, United States National Archives and Records Administration, Records of the Department of State, Record Group 59, (hereafter, USNARA/RDS).

2. Weber, *Economy and Society*, 354–74.

3. Examples include Adams, "Rule of the Father"; Adams, *Familial State*; Charrad and Adams, "Patrimonialism, Past and Present"; Charrad, "Central and Local Patrimonialism"; and Miller, *Patriarchy*, 141–45. See also Knights, *Trust and Distrust*, 59–66.

4. Adams makes this point about patrimonialism in *The Familial State*, 17, and I extend it to neopatrimonialism.

5. Accounts of Gómez's routine include Pareja y Paz Soldán, *Juan Vicente Gómez* (1951), 52–54; Ochoa Briceño, *Lo que vi*, 108; and Polanco Alcántara, *Juan Vicente Gómez*, 416.

6. Polanco Alcántara, *Juan Vicente Gómez*, 483–84; and Skurski, "Leader and the People," 155–62.

7. Polanco Alcántara, *Juan Vicente Gómez*, 275–83.
8. Polanco Alcántara, *Juan Vicente Gómez*, 357–69.
9. Parada, *De Ocumare a Miraflores*, 88.
10. Dupuy, *Propiedades*, 10–11.
11. Polanco Alcántara, *Juan Vicente Gómez*, 454–55.
12. Pareja y Paz Soldán, *Juan Vicente Gómez* (1970), 90.
13. Polanco Alcántara, *Juan Vicente Gómez*, 458–59, 472–73.
14. López Contreras, *Proceso político social*, 14.
15. Botello, *Historia de Villa de Cura*, 196–98, 206.
16. Examples include Arcaya to Gómez, September 20, 1922, in Pino Iturrieta, *Positivismo y gomecismo*, 91–92; Gil Fortoul to Gómez, February 2, 1917, in Pino Iturrieta, *Positivismo y gomecismo*, 117–18; and Vallenilla Lanz to Gómez, May 30, 1927, in Pino Iturrieta, *Positivismo y gomecismo*, 154–55.
17. Vallenilla Lanz, preface to *La Rehabilitación de Venezuela*, ii.
18. "Contestación del Congreso Nacional al Mensaje del Comandante en Jefe del Ejército," [reprinted from *El Nuevo Diario*, May 20, 1916] in Vallenilla Lanz, *La Rehabilitación de Venezuela*, 48; and "Ley Orgánica de la Hacienda Nacional," [reprinted from *El Nuevo Diario*, June 16, 1918], in Vallenilla Lanz, 167.
19. Lynch, *Caudillos*, 5.
20. Lombardi, *Venezuela*, 157–212.
21. Zahler, *Ambitious Rebels*.
22. Lynch, *Caudillos*, 68, 103, 199–200, 281–83.
23. Deas, "Colombia, Ecuador, and Venezuela," 671–73; Ewell, *Venezuela: A Century of Change*, 14–15, 20–22.
24. Salcedo-Bastardo, *Historia fundamental*, 377.
25. Ewell, *Venezuela: A Century of Change*, 20–21, 27; Deas, "Colombia, Ecuador, and Venezuela," 671.
26. Bayly, *Birth of the Modern World, 1780–1914*.
27. "Acuerdo de la Legislatura del Estado Bolívar," (January 23, 1891) in Hernández, *Recopilación de artículos y documentos*, 29, 30.
28. "Programa de la Unión Democrática," (1889) in Grases et al., *Documentos que hicieron historia*, 2:94–95.
29. Muñoz Tébar, *El personalismo i el legalismo*, 175. For Muñoz Tébar's break with Guzmán Blanco, see Olivar, *Jesús Muñoz Tébar*, 82–83, 101.
30. Velásquez, *La caída*, 157–59; García Ponce, *Política y clase media*, 184; and Ewell, *Venezuela: A Century of Change*, 24–25.
31. Lecuna, *La Revolución de Queipa*, 31–34; and Velásquez, *La caída*, 271.
32. González Escorihuela, *Las ideas políticas*; and Muñoz, "Táchira Frontier," 303–10.
33. Polanco Alcántara, *Juan Vicente Gómez*, 33–5.

34. Caballero, *Gómez, el tirano*, 43; McBeth, *Gunboats*, 10–11.
35. Polanco Alcántara, *Juan Vicente Gómez*, 479–97.
36. Gómez, *El poder andino*, 9–23.
37. Quintero, *El ocaso*, 39–70.
38. For discussion of the Libertadora and the blockade, see Velásquez, *La caída*, 383–442; and McBeth, *Gunboats*, 81–104.
39. Rangel, *Gómez: el amo del poder*, 295.
40. Picón Salas, *Los días de Cipriano Castro*, 204–05; Ewell, *Venezuela: A Century of Change*, 39.
41. Sullivan, "Rise of Despotism in Venezuela," 379–80, 402; McBeth, *Gunboats*, 106–7. For documents related to Castro and Gómez's cattle partnership, see *Boletín del Archivo Histórico de Miraflores* (hereafter, *BAHM*), no. 89 (1976): 121–33.
42. Polanco Alcántara, *Juan Vicente Gómez*, 79–80, 84–87.
43. Sullivan, "Rise of Despotism in Venezuela," 536–8; McBeth, *Gunboats*, 106–8.
44. Rodríguez Gallard, "Crisis de la economía," 139–45.
45. Harwich Vallenilla, "El modelo económico del liberalism amarillo," 242.
46. José Gil Delgado to Ministro de Estado, May 4, 1905, legajo 1808, file Caracas 1905, document no. 27, Archivo Histórico Nacional (Madrid), Ministerio de Asunto Exteriores, Serie Correspondencia, Informes de la legación de España en Caracas.
47. Paredes, *Diario de mi prisión*, 168.
48. Paredes, *Diario de mi prisión*, 321.
49. Sullivan, "Rise of Despotism in Venezuela," 402.
50. This paragraph draws on McBeth, *Gunboats*, 213–235; Polanco Alcántara, *Juan Vicente Gómez*, 89–130; and Ewell, *Venezuela and the United States*, 103–13.
51. Some of Castro's relationships with women were also rumored to be coercive. For a novelistic treatment by one of his foes, see Morantes, *El cabito*.
52. Ramón Velásquez, "Aspectos de la evolución política," 14.
53. Pedro Quartin to Ministro del Estado, January 9, 1909, Legajo 1808, file Correspondencia General, Venezuela Política, 1909, doct. no. 3, Archivo Histórico Nacional (Madrid), Ministerio de Asuntos Exteriores, Serie Correspondencia, Informes de la legación de España en Caracas.
54. Pedro Quartin to Ministro del Estado, February 16, 1909, Legajo 1808, file Correspondencia General, Venezuela Politica, 1909, doct no. 10, Archivo Historico Nacional (Madrid), Ministerio de Asunto Exteriores, Serie Correspondencia, Informes de la legación de España en Caracas.
55. "Impuestos y exclusivismos," *El Grito del Pueblo*, January 7, 1910, en-

closed in Corbett to Grey, January 12, 1910, United Kingdom National Archives, Foreign Office (hereafter, UKNA/FO) 199/232. The next sentence is based on Corbett's dispatch.

56. Gilliat-Smith to Grey, August 10, 1911, UKNA/FO 199/229.

57. Harford to Grey, November 13, 1911, UKNA/FO 371/1277.

58. "Venezuela. Annual Report, 1912," enclosed with Harford to Grey, February 13, 1913, UKNA/FO 371/1861.

59. "Memoria política acerca de posibles contingencias en el orden internacional y singularmente en relación con Venezuela," enclosed in Servet to Ministro de Estado, March 4–5, 1913, file "Correspondencia General, Venezuela, Politica, 1913," Legajo 1808, Archivo Histórico Nacional (Madrid), Ministerio de Asuntos Exteriores, Serie Correspondencia, Informes de la legación de España en Caracas.

60. Harford to Grey, January 4, 1913, UKNA/FO 371/1861.

61. Urbaneja, "El sistema politico gomecista," 61.

62. Brewer, *Sinews of Power*.

63. Centeno, *Blood and Debt*.

64. Ziems, *El gomecismo*.

65. Caffery to DS, January 17, 1912, USNARA/RDS, 831.20.

66. Harford to Grey, September 17, 1912, UKNA/FO 371/1552.

67. Pietropaoli to Cardenal Merry del Val, July 5, 1913, in Castillo Lara, *Apuntes para una historia documental*, 3:182.

68. Foucault, *Discipline and Punish*, 188; Fujitani, *Splendid Monarchy*, 105–54; and Mitchell, *Colonising Egypt*, 34–48.

69. Pietropaoli to Cardenal Merry del Val, July 6, 1913, in Castillo Lara, *Apuntes para una historia documental*, 3:183.

70. Linder, "Agriculture and Rural Society," 231–35; Gómez to Murillo, December 5, 1908, in *BAHM*, nos. 114–115 (1981–1982): 9; and Gómez to Murillo, January 16, 1909, in *BAHM*, nos. 114–115: 20.

71. Ziems, "Un ejército de alcance nacional," 133.

72. For more detailed discussion of the 1913–14 crisis, see McBeth, *Dictatorship and Politics*, 68–84; and Polanco Alcántara, *Juan Vicente Gómez*, 175–206.

73. McGill, *Poliantea*, 62, 64.

74. McGill, *Poliantea*, 67–69.

75. Siso, *Castro y Gómez*, 362.

76. López Contreras, *Proceso politico social*, 17.

77. García Jiménez, *Guigue*, 65–66.

78. Colmenter V., *Economía y política en Trujillo*, 102.

79. Ochoa Briceño, *Lo que vi*, 105, 107, 173, 175; and McGill, *Poliantea*, 217.

80. Ochoa Briceño, *Lo que vi*, 155.

81. López Contreras, *Proceso politico social*, 17.
82. Jurado de Responsabilidad Civil y Administrativa (hereafter, JRCA), *Sentencias*, 4:140–42.
83. Velásquez, *La caída*, 37.
84. McGoodwin to DS, February 15, 1915, USNARA/RDS, 831.00/718.
85. For British documentation of events in Los Caños, see the two files "Caños, Government Raid On," UKNA/FO 199/185; and "Caños, Government Raid On and Claims," UKNA/FO 199/186. See also Harford to Grey, July 16, 1915, UKNA/FO 371/2501; Harford to Grey, August 13, 1915, UKNA/FO 371/2051; Beaumont to Balfour, October 15, 1917, UKNA/FO 371/3074; and "Venezuela Annual Report, 1921," UKNA/FO 371/7325. For an anonymous Venezuelan account, see "Memorandum de los hechos realizados," Carúpano, March 17, 1915, in *BAHM*, nos. 61–63 (1969): 183–85.
86. Harford to Grey, April 28, 1915, UKNA/FO 371/2502, and enclosed memorandum.
87. Deas, "Colombia, Ecuador, and Venezuela," 678.
88. Kornblith and Quintana, "Gestión fiscal," 166–69.
89. Silva, "Pablo Ramírez: A Political Technocrat."
90. Márquez, *Presencia del Táchira*, 8.
91. Quintero, "De la alucinación a la eficiencia."
92. Ramón Velásquez, "La hacienda pública en 1921," in *BAHM*, no. 59 (1969): 67.
93. Bracho Sierra, "Cincuenta años de ingresos fiscales," 36.
94. Beaumont to Grey, September 6, 1916, UKNA/FO 371/2801.
95. Brett to DS, December 7, 1918, USNARA/RDS, 831.51/58.
96. "Historia Rentística de Venezuela, 1908–1930," enclosed with Summerlin to DS, June 17, 1931, USNARA/RDS, Box 5793, 831.51/162; and Izard, *Series estadísticas*, 214.
97. McGoodwin to DS, August 3, 1917, USNARA/RDS, 831.51/49.
98. McGoodwin to DS, September 21, 1917, USNARA/RDS, 831.51/52.
99. Dupuy, *Propiedades*, 46; and Harford to Grey, July 6, 1915, UKNA/FO 371/2502.
100. Cook to DS, June 26, 1926, USNARA/RDS, 831.00/1302; and Dupuy, *Propiedades*, 93.
101. The quotation is from Cook to DS, June 26, 1926, 831.00/1302. Other information on Hatos de Caura comes from Polanco Alcántara, *Gómez*, 476; Dupuy, *Propiedades*, 99–100; and Cook to DS, November 30, 1926, USNARA/RDS, 831.00/1316.
102. Lavin, *Halo for Gómez*, 200–01.

103. Summerlin to DS, July 15, 1931, USNARA/RDS, 831.00/1487, Box 5785.
104. Arellano-Gault, *Corruption in Latin America*, 53–101.
105. Bjarnegard, "Focusing on Masculinity," 264–65.
106. Elías Pino Iturrieta, "Estudio preliminar," in Segnini, *Los hombres del Benemérito*, 1:21–23.
107. Gobbini to Cardenal Gasparri, October 21, 1917, in Castillo Lara, *Apuntes para una historia*, 4:259.
108. Ochoa Briceño, *Lo que vi*, 107.
109. Yarrington, *Coffee Frontier*, 107.
110. Alfredo Peña, "Una ley que obligue a los partidos a mostrar publicamente el origen de sus fondos, propone el ex-presidente Caldera," *El Nacional*, September 21, 1977, C-1; and Coronil and Skurski, "Dismembering and Remembering the Nation," 297n25.
111. Yarrington, *Coffee Frontier*, 138–53.
112. "Venezuela Annual Report, 1932," UKNA/FO 371/16622.
113. "Saneamiento moral. Un jefe civil fuera de la ley," *Ecos de Torondoy* (Torondoy, Mérida) July 24, 1925.
114. Sloan to DS, April 8, 1926, USNARA/RDS, 831.00/1293.
115. Uzcátegui to Gómez, April 19, 1918, in *BAHM*, no. 120 (January–June 1985): 49–51; quote, 51.
116. For a synthesis, see Buchan and Hill, *Intellectual History*.

Chapter 2: The Gomecista Cattle Monopoly

1. Cardozo, *Sobre el cauce de un pueblo*, 328, 332, 336–39.
2. Omaña to Gómez, July 20, 1914, in *BAHM*, nos. 28–29 (1964): 148–49.
3. "Ultima hora," *El Relator* (Trujillo), March 14, 1936.
4. For a broad statement accusing Gómez of treating Venezuela as his personal possession, see "Persecutions against the Students in Venezuela," undated anonymous memo written by Venezuelan students, enclosed in Cicely Craven (Secretary, Howard League for Penal Reform, London) to Hugh Dalton (M.P. and Parliamentary Under Secretary, FO), December 8, 1930, UKNA/FO 371/14300. The students stated that Gómez "sincerely thinks . . . that the country is his private property, the realm conquered and conserved by sheer force by his sword. The natural conclusion follows up in his primitive mind that the life, liberty and property of the citizens are benefits that he has allowed them to enjoy and that he can withdraw from them at any moment he pleases." Specific parallels between Gomecista government and management of land and livestock include Cook to DS, May 11, 1925, USNARA/RDS, 831.00/1269; "Venezuela Annual Report, 1935," 2, UKNA/FO 371/19847; Joaquín Gabaldón Márquez to Laureano Vallenilla Lanz,

November 6, 1928, in Gabaldón Márquez, *Memoria y cuento*, 196; and Rangel, *Gómez*, 298–99.

5. Rourke, *Gómez*, 205–6.

6. For background on Venezuela's cattle industry, see Carvallo, *El hato venezolano*; and Briceño, *La ganadería en los llanos*.

7. Cartay, *La mesa de la meseta*, 56.

8. Febres Cordero, *Cocina criollo*.

9. Sauer to DS, March 31, 1919, USNARA/RDS, 831.00/898.

10. "Sobre exportación de ganado," *Panorama* (Maracaibo), October 1, 1919, 5.

11. "Sábados científicos," *Patria* (Mérida) August 22, 1925.

12. Williams, "Political Economy of Meat," 148.

13. Rangel, *Gómez*, 298–99.

14. Many of Gómez's property acquisitions are listed in Dupuy, *Propiedades*.

15. Harford to Grey, July 20, 1912, UKNA/FO 371/1552; Harford to Grey, July 6, 1915, UKNA/FO 371/2502; and Dupuy, *Propiedades*, 46.

16. Harford to Grey, April 28, 1915, UKNA/FO 371/2502.

17. Arévalo Cedeño, *Viva Arévalo Cedeño*, 9–11.

18. Brett to DS, September 23, 1915, USNARA/RDS, 831.00/753.

19. For Gómez's dealings with the British-owned meat plant and his control over grazing land in this region, see Yarrington, "Vestey Cattle Enterprise."

20. Dupuy, *Propiedades*, 95.

21. "Venezuela Annual Report, 1909," UKNA/FO 371/1026.

22. McBeth, *Dictatorship and Politics*, 35–39; McGill, *Poliantea*, 171; and Gil Fortoul to Gómez, February 10, 1915, in Segnini, *Los Hombres*, 1:407.

23. Rodríguez, "Gomez y el agro," 104.

24. "Venezuela Annual Report, 1912," 12, UKNA/FO 371/1861.

25. Siso, *Castro y Gómez*, 382.

26. "Intervención del Diputado Alfredo Pacheco Miranda, sobre Confiscación de los Bienes del General Juan Vicente Gómez en la sesión del 20 de abril de 1936," in *Gobierno y época del Presidente Eleazar López Contreras*, 4:125–28; and Julio Morales Lara, "Aragua para la agricultura," *El Universal*, February 16, 1946.

27. Examples include Jurado to Gómez, August 7, 1924, in Segnini, *Los hombres*, 2:85–86; Galavís to Gómez, October 2, 1910, in Segnini, *Los hombres*, 1:327–28; Quintana to Gómez, January 3, 1915, in *BAHM*, nos. 61–63 (1969): 298–300; and the examples in Linder, "Agriculture and Rural Society," 230–32, discussed in more detail below.

28. Baldó to Gómez, March 25, 1915, in *BAHM*, nos. 61–63 (1969), 72–73.

29. Jurado to Gómez, April 1, 1914, in Segnini, *Los hombres*, 2:77–78.

30. Jurado to Gómez, August 7, 1924, in Segnini, *Los hombres*, 2:85–86; and Dupuy, *Propiedades*, 115, 117.

31. Freeman to McGoodwin, September 1, 1917, enclosed in McGoodwin to DS, October 8, 1917, USNARA/RDS, 831.00/807.

32. Gómez to Murillo, January 16, 1909, in *BAHM*, nos. 114–115 (1981–82): 20. See also Gómez to Murillo, December 5, 1908, in *BAHM*, nos. 114–115 (1981–82): 9.

33. "Al General Pedro Murillo" *Patria y Unión* (Barinas) June 23, 1916.

34. Sarmiento to Gómez, June 27, 1923, in *BAHM*, nos. 133–135 (1990–91): 175–76; Uzcátegui to Gómez, April 19, 1918, in *BAHM*, no. 120 (1985): 49–51.

35. Yarrington, *Coffee Frontier*, 158; and Cardozo, "Duaca a princípios del siglo," 50.

36. When jefes civiles contradicted monopolistic expectations in the beef market, they received explicit praise in the press. See "Notas de Duaca," *Notas* (Barquisimeto), August 18, 1918; and untitled notice from San Fernando in *Notas* (Barquisimeto), April 20, 1924.

37. Pérez Soto to Gómez, April 3, 1916, in Segnini, *Los hombres*, 2:276–78.

38. Pérez Soto to Gómez, December 13, 1919, in *BAHM*, no. 75 (1973): 314–15.

39. "La Palabra del General Gomez" *El Nuevo Diario*, September 16, 1915, reprinted in Vallenilla Lanz, *La Rehabilitación*, 13–14; and "El Saneamiento Moral del País," *El Nuevo Diario*, December 21, 1915, reprinted in Vallenilla Lanz, *La Rehabilitación*, 28–29.

40. Jurado to Gómez, April 1, 1914, in Segnini, *Los Hombres*, 2:77–78.

41. Medina to Gómez, August 12, 1915, in *BAHM*, nos. 61–63 (1969): 40–41; "En práctica," *La voz de Portuguesa* (Guanare), September 24, 1915; "Noticias del interior," *El Rehabilitador* (Trujillo), October 20, 1915; Rodríguez to Gómez, November 7, 1915, in *BAHM*, no. 126 (1988): 112–13; "Acta de Instalacion de la Junta 'Gratitud a Gomez' de Criadores Zamoranos y Acuerdo," *Patria y Unión* (Barinas), December 1, 1915; and "La Voz del Jefe," *Patria y Unión* (Barinas), January 1, 1916.

42. Baldó to Gómez, December 24, 1915, in *BAHM*, nos. 61–63 (1969): 84–85.

43. Hidalgo to Gómez, September 2, 1915, in *BAHM*, nos. 61–63 (1969): 360.

44. Beaumont to Curzon, May 26, 1923, UKNA/FO 371/8530.

45. Pérez Soto to Gómez, June 26, 1915, in Segnini, *Los hombres*, 2:276.

46. Jurado to Urdaneta Maya, June 23, 1924, in Segnini, *Los hombres*, 2:85.

47. González Deluca, *Los comerciantes*, 155.

48. Caraballo Perhichi, *Obras públicas*, 42, 93; "Matadero público," *La voz de Portuguesa* (Guanare), December 19, 1915; "El 19 de Diciembre—Patrióticos festejos en toda la República," *El Nuevo Diario*, December 19, 1931; "El 19 de Diciembre en Valera, La Inauguración del Nuevo Matadero," *La Voz de Valera* (Valera), December 24 1932.

49. Gómez to Martínez Méndez, December 4, 1913, in *BAHM*, nos. 64–66 (1970): 299; and Hidalgo to Gómez, September 2, 1915, in *BAHM*, nos. 61–63 (1969): 359–60.

50. Morantes, *Puñado de guijarros*, 77–78; Work to Harford, May 14, 1915, UKNA/FO 199/224; and McGoodwin to DS, April 5, 1918, USNARA/RDS, 831.62221/2.

51. Pilcher, *Sausage Rebellion*.

52. Sarmiento to Gómez, December 3, 1923, in *BAHM*, nos. 133–135 (1990–1991): 189–90.

53. Galavís to Gómez, October 10, 1923, in Segnini, *Los Hombres*, 1:331–32.

54. Galavís to Gómez, September 24, 1925, in Segnini, *Los Hombres*, 1:333–34.

55. Galavís to Gómez, September 23, 1926, in Segnini, *Los Hombres*, 1:335–36.

56. Beaumont to Balfour, July 13, 1922, UKNA/FO 199/188.

57. Galavís to Gómez, June 13, 1922, in *BAHM*, no. 60 (1969): 203–4; and González Deluca, *Los comerciantes*, 215.

58. Beaumont to Curzon, May 1, 1923, and May 26, 1923, UKNA/FO 371/8530.

59. Siso, *Castro y Gómez*, 384–85.

60. Linder, "Agriculture and Rural Society," 230–35. Unless otherwise footnoted, all information in this paragraph and the next comes from this source. For brief biographical sketches of García, Colmenares Pacheco and Juan C. Gómez, see Segnini, *Los Hombres*, 1:175, 345, 459.

61. For other cases of political influence being used to acquire title to public lands in the Gómez era, see Yarrington, *Coffee Frontier*, 127–60.

62. Linder, "Agriculture and Rural Society," 233.

63. Donald to DS, June 6, 1916, USNARA/RDS, 831.00/773.

64. García to Gómez, January 18, 1916, in Segnini, *Los Hombres*, 1:364–66; and García to Gómez, November 14, 1916, in Segnini, *Los Hombres*, 1:366–67.

65. McGoodwin to DS, February 10, 1914, USNARA/RDS, 831.00/630.

66. Harford to Grey, February 12, 1914, UKNA/FO, 420/258.

67. Arévalo Cedeño, *Viva Arévalo*, 8 (see also pp. 9–11).

68. Sauer to DS, March 31, 1919, USNARA/RDS, 831.00/898.
69. "The Situation in Venezuela," McGoodwin to DS, March 16, 1914, USNARA/RDS, 831.00/640.
70. Gabaldón Márquez ("Jokanaán") to Leoni, October 20, 1928, in Gabaldón Márquez, *Memoria y cuento*, 181.
71. "Bola Roja," April 25, 1928, reprinted in *BAHM*, no. 7 (1960): 151–52.
72. "La Protesta," October 8, 1928, reprinted in Sanoja Hernández, *La oposición a la dictadura gomecista*, 185.
73. Pimentel, *Bajo la tiranía*, 155–56.
74. Gabaldón Márquez ("Jokanaán") to Leoni, October 20, 1928, in Gabaldón Márquez, *Memoria y cuento*, 181.
75. Pérez Contreras, "Maracay," 19; Lavin, *Halo for* Gómez, 200–201; and Summerlin to DS, July 15, 1931, USNARA/RDS, 831.00/1487, Box 5785.
76. "Venezuela Annual Report, 1932," 17, UKNA/FO 371/16622.
77. Pilcher, *Sausage Rebellion*, 1–3, 7, 10–11, 138–41, 183–85; and Rausch, *Colombia: Territorial Rule*, 177.
78. "Memorandum on the present conditions, economic and commercial, in Venezuela," enclosed in Keeling to Simon, March 2, 1934, UKNA/FO 371/17618.
79. "Memorandum on the present conditions, economic and commercial, in Venezuela," enclosed in Keeling to Simon, March 2, 1934, UKNA/FO 371/17618. At 1934 exchange rates, 11,000 bolívares was US$3,000.
80. Ramírez to Gómez, May 24, 1934, in Segnini, *Los hombres*, 2:331–32.
81. Torres, *Memorias*, 138.
82. Cartay, *Memoria de los orígenes*, 177.
83. Torres, *Memorias*, 127–30.
84. Dupuy, *Propiedades*, 80; Torres, *Memorias*, 129–37; Keeling to Simon, May 20, 1935, UKNA/FO 371/18782.
85. Torres, *Memorias*, 136.
86. Torres, *Memorias*, 127–39. Torres claimed that Gómez planned to accept lower prices from the company but that he died before changes were implemented (136).
87. "Venezuela, Annual Report, 1935," UKNA/FO 371/19847.
88. JRCA, *Sentencias*, 5:129–30.
89. Torres, *Memorias*, 138; see also Nicholson to DS, December 30, 1935, USNARA/RDS, 831.00/1557, Box 5785.

Chapter 3: Bureaucratic Reform as Anticorruption

1. The literature on tax farming is extensive; studies useful for comparative purposes include Copland and Godley, "Revenue Farming in Compar-

ative Perspective"; Salzmann, "Ancien Régime Revisited"; Kiser and Kane, "Revolution and State Structure"; and Christian, "Vodka and Corruption."

2. Rodríguez, *Los paisajes geohistóricos*; and Rodríguez, *La historia de la caña*, 112–18. Distinctions between rum and aguardiente could be blurry, so *aguardiente* sometimes referred to both.

3. Celestino Castro to Cipriano Castro, January 18, 1902, in *BAHM*, no. 6 (1960): 99–100; Briceño to Baldó, August 14, 1903, in Briceño, *Cartas sobre el Táchira*, 221–22; and Rodríguez, *La Historia de la Caña*, 118.

4. Rodríguez, *La historia*, 118; and Federico Bauder, "Tabaco y aguardiente: Consideraciones acera del decreto ejecutivo de 27 de junio sobre renta de tabaco y aguardiente" (1904), in Carrillo Batalla, *Historia de las finanzas públicas*, 1:222–25.

5. "Contrato del Ministerio de Hacienda con el Ciudadano Julio Sabres [sic], cediendo la Administración de la Renta de Licores" (1905), in Carrillo Batalla, *Historia de las finanzas públicas*, 2:418–19; and "Resolución sobre Reparto del 35% de la Renta de Licores" (1905), in Carrillo Batalla, *Historia de las finanzas públicas*, 2:420–21.

6. "Resolución sobre Remate de Renta de Licores" (1906), in Carrillo Batalla, *Historia de las finanzas públicas*, 2:432.

7. Useful works on the topic include Alexander Rodríguez, *Search for Public Policy*; Centeno, *Blood and Debt*; Rosenthal, *Salt and the Colombian State*; Deas, "Fiscal Problems of Nineteenth-Century Colombia," 294–97, 307–9; and Carey, *Distilling the Influence of Alcohol*.

8. Ministerio de Hacienda, *Exposición que dirige al Congreso Nacional . . . en 1910*, 223–24.

9. "Impuestos ilegales establecidos por los contratistas," in Ministerio de Hacienda, *Memoria* (1916), lxi; "Una Aventura de Prieto" (December 1909, Lagunillas, Mérida), and "Eminencias que se Derrumban" (January 10, 1910, Lagunillas, Mérida), Archivo Tulio Febres Cordero, Mérida, Hojas Sueltas section; and Viso C., *La epopeya del ron*, 134.

10. For the standard contract, see Ministerio de Hacienda, *Memoria* (1914), 427–28.

11. Vásquez to Márquez Bustillos, December 26, 1915, in *BAHM*, nos. 101–106 (1978): 195–97; Ministerio de Hacienda, *Memoria* (1916), 304–5, 308; and Parada, *De Ocumare a Miraflores*, 149.

12. "Eminencias que se Derrumban." This broadside published by Manuel Uzcátegui includes a copy of the subrental agreement from June 1909 and copies of correspondence among Araujo, Uzcátegui, and treasury minister Abel Santos.

13. Rondón Nucete, *Primeros años del gomecismo*, 43–44.

14. [Ramón J. Velásquez], "El Ministro Abel Santos y los Liberales de

Mérida," in *BAHM*, no. 7 (1960): 51. See also, Febres Cordero to Gómez, December 31, 1909, in *BAHM*, no. 7 (1960): 66.

15. "Eminencias que se Derrumban." Unless otherwise footnoted, all material in this paragraph is from this broadside.

16. "Una Aventura de Prieto." This broadside, published by Elpidio García, reproduces several documents related to the conflict.

17. Santos to Presidente del Estado Mérida [Cardona], December 22, 1909, in *BAHM*, no. 7 (1960): 61.

18. These letters are published in *BAHM*, no. 7 (1960), including Parra to Gómez, December 30, 1909, pp. 64–65; Nucete to Gómez, December 31, 1909, pp. 65–66; Febres Cordero to Gómez, December 31, 1909, p. 66; Paoli to Gómez, December 31, 1909, p. 68; and Chalbaud Cardona to Gómez, December 24, 1909, pp. 58–59.

19. Chalbaud Cardona to Gómez, November 26, 1909, in *BAHM*, no. 7 (1960): 55–57; and Chalbaud Cardona to Gómez, December 17, 1909, in *BAHM*, no. 7 (1960): 58.

20. Chalbaud Cardona to Gómez, December 17, 1909, in *BAHM*, no. 7 (1960): 58; and Ramón J. Velásquez, "El Ministro Abel Santos y los Liberales de Mérida," in *BAHM*, no. 7 (1960): 51.

21. "Una Aventura de Prieto."

22. Viso C., *La epopeya del ron*, 134.

23. According to Cárdenas, Zulia's pre-reform tax farmer had used his position to establish a "rigorous monopoly." Cárdenas to Santos M. Gómez, March 6, 1919, in *BAHM*, no. 72 (1972): 200.

24. In April 1915, the Ministry ordered the contractor to discontinue charging the unauthorized tax of 4 bolívares per "carga" (63 liters) of rum leaving the state. "Impuestos ilegales establecidos por los contratistas," in Ministerio de Hacienda, *Memoria de Hacienda* (1916), lxi.

25. Vásquez to Márquez Bustillos, December 26, 1915, in *BAHM*, nos. 101–106 (1978): 195–97.

26. Segnini, *La consolidación*, 55. There was no public bidding for the state-level contracts. Rarely, recipients of the contracts publicly solicited bids from those wishing to sublease tax-farming rights at the district level. "Aviso," *Patria y Unión* (Barinas), December 11, 1916.

27. Gómez to Garbi, November 8, 1910, in *BAHM*, no. 67 (1970): 27; and Yarrington, *Coffee Frontier*, 92–93, 97, 99, 101, 145.

28. Uzcátegui to Gómez, June 12, 1914, in *BAHM*, nos. 28–29 (1964): 141–42.

29. García to Gómez, May 21, 1913, in Segnini, *Los hombres*, 1:357.

30. Ministerio de Hacienda, *Memoria de Hacienda* (1914), xxi.

31. Ministerio de Hacienda, *Memoria de Hacienda* (1914), cxviii.

32. Román Cárdenas, "Introducción," in Ministerio de Hacienda, *Memoria de Hacienda* (1914), a–j. Pages in the introduction are lettered rather than numbered.
33. Cárdenas, "Introducción," f.
34. Cárdenas, "Introducción," g.
35. Cárdenas, "Introducción," f–g.
36. Cárdenas, "Introducción," f–g.
37. Cárdenas, "Introducción," g.
38. Cárdenas, "Introducción," d.
39. Ogborn, *Spaces of Modernity*, 199.
40. Cárdenas, "Introducción," f–g.
41. Segnini, *La consolidación*, 58.
42. McGoodwin to DS, August 31, 1914, USNARA/RDS, 831.00/690; and McGoodwin to DS, October 19, 1914, USNARA/RDS, 831.00/696. See also H. D. Beaumont to Foreign Office, Caracas, June 27, 1917, UKNA/FO 371/3074.
43. McBeth, *Juan Vicente Gómez*, 111.
44. "Licores," in *Memoria de Hacienda* (Caracas: El Cojo, 1915), cxxv.
45. Ministerio de Hacienda, *Ley orgánica de la renta de licores, sancionada por el congreso nacional en 1915* (Caracas: El Cojo, 1915).
46. *Ley orgánica de la renta de licores*, article 1; "Decreto sobre funcionamiento e impuesto a pagar por la industria de licores, 1906," in Carrillo Batalla, *Historia de las finanzas públicas*, 2:425–29; and Rodríguez, *La historia de la caña*,115.
47. Cárdenas, "Introducción," in Ministerio de Hacienda, *Memoria de Hacienda* (1916), d–e; and "Servicio de Licores. Renta de Licores," in *Memoria de Hacienda* (Caracas: El Cojo, 1920), cxxvii.
48. "Instrucciones para las Administraciones de la Renta de Licores," in Ministerio de Hacienda, *Memoria de Hacienda* (1916), 307–9.
49. Political considerations prevented direct administration in these four states, as explained below.
50. Román Cárdenas to Administrador de la Renta de Licores, Circular No. 947, August 2, 1915, in Ministerio de Hacienda, *Memoria de Hacienda* (1916), 311–12.
51. Román Cárdenas to Administrador de la Renta de Licores, Circular No. 110, January 17, 1916, in *Memoria de Hacienda* (Caracas: El Cojo, 1917), p. 271.
52. Román Cárdenas to Administradores de la Renta de Licores, Circular No. 98, February 4, 1919, in *Memoria de Hacienda* (Caracas: El Cojo, 1920), 410–11.
53. Román Cárdenas, "Introducción," in *Memoria de Hacienda* (Caracas: El Cojo, 1917), b.

54. Cárdenas, "Introducción," b.
55. Cárdenas, "Introducción," b–h.
56. Cárdenas, "Introducción," c.
57. "Ley orgánica de la hacienda nacional," *El Nuevo Diario*, June 16, 1918, reprinted in Vallenilla Lanz, *La Rehabilitación de Venezuela*, 167.
58. "La situación fiscal y económica de Venezuela," *El Nuevo Diario*, October 5, 1917, reprinted in Vallenilla Lanz, *La Rehabilitación de Venezuela*, 114–15.
59. Beaumont to Foreign Office, June 27, 1917, UKNA/FO, 371/3074.
60. Brett to DS, La Guaira, December 7, 1918, USNARA/RDS, 831.51/58.
61. Cárdenas to Santos M. Gómez, Caracas, March 6, 1919, in *BAHM*, no. 72 (1972): 200–201.
62. Sauer, "Data for the World's Anti-Alcoholic Congress," May 7, 1919, USNARA/RDS, Maracaibo Consular Post Records, 1919, vol. 114, section 811.4.
63. "Decreto de 30 de junio de 1919," in *Memoria de Hacienda* (Caracas: El Cojo, 1920), cxxix-cxxx. See also Sauer, "Data for the World's Anti-Alcoholic Congress," May 7, 1919, USNARA/RDS, Maracaibo Consular Post Records, 1919, vol. 114, section 811.4.
64. Sauer, "Memorandum," appended to "Data for the World's Anti-Alcoholic Congress," May 7, 1919, USNARA/RDS, Maracaibo Consular Post Records, 1919, vol. 114, section 811.4.
65. Cárdenas to Gómez, Caracas, March 2, 1919, in Segnini, *Los hombres*, 1:151–53 (quotation, 152).
66. Cárdenas to Santos M. Gómez, Caracas, March 6, 1919, in *BAHM*, no. 72 (1972): 200–201.
67. *Memoria de Hacienda* (Caracas: El Cojo, 1920), cxxix, 1–3.
68. "Compañía disuelta," *Panorama* (Maracaibo) July 16, 1919, 1; "Compañía Anónima 'Unión Destiladora,'" *Panorama*, July 12, 1919, 6; and "Un buen negocio," *Panorama*, December 16, 1919, 3.
69. "Administración de la Renta de Licores de Maracaibo," January 3, 1920, in *Memoria de Hacienda* (Caracas: El Cojo, 1920), 204–5; and "Administración de la Renta de Licores de Maracaibo," December 31, 1920, in *Memoria de Hacienda* (Caracas: El Cojo, 1921), 340–41.
70. "Administración de la Renta de Licores de Maracaibo," January 3, 1920, in *Memoria de Hacienda* (Caracas: El Cojo, 1920), 204–5.
71. "Administración de la Renta de Licores de Maracaibo," December 31, 1920, in *Memoria de Hacienda* (Caracas: El Cojo, 1921), 340–41.
72. José J. Gabaldón to Román Cárdenas, November 10, 1919, in *BAHM*, nos. 112–113 (1981): 214–15.
73. Examples include "Administración de la Renta de Licores de Ciudad

Bolívar," January 1, 1920, in *Memoria de Hacienda* (Caracas: El Cojo, 1920), 217–18; "Administración de la Renta de Licores de Maracaibo," December 31, 1921, in *Memoria de Hacienda* (Caracas: Tipografia Americana, 1922), 225–26; and "Libertad industrial," *El Rehabilitador* (Trujillo), January 11, 1919, 2.

74. "Administración de la Renta de Licores de Trujillo," January 3, 1920, in *Memoria de Hacienda* (Caracas: El Cojo, 1920), 205–7.

75. "Las grandes reformas de la hacienda actual," *La Voz de Portuguesa* (Guanare), March 18, 1916.

76. For the continuation of tax farming in these states until 1932, see "Renta de Licores," in *Memoria de Hacienda* (Caracas: Lit. y Tip. Vargas, 1932), cxvii.

77. JRCA, *Sentencias*, 3:311–14, 324–26; and Dupuy, *Propiedades del General*, 11.

78. Pimentel was not named in the contract but worked as Ramos's partner. JRCA, *Sentencias*, 3:259–62, and 5:123; for Central Tacarigua, see Cordero Velásquez, *Gómez y las fuerzas vivas*, 118.

79. "Libertad Industrial," *El Rehabilitador* (Trujillo), January 11, 1919, 2; Omaña to Gómez, February 4, 1919, in Segnini, *Los hombres*, 2: 218–19; and Cárdenas to Administrador Renta Licores (Trujillo), March 29, 1919, in *Memoria de Hacienda* (Caracas: El Cojo, 1920), 414.

80. Pérez Soto to Gómez, February 3, 1918, in *BAHM*, no. 120 (1985): 12–13.

81. Amador Uzcátegui to Gómez, Mérida, May 27, 1924, in *BAHM*, no. 77 (1974): 225–26; and Uzcátegui to Gómez, Mérida, January 4, 1921, in *BAHM* nos. 130–132 (1989–1990): 271–72.

82. Tax farming was labeled "ruinous" in "Administración de la Renta de Licores de Maracaibo," January 3, 1920, in *Memoria de Hacienda* (Caracas: El Cojo, 1920), 204–5; and "deplorable" in "Administración de la Renta de Licores de Maracaibo" January 10, 1918, in *Memoria de Hacienda* (Caracas: El Cojo, 1918), 177–78.

83. McBeth, *Juan Vicente Gómez*, 66, 70.

84. Salazar-Carrillo and West, *Oil and Development*, 58.

85. "Administración de la Renta de Licores de Maracaibo," in *Memoria de Hacienda* (Caracas: Tipografía Americana, 1923), ci; and JRCA, *Sentencias*, 5:19.

86. "Arrendamiento del impuesto de licores," in *Memoria de Hacienda* (Caracas: Tipografía Universal, 1928), lxxvi; for contractors' names, see "Nómina de los contratistas del impuesto de aguardientes," in ibid., 388.

87. "Arrendamiento del impuesto de licores," in *Memoria de Hacienda* (Caracas: Tipografía Universal, 1929), cvi; and "Nómina de los arrendatarios del impuesto de aguardientes," in ibid., 460.

88. Karl, *Paradox of Plenty*, 61.

89. "Nómina de los Contratistas del Impuesto de Aguardientes," in *Memoria de Hacienda* (Caracas: Tipografia Americana, 1923), 516. The rate was recorded as 35,000 bolívares every two weeks.

90. "Administración de la Renta de Licores de Maracaibo," in *Memoria de Hacienda* (Caracas: Tipografia Americana, 1923), ci.

91. Baldó to Gómez, November 27, 1915, in *BAHM*, no. 126 (1988): 122; Cárdenas to Gómez, September 13, 1919, in *BAHM*, no. 72 (1972): 221–22; and "Nómina de los contratistas del impuesto de aguardientes para el primer semestre de 1916, con expresión de las cuotas quincenales," in Ministerio de Hacienda, *Memoria de Hacienda* (1916), 305. For the tax farmer in Mérida passing rate increases to his subcontractors, see JRCA, *Sentencias*, 4:144–45.

92. Copland and Godley, "Revenue Farming," 59–60; and White, "From Privatized to Government-Administered Tax Collection," 661.

93. Whitehead, "State Organization in Latin America," 46–47.

94. In addition to correspondence already cited, see Juan Alberto Ramírez to Gómez, San Cristóbal, September 27, 1925, in *BAHM*, no. 69 (1971): 216. Baldó claimed that state presidents could not meet their "public and personal obligations" without the liquor contracts. JRCA, *Sentencias*, 5:47.

95. Miguel Febres Cordero to Tulio Febres Cordero, July 11 and 21, 1927, Archivo Tulio Febres Cordero, Mérida, Correspondencia section.

96. "Nómina de los contratistas del impuesto de aguardientes," in *Memoria de Hacienda* (Caracas: Tipografia Universal, 1928), 388.

97. Examples include Amador Uzcátegui to Gómez, January 4, 1921, in *BAHM*, nos. 130–132 (1989–1990): 271–72; Aranguren to Sauer, Mérida, April 11, 1919, enclosed with Sauer, "Data for the World's Anti-Alcoholic Congress"; and Emil Sauer to DS, March 31, 1919, USNARA/RDS, 831.00/898.

98. Copland and Godley, "Revenue Farming," 64–65; and Christian, *Living Water*, 117–217, 353–81.

99. "Aplicación del articulo 121 de la Ley Orgánica de la Renta de Licores," in *Memoria de Hacienda* (Caracas: El Cojo, 1916), lxi–lxii.

100. See article 7 of the contract in Ministerio de Hacienda, *Memoria de Hacienda* (1916), 301–3.

101. JRCA, *Sentencias*, 5:18–20, 23–29, and 2:284, 301–2. For more on Bozo's involvement in the liquor industry, see Pérez Soto to Gómez, November 29, 1924, in Segnini, *Los hombres*, 2:285–87.

102. JRCA, *Sentencias*, 5:242–45.

103. Treasury Minister to liquor tax farmers, May 11, 1928, in *Memoria de Hacienda* (Caracas: Tipografia Universal, 1929), 461.

104. "Administración de la Renta de Licores de Trujillo," January, 24, 1918, in *Memoria de Hacienda* (Caracas: El Cojo, 1918), 180. See also JRCA, *Sentencias*, 5:240–41.

105. Quoted in Rodríguez, *La Historia de la* Caña, 119.

106. Pérez Soto to Gómez, November 29, 1924, in Segnini, *Los hombres*, 2:285–87 (quotation, 286).

107. Deas, "Fiscal Problems," 309.

108. Eloy Montenegro, "Memorandum para el Sr Dn Emile Sauer," enclosed with Sauer, "Data for the World's Anti-Alcoholic Congress," May 7, 1919, USNARA/RDS, Maracaibo Consular Post Records, 1919, vol. 114, section 811.4. Montenegro was Eustoquio Gómez's private secretary and jefe civil of Táchira's capital, San Cristóbal. Chiossone, *Memorias de un reaccionario*, 67.

109. JRCA, *Sentencias*, 5:28–29, 249.

110. JRCA, *Sentencias*, 5:47.

111. JRCA, *Sentencias*, 3:320–21, 326.

112. H. Eric Trammell to DS, Caracas, November 25, 1930, USNARA/RDS, 831.00/1466, Box 5785.

113. Trammell to DS, November 25, 1930, USNARA/RDS, 831.00/1466, Box 5785; and Beard to Department of Overseas Trade, June 22, 1931, UKNA/FO 371/15145.

114. Summerlin to DS, June 15, 1931, USNARA/RDS, 831.00/1480, Box 5785.

115. Summerlin to DS, June 15, 1931, USNARA/RDS, 831.51/163, Box 5793.

116. "Importantes decretos presidenciales," *El Nuevo Diario* (Caracas), December 19, 1931, 1–3.

117. "Comisionado Especial—General José Félix Machado Díaz, nombrado por resolución de ayer comisionado especial para la organización de la renta de licores con jurisdicción en todo el territorio nacional," and "Importantes nombramientos del Ministerio de Hacienda," *El Nuevo Diario* (Caracas), December 23, 1931, 1.

118. Summerlin to DS, Caracas, February 4, 1932, USNARA/RDS, 831.51/174, Box 5793.

119. Summerlin to DS, Caracas, May 19, 1932, USNARA/RDS, 831.51/179, Box 5793.

120. Wilson to DS, Caracas, June 29, 1933, USNARA/RDS, 831.51/189, Box 5793.

121. Dirección de la Renta Interna, "Documento número 318," October 5, 1936, in *Memoria de Hacienda* (Caracas: Lit. y Tip. Vargas, 1937), 461; and JRCA, *Sentencias*, 5:122–23.

122. "Texto íntegro de la sensacional demanda del Procurador General de la Nación," *El Universal* (Caracas), May 4, 1936, reprinted in *Gobierno y época del Presidente Eleazar López Contreras*, 10:74–77; and JRCA, *Sentencias*, 2:241.

123. Coronil, *Magical State*.

Chapter 4: Opponents and Prisoners

1. For a discussion of the affective dimension of state formation with a focus different than mine, see Stoler, "Affective States."

2. Dupouy, "La clase media en Venezuela"; García Ponce, *Política y clase media*; and Clemente Travieso, *Mujeres venezolanas*, 55–64. The historiography on Venezuela's middle class is underdeveloped compared to larger countries such as Brazil, Mexico, Argentina, Peru, and Colombia.

3. Owensby, *Intimate Ironies*; and Porter, *From Angel to Office Worker*.

4. For a novelistic treatment set during the Gómez era, see Palacios, *Ana Isabel, una niña decente*. For comparative Latin American cases, see Parker, *Idea of the Middle Class*; and Suárez Findlay, *Imposing Decency*.

5. Holmes, *Corruption*, 4–17, and works cited therein.

6. Exceptions include Smith, *Culture of Corruption*; and Heinzen, *Art of the Bribe*.

7. Prieto, "Corrupt and Rapacious"; Smith, "Paradoxes of the Public Sphere"; and Knights, *Trust and Distrust*, 313–18.

8. This definition of emotions is adapted from Strange and Cribb, "Historical Perspectives," which states, "emotions are processed feelings, sensed, experienced and expressed distinctly through historically situated language and modes of expression" (4).

9. Frevert, *Emotions in History*, 12. See also Frevert, *Politics of Humiliation*, 1–76.

10. Plamper, *History of Emotions*, 68–71, 303.

11. This definition is Julian Pitt-Rivers's, as quoted in Piccato, *City of Suspects*, 80.

12. Johnson and Lipsett-Rivera, "Introduction," in *Faces of Honor*, 3.

13. Burkholder, "Honor and Honors."

14. Chambers, *From Subjects to Citizens*, 161–242; and Uribe-Uran, *Honorable Lives*.

15. Drinot, *Sexual Question*; Sippial, *Prostitution*, 148–79; and Beattie, *Tribute of Blood*.

16. Chambers, *From Subjects to Citizens*, 193.

17. Zahler, *Ambitious Rebels*, 137.

18. Zahler, *Ambitious Rebels*, 12–149; and Piccato, *City of Suspects*, 77–102.

19. Caulfield, Chambers, and Putnam, *Honor, Status, and Law*.

20. Zahler, *Ambitious Rebels*, 150–85; and Chambers, *From Subjects to Citizens*, 180–215.

21. Skurski, "Leader and the 'People,'" 134–73.

22. Díaz, *Female Citizens*, 173–74.

23. Gómez referred to himself as "first agriculturalist, first rancher, first military man, first organizer, and first worker of Venezuela." Polanco Alcántara, *Juan Vicente Gómez*, 480. In his rare public utterances, Gómez also portrayed himself as dedicated more to agrarian work than to politics. See "Un discurso del General Gómez," in Velásquez, *Memorias de Venezuela*, 346.

24. "Impresiones de Maracay," *El nuevo diario,* July 29, 1915 in Vallenilla Lanz, *La Rehabilitación de Venezuela*, 5–7.

25. Veloz Goiticoa, *Maracay*, 6, 8, 14–15.

26. "El General Gómez y los hombres de trabajo," pamphlet, 1914, enclosed in McGoodwin to DS, February 23, 1914, USNARA/RDS, 831.00/633.

27. "Protección a las Clases Laboriosas," *El Nuevo Diario*, May 24, 1918, in Vallenilla Lanz, *La Rehabilitación de Venezuela*, 148.

28. "La Evolución Industrial de Venezuela" *El Nuevo Diario*, August 25, 1915, in Vallenilla Lanz, *La Rehabilitación de Venezuela*, 11.

29. Capriles, *Jira patriótica*, 13, 23, 83. For a discussion drawing on some of these quotations, see Caraballo Perichi, *Obras públicas, fiestas y mensajes*, 118–19.

30. "La Voz del Jefe" *Patria y Unión* (Barinas) January 1, 1916; Polanco Alcántara, *Juan Vicente Gómez*, 355–56; and Pereira, *En la prisión*, 136.

31. Arévalo Cedeño, *Viva Arévalo Cedeño*, 3–11.

32. Arévalo Cedeño, *Viva Arévalo Cedeño*, 26.

33. Arévalo Cedeño, *Viva Arévalo Cedeño*, 7.

34. Arévalo Cedeño, *Viva Arévalo Cedeño*, 9–11.

35. Arévalo Cedeño, *Viva Arévalo Cedeño*, 11, emphasis in original.

36. Arévalo Cedeño, *Viva Arévalo Cedeño*, 8.

37. For an overview of race relations in this period, see Wright, *Café con leche*, 69–96.

38. Santos to Gómez, March 23, 1921, and Coronil to Gómez, March 23, 1921, both in *BAHM*, nos. 130–132 (1989): 170.

39. Arévalo Cedeño, "Carta Abierta," September 22, 1914, in *Viva Arévalo Cedeño*, 384. Similarly, Arévalo Cedeño denounced Gómez's monopolies in a public letter to an aide of the dictator in 1917, in *Viva Arévalo Cedeño*, 387.

40. Arévalo Cedeño, *Viva Arévalo Cedeño*, 52.

41. Arévalo Cedeño, *Viva Arévalo Cedeño*, 8.

42. Arévalo Cedeño, *Viva Arévalo Cedeño*, 5.
43. Jacinto López, "Dictadura perpetua en Venezuela" (1922), in Ciudad de Castro, *Juan Vicente Gómez ante la historia*, 61–63.
44. Arévalo Cedeño, *Viva Arévalo Cedeño*, 38.
45. Arévalo Cedeño, *Viva Arévalo Cedeño*, 95.
46. Chamberlin and Gilman, *Degeneration*; Sarah Watts, *Rough Rider*; Nye, *Masculinity*, 72–126; Borges, "'Puffy, Ugly, Slothful, and Inert,'" 235.
47. Arévalo Cedeño, *Viva Arévalo Cedeño*, 5, 19, 28, 78.
48. Arévalo Cedeño, *Viva Arévalo Cedeño*, 155.
49. Arévalo Cedeño, *Viva Arévalo Cedeño*, 155.
50. Arévalo Cedeño, *Viva Arévalo Cedeño*, 156.
51. López, "Dictadura perpetua," 62.
52. Magda Portal, "Un alerta a la juventud de América Latina" (1929), in Sosa A. and Lengrand, *Del Garibaldismo estudiantil*, 425. For Portal's association with Gómez's opponents, see Weaver, *Peruvian Rebel*, 77–78.
53. Arévalo Cedeño, *Viva Arévalo Cedeño*, 311. This passage is from Arévalo Cedeño's 1931 tribute to a fallen comrade.
54. An overview of political imprisonment under Gómez is Sanoja Hernández, "Largo viaje hacia la muerte."
55. Pocaterra, *Gómez, the Shame of America*, 125.
56. Historian Manuel Caballero notes the parallel between Gómez's literal and figurative emasculation of opponents but does not link either to corruption. Caballero, *Gómez, el tirano liberal*, 242.
57. The original Spanish reads, "lo amarraron por sus partes con un cordel y lo colgaron ignominiosamente hasta desgarrarle la carne." Vallenilla de Aguirre to Gómez, January 13, 1913, in *BAHM*, no. 31 (1964), 55. For a similar incident, see Prato to Gómez, April 7, 1912, in *BAHM*, no. 31 (1964), 61.
58. Pocaterra, *Gómez, the Shame of America*, 138.
59. Pocaterra, *Gómez, the Shame of America*, 30, 87, 150.
60. McGoodwin to DS, March 8, 1919, USNARA/RDS, 831.00/894; and Pocaterra, *Gómez, the Shame of America*, 97.
61. Declaration of John Baptist Howell, July 12, 1933, Police Court, Port of Spain, Trinidad, in file "Holder E., [and] Howell J., imprisonment of at Puerto Cabello," UKNA/FO 199/268; and declaration of George Roseberry Campbell Weekes, June 18, 1935, Port of Spain, in file A7619, UKNA/FO 371/18784.
62. Luciani, *La dictadura*, 72, 135. This book was first published in a rare 1930 edition.
63. Luciani, *La dictadura*, 33.
64. Luciani, *La dictadura*, 56–57.
65. Luciani, *La dictadura*, 57.

66. All quotations in this paragraph are from García Naranjo, *Venezuela and Its Ruler*, 97.
67. García Naranjo, *Venezuela and Its Ruler*, 98.
68. García Naranjo, *Venezuela and Its Ruler*, 98.
69. Brett to DS, September 15, 1915, USNARA, 831.00/753, 7–8.
70. Beaumont to Balfour, September 8, 1917, UKNA/FO 199/232.
71. M. Flores Cabrera, *Siniestro recuento: prisiones y destierros bajo la dictadura del Gral. Juan Vicente Gómez* (Santo Domingo: Imprenta La Cuna de América, 1914), 17–21, enclosed with McGoodwin to DS, February 15, 1915, USNARA/RDS, 831.00/719; and Lisandro Alvarado, *Archivo de la Rotunda*, 35–54, 65–66.
72. Zinoman, *Colonial Bastille*, 76, 93–95; and O'Brien, "Prison on the Continent," 184.
73. Garbi Sánchez, *Alzamientos*, 114, 117, 128.
74. Velasco Jaime to Tarazona, April 11, 1913, in *BAHM*, no. 31 (1964): 62–64. According to Velasco, the budget allowed for 75 céntimos per prisoner per day for the purchase of food, and there were presently 153 prisoners "entre causas comunues, detenidos y algunos de la Escuela." For exchange rates, see Keyse Rudolph and Rudolph, *Historical Dictionary of Venezuela*, 233. Officials guarding political prisoners working on the highways in 1929 reportedly pocketed up to two-thirds of the money budgeted for food; Pereira, *En la prisión*, 61–62.
75. McGoodwin to DS, April 13, 1914, USNARA/RDS, 831.00/650.
76. Pimentel, *Bajo la tiranía*, 46–47, 72; and Pereira, *En la prisión*, 153.
77. Pocaterra, *Gómez, the Shame of America*, 110, 158, 187–88, 202–3.
78. Garbi Sánchez, *Alzamientos*, 131.
79. Brett to DS, September 23, 1915, USNARA/RDS, 831.00/753; Julio Delgado Chalbaud to Henry Fry Tenant, September 4, 1913, enclosed with Tenant to DS, September 15, 1913, USNARA/RDS, 831.00/605; MacGregor to Eden, February 11, 1936, UKNA/FO 371/19845.
80. Flores, *Gómez, patriarca del crimen*, 79–80; and Pereira, *En la prisión*, 153.
81. Flores, *Gómez, patriarca del crimen*, 80.
82. The original expression, according to Rafael Caldera, is "Yo no pido que me den, sino que me pongan donde haiga." Alfredo Peña, "Una ley que obligue a los partidos a mostrar publicamente el origen de sus fondos, propone el ex-presidente Caldera," *El Nacional*, September 21, 1977.
83. Garbi Sánchez, *Alzamientos*, 123–24, 127–28.
84. Garbi Sánchez, *Alzamientos*, 123.
85. Garbi Sánchez, *Alzamientos*, 124.
86. Garbi Sánchez, *Alzamientos*, 124.
87. "Crimes brought about by President Gómez of Venezuela in the

persons of prisoners to keep himself in power." Enclosed with Fairchild [US House of Representatives] to Hughes [Secretary of State], May 19, 1921, USNARA/RDS, 831.00/993. Gomecistas' use of *vago* and *vagabundo* closely parallels usage of these terms in the mid-nineteenth century, when they referred to individuals deemed to be lazy, without virtue, and averse to productive labor. Zahler, *Ambitious Rebels*, 141–45.

88. Skurski, "Leader and the 'People,'" 172.

89. Pocaterra, *Gómez, the Shame of America*, 120, 158, 168, 174.

90. Garbi Sánchez, *Alzamientos*, 131.

91. The theme of transcendence appears often in prison literature, according to Carnochan, "Literature of Confinement," 381–406.

92. For a similar point about Brazilian men separated from their families by military conscription, see Beattie, *Tribute of Blood*, 219.

93. Pimentel, *Bajo la tiranía*, 46, 48, 65, 110.

94. Pimentel, *Bajo la tiranía*, 48–49. Pimentel claims that other lawyers refused the owner's request to initiate judicial proceedings to evict her family, implying that they viewed this as disreputable work.

95. Pimentel, *Bajo la tiranía*, 116. The house rented for 80 bolívares a month and lacked sewers, which may have caused the death of Cecilia's younger brother, Vicente, from typhus (120).

96. Pimentel, *Bajo la tiranía*, 116.

97. Pimentel, *Bajo la tiranía*, 116.

98. Pimentel, *Bajo la tiranía*, 117.

99. Pimentel, *Bajo la tiranía*, 194.

100. One journalist stated that Caracas women from "decent families" who worked at a tobacco company beginning in 1908 were "pioneers" driven by economic necessity. "In those times, the work of women in the street was an infamous disgrace (*baldón infamante*)." Clemente Travieso, *Mujeres venezolanas*, 57. The author implies (59–60) that attitudes began to change gradually after Gómez's death.

101. Porter, *From Angel to Office Worker*, 128. For more on this theme, see Lauderdale Graham, *House and Street*.

102. McGoodwin to DS, April 13, 1914, USNARA/RDS, 831.00/650. According to McGoodwin, "these payments [for extra rations] must be made at the exact moment demanded by the governor of the prison and must be brought to him at the prison, to his private office, by the nearest relative of the prisoner, usually the wife, if she be attractive."

103. Pimentel, *Bajo la tiranía*, 47.

104. Flores, *Gómez, patriarca del crimen*, 73, 75; and Pereira, *En la prisión*, 153.

105. In the original, "chácharos," members of La Sagrada, Gómez's political police.

106. Pimentel, *Bajo la tiranía*, 292–93.

107. This episode coincides with the argument that studies of corruption should include sexual extortion as well as financial extortion. Merkle, "Gender and Corruption."

108. Martz, "Venezuela's 'Generation of '28,'" 18–20. For an extended discussion of the students' opposition discourse, including Betancourt's intertwining of populism and masculinity, see Skurski, "Leader and the 'People,'" 175–203.

109. Multiple telegrams dated February 24, 1928, from Rafael María Velasco and Efraín González to Gómez, in Betancourt Valverde, *Papers of Rómulo Betancourt*, tomo I, anexo E, roll 1 (microfilm). For women's participation, see also Clemente Travieso, *Mujeres venezolanas*, 17–25.

110. Engert to DS, March 7, 1928, USNARA/RDS, 831.00/1350.

111. Venezuela, Annual Report, 1928, p. 3, PRO/FO 371/13558.

112. Ochoa Briceño, *Lo que vi*, 175; McGill, *Poliantea*, 217; and Rourke, *Gómez, Tyrant of the Andes*, 229.

113. Quoted in Polanco Alcántara, *Juan Vicente Gómez*, 355–56.

114. Pereira, *En la prisión*, 236; Gonzalo Carnevali, "La charla desordenada sobre Gómez y el gomecismo (1928)," in Suárez Figueroa, *La oposición a la dictadura gomecista*, 256; and Flores, *Gómez, patriarca del crimen*, 73.

115. Miguel Febres Cordero to Tulio Febres Cordero, April 24, 1928, Archivo Tulio Febres Cordero. See also Jokanaán (Joaquín Gabaldón Márquez) to Leoni, October 20, 1928, in Gabaldón Márquez, *Memoria y cuento*, 181.

116. "Carta Abierta," in *BAHM*, no. 7 (1960): 147–49; and "Carta Abierta. A los Senadores y Diputados al Congreso Nacional de 1928," in *BAHM*, no. 7 (1960): 149–50.

117. "Bola Roja," in *BAHM*, no. 7 (1960): 151–52.

118. "A los Obreros y Campesinos de Venezuela," in *BAHM*, no. 7 (1960): 153–54.

119. "Ejército Nacional," in *BAHM*, no. 7 (1960): 155–56.

120. "Venezolanos!! El Día de Hacer Valer Nuestros Derechos Ha Llegado," in *BAHM*, no. 7, (1960): 145–46.

121. Examples include Caballero, *Gómez, el tirano liberal*, 298–301, 339, 355; and Martz, "Venezuela's 'Generation of '28.'"

122. Un Venezolano (Gabaldón Márquez) to Vallenilla Lanz, November 6, 1928, in Gabaldón Márquez, *Memoria y cuento*, 196, 198–99.

123. Gabaldón Márquez to Leoni, October 20, 1928, in Gabaldón Márquez, *Memoria y cuento*, 183.

124. Rómulo Betancourt and Miguel Otero Silva, "En las huellas de la pezuña" [1929], in Sosa and Lengrand, *Del garibaldismo*, 324.

125. The context and content of the Plan of Barranquilla are discussed

in Carrera Damas, *Rómulo histórico*, 89–104; and Alexander, *Rómulo Betancourt*, 49–66.

126. Rómulo Betancourt et al., "El Plan de Barranquilla" (1931), in Sosa and Lengrand, *Del garibaldismo*, 465.

127. Rómulo Betancourt et al., "El Plan de Barranquilla" (1931), in Sosa and Lengrand, *Del garibaldismo*, 460.

128. Betancourt to "Gordito" [Germán Herrera Umérez], August 13, 1931, in Suárez Figueroa, *Rómulo Betancourt: selección de escritos*, 57.

129. Betancourt to "Gordito," August 13, 1931, 57.

130. Rómulo Betancourt, "Con quién estamos y contra quién estamos" (1932), in Sosa and Lengrand, *Del garibaldismo*, 474–75.

131. Betancourt, "Con quién estamos," 501.

Chapter 5: Oil Money

1. Coronil, *Magical State*, 1–5, 353–57; Karl, *Paradox of Plenty*, 56–58, 184.

2. Lieuwen, *Petroleum in Venezuela*, 1–32; and Mommer, *Global Oil*, 107–9.

3. "Important Events in the Venezuelan Oilfields during the First Four Months of 1924," 1, enclosed with Sanders to DS, May 23, 1924, US-NARA/RDS, 831.6363/204.

4. Lieuwen, *Petroleum in Venezuela*, 35.

5. "Venezuela. Annual Report, 1913," 8, April 13, 1914, UKNA/FO 199/238, file "Reports Annual."

6. Harford to Grey, November 13, 1911, UKNA/FO 371/1277.

7. Harford to Grey, January 4, 1913, UKNA/FO 371/1861, file 3958.

8. "Venezuela. Annual Report, 1912," 4. Enclosed with Harford to Grey, February 13, 1913, UKNA/FO 371/1861, file 10075.

9. J. M. Snow, Foreign Office Minutes, February 13, 1930, UKNA/FO 371/14300, File A1256.

10. Harford to Grey, January 4, 1913, UKNA/FO 371/1861, file 3958.

11. McBeth, *Juan Vicente Gómez and the Oil Companies*, 70.

12. Trujillo, "Resumen de los documentos de traspaso de concesiones"; and Mommer, *Global Oil*, 111.

13. Lieuwen, *Petroleum in Venezuela*, 11.

14. Salazar-Carrillo and West, *Oil and Development*, 38.

15. Yergin, *Prize*, 212–26.

16. Salazar-Carrillo and West, *Oil and Development*, 58–59.

17. Mommer, *Global Oil*, 110.

18. Torres, *Memorias*, 67, 76, 179, 199–200.

19. López Contreras, *Páginas para la historia militar*, 241–42.

20. "Plan de Barranquilla," in Sosa A. and Lengrand, *Del garibaldismo*,

465–66; and Rómulo Betancourt, "Dos libros de Picón-Salas," and "La situación económico-fiscal de Venezuela," in Gómez, *Rómulo Betancourt*, 136, 161–62.

21. McBeth, *Juan Vicente Gómez and the Oil Companies*, 17.

22. McBeth, *Juan Vicente Gómez and the Oil Companies*, 46–47; and JRCA, *Sentencias*, 2:193.

23. The tribunal that investigated corruption in 1945–46 found that Méndez's private correspondence mentioned so many *testaferros* that "it is impossible to enumerate them." JRCA, *Sentencias*, 1:170.

24. British Legation, Caracas, to Chamberlain, December 14, 1928, and enclosure, UKNA/FO 199/273, file "Personalities."

25. "Report on the Leading Personalities in Venezuela," 23, enclosed with Keeling to Simon, January 2, 1935, UKNA/FO 371/18782, file A 827.

26. "Venezuela. Annual Report, 1935," 2, enclosed with Keeling to Eden, April 6, 1936, UKNA/FO 371/19847, file A 4525.

27. MacGregor to Eden, January 24, 1936, UKNA/FO 371/19845, file A 1370.

28. Torres, *Memorias*, 179.

29. McGoodwin to DS, May 27, 1921, USNARA/RDS, 831.6363/61; see also Beaumont to Curzon, July 15, 1921, UKNA/FO 371/5721, file A 5977.

30. Torres, *Memorias*, 199.

31. McBeth, *Juan Vicente Gómez and the Oil Companies*, 92; see also JRCA, *Sentencias*, 1:103–4.

32. McBeth, *Juan Vicente Gómez and the Oil Companies*, 32.

33. "Leading Personalities in Venezuela," enclosed with Hutcheon to Secretary of State for Foreign Affairs, December 3, 1932, UKNA/FO 199/273, file "Personalities."

34. "Leading Personalities in Venezuela."

35. Engert to DS, March 8, 1928, USNARA/RDS, 831.6363/376, and enclosed copy of *Gaceta Oficial*, March 3, 1928.

36. Trujillo, "Resumen de los documentos de traspaso de concesiones," 232–33.

37. McBeth, *Juan Vicente Gómez and the Oil Companies*, 86–87.

38. JRCA, *Sentencias*, 4:17.

39. "Venezuela. Annual Report, 1913," April 13, 1914, in UKNA/FO 199/238, file "Reports Annual."

40. JRCA, *Sentencias*, 2:186–87. For Pérez's status as José Vicente's lawyer, see McBeth, *Juan Vicente Gómez and the Oil Companies*, 67.

41. Yergin, *Prize*, 217–18.

42. Cook to DS, June 8, 1922, USNARA/RDS, 831.6363/103; and "Venezuelan Oil Held Up By Lack of Transport," *Oil Trade Journal*, Au-

gust 1922, enclosed with Cook to DS, September 4, 1922, USNARA/RDS, 831.6363/114.

43. Lieuwen, *Petroleum in Venezuela*, 18–24.

44. McBeth, *Gómez and the Oil Companies*, 35.

45. Lieuwen, *Petroleum in Venezuela*, 24–25, 34.

46. McGoodwin to DS, May 27, 1921, USNARA/RDS, 831.6363/61.

47. McGoodwin to DS, May 27, 1921, USNARA/RDS, 831.6363/61.

48. McBeth, *Gómez and the Oil Companies*, 49; and Lieuwen, *Petroleum in Venezuela*, 26.

49. Márquez Bustillos to Urdaneta Maya, April 27, 1921, in Segnini, *Los hombres*, 2:148.

50. Márquez Bustillos to Urdaneta Maya, April 27, 1921, in Segnini, *Los hombres*, 2:147.

51. Lieuwen, *Petroleum in Venezuela*, 27.

52. McGoodwin to DS, October 17, 1921, USNARA/RDS, 831.6363/79.

53. Dormer (Caracas) to Beaumont, October 20, 1919, UKNA/FO 199/181, file "British Enterprises in Venezuela."

54. Dormer to Curzon, June 25, 1920, UKNA/FO 199/229, file "Oilfields Venezuelan."

55. Beaumont to Curzon, July 15, 1921, UKNA/FO 371/5721, file A5977.

56. Beaumont to Balfour, June 15, 1922, UKNA/FO 199/225, file "Mining Law."

57. McBeth, *Juan Vicente Gómez and the Oil Companies*, 60; see also Lieuwen, *Petroleum in Venezuela*, 27–29.

58. These attempts are recorded in the documents gathered in the file "Anglo-Persian Oil Co.," UKNA/FO 199/259; and in Sir John Cadman (Anglo-Persian) to Sir Robert Vansittart (FO), March 23, 1934, UKNA/FO 371/17619, file A2508; and "Venezuela. Annual Report, 1934," enclosed with Keeling to Simon, January 21, 1935, UKNA/FO 371/18784, file A1840.

59. US Consulate (Caracas) to DS, July 3, 1922, USNARA/RDS, 831.6363/108.

60. Sanders to DS, December 22, 1922, USNARA/RDS, 831.6363/119.

61. Medrano, *Juan Vicente Gómez*, 100.

62. Cook to DS, July 3, 1923, USNARA/RDS, 831.6363/138, and enclosures.

63. US legation's translation of "Fundación de una Empresa con Capital del País," *El Universal*, June 28, 1923, enclosed in Cook to DS, July 3, 1923, USNARA/RDS, 831.6363/138.

64. Bennett to MacDonald, April 28, 1924, UKNA/FO 199/232, file "Political."

65. Chabot to DS, April 14, 1924, USNARA/RDS, 831.6363/178.

66. Cook to DS, February 25, 1924, USNARA/RDS, 831.6363/157.

67. Hardwicke (Caracas) to Stone (Pittsburgh), June 7, 1924, enclosed with Chabot to DS, June 14, 1924, USNARA/RDS, 831.6363/211.

68. Harrison to Chabot, May 17, 1924, USNARA/RDS, 831.6363/183; and Chabot to DS, July 10, 1924, USNARA/RDS, 831.6363/223.

69. P. T. C. (Economic advisor, Department of State), "Venezuelan Petroleum Law—1922," memo dated April 19, 1924, USNARA/RDS, 831.6363/237.

70. Rabe, *Road to OPEC*, 30; and McBeth, *Juan Vicente Gómez and the Oil Companies*, 99–101.

71. Cook to DS, March 7, 1924, USNARA/RDS, 831.6363/160.

72. Chabot to DS, July 10, 1924, USNARA/RDS, 831.6363/223.

73. Chabot to DS, April 13, 1924, USNARA/RDS, 831.6363/172; and Chabot to DS, April 14, 1924, USNARA/RDS, 831.6363/178.

74. Chabot to DS, May 9, 1924, USNARA/RDS, 831.6363/196.

75. Rabe, *Road to OPEC*, 30.

76. McBeth, *Juan Vicente Gómez and the Oil Companies*, 100–101.

77. Examples include Cook to DS, February 25, 1924, USNARA/RDS, 831.6363/157; Cook to DS, March 7, 1924, USNARA/RDS, 831.6363/160; Voetter to DS, March 13, 1924, USNARA/RDS, 831.6363/162; and Chabot to DS, April 29, 1924, USNARA/RDS, 831.6363/181.

78. McBeth, *Juan Vicente Gómez and the Oil Companies*, 99.

79. Chabot to DS, June 7, 1924, USNARA/RDS, 831.6363/206.

80. Polanco Alcántara, *Juan Vicente Gómez*, 468–74.

81. McBeth, *Juan Vicente Gómez and the Oil Companies*, 107.

82. JRCA, *Sentencias*, 3:320.

83. JRCA, *Sentencias*, 2:251, 315; 3:69; and 4:11.

84. JRCA, *Sentencias*, 3:262.

85. O'Reilly to Wilson, October 13, 1930, UKNA/FO 199/259, file "Anglo-Persian Oil Co."

86. "Texto íntegro de la sensacional demanda del Procurador General de la Nación," *El Universal*, May 4, 1936, in *Gobierno y epóca del Presidente Eleazar López Contreras* 10:63–79.

87. Arcaya, *Cuenta que el Dr. Pedro Manuel Arcaya rinde*, 2:745.

88. "Texto íntegro de la sensacional demanda," 65.

89. Arcaya, *La pena de la confiscación*, 110–14, 118–20.

90. JRCA, "Remitido," *El Universal*, August 1, 1946.

91. Theobald, *Corruption, Development, and Underdevelopment*, 19–21.

92. Rómulo Betancourt, "Con quién estamos y contra quién estamos," in Sosa A. and Lengrand, *Del garibaldismo*, 484–85; and Arcaya, *La pena de la confiscación*, 55.

93. Harford to Grey, January 23, 1912, UKNA/FO 371/1552.

94. Arcaya, *La pena de la confiscación*, 103.

95. Arcaya, *Cuenta que el Dr. Pedro Manuel Arcaya rinde.*

96. "Texto íntegro de la sensacional demanda del Procurador General de la Nación," *El Universal* May 4, 1936, in *Gobierno y época del Presidente Eleazar López Contreras*, 10:63–79; and JRCA, *Sentencias*, 2:112 and 4:73.

97. Arcaya, *Cuenta que el Dr. Pedro Manuel Arcaya rinde*, xlv.

98. Arcaya, *La pena de la confiscación*, 140–41.

99. "Defensa del Señor Baldomero Uzcátegui: Sus Relaciones con el Capítulo VII," *El Universal*, April 1, 1946; and JRCA, *Sentencias*, 4:89.

100. Siso, *Castro y Gómez*, 362.

101. Siso, *Castro y Gómez*, 363.

102. López Contreras, *Proceso Político Social*, 14.

103. Arcaya, *Cuenta que el Dr. Pedro Manuel Arcaya rinde*, 1:xxix, 75–151.

104. Trinkunas, *Crafting Civilian Control of the Military*, 31–32.

105. Ziems, *El gomecismo*, 225–226; and "Venezuela. Annual Report, 1936," enclosed with Gye to Eden, March 14, 1937, UKNA/FO 371/20676, file 2632.

106. Ziems, *El gomecismo*, 228–30.

107. Siso, *Castro y Gómez*, 363; and Andrés Eloy Blanco, "Cuentas claras," *El Universal*, November 30, 1945.

108. Skurski, "Leader and the 'People,'" 223; and Segnini, *Las luces del gomecismo*, 313–15.

109. Arcaya, *Cuenta que el Dr. Pedro Manuel Arcaya rinde*, 2:ix, 727.

110. Arcaya, *La pena de la confiscación*, 146.

111. Arcaya, *Cuenta que el Dr. Pedro Manuel Arcaya rinde*, 1:59–62, 65–72, 199–213; and 2:732–33, 737–38.

112. JRCA, *Sentencias*, 2:154, 185–86, 285.

113. Pedro Manuel Arcaya, "Al Pueblo de Venezuela. Comunicado No. 1 del Doctor Pedro Manuel Arcaya," *El Universal*, July 28, 1946, 4; "Remitido. Escrito presentado por el Doctor César González a la Comisión prevista en el decreto de la Asamblea Nacional Constituyente, sobre acusaciones del Jurado de Responsabilidad Civil y Administrativa," *El Universal*, February 3, 1948, 10.

114. Andrés Eloy Blanco, "Cuentas claras," *El Universal*, November 30, 1945, 4. See also Ramírez, *Biografía de Andrés Eloy Blanco*, 3–7, 308–10.

115. Arcaya, *Cuenta que el Dr. Pedro Manuel Arcaya rinde*, 1:xxxv, 192–94.

116. Pimentel, *Bajo la tiranía*, 122.

Chapter 6: Transition, 1935–45

1. Torres, *Memorias*, 163.

2. Polanco Alcántara, *Juan Vicente Gómez*, 526–27. Public announcement of López Contreras's position was delayed until after Gómez's death.

3. Torres, *Memorias*, 164.

4. Torres, *Memorias*, 164.

5. Torres, *Memorias*, 165.

6. For Ewell's discussion of "the Gómez system," see her *Venezuela: A Century of Change*, 69–78. A useful discussion of the historiography through the early 1990s is Ellner, "Venezuelan Revisionist Political History." A recent work in this tradition is Bruni Celli, *El 18 de octubre*.

7. Ellner, "Venezuelan Revisionist Political History," 100–104.

8. For an essay criticizing the 1945 coup by a member of Medina Angarita's government writing from a Burkean perspective, see Uslar Pietri, *Golpe y estado*, 21–86.

9. Yarrington, "Political Transition in an Age of Extremes," 160–87.

10. "Programa de Febrero del Presidente Eleazar López Contreras," in Suárez Figueroa, *Programas políticas*, 1:123–134 (quotation on 125).

11. "Proyecto de Programa del Partido Republicano Progresista," in Suárez Figueroa, *Programas políticas*, 1:138–39.

12. "Manifiesto-Programa del Movimiento de Organización Venezolana," in Suárez Figueroa, *Programas políticas*, 1:142.

13. "Manifiesto-Programa del Movimiento de Organización Venezolana," in Suárez Figueroa, *Programas políticas*, 1:144.

14. Alexander, *Rómulo Betancourt*, 93, 97–99; Friedman, *Unfinished Transitions*, 65–66, 72–73; and Ewell, *Venezuela*, 84–85.

15. Herman, *Christian Democracy*, 3–22.

16. Yarrington, "Political Transition in an Age of Extremes."

17. "Mensaje de la Federación de Estudiantes de Venezuela," enclosed in Nicholson to DS, December 21, 1935, USNARA/RDS, 831.00/1547; and Macgregor to FO, December 20, 1935, UKNA/FO 371/18782, file A 10739.

18. Torres, *Memorias*, 138.

19. MacGregor to Eden, December 24, 1935, UKNA/FO 371/19845.

20. Nicholson to DS, December 21, 1935, USNARA/RDS, 831.00/1547.

21. MacGregor to Eden, December 24, 1935, UKNA/FO 371/19845.

22. Parada, *De Ocumare a Miraflores*, 200–01.

23. López Contreras, *Proceso político social*, 91–115; and Lovera, *Un hombre*, 313.

24. Yarrington, *Coffee Frontier*, 181–92.

25. MacGregor to Eden, January 24, 1936, UKNA/FO 371/19845.

26. "Venezuelan Mob Sacks Coffee Estate of Gómez," *New York Times*, February 24, 1936, 10. For Gómez's acquisition of the estate, see "Venezuela Annual Report," 1926, UKNA/FO 371/12063, 8.

27. Betancourt, *El 18 de Octubre*, 336.

28. MacGregor to Eden, 24 December 1935, UKNA/FO 371/19845.

29. López Contreras, *Proceso político social*, 91–115; Botello, *Historia de Villa de Cura* (2005), 288–91; Yarrington, *Coffee Frontier*, 184–86.

30. Macgregor to Secretary of State for Foreign Affairs, January 6, 1936, UKNA/FO 371/19845; Tinker Salas, *Enduring Legacy*, 102–5; and anonymous, "Extract of letter to Mr. N. Carr, Caribbean Petroleum Co.," undated, enclosed with British Legation, Caracas, to American Department, UKNA/FO 371/19845, File A 1371.

31. Nicholson to DS, December 30, 1935, USNARA/RDS, 831.00/1557, Box 5785.

32. MacGregor to Eden, February 11, 1936, UKNA/FO 371/19845.

33. "Venezuela. Annual Report, 1936," 10–11, enclosed with Gye to Eden, March 14, 1937, UKNA/FO 371/20676, file 2632; Ochoa Briceño, *Lo que vi*, 149, 155, 173.

34. Torres, *Memorias*, 169.

35. Emilio Arévalo Cedeño, "Discurso pronunciado por el General Emilio Arévalo Cedeño . . . el día 10 de mayo de 1936," broadsheet in Betancourt Valverde, *Papers of Rómulo Betancourt*, tomo 5, anexo B.

36. MacGregor to Eden, January 2, 1936, UKNA/FO 371/19845.

37. "Noticias generales," *El Relator* (Trujillo), February 12, 1936.

38. MacGregor to Eden, January 24, 1936, UKNA/FO 371/19845, with enclosures.

39. Bruzaud, "Memorandum," 5, enclosed with Wiswould to Troutbeck, January 23, 1936, UKNA/FO 371/19845.

40. MacGregor to Eden, January 24, 1936, UKNA/FO 371/19845.

41. Gonzalo Barrios, "Confiscación de los bienes de Gómez," *Ahora*, April 12, 1936, reprinted in Velásquez, *El debate político*, 1:373–77; and "Proyecto de Programa del Partido Republicano Progresista," in Suárez Figueroa, *Programas políticas*, 1:134–41.

42. Coronil, *Magical State*, 94, 97, 99.

43. The confiscation measure is reprinted in Dupuy, *Propiedades*, 147–49.

44. "Programa de Febrero del Presidente Eleazar López Contreras," in Suárez Figueroa, *Programas políticas*, 1:131.

45. "Ante el actual gobierno, a la izquierda no le queda sino un sitio: la oposición," *ORVE*, November 29, 1936, in Velázquez, *El debate político*, 2:736.

46. "Ante el actual gobierno, a la izquierda no le queda sino un sitio: la oposición," ORVE, November 29, 1936, in Velázquez, *El debate político*, 2:735–36.

47. Translation of article from *La Esfera*, January 22, 1936, enclosed in MacGregor to Eden, January 24, 1936, UKNA/FO, 371/19845, file A 1370.

48. ORVE, "El problema nacional de instrucción pública," *Ahora*, May 9, 1936, reprinted in Velásquez, *El debate político*, 1:515.

49. Arcaya, *Defensa del Doctor Pedro Manuel Arcaya*, 79–91, 205.

50. "El Capítulo VII: Ubre de parásitos," *Izquierdas*, September 1938, reprinted in Sosa A., ed., *Papeles clandestinos*, 567–68.

51. "Contra la represión," *Izquierdas*, July 1938, reprinted in Sosa A., *Papeles clandestinos*, 547–49; "Los manejos en la inversion de los fondos públicos. Nuestra posición ante las recientes actuaciones de la Junta Reguladora," in *Boletín* July 20, 1940, reprinted in Sosa A., *Papeles clandestinos*, 481–84; and "Un monopolio de Mibelli y Galavís," in *Izquierdas*, September 1938, reprinted in Sosa A., *Papeles clandestinos*, 559.

52. Arcaya, *Defensa del Doctor Pedro Manuel Arcaya*, 40, 112, 139, 226, 417–20, and passim; Arcaya, *Cuenta que el Dr. Pedro Manuel Arcaya rinde*, 2: 749–774. Most of these charges were repeated in Arcaya, *La pena de la confiscación*, 73, 78–79, 104, 114–15, 118–20, 152.

53. "El Capítulo VII: Ubre de parásitos," *Izquierdas*, September 1938, reprinted in Sosa A., *Papeles clandestinos*, 567–68.

54. Interview with Villalba in 1940, quoted in Carrillo Batalla, *El régimen del General*, 424–25.

55. Arcaya, *Defensa del Doctor Pedro Manuel Arcaya*, 417–20.

56. JRCA, *Sentencias*, 1:303–34; and Eleazar López Contreras, "Remitido," *El Universal*, April 28, 1946, 5. López Contreras's use of Chapter VII funds is discussed further in the next chapter.

57. Corrigan to DS, March 19, 1946, USNARA/RDS, 831.00/3–1946.

58. "Ley Orgánica de Hacienda Nacional del 15 de Julio de 1938 (Extracto)," reprinted in Contraloría General de la República, *Historia*, 2:207–220 (quotation on 210). See also Arcaya, *Defensa del Doctor Pedro Manuel Arcaya*, 104.

59. Silva, *Public Probity*, 138; and Drake, *The Money Doctor in the Andes*, 103–4.

60. Gumersindo Torres, "Informe del Contralor General," in Contraloría General de la Nación, *Informe*, viii.

61. Torres, "Informe," xviii–xix; and Mayobre, *Gumersindo Torres*, 121–25.

62. Quoted in Caldera, *Eleazar López Contreras*, 89–90.

63. Rufino Blanco Fombona, "El gran presidente que nos deja," *La esfera*, April 16, 1941, reprinted in López Contreras, *El triunfo de la verdad*, 258–59.

64. Caldera, *Los causahabientes*, 90.

65. Battaglini, *El medinismo*, 63–80; and Rabe, *Road to OPEC*, 60, 77–87.

66. Ewell, "Venezuela since 1930," 733, 742.

67. Isaías Medina A., "Alocución del General Isaías Medina Angarita al Tomar Posesión de la Presidencia de la República," (1941) reprinted in

Gobierno y época del Presidente Isaías Medina Angarita [hereafter, *GEPIMA*], 1:73–79 (quotation on 77).

68. "Continua la segunda discusión del Proyecto de Ley de Presupuesto General de Rentas y Gastos Públicos, 1941–1942. Sesión del día 29 de mayo de 1941," reprinted in *GEPIMA*, 4:121–56.

69. Montilla served as state president in the provisional government headed by Betancourt, and then minister of agriculture under president Rómulo Gallegos. Kolb, *Democracy and Dictatorship in Venezuela*, 27.

70. "Continua la segunda discusión," 132–33.

71. "Continua la segunda discusión," 136.

72. "Continua la segunda discusión," 140.

73. "Continua la segunda discusión," 155.

74. Rómulo Betancourt, "Discurso de Rómulo Betancourt," in Catalá, *Acción Democrática, primeros años*, 116.

75. "Inmoralidad: Lepra Administrativa en Venezuela," *Acción Democrática*, August 29, 1942, reprinted in *GEPIMA*, 10:514–15.

76. "El doctor Carlos A. D'Ascoli habla sobre la reforma tributaria," *Acción Democrática*, May 16, 1942, reprinted in *GEPIMA*, 17:141–45.

77. Rómulo Betancourt, "La palabra de Rómulo Betancourt en el Metropolitano" (1944), in Soteldo, *Rómulo Betancourt: Antología política*, 504.

78. "Report on Leading Personalities in Venezuela 1946." Enclosed with Ogilvie-Forbes to Bevin, June 26, 1946, UKNA/FO 371/52227, File AS-3946/47.

79. Pérez, *La verdad inédita*, 10–11.

80. "El peculado, flangelo nacional," in *La Esfera*, February 5, 1943, reprinted in *GEPIMA*, 10:519.

81. Ramón David León, "'Todos con Medina contra la reacción!,'" *La Esfera*, September 28, 1944, reprinted in *GEPIMA*, 12:207.

82. "El peculado, flangelo nacional," 519–20.

83. "Hay que exterminar el peculado," *La Esfera*, July 10, 1945, reprinted in *GEPIMA*, 10:536.

84. "El peculado, flangelo nacional," 519.

85. Ramón David León, "'Todos con Medina contra la reacción!,'" *La Esfera*, September 28, 1944, reprinted in *GEPIMA*, 12:204.

86. "Incompatibilidad y dignidad nacional," *Acción Democrática*, May 13, 1944, reprinted in *GEPIMA*, 10:159.

87. "Hay que exterminar el peculado," *La Esfera*, July 10, 1945, reprinted in *GEPIMA*, 10:536.

88. "En Senado Rechazan la Ley sobre Enriquecimiento Ilícito de Funcionarios tras Largo Debate," *La Esfera*, July 17, 1945, reprinted in *GEPIMA*, 10:539–45.

89. "El Incondicionalismo del Congreso," *La Esfera*, July 18, 1945, 1, reprinted in *GEPIMA*, 10:548.

90. Trinkunas, *Crafting Civilian Control*, 34; Pérez, *La verdad inédita*, 11; and Siso, *Castro y Gómez*, 130.

91. Pérez, *La verdad inédita*, 106–7.

92. Pérez, *La verdad inédita*, 98.

93. Corrigan to DS, October 26, 1945, USNARA/RDS, 831.00/10-2645, Box 5379.

94. Ewell, *Venezuela: A Century of Change*, 94–95.

95. Betancourt, *Venezuela: Oil and Politics*, 94.

96. Velásquez, "Aspectos de la evolución política," 77.

97. Pérez, *La verdad*, 12.

98. Velásquez, "Aspectos de la evolución política," 75–76.

99. Burggraaff, *Venezuelan Armed Forces*, 52–54.

100. "Opinión Nacional: Nuestra Consigna," *Ahora*, September 8, 1945, reprinted in *GEPIMA*, 14:23–26.

101. Jiménez M., *Choque de generales*, 307–9.

102. Jiménez M., *Choque de generales*, 308–37.

103. "Discurso del mitin del 17 de octubre de 1945," in Suárez Figueroa, *Rómulo Betancourt: selección de escritos políticos*, 173.

104. "Discurso del mitin del 17 de octubre de 1945," 182.

105. Velásquez, "Apectos de la evolución política," 81–82; Ewell, *Venezuela: A Century of Change*, 94–95.

Chapter 7: The Corruption Trials, Public Opinion, and the Middle Class

1. Arráiz Lucca, *El trienio adeco*, 59–65.

2. Junta Revolucionario del Gobierno, "Decreto No. 6," in JRCA, *Sentencias*, 1:3.

3. Rómulo Betancourt, "La razón y propósito de la 'Revolución de Octubre,' explicados por Betancourt, Presidente de la Junta Revolucionaria de Gobierno en alocución al país," October 30, 1945, in Suárez Figueroa, ed., *Rómulo Betancourt: selección de escritos políticos*, 185.

4. Betancourt, "La razón y propósito," 186.

5. Morillo, *El enriquecimiento ilícito*, 46–47.

6. Gómez, *El origen del estado democrático*, 175–79; Luzardo, *Notas historico-economicas*, 158–59; and Olivar, "El Jurado de Responsabilidad Civil y Administrativa."

7. Smith, "Paradoxes of the Public Sphere."

8. Karl, "Petroleum and Political Pacts," 70; García Ponce, *Política y clase media*, 63; and Tinker Salas, *Enduring Legacy*, 185–86.

9. Clemente Travieso, *Mujeres venezolanas*, 57–64.

10. Clemente Travieso, *Mujeres venezolanas*, 61.
11. Friedman, *Unfinished Transitions*, 83–89.
12. Ewell, "Ligia Parra Jahn."
13. Luque, *Educación, estado y nación*, 298–312, 319–34; and Herman, *Christian Democracy*, 32–36.
14. Arráiz Lucca, *El trienio adeco*, 65–68.
15. Brito Cornieles and Cancela Cambon, "Desarrollo de la prensa," 76.
16. Dupouy, "La clase media en Venezuela," 77.
17. Dupouy, "La clase media en Venezuela," 95.
18. Díaz Rangel, *La prensa venezolana*, 81; and Brito Cornieles and Cancela Cambon, "Desarrollo de la prensa," 78.
19. Francis to FO, September 18, 1946, UKNA/FO 371/52209, File AS 6003/48.
20. Pérez, *La verdad inédita*, 10–11.
21. "Liquidación de una inmensa cuenta," *La Esfera*, October 24, 1945, enclosed in Corrigan to DS, October 27, 1945, USNARA/RDS, 831.00/10–2745, Box 5379.
22. Alfredo Silva Heredia, "Contra el arraigado vicio del peculado," *La Esfera*, October 30, 1945, reprinted in *Gobierno y época de la Junta Revolucionaria*, 19:116.
23. Luis Ramón Hernández, "Lucha contra el peculado," *El Universal*, November 19, 1945, 20.
24. This paragraph is based on Herman, *Christian Democracy*, 6–24.
25. "La necesidad de castigar el peculado es indiscutible declara el Procurador General Rafael Caldera," *El País*, 6 November 1945, reprinted in *Gobierno y época de la Junta Revolucionaria*, 19:129–30.
26. Humberto Cuenca, "La Prescripción en el Delito de Peculado. Al Márgen del Decreto No. 6," *El Universal*, October 27, 1945.
27. This language appears in article 35 of the constitutions of 1925 and 1928 and was maintained in subsequent constitutions of the Gómez era. For a discussion, see "Intervención del Diputado Juan Carmona, sobre Confiscación de los Bienes del General Juan Vicente Gómez, sesión del 20 ad Abril de 1936," reprinted in *Gobierno y Época del Presidente Eleazar López Contreras*, 4:130.
28. Humberto Cuenca, "La Prescripción en el Delito de Peculado. Al Márgen del Decreto No. 6," *El Universal*, October 27, 1945.
29. "El tribunal extraordinario para delitos contra la nación," *El País*, November 6, 1945, reprinted in *Gobierno y época de la Junta Revolucionaria*, 19:125–27.
30. Corrigan to DS, November 3, 1945, USNARA/RDS, 831.00/11–345, Box 5379.
31. "La necesidad de castigar el peculado es indiscutible declara el

Procurador General Rafael Caldera," *El País*, November 6, 1945, in *Gobierno y época de la Junta Revolucionaria*, 19:129.

32. Federico Lesamann Vera, "La Contraloría General de la Nación y el peculado," *El Universal*, November 11, 1945.

33. Corrigan to DS, November 14, 1945, USNARA/RDS, Box 5379, 831.00/11–1445.

34. Corrigan to DS, October 30, 1945, USNARA/RDS, Box 5379, 831.00/10–3045.

35. Betancourt, "La razón y propósito," 187.

36. "Plausible actitud del M. R. I. sobre listas del Capítulo Séptimo para la publicidad," *El Universal*, November 11, 1945.

37. "Plausible precaución moral del Ministro de Interior," *El Universal*, November 12, 1945.

38. "Resolución de la Comisión Calificadora de Funcionarios Públicos," and "Decreto no. 54 de la Junta Revolucionaria de Gobierno," in JRCA, *Sentencias*, 1:10–17.

39. "Decreto no. 54," 16.

40. Corrigan to DS, November 19, 1945, USNARA/RDS, Box 5379, 831.00/11–1945.

41. Corrigan to DS, November 13, 1945, USNARA/RDS, Box 5379, 831.00/11–1345.

42. Andrés Eloy Blanco, "Cuentas claras," *El Universal*, November 30, 1945.

43. "La Comisión que conoce de pensiones del Capítulo VII rendirá Informe al respeto," *El Universal*, November 15, 1945.

44. "Decreto no. 64 de la Junta Revolucionaria de Gobierno," in JRCA, *Sentencias*, 1:19.

45. "Decreto no. 64 de la Junta Revolucionaria de Gobierno," in JRCA *Sentencias*, 1:19–20.

46. "Decreto no. 64 de la Junta Revolucionaria de Gobierno," in JRCA, *Sentencias*, 1:21.

47. "Decreto no. 64 de la Junta Revolucionaria de Gobierno," in JRCA, *Sentencias*, 1:18.

48. Corrigan to DS, November 28, 1945, USNARA/RDS, Box 5379, 831.00/11–2845.

49. *El Nacional* published a photo of crowds outside the congressional chambers where the jury presented its verdicts with the caption: "El público, ávido de conocer los pormenores del proceso, llena los pasillos de los hemiciclos parlamentarios durante el desarrollo del proceso de juicios por peculado." See "Condenado Rafael S. Urbina," *El Nacional*, January 4, 1946.

50. JRCA, *Sentencias*, 1:84–91.

51. "Condenado Pérez Soto a pagar más de 20 millones," *El Nacional*, February 8, 1946.
52. JRCA, *Sentencias*, 1:145.
53. JRCA, *Sentencias*, 1:144.
54. JRCA, *Sentencias*, 1:145, 152.
55. "Más de Bs. 13.000.000 deberá devolver el Gral. Pérez Soto," *El Heraldo*, February 8, 1946, enclosed in Dawson to DS, February 9, 1946, USNARA/RDS, 831.00/2–946.
56. Fernando Carrasquel, "Balance del IV Mes: Afirmación de la Confianza Nacional," *El Universal*, February 20, 1946.
57. "Las Tareas del Jurado de Responsabilidad Civil y Administrativa," *El Universal*, February 21, 1946.
58. "La revolución de octubre no cobra rencores, su honrada propósito es que se haga justicia," *La Esfera*, February 23, 1946.
59. JRCA, *Sentencias*, 1:326.
60. Eleazar López Contreras, "Remitido," *El Universal*, April 28, 1946.
61. Ochoa Briceño, *Lo que vi*, 149, 171–72; and Siso, *Castro y Gómez*, 363.
62. Corrigan to DS, October 26, 1945, USNARA/RDS, Box 5379, 831.00/10–2645.
63. JRCA, *Sentencias*, 1:309.
64. Betancourt, *El 18 de octubre de 1945*, 343.
65. Corrigan to DS, December 14, 1945, USNARA/RDS, Box 5379, 831.00/12–1445.
66. Reprinted in Cárdenas, *COPEI en el trienio populista*, 410.
67. JRCA, *Sentencias*, 1:305–11, 327–29, 333.
68. "Remitido," *El Universal*, April 28, 1946.
69. Arcaya, *Cuenta que el Dr. Pedro Manuel Arcaya rinde*, 1:li–lii.
70. Corrigan to DS, March 21, 1946, USNARA/DS, 831.00/3–2146.
71. JRCA, *Sentencias*, 4:84–90; "Defensa del Señor Baldomero Uzcátegui: sus relaciones con el Capítulo VII," *El Universal*, April 1, 1946; and McBeth, *Juan Vicente Gómez and the Oil Companies*, 46–47.
72. Corrigan to DS, March 21, 1946, USNARA/RDS, 831.00/3–2146; and "Defensa del Señor Baldomero Uzcátegui: sus relaciones con el Capítulo VII," *El Universal*, April 1, 1946.
73. Corrigan to DS, March 21, 1946, USNARA/DS, 831.00/3–2146.
74. "Sensible desaparición," *La Esfera*, March 21, 1946.
75. "Lamentable desaparición," *El Universal*, March 21, 1946.
76. "Lamentable desaparición," *El Universal*, March 21, 1946.
77. Gortazar to Ministro de Asuntos Exteriores, April 1, 1946, Archivo General de la Administración, Alcalá de Henares, Spain, Ministerio de Asuntos Exteriores, Box 82/05345, File R. 1754–13, Venezuela, Política.

78. "Defensa del Señor Baldomero Uzcátegui: sus relaciones con el Capítulo VII," *El Universal*, April 1, 1946.

79. Arráiz Lucca, *Arturo Uslar Pietri*.

80. JRCA, *Sentencias*, 1:287–302.

81. Uslar Pietri to Betancourt, March 26, 1946 (printed broadsheet), enclosed with Uslar Pietri to Braden, April 25, 1946, USNARA/RDS, 831.00/4–2546. All quotations in this paragraph and the next are from this broadsheet.

82. Corrigan to DS, May 10, 1946, USNARA/RDS, 831.00/5–1046; and "Los directores de diarios y representantes de la A. V. P. y del Sindicato de Periodistas, opinan acerca de detenciones motivadas por publicación de la carta de Arturo Uslar Pietri," *El Nacional*, May 7, 1946.

83. Manuel Vicente Tinoco, "Al Presidente de la Junta Revolucionario de Gobierno," *El Universal*, May 8, 1946. Tinoco later directed press censorship under the military government that took power in 1948, according to Herman, *Christian Democracy*, 37.

84. Martín Fierro [pseudonym of Otero Silva], "La carta," *El Nacional*, May 9, 1946.

85. "Por la libertad de la prensa," *La Esfera*, May 7, 1946.

86. Corrigan to DS, May 10, 1946, USNARA/RDS, 831.00/5–1046.

87. Cartay Ramírez, *Caldera y Betancourt*, 100–02, 112.

88. *COPEI* stands for Comité de Organización Política Electoral Independiente (Committee of Independent Political Electoral Organization). It is widely regarded as a Christian democratic or social Christian party, despite the lack of any religious reference in its name. García Ponce, *Política y clase media*, 264–65.

89. Cartay Ramírez, *Caldera y Betancourt*, 93.

90. JRCA, *Sentencias*, vols. 1–5; statistics generated by the author. In cases where the jury required multiple heirs of a deceased official to demonstrate the licit origin of their wealth, I have counted each named heir as an individual.

91. JRCA, *Sentencias*, 1:113.

92. JRCA, *Sentencias*, 3:187.

93. JRCA, *Sentencias*, 2:88.

94. Examples include JRCA, *Sentencias*, 2:186; 4:206–7; and 5:148–49, 259.

95. Examples include JRCA, *Sentencias*, 1:312; 2:16–19, 34–35; and 5:258–65.

96. JRCA, *Sentencias*, 4:208; and 5:265–68.

97. Peña, *Conversaciones con Uslar Pietri*, 50–51.

98. JRCA, *Sentencias*, 1:198–99, 286; 5:176–77; and 4:222. See also JRCA, *Sentencias*, 1:65–73.

99. JRCA, *Sentencias*, 1:326; 2:27, 41–42, 88; 3:187; and 4:99.

100. Eduardo Gallego Mancera resigned from the jury in part because he believed the trials lacked "a uniform criterion for the selection of individuals who should be tried." Eduardo Gallegos Mancera, "Mi actuación en el Tribunal de Responsabilidad," *El Nacional*, May 29, 1946.

101. Examples include JRCA, *Sentencias*, 1:145; 2:284, 301; 3:250, 251, 261; 5:19, 25, 26, 29, 128–30, 151–52, 205–6, 243, and 247.

102. "Sentencias del Jurado de Responsabilidad Civil y Administrativa," *La Esfera*, July 16, 1946; "Los procesos por peculado," *La Esfera*, July 18, 1946; "Los Juicios por Responsabilidad Civil y Administrativa," *El Universal*, July 19, 1946; and "Sentencias del Jurado de Responsabilidad Civil y Administrativa," *La Esfera*, July 22, 1946.

103. JRCA, *Sentencias*, 2:251, 315, 328–29; 3:69, 270–329.

104. JRCA, *Sentencias*, 3:319.

105. JRCA, *Sentencias*, 1:105–6, 170–71; 2:302; 4:17.

106. "Los procesos por peculado," *La Esfera*, July 18, 1946.

107. "Los Juicios por Responsabilidad Civil y Administrativa," *El Universal*, July 19, 1946.

108. Corrigan to DS, 19 July 1946, 831.00/7–1946, in US Department of State, *Foreign Relations*, 11:1,303.

109. Domingo Alberto Rangel, "El derecho revolucionario y los juicios por peculado," *El País*, February 5, 1947.

110. Corrigan to DS, 18 November 1946, USNARA/RDS, Box 3581, 831.00/11–1846.

111. These current and former officers included graduates of the military academy and non-graduates who won military titles in civil wars around the turn of the twentieth century.

112. "Los juicios contra el peculado," *El País*, October 17, 1947; and "Ayer tarde recibió la Comisión Permanente de la ANC el informe elaborado por la comisión que revisó los juicios por peculado," *La Esfera*, January 31, 1948.

113. Vargas to Betancourt, October 29, 1947, in Betancourt Valverde, *Papers of Rómulo Betancourt*, tomo VI; Alexander, *Rómulo Betancourt*, 297; and JRCA, *Sentencias*, 1:208–12.

114. Revenga to Betancourt, undated, filed with letters from October 1947, in Betancourt Valverde, *Papers of Rómulo Betancourt*, tomo VI.

115. Chiossone, *Memorias*, 225–26; and JRCA, *Sentencias*, 3:183–89.

116. "Dirigentes obreros se pronuncian contra la propuesta nulidad de sentencias del Jurado de Responsabilidad Civil y Administrativa," *El País*, February 3, 1948.

117. "Comisión de A.N.C. conoció informe sobre los juicios de peculado," *El País*, February 2, 1948; "Devueltos los bienes de 23 enjuiciados por peculado," *El Nacional*, August 31, 1948.

118. "La Revisión de los Juicios de Responsabilidad," *El Universal*, February 6, 1948; and J. M. Rosales Aranguren, "Revisión de los juicios de peculado," *El Universal*, February 12, 1948.

119. This last defendant was Colonel José María Márquez Iragorry, the son of Provisional President Márquez Bustillos. Col. Márquez Iragorry was credited with securing the release of numerous political prisoners under Gómez, and they believed he deserved promotion to general. JRCA, *Sentencias*, 3:200–210; and Andrés Eloy Blanco, "El General Márquez Iragorry," *El Universal*, June 22, 1945.

120. "Remitido. En defensa del Doctor Manuel Silveira y de su esposa la Señora Isabel Oteyza de Silveira," *El Universal*, April 11, 1946.

121. Luzardo, *Notas historico-economicas*, 158; Ewell, *Venezuela: A Century of Change*, 94–107; Luque, *Educación, estado y nación*, 349–77.

122. Leddy to DS, September 22, 1949, USNARA/RDS, Box 5383, 831.00/9-2249

123. Quoted in Leddy to DS, September 22, 1949, USNARA/RDS, Box 5383, 831.00/9-2249.

124. Owensby, *Intimate Ironies*, 72–99; Owensby, "Middle Class Politics"; and Porter, *From Angel to Office Worker*, 111–39.

Conclusion: Twentieth-Century Venezuela and the Historical Study of (Anti)Corruption

1. This definition of historical memory is derived from Stern, *Battling for Hearts and Minds*, 5: "Memory is the meaning we attach to experience, not simply the recall of the events and emotions of experience." Stern's definition has become a central point of reference in the literature on historical memory in Latin American studies.

2. Betancourt, *Venezuela: Oil and Politics*, 121; and Betancourt, *El 18 de Octubre de 1945*, 336–42.

3. Ewell, *Indictment of a Dictator*, 45–46, 52–53.

4. Ewell, *Indictment of a Dictator*, 141–42.

5. Karl, "Petroleum and Political Pacts."

6. Ewell, *Indictment of a Dictator*, 46, 52–53, 96. See also Morillo, *El enriquecimiento ilícito*, 43–94.

7. Ewell, *Indictment of a Dictator*, 127.

8. Silva Michelena, "Venezuelan Bureaucrat," 114, 118.

9. Sanin [Alfredo Tarre Murzi], *Venezuela saudita*; Frielich de Segal, *La venedemocracia*, 30–31; Cañizales Márquez, *Así somos los venezolanos*, 103–04, 110–11, 155–58; Peña, *Democracia y reforma*, 355–418. See also Ewell, *Indictment of a Dictator*, 72–74.

10. Coppedge, *Strong Parties and Lame Ducks*.

11. Rómulo Betancourt, "Un enfoque de la realidad económica, políti-

ca y social de América Latina," Caracas, May 23, 1976, in Suárez Figeroa, *Rómulo Betancourt: selección de escritos políticos*, 424–26.

12. Rómulo Betancourt, "Discurso ante la convención extraordinaria de A.D.," August 27, 1977, in Suárez Figeroa, *Rómulo Betancourt: selección de escritos políticos*, 436–38.

13. Alfredo Peña, "Una ley que obligue a los partidos a mostrar publicamente el origen de sus fondos, propone el ex-presidente Caldera," *El Nacional*, September 21, 1977.

14. Frielich de Segal, *La venedemocracia*, 88–89.

15. Peña, *Conversaciones con Uslar Pietri*, 49–54.

16. Peña, *Conversaciones con Uslar Pietri*, 53.

17. Alfredo Peña, "La corrupción administrativa: el pueblo pierde fe en los políticos que prometen acabar con el mal mientras el fenómeno se extiende como hierba maldita," *El Nacional*, September 24, 1977.

18. Rey, "Corruption and Political Illegitimacy."

19. Pérez Perdomo, "Corruption and Political Crisis," 326–28.

20. Beroes, *RECADI: La gran estafa*. RECADI stands for Régimen de Cambios Diferenciales (Regime of Differential Exchange Rates).

21. The image of PDVSA as a meritocracy became controversial under Chávez. See Wiseman and Béland, "Politics of Institutional Change," 151–58.

22. For a translation of the manifesto, see Naím, *Paper Tigers and Minotaurs*, 155–56.

23. Gates, *Electing Chávez*, 15–18.

24. Rivero, *La rebelión de los náufragos*, 238–39, 355, 362–63, 387, 394–95.

25. De Graaf, Wagenaar, and Hoenderboom, "Constructing Corruption"; Knights, *Trust and Distrust*; and Kerkhoff et al., "Dutch Political Corruption."

26. Transparency International, "What Is Corruption?" https://www.transparency.org/en/what-is-corruption, accessed January 3, 2024.

27. Scholarly critiques of TI's definition and its role in anticorruption include Brown and Cloke, "Neoliberal Reform"; Walton, *Anti-Corruption and Its Discontents*; and Pierce, *Moral Economies of Corruption*, 6–9.

28. See Buchan and Hill, *Intellectual History*, and works cited therein.

29. Heywood, "Rethinking Corruption"; Conaghan, "Prosecuting Presidents," 676; and Bussell, "Typologies of Corruption."

30. Muir and Gupta, "Rethinking the Anthropology of Corruption"; Knights, *Trust and Distrust*; and Heinzen, *Art of the Bribe*.

31. Bjarnegard, "Focusing on Masculinity"; Merkle, "Gender and Corruption"; and Smith, "Paradoxes of the Public Sphere."

32. Adams, "Rule of the Father"; and Charrad, "Central and Local Patrimonialism."

33. Studies that exemplify this approach include Knights, *Trust and Distrust*; Kroeze, Vitória, and Geltner, *Anticorruption in History*; and Heinzen, *Art of the Bribe*.

BIBLIOGRAPHY

Abbreviations

BAHM	*Boletín del Archivo Histórico de Miraflores*
GEPIMA	*Gobierno y época del Presidente Isaías Medina Angarita*
JRCA	Jurado de Responsabilidad Civil y Administrativa
UKNA/FO	United Kingdom National Archives, Foreign Office
USNARA/RDS	United States National Archives and Records Administration, Records of the Department of State

Archives

Archivo Histórico Nacional, Ministerio de Asuntos Exteriores. Madrid, Spain.
Archivo General de la Administración, Ministerio de Asuntos Exteriores. Alcalá de Henares, Spain.
Archivo Tulio Febres Cordero. Mérida, Venezuela.
United Kingdom National Archives, Foreign Office, 1908–1948 (UKNA/FO). Kew, United Kingdom.
United States National Archives and Records Administration, Records of the Department of State, 1910–1948 (USNARA/RDS). Washington, DC, and College Park, Maryland, USA.

Newspapers

Ecos de Torondoy (Torondoy, Mérida)
El Nacional (Caracas)
El Nuevo Diario (Caracas)
El País (Caracas)
El Rehabilitador (Trujillo)
El Relator (Trujillo)
El Universal (Caracas)
La Esfera (Caracas)

La Voz de Portuguesa (Guanare)
La Voz de Valera (Valera)
Notas (Barquisimeto)
Panorama (Maracaibo)
Patria (Mérida)
Patria y Unión (Barinas)

Published Collections of Documents

Archivo Histórico de Miraflores. *Boletín del Archivo Histórico de Miraflores.* Caracas: Archivo Histórico de Miraflores, 1959–2004 (*BAHM*).
Betancourt Valverde, Virginia, ed. *The Papers of Rómulo Betancourt.* Wilmington, DE: Scholarly Resources, 2003 (microfilm).
Carrillo Batalla, Tomás Enrique, ed. *Historia de las finanzas públicas en Venezuela, siglo xx.* 83 vols. Caracas: Academia Nacional de la Historia, 1988.
Castillo Lara, Lucas Guillermo, ed. *Apuntes para una historia documental de la iglesia venezolana en el archivo secreto vaticano (1900–1922).* 4 vols. Caracas: Academia Nacional de la Historia, 2000.
Catalá, José Agustín, ed. *Acción Democrática, primeros años: oposición y poder, 1941–1948.* Caracas: Centauro, 1987.
Contraloría General de la República. *Historia de la Contraloría de la República.* 2 vols. Caracas: La Contraloría General de la República, 1988.
Gobierno y época de la Junta Revolucionaria. 25 vols. Caracas: Congreso de la República, 1989.
Gobierno y época del Presidente Eleazar López Contreras. 16 vols. Caracas: Congreso de la República, 1985.
Gobierno y época del Presidente Isaías Medina Angarita. 17 vols. Caracas: Congreso de la República, 1987 (*GEPIMA*).
Gómez, Alejandro, ed. *Rómulo Betancourt contra la dictadura de Juan Vicente Gómez, 1928–1935.* Caracas: Ediciones Centauro, 1982.
Grases, Pedro, Ramón J. Velásquez, Manuel Pérez Vila, and Horacio Jorge Becco, eds. *Documentos que hicieron historia.* 5 vols. Caracas: Presidencia de la República, 1988.
Hernández, José Manuel, ed. *Recopilación de artículos y documentos relativos a los derechos del territorio Yuruary y autonomía del estado Bolívar.* Caracas: Impr. de la Patria, 1891.
Jurado de Responsabilidad Civil y Administrativa (JRCA). *Sentencias.* 5 vols. Caracas: Imprenta Nacional, 1946.
López Contreras, Eleazar. *El triunfo de la verdad: documentos para la historia venezolana.* México: Genio Latino, 1949.
Sanoja Hernández, Jesús, ed. *La Oposición a la dictadura gomecista: la prensa clandestina y otros documentos.* Caracas: Congreso de la República, 1983.

Segnini, Yolanda, ed. *Los hombres del Benemérito: epistolario inédito*. 2 vols. Caracas: Instituto de Estudios Hispanoamericanos, Universidad Central de Venezuela, 1985–86.
Sosa A., Arturo, ed. *Papeles clandestinos del Partido Democrático Nacional (1937–1941): documentos del archivo de Juan Bautista Fuenmayor*. Caracas: Ediciones de la Presidencia de la República, 1995.
Soteldo, Patricia, ed. *Rómulo Betancourt: antología política, 1941–1945*. Caracas: Fundación Rómulo Betancourt, 1999.
Suárez Figueroa, Naudy, ed. *La oposición a la dictadura gomecista: el movimiento estudiantil de 1928, antología documental*. Caracas: Congreso de la República, 1983.
Suárez Figueroa, Naudy, ed. *Programas políticas venezolanos de la primera mitad del siglo xx*, 2 vols. Caracas: Universidad Católica Andrés Bello, 1977.
Suárez Figueroa, Naudy, ed. *Rómulo Betancourt: selección de escritos políticos, 1929–1981*. Caracas: Fundación Rómulo Betancourt, 2006.
Vallenilla Lanz, Laureano, ed. *La rehabilitación de Venezuela: campañas políticas de "El Nuevo Diario" 1915 a 1926*. Caracas: Lit. y Tip. Vargas, 1926.
Velásquez, Ramon J., ed. *El debate político en 1936*. 3 vols. Caracas: Congreso de la República, 1983.

General Works

Adams, Julia. *The Familial State: Ruling Families and Merchant Capitalism in Early Modern Europe*. Ithaca, NY: Cornell University Press, 2005.
Adams, Julia. "The Rule of the Father: Patriarchy and Patrimonialism in Early Modern Europe." In *Max Weber's Economy and Society: A Critical Companion*, edited by Charles Camic, Philip S. Gorski, and David M. Trubek, 237–266. Stanford, CA: Stanford University Press, 2005.
Alexander, Robert. *Rómulo Betancourt and the Transformation of Venezuela*. New Brunswick [NJ]: Transaction Books, 1982.
Alexander Rodríguez, Linda. *The Search for Public Policy: Regional Politics and Government Finances in Ecuador, 1830–1940*. Berkeley: University of California Press, 1985.
Arcaya, Pedro Manuel. *Cuenta que el Dr. Pedro Manuel Arcaya rinde al pueblo venezolano de los fondos del Capítulo VII y créditos adicionales al mismo del presupuesto de gastos del despacho de Relaciones Interiores, erogados desde el 13 de enero de 1925 hasta el 19 de abril de 1929, siendo Arcaya ministro de dicho despacho*. 2 vols. Caracas: Impresos Unidos, 1941.
Arcaya, Pedro Manuel. *Defensa del Doctor Pedro Manuel Arcaya en los juicios civiles que contra él y otros intentó el Doctor Juan José Abreu, Procurador General de la Nación*. Caracas: Tip. del Comercio, 1939.

BIBLIOGRAPHY

Arcaya, Pedro Manuel. *La pena de la confiscación general de bienes en Venezuela: estudio de historia y derecho*. Caracas: Impresores Unidos, 1945.

Arellano-Gault, David. *Corruption in Latin America*. New York: Routledge, 2020.

Arévalo Cedeño, Emilio. *Viva Arévalo Cedeño! (el libro de mis luchas)*. 1936. Caracas: Seleven, 1979.

Arráiz Lucca, Rafael. *Arturo Uslar Pietri*. Caracas: El Nacional, 2006.

Arráiz Lucca, Rafael. *El trienio adeco (1945–1948) y las conquistas de la ciudadanía*. Caracas: Editorial Alfa, 2016.

Bach, Daniel C. "Patrimonialism and Neopatrimonialism: Comparative Receptions and Transcriptions." In *Neopatrimonialism in Africa and Beyond*, edited by Daniel C. Bach and Mamoudou Gazibo, 25–45. New York: Routledge, 2012.

Battaglini, Oscar. *El medinismo: modernización, crisis política, y golpe de estado*. Caracas: Monte Ávila Editores, 1997.

Bayly, C. A. *The Birth of the Modern World, 1780–1914*. Oxford: Blackwell, 2004.

Beattie, Peter M. *The Tribute of Blood: Army, Honor, Race, and Nation in Brazil, 1864–1945*. Durham, NC: Duke University Press, 2001.

Beroes, Agustín. *RECADI: La gran estafa*. Caracas: Planeta, 1990.

Betancourt, Rómulo. *El 18 de Octubre de 1945: Génesis y realizaciones de una revolución democrática*. Barcelona: Seix Barral, 1979.

Betancourt, Rómulo. *Venezuela: Oil and Politics*. Translated by Everett Bauman. Boston: Houghton Mifflin, 1979. (Original Spanish edition, 1956.)

Bjarnegard, Elin. "Focusing on Masculinity and Male-Dominated Networks in Corruption." In *Gender and Corruption: Historical Roots and New Avenues for Research*, edited by Helena Stensöta and Lena Wängnerud, 257–73. Cham, Switzerland: Palgrave Macmillan, 2018.

Borges, Dain. "'Puffy, Ugly, Slothful, and Inert': Degeneration in Brazilian Social Thought." *Journal of Latin American Studies* 25, no. 2 (1993): 235–56.

Botello, Oldman. *Historia de Villa de Cura: tránsito por la vida de un pueblo*. Maracay: Ediciones de la Asamblea Legislativa del Estado Aragua, 1971.

Botello, Oldman. *Historia de Villa de Cura: tránsito por la vida de un pueblo*. Villa de Cura: Publicaciones de la Alcaldía del Municipio Zamora, 2005.

Bracho Sierra, J. J. "Cincuenta años de ingresos fiscales, 1910–1960." *Revista de Hacienda*, no. 48 (1964): 31–69.

Bratsis, Peter. "The Construction of Corruption, or Rules of Separation and Illusions of Purity in Bourgeois Societies." *Social Text* 21, no. 4 (Winter 2003): 9–33.

Brewer, John. *Sinews of Power: War, Money, and the English State, 1688–1783.* New York: Knopf, 1989.

Briceño, Santiago. *Cartas sobre el Táchira.* Caracas: Biblioteca de Autores y Temas Tachirenses, 1960.

Briceño, Tarcila. *La ganadería en los llanos centro-occidentales venezolanos, 1910–1935.* Caracas: Academia Nacional de la Historia, 1985.

Brito Cornieles, Judith, and Herminia Cancela Cambon. "Desarrollo de la prensa diaria regional (1946–1986)." In *40 años de comunicación social en Venezuela,* edited by Eleazar Díaz Rangel, 57–120. Caracas: Congreso de la República, 1988.

Brown, Ed, and Jonathan Cloke. "Neoliberal Reform, Governance, and Corruption in the South: Assessing the International Anti-Corruption Crusade." *Antipode* 36, no. 2 (Mar. 2004): 272–94.

Bruni Celli, Marco Tulio. *El 18 de octubre de 1945.* Caracas: La Hoja del Norte/Cyngular, 2014.

Buchan, Bruce, and Lisa Hill. *An Intellectual History of Political Corruption.* Basingstoke: Palgrave Macmillan, 2014.

Burggraaff, Winfield J. *The Venezuelan Armed Forces in Politics, 1935–1959.* Columbia: University of Missouri Press, 1972.

Burkholder, Mark. "Honor and Honors in Colonial Spanish America." In Johnson and Lipsett-Rivera, *Faces of Honor,* 18–44.

Bussell, Jennifer. "Typologies of Corruption: A Pragmatic Approach." In *Greed, Corruption, and the Modern State: Essays in Political Economy,* edited by Susan Rose-Ackerman and Paul Lagunes, 21–45. Cheltenham: Edward Elgar, 2015.

Caballero, Manuel. *Gómez, el tirano liberal (vida y muerte del siglo xix).* Caracas: Monte Avila, 1993.

Caldera, Rafael. *Eleazar López Contreras: camino a la democracia (al ciudadano Presidente Eleazar López Contreras, en el centenario de su nacimiento, 1883–1983).* N.p.: Fondo Editorial del Estado Táchira, 1983.

Caldera, Rafael. *Los causahabientes: De Carabobo a Punto Fijo.* Caracas: Panapo, 1999.

Cañizales Márquez, José. *Así somos los venezolanos.* Caracas: Editorial Fuentes, 1977.

Capriles, Raúl. *Jira patriótica: la obra progresista del General Gómez.* Caracas: Litografía del Comercio, 1916.

Caraballo Perichi, Ciro. *Obras públicas, fiestas y mensajes: un puntal del régimen gomecista.* Caracas: Academia Nacional de la Historia, 1981.

Cárdenas, Rodolfo José. *COPEI en el trienio populista, 1945–1948.* Madrid: Hijos de E. Minuesa, 1987.

Cardozo, Arturo. *Sobre el cauce de un pueblo: un siglo de historia trujillana, 1830–1930.* Trujillo: Fondo Editorial Arturo Cardozo, 2001.

Cardozo, Orlando. "Duaca a princípios del siglo." In *San Juan Bautista de Duaca*, edited by Francisco Cañizales Verde, 44–65. Barquisimeto: Fundación Buría, 1991.

Carey, David, ed. *Distilling the Influence of Alcohol: Aguardiente in Guatemalan History*. Gainesville: University of Florida Press, 2012.

Carnochan, W. B. "The Literature of Confinement." In *The Oxford History of the Prison: The Practice of Punishment in Western Society*, edited by Norval Morris and David J. Rothman, 381–406. New York: Oxford University Press, 1998.

Carrera Damas, Germán. *Rómulo histórico*. Caracas: Editorial Alfa, 2013.

Carrillo Batalla, Tomás Enrique. *El régimen del General Eleazar López Contreras*. Caracas: Academia Nacional de la Historia, 2008.

Cartay, Rafael. *La mesa de la meseta: historia gastronómica de Mérida*. Mérida: Editorial Venzolana, 1988.

Cartay, Rafael. *Memoria de los orígenes: economía y sociedad en Barinas, 1786–1937*. Caracas: Academia Nacional de Ciencias Económicas, 1990.

Cartay Ramírez, Gehard. *Caldera y Betancourt, constructores de la democracia*. Caracas: Dahbar/Cyngular, 2018.

Carvallo, Gastón. *El hato venezolano, 1900–1980*. Caracas: Tropykos, 1985.

Caulfield, Sueann, Sarah Chambers, and Laura Putnam, eds. *Honor, Status, and Law in Modern Latin America*. Durham, NC: Duke University Press, 2005.

Centeno, Miguel Angel. *Blood and Debt: War and the Nation-State in Latin America*. University Park: Penn State University Press, 2002.

Centeno, Miguel A., and Agustin Ferraro, eds. *State and Nation Making in Latin America and Spain: Republics of the Possible*. Cambridge: Cambridge University Press, 2013.

Chamberlin, J. Edward, and Sander L. Gilman, eds. *Degeneration: The Dark Side of Progress*. New York: Columbia University Press, 1985.

Chambers, Sarah. *From Subjects to Citizens: Honor, Gender, and Politics in Arequipa, Peru, 1780–1854*. University Park: Penn State University Press, 1999.

Charrad, Mounira, and Julia Adams. "Patrimonialism, Past and Present." *Annals of the American Academy of Political and Social Science*, no. 636 (July 2011): 6–15.

Charrad, Mounira. "Central and Local Patrimonialism: State-Building in Kin-Based Societies." *Annals of the American Academy of Political and Social Science*, no. 636 (July 2011): 49–68.

Chehabi, H. E., and Juan Linz. "A Theory of Sultanism 1: A Type of Nondemocratic Rule." In *Sultanistic Regimes*, edited by Houchang Chehabi and Juan Linz, 3–25. Baltimore: Johns Hopkins University Press, 1998.

Chiossone, Tulio. *Memorias de un reaccionario*. Caracas: Congreso de la Republica, 1988.

Christian, David. *Living Water: Vodka and Russian Society on the Eve of Emancipation*. Oxford: Clarendon Press, 1990.

Christian, David. "Vodka and Corruption in Russia on the Eve of Emancipation." *Slavic Review* 36, nos. 3–4 (1987): 471–88.

Ciudad de Castro, Carmen, ed. *Juan Vicente Gómez ante la historia*. San Cristóbal: Biblioteca de Autores y Temas Tachirenses, 1986.

Clemente Travieso, Carmen. *Mujeres venezolanas y otros reportajes*. Caracas: Avila Gráfica, 1951.

Colmenter V., Felipe S. *Economía y política en Trujillo durante el guzmancismo, 1870–1887*. [Caracas]: Fundación para el Rescate del Acervo Documental Venezolano, 1983.

Conaghan, Catherine M. "Prosecuting Presidents: The Politics within Ecuador's Corruption Cases." *Journal of Latin American Studies* 44, no. 4 (2012): 649–78.

Contraloría General de la Nación. *Informe presentado al Congreso Nacional en las sesiones de 1939*. Caracas: n.p., 1939.

Copland, Ian, and Michael R. Godley. "Revenue Farming in Comparative Perspective: Reflections on Taxation, Social Structure and Development in the Early-Modern Period." In *The Rise and Fall of Revenue Farming: Business Elites and the Emergence of the Modern State in Southeast Asia*, edited by John Butcher and Howard Dick, 45–68. New York: St. Martin's Press, 1993.

Coppedge, Michael. *Strong Parties and Lame Ducks: Presidential Partyarchy and Factionalism in Venezuela*. Stanford, CA: Stanford University Press, 1994.

Cordero Velásquez, Luis. *Gómez y las fuerzas vivas*. Caracas: Doneme, 1971.

Coronil, Fernando. *The Magical State: Nature, Money, and Modernity in Venezuela*. Chicago: University of Chicago Press, 1997.

Coronil, Fernando, and Julie Skurski. "Dismembering and Remembering the Nation: The Semantics of Political Violence in Venezuela." *Comparative Studies in Society and History* 33, no. 2 (Apr. 1991): 288–337.

Cromwell, Jesse. *The Smugglers' World: Illicit Trade and Atlantic Communities in Eighteenth-Century Venezuela*. Chapel Hill: University of North Carolina Press, 2018.

De Graaf, Gjalt, Pieter Wagenaar, and Michel Hoenderboom. "Constructing Corruption." In *The Good Cause: Theoretical Perspectives on Corruption*, edited by Gjalt De Graaf, Patrick von Maravic, and Pieter Wagenaar, 98–114. Farmington Hills, MI: Barbara Budrich, 2010.

Deas, Malcolm. "Colombia, Ecuador, and Venezuela, c. 1880–1930." In

The Cambridge History of Latin America, edited by Leslie Bethell, vol. 5, 641–84. Cambridge: Cambridge University Press, 1984.

Deas, Malcolm. "The Fiscal Problems of Nineteenth-Century Colombia." *Journal of Latin American Studies* 14, no. 2 (Nov. 1982): 287–328.

Derby, Lauren. *The Dictator's Seduction: Politics and the Popular Imagination in the Era of Trujillo*. Durham, NC: Duke University Press, 2009.

Díaz, Arlene J. *Female Citizens, Patriarchs, and the Law in Venezuela, 1789–1904*. Lincoln: University of Nebraska Press, 2004.

Díaz Rangel, Eleazar. *La prensa venezolana en el siglo XX*. Caracas: Fundación Neumann, 1994.

Drake, Paul W. *The Money Doctor in the Andes: U.S. Advisors, Investors, and Economic Reform in Latin America from World War I to the Great Depression*. Durham, NC: Duke University Press, 1989.

Drinot, Paulo. *The Sexual Question: A History of Prostitution in Peru, 1850s–1950s*. Cambridge: Cambridge University Press, 2020.

Dupouy, Walter. "La clase media en Venezuela." In *La clase media en Costa Rica, Haiti y Venezuela: cinco colaboraciones*, edited by Theo R. Crevenna, 68–102. Washington, DC: Unión Panamericana, 1951.

Dupuy, Crisalida. *Propiedades del General Juan Vicente Gómez*. Caracas: Contraloría General de la República, 1983.

Ellner, Steve. "Venezuelan Revisionist Political History, 1908–1958: New Motives and Criteria for Analyzing the Past." *Latin American Research Review* 30, no. 2 (1995): 91–121.

Engels, Jens Ivo. "Corruption and Anticorruption in the Era of Modernity and Beyond." In Kroeze, Vitória, and Geltner, *Anticorruption in History*, 167–80. Oxford: Oxford University Press, 2018.

Erdmann, Gero, and Ulf Engel. "Neopatrimonialism Reconsidered: Critical Review and Elaboration of an Elusive Concept." *Commonwealth and Comparative Politics* 45, no. 1 (2007): 95–119.

Ewell, Judith. "Ligia Parra Jahn: The Blonde with the Revolver." In *The Human Tradition in Latin America: The Twentieth Century*, edited by William Beezley and Judith Ewell, 151–166. Wilmington, DE: Scholarly Resources, 1987.

Ewell, Judith. *The Indictment of a Dictator: The Extradition and Trial of Marcos Pérez Jiménez*. College Station: Texas A&M Press, 1981.

Ewell, Judith. *Venezuela: A Century of Change*. Stanford, CA: Stanford University Press, 1984.

Ewell, Judith. "Venezuela since 1930." In *The Cambridge History of Latin America*, edited by Leslie Bethell, vol. 8, 727–90. Cambridge: Cambridge University Press, 1991.

Ewell, Judith. *Venezuela and the United States: From Monroe's Hemisphere to Petroleum's Empire*. Athens: University of Georgia Press, 1996.

Febres Cordero, Tulio. *Cocina criollo o guía del ama de casa para disponer la comida diaria con prontitud y acierto.* 1899. N.p.: Corporación de los Andes, 1979.

Flores, Carlos M. *Gómez, patriarca del crimen: el terror y el trabajo forzado en Venezuela.* 1933. Caracas: Ateneo de Caracas, 1980.

Foucault, Michel. *Discipline and Punish: The Birth of the Prison.* Translated by Alan Sheridan. New York: Vintage, 1977.

Frevert, Ute. *Emotions in History, Lost and Found.* Budapest: Central European University Press, 2011.

Frevert, Ute. *The Politics of Humiliation: A Modern History.* Translated by Adam Bresnahan. Oxford: Oxford University Press, 2020.

Friedman, Elisabeth J. *Unfinished Transitions: Women and the Gendered Development of Democracy in Venezuela.* University Park: Penn State University Press, 2000.

Frielich de Segal, Alicia, ed. *La venedemocracia.* Caracas: Monte Avila Editores, 1978.

Fujitani, Takashi. *Splendid Monarchy: Power and Pageantry in Modern Japan.* Berkeley: University of California Press, 1996.

Gabaldón Márquez, Joaquín. *Memoria y cuento de la generación del 28.* Caracas: n.p., 1958.

Garbi Sánchez, José. *Alzamientos, cárceles, y experiencias.* N.p.: Caracas, 1979.

García Jiménez, Luis Rafael. *Güigüe: historia social de un atraso, 1936–1994.* Valencia: Universidad de Carabobo, 2004.

García Naranjo, Nemesio. *Venezuela and Its Ruler.* Translated by Calla Wheaton Esteva. New York: Carranza, 1927.

García Ponce, Guillermo. *Política y clase media.* Caracas: Editorial Domingo Fuentes, 1969.

Gates, Leslie. *Electing Chávez: The Business of Anti-neoliberal Politics in Venezuela.* Pittsburgh: University of Pittsburgh Press, 2010.

Giraudy, Agustina, Jonathan Hartlyn, Claire Dunn, and Emily Carty. "The Impact of Neopatrimonialism on Poverty in Contemporary Latin America." *Latin American Politics and Society* 62, no. 1 (2020): 73–96.

Goldstein, Donna, and K. Drybread. "The Social Life of Corruption in Latin America." *Culture, Theory, and Critique* 59, no. 4 (2018): 299–311.

Gómez, Carlos Alarico. *El origen del estado democrático en Venezuela (1941–1948).* Caracas: Biblioteca de autores y temas tachirenses, 2004.

Gómez, Carlos Alarico. *El poder andino: de Cipriano Castro a Medina Angarita.* Caracas: El Nacional, 2007.

González Deluca, María Elena. *Los comerciantes de Caracas: Cien años de acción y testimonio de la Cámara de Comercio de Caracas.* Caracas: Cámara de Comercio de Caracas, 1994.

González Escorihuela, Ramón. *Las ideas políticas en el Táchira: de los años 70 del siglo xix a la segunda década del siglo xx*. Caracas: Biblioteca de Autores y Temas Tachirenses, 1994.

Graham, Richard. *Patronage and Politics in Nineteenth-Century Brazil*. Stanford, CA: Stanford University Press, 1990.

Harwich Vallenilla, Nikita. "El modelo económico del liberalismo amarillo: historia de un fracaso, 1888–1908." In *Política y economía en Venezuela, 1810–1976*, edited by Miguel Izard, 205–43. Caracas: Fundación John Boulton, 1976.

Heidenheimer, Arnold J. "Perspectives on the Perception of Corruption" [1970]. In *Political Corruption: Concepts and Contexts*, 3rd ed., edited by Arnold J. Heidenheimer and Michael Johnston, 141–54. New Brunswick [NJ]: Transaction Publishers, 2002.

Heinzen, James. *The Art of the Bribe: Corruption under Stalin, 1943–1953*. New Haven, CT: Yale University Press, 2016.

Herman, Donald. *Christian Democracy in Venezuela*. Chapel Hill: University of North Carolina Press, 1980.

Herrera, Claudia, and Agustín Ferraro. "Friends' Tax: Patronage, Fiscality, and State Building in Argentina and Spain." In Centeno and Ferraro, *State and Nation Making*, 157–80.

Heywood, Paul M. "Rethinking Corruption: Hocus-Pocus, Locus and Focus." *Slavonic and East European Review* 95, no. 1, special issue, "Innovations in Corruption Studies" (2017): 21–48.

Holmes, Leslie. *Corruption: A Very Short Introduction*. New York: Oxford University Press, 2015.

Izard, Miguel. *Series estadísticas para la historia de Venezuela*. Mérida: Universidad de los Andes, 1970.

Jiménez M., Rafael Simón. *Choque de generales: López Contreras—Medina Angarita: la ruptura que liquidó la hegemonía andina*. Caracas: Centauro, 2010.

Johnson, Lyman L., and Sonya Lipsett-Rivera, eds. *The Faces of Honor: Sex, Shame, and Violence in Colonial Latin America*. Albuquerque: University of New Mexico Press, 1998.

Johnston, Michael. "The Definitions Debate: Old Conflicts in New Guises." In *The Political Economy of Corruption*, edited by Arvind K. Jain, 11–31. New York: Routledge, 2001.

Johnston, Michael. "The Search for Definitions: The Vitality of Politics and the Issue of Corruption." *International Social Science Journal*, no. 149 (1996): 321–35.

Joseph, Gilbert M., and Daniel Nugent, eds. *Everyday Forms of State Formation: Revolution and the Negotiation of Rule in Modern Mexico*. Durham, NC: Duke University Press, 1994.

Karl, Terry Lynn. "Petroleum and Political Pacts: The Transition to Democracy in Venezuela." *Latin American Research Review*, 22, no. 1 (1987): 63–94.

Karl, Terry Lynn. *The Paradox of Plenty: Oil Booms and Petro-States.* Berkeley: University of California, 1997.

Katzarova, Elitza. *The Social Construction of Global Corruption: From Utopia to Neoliberalism.* Cham, Switzerland: Palgrave Macmillan, 2019.

Kay, Cristóbal. "Modernization and Dependency Theory." In *The Routledge Handbook of Latin American Development*, edited by Julie Cupples, 15–28. London: Routledge, 2018.

Kerkhoff, Antoon D. N., Michel P. Hoenderboom, Ronald Kroeze, and Pieter Wagenaar. "Dutch Political Corruption in Historical Perspective: From Eighteenth-Century Value Pluralism to a Nineteenth-Century Dominant Liberal Value System and Beyond." In *Korruption: Historische Annäherungen an eine Gundfigur Politischer Kommunikation*, edited by Niels Grüne and Smona Slanička, 443–67. Gottingen: Vandenhoeck & Ruprecht, 2010.

Kerkhoff, Toon, Ronald Kroeze, and Pieter Wagenaar. "Corruption and the Rise of Modern Politics in Europe in the Eighteenth and Nineteenth Centuries." *Journal of Modern European History* 11, no. 1 (2013): 19–30.

Keyse Rudolph, Donna, and G. A. Rudolph. *Historical Dictionary of Venezuela.* 2nd ed. Lanham, MD: Scarecrow Press, 1996.

Kiser, Edgar, and Joshua Kane. "Revolution and State Structure: The Bureaucratization of Tax Administration in Early Modern France and England." *American Journal of Sociology* 107, no. 1 (2001): 183–223.

Knights, Mark. *Trust and Distrust: Corruption in Office in Britain and Its Empire, 1600–1850.* Oxford: Oxford University Press, 2021.

Kolb, Glen L. *Democracy and Dictatorship in Venezuela, 1945–1958.* Hamden, CT: Archon, 1974.

Kornblith, Miriam, and Luken Quintana. "Gestión fiscal y centralización del poder político en los gobiernos de Cipriano Castro y de Juan Vicente Gómez." *Politeia*, no. 10 (1981): 143–225.

Kroeze, Ronald, André Vitória, and G. Geltner, eds. *Anticorruption in History: From Antiquity to the Modern Era.* Oxford: Oxford University Press, 2018.

Kroeze, Ronald, André Vitória, and G. Geltner. "Introduction: Debating Corruption and Anticorruption in History." In Kroeze, Vitória, and Geltner, *Anticorruption in History*, 1–17. Oxford: Oxford University Press, 2018.

Lauderdale Graham, Sandra. *House and Street: The Domestic World of Servants and Masters in Nineteenth-Century Rio de Janeiro.* New York: Cambridge University Press, 1988.

Lavin, John. *A Halo for Gómez.* New York: Pageant Press, 1954.

Lecuna, Vicente. *La Revolución de Queipa*. Caracas: n.p., 1991.
Lieuwen, Edwin. *Petroleum in Venezuela: A History*. New York: Russell & Russell, 1954.
Linder, Peter S. "Agriculture and Rural Society in Pre-petroleum Venezuela: The Sur del Lago Zuliano, 1880–1920." PhD diss., University of Texas, 1992.
Lisandro Alvarado, Aníbal, ed. *Archivo de la Rotunda*. Caracas: Ediciones Garrido, 1954.
Lombardi, John V. *Venezuela: The Search for Order, The Dream of Progress*. Oxford: Oxford University Press, 1982.
López, A. Ricardo, and Barbara Weinstein. "Introduction: We Shall Be All: Toward a Transnational History of the Middle Class." In *The Making of the Middle Class*, edited by A. Ricardo López and Barbara Weinstein, 1–25. Durham, NC: Duke University Press, 2012.
López, Jacinto. "Dictadura perpetua en Venezuela." (Originally published, 1922.) In *Juan Vicente Gómez ante la historia*, edited by Carmen Ciudad de Castro, 51–63. Caracas: Biblioteca de Autores y Temas Tachirenses, 1986.
López Contreras, Eleazar. *Páginas para la historia militar de Venezuela*. Caracas: Tipografía Americana, 1944.
López Contreras, Eleazar. *Proceso político social, 1928–1936*. 2nd ed. Caracas: Editorial Ancora, 1955.
López Maya, Margarita. *El ocaso del chavismo: Venezuela, 2005–2015*. Caracas: Editorial Alfa, 2016.
López Maya, Margarita. "Populism, 21st-Century Socialism, and Corruption in Venezuela." *Thesis Eleven* 149, no. 1 (2018): 67–83.
Lovera, Ildemaro. *Un hombre, un país*. Caracas: n.p., 1984.
Luciani, Jorge. *La dictadura perpetua de Gómez y sus adversaries*. 2nd ed. Caracas: Cooperativa de Artes Gráficas, 1936.
Luque, Guillermo. *Educación, estado y nación: una historia política de la educación oficial venezolana, 1928–1958*. Caracas: Monte Avila, 2009.
Luzardo, Rodolfo. *Notas histórico-económicas, 1928–1963*. Caracas: Editorial Sucre, 1963.
Lynch, John. *Caudillos in Spanish America, 1800–1850*. Oxford: Clarendon Press, 1992.
Márquez, Abdelkader. *Presencia del Táchira en la hacienda pública venezolana*. Caracas: Contraloría General de la República, 1982.
Martz, John D. *Acción Democrática: Evolution of a Modern Political Party in Venezuela*. Princeton, NJ: Princeton University Press, 1966.
Martz, John D. "Venezuela's 'Generation of '28': The Genesis of Political Democracy." *Journal of Inter-American Studies* 6, no. 1 (1964): 17–32.
Mayobre, Eduardo. *Gumersindo Torres*. Caracas: El Nacional, 2007.

BIBLIOGRAPHY

McBeth, Brian S. *Dictatorship and Politics: Intrigue, Betrayal, Survival in Venezuela, 1908–1935.* Notre Dame, IN: University of Notre Dame Press, 2008.

McBeth, Brian S. *Gunboats, Corruption, and Claims: Foreign Intervention in Venezuela, 1899–1908.* Westport, CT: Greenwood Press, 2001.

McBeth, Brian S. *Juan Vicente Gómez and the Oil Companies in Venezuela, 1908–1935.* Cambridge: Cambridge University Press, 1983.

McFarlane, Anthony. "Political Corruption and Reform in Bourbon Spanish America." In *Political Corruption in Europe and Latin America*, edited by Walter Little and Eduardo Posada-Carbó, 41–63. St. Martin's: New York, 1996.

McGill, Samuel. *Poliantea: Desarrollos Históricos, 1900–1950.* Caracas: Imprenta Nacional, 1978.

Medrano, José Miguel. *Juan Vicente Gómez.* Madrid: Ediciones Quorum, 1987.

Merkle, Ortrun. "Gender and Corruption: What We Know and Ways Forward." In *A Research Agenda for Studies of Corruption*, edited by Alina Mungiu-Pippidi and Paul Heywood, 75–89. Cheltenham: Edward Elgar, 2020.

Miller, Pavla. *Patriarchy.* London: Routledge, 2017.

Ministerio de Hacienda. *Exposición que dirige al Congreso Nacional de los Estados Unidos de Venezuela el Ministro de Hacienda y Crédito Público en 1910.* Caracas: El Cojo, 1910.

Ministerio de Hacienda, *Ley orgánica de la renta de licores, sancionada por el congreso nacional en 1915.* Caracas: El Cojo, 1915.

Ministerio de Hacienda. *Memoria de Hacienda.* Caracas: various publishers, 1914–1937.

Mitchell, Timothy. *Colonising Egypt.* Berkeley: University of California Press, 1988.

Mommer, Bernard. *Global Oil and the Nation State.* Oxford: Oxford University Press, 2002.

Morantes, Pedro María [Pío Gil]. *El cabito, novela venezolana contemporánea.* Valencia: Imprenta F. Vives Mora, 1910.

Morantes, Pedro María. *Puñado de guijarros: los áulicos de palacio en 1914.* 1914. Caracas: Ediciones Centauro, 1988.

Morillo, Gilberto. *El enriquecimiento ilícito: referencias a la legislación venezolana.* Caracas: Fuerza Democrática Popular, 1965.

Muir, Sarah, and Akhil Gupta. "Rethinking the Anthropology of Corruption." *Current Anthropology* 59, suppl. 18 (April 2018): S4–S15.

Mungiu-Pippidi, Alina. *The Quest for Good Governance: How Societies Develop Control of Corruption.* Cambridge: Cambridge University Press, 2015.

Muñoz, Arturo Guillermo. "The Táchira Frontier, 1881–1899: Regional

Isolation and National Integration in the Venezuelan Andes." PhD diss., Stanford University, 1977.

Muñoz Tébar, Jesús. *El personalismo i el legalismo*. New York: A. E. Hernández, 1890.

Myrup, Erik. *Power and Corruption in the Early Modern Portuguese World*. Baton Rouge: Louisiana State University Press, 2015.

Naím, Moisés. *Paper Tigers and Minotaurs: The Politics of Venezuela's Economic Reforms*. Washington, DC: Carnegie Endowment for International Peace, 1993

Niblo, Stephen. *Mexico in the 1940s: Modernity, Politics, and Corruption*. Wilmington, DE: Scholarly Resources, 1999.

Nye, Robert A. *Masculinity and Male Codes of Conduct in Modern France*. Berkeley: University of California Press, 1993.

O'Brien, Patricia. "The Prison on the Continent: Europe, 1865–1965." In *The Oxford History of the Prison: The Practice of Punishment in Western Society*, edited by Norval Morris and David J. Rothman, 178–201. New York: Oxford University Press, 1998.

Ochoa Briceño, Santiago. *Lo que vi, oí, e hice. Del andinismo a la democracia. Memorias*. Caracas: Ediciones de la Presidencia de la República, 1994.

Ogborn, Miles. *Spaces of Modernity: London's Geographies, 1680–1780*. London: Guilford Press, 1998.

Olivar, José Alberto. "El Jurado de Responsabilidad Civil y Administrativa, 1946: caso Román Cárdenas. Los excesos de una revolución." In *"Dádivas, dones y dineros": aportes a una nueva historia de la corrupción en América Latina*, edited by Christoph Rosenmüller and Stephan Ruderer, 233–46. Madrid: Iberoamericana, 2016.

Olivar, José Alberto. *Jesús Muñoz Tébar*. Caracas: El Nacional, 2008.

Owensby, Brian P. *Intimate Ironies: Modernity and the Making of Middle-Class Lives in Brazil*. Stanford, CA: Stanford University Press, 1999.

Owensby, Brian P. "Middle Class Politics in Revolution." In *The Making of the Middle Class: Toward a Transnational History*, edited by A. Ricardo López and Barbara Weinstein, 288–95. Durham, NC: Duke University Press, 2012.

Palacios, Antonia. *Ana Isabel, una niña decente*. 1949. Caracas: Monte Avila Editores, 2004.

Parada, Nemecio. *De Ocumare a Miraflores*. Caracas: Imprenta Nacional, 1975.

Paredes, Antonio. *Diario de mi prisión en San Carlos. 1901*. Port of Spain, Trinidad: Davidson and Todd, 1907.

Pareja y Paz Soldán, José. *Juan Vicente Gómez: un fenómeno telúrico*. Caracas: Avila Gráfica, 1951.

Pareja y Paz Soldán, José. *Juan Vicente Gómez, un fenómeno telúrico*. Caracas: Ediciones Centauro, 1970.
Parker, D. S. *The Idea of the Middle Class: White Collar Workers and Peruvian Society, 1900–1950*. University Park: Penn State University Press, 1998.
Peña, Alfredo. *Conversaciones con Uslar Pietri*. Caracas: Ateneo de Caracas, 1978.
Peña, Alfredo. *Democracia y reforma del estado*. Caracas: Editorial Jurídica Venezolana, 1978.
Pereira, Pedro N. *En la prisión: los estudiantes de 1928*. Caracas: Avila Gráfica, 1952.
Pérez, Ana Mercedes. *La verdad inédita: historia de la Revolución de Octubre con nuevos documentos*. 3rd ed. Caracas: Ernesto Armitano, 1975.
Pérez Contreras, Zandra. "Maracay, centro de industrias agrícolas y pecuarias bajo la influencia del general Juan Vicente Gómez." *Tiempo y espacio* 23, no. 59 (2013): 1–32.
Pérez Perdomo, Rogelio. "Corruption and Political Crisis." In *Lessons of the Venezuelan Experience*, edited by Louis W. Goodman, Johanna Mendelson Forman, Moisés Naím, Joseph S. Tulchin, and Gary Bland, 311–33. Washington, DC: Woodrow Wilson Center Press, 1995.
Piccato, Pablo. *City of Suspects: Crime in Mexico City, 1900–1931*. Durham, NC: Duke University Press, 2001.
Pierce, Steven. *Moral Economies of Corruption: State Formation and Political Culture in Nigeria*. Durham, NC: Duke University Press, 2016.
Picón Salas, Mariano. *Los días de Cipriano Castro*. Caracas: Ediciones Garrido, 1953.
Pilcher, Jeffrey. *The Sausage Rebellion: Public Health, Private Enterprise, and Meat in Mexico City, 1890–1917*. Albuquerque: University of New Mexico Press, 2006.
Pimentel, Cecilia. *Bajo la tiranía*. Caracas: n.p., 1970.
Pino Iturrieta, Elías, ed. *Juan Vicente Gómez y su época*. Caracas: Monte Avila, 1988.
Pino Iturrieta, Elías. *Positivismo y gomecismo*. Caracas: Editorial Alfa, 2015.
Plamper, Jan. *The History of Emotions: An Introduction*. Translated by Keith Tribe. Oxford: Oxford University Press, 2015.
Pocaterra, José Rafael. *Gómez, the Shame of America*. Paris: André Delpeuch, 1929.
Polanco Alcántara, Tomás. *Juan Vicente Gómez, aproximación a una biografía*. Caracas: Grijalbo, 1990.
Porter, Susie. *From Angel to Office Worker: Middle-Class Identity and Female Consciousness in Mexico, 1890–1950*. Lincoln: University of Nebraska Press, 2018.

Pozsgai-Alvarez, Joseph, ed. *The Politics of Anti-Corruption Agencies in Latin America*. New York: Routledge, 2021.

Prieto, Moisés. "Corrupt and Rapacious: Colonial Spanish-American Past through the Eyes of Early Nineteenth-Century Contemporaries: A Contribution from the History of Emotions." In *Corruption, Empire, and Colonialism in the Modern Era: A Global Perspective*, edited by Ronald Kroeze, Pol Dalmau, and Frédéric Monier, 105–39. Singapore: Springer, 2021.

Quintero, Inés. "De la alucinación a la eficiencia: Román Cárdenas en el Ministerio de Hacienda." *Tierra Firme* 3, no. 12 (1985): 599–611.

Quintero, Inés. *El ocaso de una estirpe*. Caracas: Alfadil Ediciones, 1989.

Quiroz, Alfonso W. *Corrupt Circles: A History of Unbound Graft in Peru*. Baltimore: Johns Hopkins University Press, 2008.

Rabe, Stephen G. *The Road to OPEC: United States Relations with Venezuela, 1919–1976*. Austin: University of Texas Press, 1982.

Ramírez, Alfonso. *Biografía de Andrés Eloy Blanco y memoria de su época*. Caracas: El Centauro, 1997.

Rangel, Domingo Alberto. *Gómez: el amo del poder*. 2nd ed. Valencia: Mérida Editores, 2005.

Rausch, Jane M. *Colombia: Territorial Rule and the Llanos Frontier*. Gainesville: University of Florida Press, 1999.

Rey, Juan Carlos. "Corruption and Political Illegitimacy in Venezuelan Democracy." In *Reinventing Legitimacy: Democracy and Political Change in Venezuela*, edited by Damarys Canache and Michael R. Kulisheck, 113–35. Westport, CT: Greenwood Press, 1998.

Rivero, Mirtha. *La rebelión de los náufragos*. Caracas: Alfa, 2010.

Rodríguez, José Ángel. *La historia de la caña: azúcares, aguardientes y rones, siglos xvi–xx*. Caracas: Alfadil, 2005.

Rodríguez, José Ángel. *Los paisajes geohistóricos cañeros en Venezuela*. Caracas: Academia Nacional de la Historia, 1986.

Rodríguez, Luis Cipriano. *Gómez: agricultura, petróleo y dependencia*. Caracas: Tropykos, 1983.

Rodríguez, Luis Cipriano. "Gómez y el agro." In Pino Iturrieta, *Juan Vicente Gómez y su época*, 91–114.

Rodríguez Gallard, Irene. "Crisis de la economía en tiempos de la Restauración Liberal." In *Cipriano Castro y su época*, edited by Elías Pino Iturrieta, 131–46. Caracas: Monte Avila, 1991.

Rondón Nucete, Jesús. *Primeros años del gomecismo*. Mérida: Universidad de los Andes, 2003.

Rosenmüller, Christoph, and Stephan Ruderer. "Introducción." In *Dádivas, dones y dineros: aportes a una nueva historia de la corrupción en América Latina*, edited by Christoph Rosenmüller and Stephan Ruderer, 7–25. Madrid: Iberoamericana, 2016.

Rosenmüller, Christoph. *Corruption and Justice in Colonial Mexico, 1650–1755*. Cambridge: Cambridge University Press, 2019.

Rosenmüller, Christoph, ed. *Corruption in the Iberian Empires: Greed, Custom, and Colonial Networks*. Albuquerque: University of New Mexico Press, 2017.

Rosenthal Joshua M. *Salt and the Colombian State: Local Society and Regional Monopoly in Boyacá, 1821–1900*. Pittsburgh: University of Pittsburgh Press, 2012.

Rourke, Thomas. *Gómez, Tyrant of the Andes*. New York: William Morrow, 1941.

Salazar-Carrillo, Jorge, and Bernadette West. *Oil and Development in Venezuela during the 20th Century*. Westport, CT: Praeger, 2004.

Salcedo-Bastardo, J. L. *Historia fundamental de Venezuela*. 7th ed. Caracas: Fundación Gran Mariscal de Ayacucho, 1977.

Salvatore, Ricardo. "Between Empleomanía and the Common Good: Expert Bureaucracies in Argentina (1870–1930)." In Centeno and Ferraro, *State and Nation Making*, 225–46.

Salzmann, Ariel. "An Ancien Régime Revisited: 'Privatization' and Political Economy in the Eighteenth-Century Ottoman Empire." *Politics and Society* 21, no. 4 (1993): 393–423.

Sanín [Alfredo Tarre Murzi]. *Venezuela saudita*. Valencia: Vadell Hermanos, 1978.

Sanoja Hernández, Jesús. "Largo viaje hacia la muerte." In Pino Iturrieta, *Juan Vicente Gómez y su época*, 144–155.

Segnini, Yolanda. *La consolidación del régimen de Juan Vicente Gómez*. Caracas: Academia Nacional de la Historia, 1982.

Segnini, Yolanda. *Las luces del gomecismo*. Caracas: Alfadil Ediciones, 1987.

Shore, Cris, and Dieter Haller. "Sharp Practice: Anthropology and the Study of Corruption." In *Corruption: Anthropological Perspectives*, edited by Dieter Haller and Cris Shore, 1–26. London: Pluto Press, 2005.

Silva, Patricio. "Pablo Ramírez: A Political Technocrat Avant-la-Lettre." In *The Politics of Expertise in Latin America*, edited by Miguel Centeno and Patricio Silva, 52–76. London: Palgrave Macmillan, 1998.

Silva, Patricio. *Public Probity and Corruption in Chile*. New York: Routledge, 2019.

Silva Michelena, José A. "The Venezuelan Bureaucrat." In *A Strategy for Research on Social Policy*, edited by Frank Bonilla and José A. Silva Michelena, 86–119. Vol. 1 of *The Politics of Change in Venezuela*. Cambridge, Mass: MIT Press, 1967.

Sippial, Tiffany. *Prostitution, Modernity, and the Making of the Cuban Republic, 1840–1920*. Chapel Hill: University of North Carolina Press, 2013.

Siso, Carlos. *Castro y Gómez: importancia de la hegemonía andina*. Caracas: Editorial Arte, 1985.
Skurski, Julie. "The Leader and the 'People': Representing the Nation in Postcolonial Venezuela." PhD diss., University of Chicago, 1993.
Smith, Benjamin T. "The Paradoxes of the Public Sphere: Journalism, Gender, and Corruption in Mexico, 1940–70." *Journal of Social History* 52, no. 4 (2019): 1330–54.
Smith, Daniel Jordan. *A Culture of Corruption: Everyday Deception and Popular Discontent in Nigeria*. Princeton, NJ: Princeton University Press, 2007.
Sosa A., Arturo, and Eloi Lengrand. *Del garibaldismo estudiantil a la izquierda criolla*. Caracas: Ediciones Centauro, 1981.
Stern, Steve J. *Battling for Hearts and Minds: Memory Struggles in Pinochet's Chile, 1973–1988*. Durham, NC: Duke University Press, 2006.
Stoler, Ann Laura. "Affective States." In *A Companion to the Anthropology of Politics*, edited by David Nugent and Joan Vincent, 4–20. Oxford: Blackwell, 2004.
Strange, Carolyn, and Robert Cribb. "Historical Perspectives on Honour, Violence, and Emotion." In *Honour, Violence, and Emotions in History*, edited by Carolyn Strange, Robert Cribb, and Christopher E. Forth, 1–22. London: Bloomsbury, 2014.
Suárez Findlay, Eileen J. *Imposing Decency: The Politics of Sexuality and Race in Puerto Rico, 1870–1920*. Durham, NC: Duke University Press, 1999.
Sullivan, William. "The Rise of Despotism in Venezuela: Cipriano Castro, 1899–1908." PhD diss., University of New Mexico, 1974.
Theobald, Robin. *Corruption, Development, and Underdevelopment*. Durham, NC: Duke University Press, 1990.
Tinker Salas, Miguel. *The Enduring Legacy: Oil, Culture, and Society in Venezuela*. Durham, NC: Duke University Press, 2009.
Torres, Gumersindo. *Memorias de Gumersindo Torres, un funcionario incorruptible en la dictadura del General Gómez*, edited by José Agustín Catalá. Caracas: Presidencia de la República, 1996.
Trinkunas, Harold. *Crafting Civilian Control of the Military in Venezuela: A Comparative Perspective*. Chapel Hill: University of North Carolina Press, 2005.
Trujillo, Gonzalo. "Resumen de los documentos de traspaso de concesiones de hidrocarburos, del año 1920 al 1938 inclusive." *Revista del Ministerio de Fomento* 2, no. 8 (1939): 161–274.
Urbaneja, Diego Bautista. "El sistema político gomecista." In Pino Iturrieta, *Juan Vicente Gómez y su época*, 51–67.
Uribe-Uran, Victor M. *Honorable Lives: Lawyers, Family, and Politics in Colombia, 1780–1850*. Pittsburgh: University of Pittsburgh Press, 2000.

US Department of State. *Foreign Relations of the United States 1946*. 11 vols. Washington, D.C.: Government Printing Office, 1969.

Uslar Pietri, Arturo. *Golpe y estado en Venezuela*. Caracas: Grupo Editorial Norma, 1992.

Velásquez, Ramón J. "Aspectos de la evolución política de Venezuela en el último medio siglo." In *Venezuela moderna: medio siglo de historia, 1926–1976*, edited by Ramón J. Velásquez, 13–436. Caracas: Editorial Ariel, 1979.

Velásquez, Ramón J. *Confidencias imaginarias de Juan Vicente Gómez*. 1979. Caracas: Biblioteca de Autores y Temas Tachirenses, 1999.

Velásquez, Ramón J. *La caída del liberalismo amarillo: tiempo y drama de Antonio Paredes*. 6th ed. Caracas: Ediciones de la Presidencia de la República, 1988 (originally published, 1972).

Velásquez, Ramón J. *Memorias de Venezuela*. Caracas: Ediciones Centauro, 1991.

Veloz Goiticoa, N. *Maracay, sus cultivadas dehesas*. Caracas: Tip. Universal, 1916.

Viso C., Carlos. *La epopeya del ron de Carúpano*. Caracas: ExLibris, 2004.

Walton, Grant. *Anti-Corruption and Its Discontents: Local, National, and International Perspectives on Corruption in Papua New Guinea*. London: Routledge, 2018.

Watts, Sarah. *Rough Rider in the White House: Theodore Roosevelt and the Politics of Desire*. Chicago: University of Chicago Press, 2003.

Wiseman, Colin, and Daniel Béland. "The Politics of Institutional Change in Venezuela: Oil Policy during the Presidency of Hugo Chávez." *Canadian Journal of Latin American and Caribbean Studies* 35, no. 70 (2010): 141–64.

Weaver, Kathleen. *Peruvian Rebel: The World of Magda Portal, with a Selection of Her Poems*. University Park: Penn State University Press, 2009.

Weber, Max. *Economy and Society: A New Translation*. Translated and edited by Keith Tribe. Cambridge: Harvard University Press, 2019.

White, Eugene N. "From Privatized to Government-Administered Tax Collection: Tax Farming in Eighteenth-Century France." *Economic History Review* 57, no. 4 (2004): 636–63.

Whitehead, Laurence. "State Organization in Latin America since 1930." In *The Cambridge History of Latin America: 1930 to the Present: Economy, Society and Politics*, vol. 6, part 2, edited by Leslie Bethell, 3–95. Cambridge: Cambridge University Press, 1994.

Williams, Marc. "The Political Economy of Meat: Food, Culture and Identity." In *Political Economy, Power and the Body: Global Perspectives*, edited by Gillian Youngs, 135–58. London: MacMillan, 2000.

Woodfine, Philip. "Tempters or Tempted? The Rhetoric and Practice of

Corruption in Walpolean Politics." In *Corrupt Histories*, edited by Emmanuel Kreike and William Chester Jordan, 167–196. Rochester, NY: University of Rochester Press, 2004.

Wright, Winthrop. *Café con leche: Race, Class, and National Image in Venezuela*. Austin: University of Texas Press, 1990.

Yarrington, Doug. *A Coffee Frontier: Land, Society, and Politics in Duaca, Venezuela, 1830–1936*. Pittsburgh: University of Pittsburgh Press, 1997.

Yarrington, Doug. "Political Transition in an Age of Extremes: Venezuela in the 1930s." In *The Great Depression in Latin America*, edited by Paulo Drinot and Alan Knight, 160–87. Durham, NC: Duke University Press, 2014.

Yarrington, Doug. "Tax Farming, Liquor, and the Quest for Fiscal Modernity in Venezuela, 1908–1935." *Hispanic American Historical Review* 94, no. 2 (2014): 237–69.

Yarrington, Doug. "The Vestey Cattle Enterprise and the Regime of Juan Vicente Gómez, 1908–1935." *Journal of Latin American Studies* 35, no. 1 (2003): 89–115.

Yergin, Daniel. *The Prize: The Epic Quest for Oil, Money, and Power*. New York: Free Press, 2008.

Zahler, Reuben. *Ambitious Rebels: Remaking Honor, Law, and Liberalism in Venezuela, 1780–1850*. Tucson: University of Arizona Press, 2013.

Ziems, Angel. *El gomecismo y la formación del ejército nacional*. Caracas: Ateneo de Caracas, 1979.

Ziems, Angel. "Un ejército de alcance nacional." In Pino Iturrieta, *Juan Vicente Gómez y su época*, 115–39.

Zinoman, Peter. *The Colonial Bastille: A History of Imprisonment in Vietnam, 1862–1940*. Berkeley: University of California Press, 2001.

INDEX

Note: Page numbers in *italics* indicate illustrative materials.

Abreu, Juan José, 146–47, 149, 168, 169–70
Acción Democrática (AD). *See* Democratic Action Party
adecos, 175, 184, 193, 202, 204, 212
aguardiente (alcoholic beverage), 75–76; distribution of revenue contracts, 81; lack of centralized bureaucracy, 76; legal and illegal profits, 76–77; liquor-tax contracts, 77–79; monthly payments by liquor tax farmers to treasury, *80*; subcontract for liquor tax, 80–81
aguinaldos, 151
ambiguous corruption. *See* financial corruption
Andrade, Ignacio, 29
Anglo-Persian Oil Company, 141
anticorruption, 12, 14, 119–25, 184–86, 225–26; Cárdenas, bureaucratization and, 81–87; controversy over trials, 18; definition of, 7; early reaction to anticorruption campaign, 188–94; failure of trials, 13; history of, 6–7, 14, 19, 222; interdisciplinary analyses of, 15, 221; in patrimonialism, 11, 12; rhetoric and actions of Betancourt, 14–15; sentiment against Gomecista cattle monopoly, 64–68, 72; trials, 5, 18
Apure state: animosities by fiscal transition, 90; Gomecista cattle monopoly, 54–55, 57, 195; jefe civil, 47; La Candelaria acquisition in, 43; property acquisitions by Gómez, 54, 55; reduction in cattle taxes, 69
Araujo, José Eliseo, 77
Arcaya, Pedro Manuel, 169–70, 192, 199, 226; Abreu's lawsuit against, 169; accusation against López Contreras, 169–70; Chapter VII expenditures, 146–47, 151–53, 155–56; defense of discretionary payments, 226; about Gómez's "inherent" obligation, 150; misuse of Chapter VII funds, 167; patrimonial view, 147
Arellano-Gault, David, 45
Arévalo Cedeño, Emilio, 65, 112, 114, 165; honor of "whining exiles," 108; invasions of Vene-

zuela, 105–6, 108; metaphorical emasculation of men, 110; opposition discourse of, 105–7; sale of animals, 124
army/military control under Gómez, 34, 150–51; 1910–13 reform, 12; creation of "fiscal-military" states, 35; exploitation of military forces, 38; military reform, 35–37; profiteering activities, 39–40; promotion of impersonal criteria, 34–35. *See also* military coup

Baldó, José Antonio, 52, 57, 59
Baptista Galindo, Francisco, 153–54
Baptista, Leopoldo, 49–50
Beaumont, H. D., 42, 141
Bello, Dionisia, 23, 39
Betancourt, Rómulo, 15–17, 119–20, 160, 182, 216; anticorruption measures in Venezuela, 122–24, 180–81, 191, 218; class-based analysis, 124; contact with dissident members, 120–21; exiles' intellectual evolution, 123; justification for corruption trials, 184; and López Contreras, 162, 164, 170; Pact of Punto Fijo agreement, 217; proposal for new jury, 218–20; review of jury's verdicts, 209–10; struggle over public memory of trials, 221
Bjarnegard, Elin, 45
Blanco, Andrés Eloy, 153, 166, 177, 193; parents, 15–54
Blanco Fombona, Rufino, 172
bourgeois honor, 16, 100; dictator as personification of, 102; Gómez's portrayal as embodiment of, 104
bourgeois masculine values in Venezuela, 103–4

bribery in oil sector of Venezuelan officials, 128
British legation in Caracas, 112, 129, 148
Bueno, Adolfo, 133–34, 137
bureaucratic reform of liquor tax: aguardiente and tax farming, 75–81; Cárdenas, anticorruption and bureaucratization, 81–87; liquor-tax contracts, 73–74; tax farming, 75–81, 91–95; transition to direct administration, 95–98; Unión Destiladora and trials of direct administration, 87–91. *See also* anticorruption

Caldera, Rafael, 161, 217–19; about López Contreras, 173; and National Action Party, 189–90; resignation from AD's government, 204; stand against AD, 213; UNE, 161–62
Camero, Paulino, 118–19, 164
Caracas: anonymous flyers in, 121–22; cattle and beef market, 52, 55; Chamber of Commerce, 62; Galavís's access to cattle market in, 61–62; Gómez's control over beef consumption in, 65–68
Cárdenas, Román, 11, 40–41, 74, 87–90, 97, 148; anticorruption and bureaucratization, 12, 81–87; treasury reforms in Venezuela, 41–43; vision of fiscal modernity, 14, 16
Carnevali Picón, Tulio, 90–91
Castillo in Puerto Cabello, prison in, 112, 114–15, 118–19, 166
Castro, Cipriano, 28, 29, 76, 110; Gómez's role in command, 29–30; and politics of monopolies, 30–34; uprising (1899), 45

INDEX

cattle monopoly, 15–16, 49–50, 136; and anticorruption sentiment, 64–68; *Compañía Ganadera Industrial Venezolana*, 68–73; control of livestock herds and ranchlands in plains, 52; control over cattle and beef market, 50–51, 54–68; demand of Venezuelan consumers, 52–54; in plains and center-north, 54–63; political and economic power in cattle cartel, 73–74; political centralization, 51–52; in Zulia, 63–64

caudillismo (practice of caudillo politics), 16, 47, 119; Castro's role, 28, 29–30; *caudillos*' influence in Venezuelan politics, 26; Guzmán Blanco's role, 27–29; political liberalism, 27

Centeno, Melchor, 153, 169

Centeno, Miguel, 35

Chalbaud Cardona, Esteban, 77–79

Chapter VII of budget of Ministry of Interior Relations, 13, 17, 156, 170–72; beneficiaries of, 126–28, 155; for civilian supporters, 151–52; controversies over expenditures, 146–49; discretionary presidential payments, 18, 148, 159, 168–69, 171, 174–77; functioning of funds, 145–46; Gómez's generosity to military officers, 150–51; for middle-class lifestyle maintenance, 151; for natural disasters and public-health emergencies, 149; to officials' illicit enrichment, 152–53, 154; for personal and political motivations, 149–50, 155; public attention to, 159, 168–70; to support Venezuelan

women, 152, 153–54. *See also* corruption; López Contreras, Eleazar; Medina Angarita, Isaías

Chávez, Hugo, 13, 220–21

Clemente Travieso, Carmen, 116–17

Cocina criolla o guia del ama de casa para disponer la comida diaria con prontitud y acierto (Febres Cordero), 52–53

Colmenares Pacheco, Francisco Antonio, 36, 37, 44, 63

Compañía Ganadera Industrial Venezolana, 4, 68; Gumersindo Torres reorganizing, 70–71; managerial and financial problems, 70; reduction in cattle taxes, 69

Compañía Venezolana de Petróleo (CVP), 142–45, 208

COPEI (Christian democratic party), 204, 217–20

Corao, Manuel, 33, 55–56

Coronil, Fernando, 13, 17, 98, 155

corruption, 9–11, 39–41, 48, 64, 72, 99–100, 107, 125, 127, 148, 156, 164, 174, 223, 226; AD's campaign against, 204, 216; constructivist approach to, 222–23; costs of, 116–19; definition of, 7, 222; democratic reformers' condemnations, 15; disaggregating, 223–24; emic approaches/perspective to, 8; of Guzmán Blanco, 28; history of, 6–7, 19; interdisciplinary analysis, 15; oil sector, 128–29; of members of Pérez's cabinet, 95, 221–22; in opposition discourse of Arévalo Cedeño, 105–9; Quiroz's history of, 231n38; in patrimonialism, 11, 12; prisons and masculine honor, 109–16; social meaning of, 8; through cattle and beef market, 56–58; Torres's memoir about, 3–5; types, 224; Venezuelan jefes civiles and, 44–48; "universal" concept of, 9, 227. *See also* anticorruption; cattle monopoly; Chapter VII of budget of Ministry of Interior Relations; financial corruption; predatory corruption

corruption trials of former officials, 184, 189–190; beginning of, 194–96; connection with controversies over gendered roles, 187–88; convictions for predatory corruption, 185, 190; financial *vs.* predatory corruption in, 205–8; public opinion, 184–85; public opinion turns against, 196–205; of trienio, 186. *See also* anticorruption

Crespo, Joaquín, 29, 134

CVP. *See* Compañía Venezolana de Petróleo

Delgado Chalbaud, Carlos, 209
Delgado Chalbaud, Román, 33, 114, 116
D'Elía, José, 78–79
Democratic Action Party, 18, 159, 173, 175–76, 179, 183, 204, 213, 216. See also *trienio*
Díaz, Arlene, 103
dishonor of middle-class people, 99–101
Dormer, Cecil, 140–41
Doyle, William T. S., 142
Ducharne, Horacio, 39
Dupouy, Walter, 188

El Nuevo Diario newspaper, 25–26, 86, 96, 163

El personalismo i el legalismo (Muñoz Tébar), 28

El Universal newspaper, 188–90, 209; about corruption trials, 195–96; appreciation from *La Esfera*, 196; articles about financial corruption, 190–92; praise for Uzcátegui, 200; review of jury's verdicts, 208–9

embezzlement (*peculado*), 11, 95, 122, 169, 178, 184, 189, 218, 231n28

emotional economy of anticorruption, 101, 105–6, 122, 124, 156, 172

Engels, Jens Ivo, 9
Escobar Llamozas, Gustavo, 133–34
Ewell, Judith, 159, 216

Falcón, Juan Crisóstomo, 148
Febres Cordero, Miguel, 121
Febres Cordero, Tulio, 52–53
February Program 160, 162, 167, 171–72
financial corruption, 9–10, 17, 172, 176, 181, 185, 186, 191, 193, 213, 223, 230n22; comparison of prosecutions for, 205; convictions for, 211; CVP in, 208, 211; engagement of officials in Angarita's government, 177; jury's intolerance of, 208 in trials, 205–8; "embezzlement" (*peculado*), 11, 95, 122, 169, 178, 184, 189, 218, 231n28. *See also* predatory corruption
fiscal modernization (modernización fiscal), 26, 86; fiscal modernity, 75, 82–83, 86, 88
foreign investment under Gómez's rule, 128–30
Frevert, Ute, 101

INDEX

Gabaldón Márquez, Joaquín, 66–67, 119, 122

Galavís, Félix, 35, 37, 45, 54, 56, 65, 136, 196; military reviews at Hipódromo, 36–37; monopolizing liquor sales in Yaracuy, 94; profits from liquor-revenue contracts, 95; request to access Caracas market, 61–62

Gallegos, Rómulo, 151, 173, 210, 212

Garbi Sánchez, José, 79, 80, 113–16, 124

García, José María, 36, 63, 81, 87, 136, 168

García Naranjo, Nemesio, 111–12

generally condemned corruption. *See* predatory corruption

gente decente (decent people), 100, 118, 119, 152, 154, 156

Gimón, David, 136, 158

Gómez, Eustoquio, 58, 89, 95, 164, 199

Gómez, José Vicente, 23, 29, 37, 121, 196, 200, 202; oil concessions, 132, 136–37

Gómez, Juan Crisóstomo ("Juancho"), 63, 131–32, 140

Gómez, Juan Vicente, 3, 37, 100, 103, 126; anti-monopoly policy, 33; arguments of defenders and oppositions, 10; army/military control under Gómez, 34–40; and Chapter VII payments, 145–56; collaborators, 11–12; daily routine of, 22–26; death of, 158–59; discretionary presidential payments, 148; early history of petroleum and foreign investment, 128–30; generosity to military officers, 150; military reviews at Hipódromo, 36; modes of spreading nation's oil wealth, 127; neopatrimonial treasury under Gómez, 40–44; oil/petroleum concessions, 130–37, 155–56; patrimonial rule in Venezuela, 21–22; and politics of monopolies, 30–34; role in Castro's command, 29–30; self-declaration, 250n23; Venezuela during Gómez era, *53*

Gómez, Santos Matute, 69, 88

gray corruption. *See* financial corruption

Gulf Oil, 128, 130

Guzmán Blanco, Antonio, 27–29

Hernández, José Manuel, 28–29

"hombre de trabajo", ideal of, 102–4, 114, 120

humiliation, 14; economic loss leading to, 100–101; emotional economy of anticorruption, 105-6, 124, 156; López Contreras's ending of ubiquitous predation, 172–73; submission to Gomecista predation causes, 16, 99, 101; victims of predatory corruption experienced, 16, 65, 68, 115, 122, 164, 185, 223–24

"incompatibility" principle, 177

jefes civiles, 44–48, 58, 78, 79, 163, 194

Johnson, Lyman, 102

Johnston, Michael, 7

Juliac, Josefina, 119

Jurado, León, 57, 60

Jury of Civil and Administrative Responsibility (Jurado de Responsabilidad Civil y Administrativa), 193–213; controversial cases,

196–204, 213-14; first cases, 194–96; formation of 193–94; post-1948 criticism of, 215–16, 219–21; treatment of financial *vs.* predatory corruption, 205–8; verdicts reviewed, 208–13

La Candelaria, 43–44, 106
La Esfera, 168, 174, 176, 178, 188–89, 196; anti–Medina Angarita stance of, 176–78; appreciating *El Universal*, 196; review of jury's verdicts and 1948 Coup, 208–14
La Rotunda, 110–12, 166
Las Delicias (Gómez's estate), 24
Lecuna, Vicente, 131
Leoni, Raúl, 119, 217
León, Ramón David, 174, 176, 189
Lieuwen, Edwin, 130
Linares Alcántara, Francisco, 148, 230n23
Linder, Peter, 63, 64
liquor-tax contracts, 74, 80, 81; under Gómez, 97; for Mérida, 77, 78; Uzcátegui subcontracted share of Araujo, 78; in Zulia, 87. *See also* aguardiente (alcoholic beverage); bureaucratic reform on liquor tax; tax farming/farmers in Venezuela
Lizarraga, Pedro, 52
López Contreras, Eleazar, 5, 121, 157, 183, 196; Arcaya's allegation against, 169–70; authorizing ceremony at Castillo prison, 166; Blanco Fombona's statement, 172–73; calls for confiscation, 166–67; corruption trials against, 184, 191, 196–205; curtailment of predatory corruption, 17; debates over continuation of Chapter VII, 17–18, 158–59, 168; debates over post-Gómez transition, 159–60; defense of discretionary payments, 226; disapproved of concessions trade, 131; ending predatory profiteering/practices, 158–59, 165, 167, 182; failure of Chapter VII reform, 168–69; February Program, 160, 162, 167, 171–72; financial corruption in administration, 191; handling of university student's protest, 164–65; hypocrisy in allowing Abreu, 169; Left, criticism from, 168, 172; misuse of Chapter VII, 170–72; against patrimonialism, 12; PDN, political liberalization, 181; possibility of returning to presidency, 179–80; reactions from Gómez's clan, 167–68; release of political prisoners, 166; suspension of oil concessions by, 173; warning of exploitation of military forces, 38. *See also* Chapter VII of budget of Ministry of Interior Relations; Medina Angarita, Isaías; post-Gómez transition (1935–45)
López Maya, Margarita, 13
Los Hatos del Caura, 44
Luciani, Jorge, 111
Lynch, John, 27; characterization of *caudillismo*, 26; description about Páez, 27

malfeasance. *See* corruption
Maracaibo beef market, monopolized access to, 64
Maracay: property acquisitions by Gómez, 55–56; Venezuelan Industrial Cattle Company at, 68–69

INDEX

Márquez Bustillos, Victorino, 133, 137, 139–40, 142, 153
Márquez Iragorry, José María, 270n119
Márquez, Ovidio, 91, 93, 95
masculine honor: in discourse of Arévalo Cedeño, 105–9; and ideal of "hombre de trabajo," 102–4; prisons, corruption and, 109–16
McBeth, Brian S., 130, 132, 141, 230n23; and CVP, 144–45; financial history of Bueno's concessions, 133
McGill, Samuel, 35–37
McGoodwin, Preston, 43, 58, 139–40
McKay (Mr.), 140–41
Medina Angarita, Isaías, 5, 13, 151, 173, 183; 1943 oil law, 158; 1945 coup overthrow, 180–82; and AD, 175–76, 179; anti–Medina Angarita stance of *La Esfera*, 176–78; challenges from political groups, 173–74; change in public anticorruption discourse, 176; cooperation with opposition parties, 173; criticism on continuing "personalist" practices of Gómez, 13; debates over continuation of Chapter VII, 17–18, 158–59; legalizing voter rights to women, 187; Montilla's accusations of corruption, 175; PDV creation, 176; reform agenda, 174; and UPM, 178–79. *See also* Chapter VII of budget of Ministry of Interior Relations; López Contreras, Eleazar; post-Gómez transition (1935–45)
Medrano, José Miguel, 142
Méndez, Julio, 132, 140
Meyerheim, Cecil, 39

middle-class honor, 100, 101; emotional dimension of, 102; new republican understanding, 103
middle-class Venezuelans, 151; changes in gender roles, 186–87; dishonor of, 99–101; opposition to Gomecista predation, 99–100, 102, 105, 109, 124, 125; women for voting rights, 187
military. *See* army/military control under Gómez
military coup: 1945 coup, 180–82; 1948 coup, 208–14, 215, 217; 1992 coup attempt, 220
Miller, William Ian, 102
mining taxes, *85*, 91
modernization theory, 15, 232n42
modern state, 18, 47, 161, 203; based on universal suffrage and bureaucratic principles, 173, 196; corruption as antithesis, 15; pillars, 12; promise of Medina Angarita, 174
monopolies in Venezuelan politics: Castro's role in, 30–32; concessions in Venezuela, 8; Gómez's dictatorship move in, 31, 32–34; monopoly over cattle markets, 12; Spanish legation in Caracas, 32, 33; women's criticism of beef monopoly, 66. *See also* cattle monopoly
Moros, Eulogio, 55, 106
Movimiento de Organización Venezolano (ORVE), 160–61, 167
Muñoz Tébar, Jesús, 28
Murillo, Pedro, 36, 45, 58

National Action Party, 189
National Student Union. *See* Unión Nacional Estudiantil (UNE)

neopatrimonialism, 13, 230n25, 231n26; Gómez's daily routine, 22–26; changing nature of, 231n35
neopatrimonial state formation, 5, 10–11, 15, 21, 75, 99, 149, 214; anticorruption in, 11, 12; army/military control under Gómez, 34–40; corruption in, 11, 12; neopatrimonial treasury under Gómez, 40–44; politics of monopolies, 30–34; state presidents and jefes civiles contribution, 44–48
neopatrimonial treasury, 40–44; Cárdenas's reforms in, 40–43; personal investments in properties, 43–44; professionalization and bureaucratization, 40
neosultanism, 231n26
Nicholson, Meredith, 165
1935–36 protests: in Caracas, 162–63; in Crespo district, 164; responsibility of López Contreras to control, 164–65; in Valencia, 163–64
Núñez, Dolores Amelia, 23

Odebrecht (Brazilian firm), 6
oil boom in Venezuela (1923–29), 17, 22, 25
oil legislation: 1922 legislation, 131, 137–42; 1943 legislation, 181
oil money, 127, 156; bribery in oil sector of Venezuelan officials, 127–28; and Chapter VII payments, 145–56; and Compañía Venezolana de Petróleo, 142–45, 208; early history of petroleum and foreign investment, 128–30; private interests in making of 1922 oil law, 137–42

oil/petroleum concessions, 8, 17, *135*, 155–56; beneficiaries of, 126–27; CVP receiving, 208; during Gómez regime, 130–37
Omaña, Timoleón, 49–51, 66, 79, 90
OPEC. *See* Organization of Petroleum Exporting Countries
Organic Law to Safeguard the Public Patrimony (1982), 220
Organization of Petroleum Exporting Countries (OPEC), 217
ORVE. *See* Movimiento de Organización Venezolano
Otero Silva, Miguel, 119, 122, 204

pacted democracy of Venezuela, 217, 218, 221
Páez, José Antonio, 27
Palacios, Antonia, 119, 249n4
Parada, Nemecio, 24
Paredes, Antonio, 32
Parra Jahn, Ligia, 187
Partido Comunista de Venezuela (PCV), 173
Partido Democrático Nacional (PDN), 169, 170
Partido Democrático Venezolano (PDV), 176, 178
Partido Republicano Progresista (PRP), 160–62, 167–68
patriarchy, 103, 154, 187; and honor, 16, 103, 105, 109, 125, 200, 201; connection to patrimonialism, 21–22, 152, 225; Gómez as patriarchal figure, 25, 121, 128, 152, 154, 225; patriarchal households, 22, 68, 102, 214, 226
patrimonialism, 11–12, 214, 225; and caudillismo, 26–30; Weber's concept, 21–22. *See also* neopatrimonialism

INDEX

Patriotic Military Union. *See* Unión Patriótica Militar (UPM)
PCV. *See* Partido Comunista de Venezuela
PDN. *See* Partido Democrático Nacional
PDV. *See* Partido Democrático Venezolano
PDVSA. *See* Petróleos de Venezuela
peculado. See embezzlement
Pérez, Ana Mercedes, 176, 189
Pérez Jimenez, Marcos, 212, 216, 217
Pérez, Juan Bautista, 95, 168
Pérez Soto, Vincencio, 58–60, 90–91, 94, 136, 194–95
"personalism" (*personalismo*), 11, 18, 27, 177, 181, 217, 225
Petróleos de Venezuela (PDVSA), 220, 271n21
petroleum: early history of, 128–30; petroleum-related corruption, 127; Venezuela's petroleum industry, 128. *See also* oil/petroleum concessions
Pietropaoli, Carlo, 36
Pimentel, Antonio, 40, 44, 55, 96, 148, 163, 196, 253n94
Pimentel, Cecilia, 116–19, 125, 153–54
Pimentel, Francisco, 116
Pimentel, Luis Rafael, 116–19
Pimentel, Tancredo, 116, 118, 119
Pimentel, Vicente, 117
Pino Iturrieta, Elías, 45
Plan of Barranquilla (Betancourt), 123
playa system, 60–62
Pocaterra, José Rafael, 109, 110
Polanco Alcantara, Tomás, 145, 230n23
political liberalism, 27–28

Portal, Magda, 108
post-Gómez transition (1935–45), 160; 1935–36 protests, 162–65; Contreras and, 158–59, 160, 166–73; under Medina Angarita, 159, 173–82; and ORVE, 160–62; and PRP, 160–62; and UNE, 161–62
predatory corruption, 9–10, 14, 17, 57, 100–2, 124, 156, 158, 181–82, 185, 190, 213, 231n26; Contreras and, 17, 162–73; ending predatory profiteering/practices, 158–59, 165, 167, 182; in trials, 205–8; victims by predatory corruption experienced, 223–24; visceral denunciations of, 224. *See also* corruption
predatory neopatrimonialism, 231n35
prisons, 109–16; Castillo in Puerto Cabello, 112, 114–15, 118–19, 166; connection between profiteering and prison system, 112–13; corruption in, 113–14; functions in regime's systematic profiteering, 112; Garbi Sánchez's indignation over exploitation, 114–15; García Naranjo's writings about, 111–12; insults to prisoners, 115–16; La Rotunda prison in Caracas, 110–12; Pocaterra prison in Caracas, 110; and prisoners' families, 116–19
profiteering. *See* corruption
PRP. *See* Partido Republicano Progresista
Puerto Cabello, 52, 164; Castillo prison in, 112, 114–15, 118–19, 166; cattle markets, 52; property acquisitions by Gómez, 55–56

Quiroz, Alfonso, 231n38

Ramírez, Roberto, 89, 95, 143, 145
Ramos, Ramón, 89, 96, 145, 163–64
Rangel, Domingo Alberto, 54, 209
regulated neopatrimonialism, 231n35
republican honor: studies of, 102; values of, 105
Revenga de Gómez, Josefina, 132, 200, 210
Revolución Libertadora (Liberating Revolution), 30, 35, 40, 45
Rincón, Onésimo, 63–64
Rivero, Mirtha, 221
Rodríguez, Elías, 137, 139
Rodríguez, Valmore, 191
Roosevelt, Theodore, 32
Royal Dutch Shell, 123, 128, 130

Santos, Abel, 40, 77–79
Sarmiento, Manuel, 58, 61, 62
Sauer, Carl, 53
Sauer, Emile, 94–95
Schlesinger, Arthur, 230n24
Shell (company), 123, 128, 130
Siso, Carlos, 12, 37, 56, 62–63, 150
Skurski, Julie, 103
Smith, Benjamin, 186
Standard Oil, 123, 128, 130, 144
state formation. *See* neopatrimonial state formation
Stinnes, Hugo, 143–44
Substantiating Commission, 192–94, 198
Sullivan, William, 32
sultanism, 231n26

taxation: liquor tax revenues, *80*, *85*; mining taxes, *85*, 91; reduction in cattle taxes, 69; taxes on livestock crossing state borders, 59–60

tax farming/farmers in Venezuela, 83, 94; aguardiente and, 75–81; Cárdenas argument to replace, 74, 82; jefes civiles as, 46; legal and illegal profits, 76–77, 93; monopolized regional markets, 83; patrimonial contract system, 92; payments by liquor tax farmers to treasury, *80*, 81; political connections to Gómez, 77; rights, 81; selling untaxed aguardiente, 79. *See also* liquor-tax contracts
TI. *See* Transparency International
Tinoco, Manuel Vicente, 175, 203
Torres, Gumersindo, 11, 70–71, 131, 138–40, 158, 160, 165, 171; engagement with systemic corruption issue, 4–5; overview of memoir, 3–4, 133; study of corruption–state formation relationship, 5
Transparency International (TI), 6, 222
treasury. *See* neopatrimonial treasury
trienio, 184, 186, 188, 190, 218–19, 221; changes in Venezuelan middle class, 185; controversies surrounding anticorruption efforts of, 219, 222, 226

UNE. *See* Unión Nacional Estudiantil
Unión Destiladora, 87–91, 93
Unión Patriótica Militar (UPM), 178–79
UPM. *See* Unión Patriótica Militar
Urbaneja, Diego Bautista, 35
Uslar Pietri, Arturo, 202, 219
Uzcátegui, Amador, 47, 81, 89
Uzcátegui, Baldomero, 200–3, 213–14
Uzcátegui, Manuel, 77–79, 242n12

"vagos," 115, 116
Valencia: cattle markets, 52; property acquisitions by Gómez, 55–56; reduction in beef prices at, 69
Vallenilla Lanz, Laureano, 25
Velasco, Rafael María, 66, 163
Velásquez, Ramón, 230n23
Venezuela: política y petróleo (Betancourt), 216
Venezuelan Communist Party. *See* Partido Comunista de Venezuela (PCV)
Venezuelan Industrial Cattle Company. *See* Compañía Ganadera Industrial Venezolana
Venezuelan Navigation Company, 62
Venezuelan Telephone Company, 129
Venezuela Oil Concessions, 142
Venezuela y su gobernante (*Venezuela and Its Ruler*) (García Naranjo), 111
Villalba, Jóvito, 119–20, 170, 217, 219
Vivas, Ezequiel, 129
voting rights for Venezuelan women, 186–87

Weber, Max, 21–22
women in Venezuela: changes in gender roles, 186–87; criticism on beef monopoly, 66; Gomecismo's impact on, 125; into higher-paid professions, 187; participation in public world of business, 187; receiving Chapter VII funds, 152; references to "street work," 118; suffering under the predatory corruption, 14; voting rights, 186–87
W. R. Grace and Company, 58

Yergin, Daniel, 137

Zahler, Reuben, 27, 103
Ziems, Angel, 35
Zulia state: cattle monopoly in, 63–64, 195; liquor tax in, 87–91; state president and jefe civil, 47; statewide liquor monopoly, 79; treasury officials in, 88